Vital Records
of the Towns of
Barnstable *and* Sandwich

An authorized facsimile reproduction of
records published serially 1901-1935 in
The Mayflower Descendant.

With Added Index of Names by

COL. LEONARD H. SMITH JR.
&
NORMA H. SMITH

CLEARFIELD

Copyright © 1976, 1982
by Leonard H. Smith, Jr.
All Rights Reserved.

Reprinted for
Clearfield Company, Inc. by
Genealogical Publishing Co., Inc.
Baltimore, Maryland
1992, 1994, 1996, 2003

International Standard Book Number: 0-8063-4614-0

Made in the United States of America

Contents

Preface	4
Historical Data - Barnstable	5
Historical Data - Sandwich	6

Part I - Barnstable

Volume 2 (1900)	9
Volume 3 (1901)	12
Volume 4 (1902)	18
Volume 5 (1903)	24
Volume 6 (1904)	28
Volume 10 (1908)	36
Volume 11 (1909)	38
Volume 12 (1910)	44
Volume 14 (1912)	46
Volume 19 (1917)	51
Volume 20 (1918)	60
Volume 23 (1921)	62
Volume 25 (1923)	65
Volume 27 (1925)	71
Volume 31 (1933)	74
Volume 32 (1934)	90
Volume 33 (1935)	101
Volume 34 (1937)	117

Part II - Sandwich

Volume 14 (1912)	125
Volume 29 (1931)	135
Volume 30 (1932)	146

Index

Barnstable	159
Sandwich	214

Preface

In 1900 the Society of Mayflower Descendants in Massachusetts began printing in its quarterly, *The Mayflower Descendant,* the vital records of Barnstable, Mass., as they had been literally transcribed from the original records by George Robert Bowman. The printing of the records of Sandwich was begun in 1912. The printing continued, irregularly, until the demise of the quarterly in 1935. Unfortunately, the printing of the transcripts was not completed.

The earliest event noted in the Barnstable printed record is 1688, the latest 1729. The earliest event noted in the Sandwich printed record is 1636, the latest 1720. Not all events between those two dates are included.

This volume is a facsimile reproduction of the town records which were published, with the addition of a name index for each town. Some early events may be recorded in Plymouth Colony records.

The Barnstable index was first published, separately, in 1975. The Sandwich index (with an index for the town of Wareham) was published the same year. The production of a limited number of copies of a combined edition of records and indexes in 1986 accounts for the unconventional inclusion of the front matter in the arabic pagination.

The publication of the present volume is the result of the gracious consent of the Society of Mayflower Descendants in Massachusetts, for which our thanks are extended.

Our thanks are also extended to the State Street Trust Company of Boston, Mass., for its permission to use its illustration of the town seal of Barnstable and to the Town Clerk of Sandwich for supplying an example of the seal of that town.

BARNSTABLE HISTORICAL DATA

1538 Mar 5*   Mentioned in a list of those "allowed to exercise men in Armes", ... "ffor Barnstable ... Mr. Thom Dimmack ..." (Ply. Col. Rec., Vol. XI, p. 30.)

1641 Jun 17*   Bounds between Barnstable and Yarmouth established.

1652 Mar 2*   Bounds between Barnstable and Sandwich to be established.

1658 Mar 11*   Barnstable and Yarmouth agreed upon bounds.

1662 Jun 3*   Additional lands granted to Barnstable.

1662 Jun 10*   Bounds between Barnstable and Sandwich to be established.

1672 Oct 29*   Bounds between Barnstable and Sandwich established.

1795 Jan 22   Bounds between Barnstable and the district of Mashpee established.

1894 Mar 28   Bounds between Barnstable and Mashpee established.

1916 Apr 24   Bounds between Barnstable and Mashpee established and part of Sandwich annexed.

*Old Style, or according to the Julian calendar. The present calendar, the Gregorian or New Style, was adopted by an Act of Parliament of Great Britain. It was ordered that September 3, 1752, should become September 14 and that the legal year should commence with the first of January, instead of March 25, beginning January 1, 1752. To change Old Style to New Style add 10 days to a 17th century date and 11 to an 18th century date.

(From "Historical Data Relating to Counties, Cities and Towns in Massachusetts", by Kevin H. White.)

SANDWICH HISTORICAL DATA

1638 Mar 6*	Certain persons were ordered to "...goe to Sanditch, and set forth their bounds of the lands graunted to them". (Ply. Col. Rec., Vol. 1, p. 80.)
1652 Mar 2*	Bounds between Sandwich and Barnstable to be established.
1662 June 10*	Bounds between Sandwich and Barnstable to be established.
1670 June 7*	Bounds between Sandwich and Plymouth as established Jan. 19,* 1663, ordered to be recorded.
1672 Oct 29*	Bounds between Sandwich and Barnstable established.
1681 July 7*	Bounds between Sandwich and "Suckanesset" established.
1684 Oct 28*	Bounds established.
1735 Nov 28*	Bounds between Sandwich and lands of the proprietors of Mashpee confirmed.
1811 Feb 26	Part of the plantation of "Marshpee" annexed.
1859 Apr 1	Part of the district of "Marshpee" annexed.
1860 Mar 13	Part of the district of "Marshpee" annexed.
1872 Mar 19	Part re-annexed to Mashpee.
1880 Mar 19	Bounds between Sandwich and Falmouth established.
1884 Apr 2	Part established as Bourne.
1887 May 27	Bounds between Sandwich and Mashpee established and part annexed to Mashpee.
1905 Apr 20	Bounds between Sandwich and Mashpee established and part annexed to Mashpee.
1916 Apr 24	Part annexed to Barnstable.

*Old Style, or accoridng to the Julian calendar. The present calendar, the Gregorian or New Style, was adopted by an Act of Parliament of Great Britian. It was ordered that September 3, 1752, should become September 14 and that the legal year should commence with the first of January, instead of March 25, beginning January 1, 1752. To change Old Style to New Style add 10 days to a 17th century date and 11 to an 18th century date.

(From "Historical Data Relating to Counties, Cities and Towns in Massachusetts", by Kevin H. White.)

Part I
Barnstable

THE MAYFLOWER DESCENDANT

A Quarterly Magazine

OF

Pilgrim Genealogy and History

1900

VOLUME II

BOSTON
PUBLISHED BY THE
MASSACHUSETTS SOCIETY OF MAYFLOWER DESCENDANTS
1900

BARNSTABLE, MASS., VITAL RECORDS.

Transcribed from the original records,

By GEORGE ERNEST BOWMAN.

Volume I of the Barnstable town records is not the original, but a copy made in 1736, in accordance with the following vote recorded on the first page: "At a Meeting of y*e* Inhabitants of the Town of Barnstable June 30th John Thacher Esq*r* Moderator Then Voted that y*e* old Town Book as to y*e* Articles Contained in the Same to be of future Use be Transcribed by y*e* Town Clerk into a New Book to be procured by him with as Much Speed as Conveniently May.

"Barnstable Town Book Anno. 1736 bought p*r* David Crocker Town Clerk. pretium £13 12*s*"

The vital records in the copy were arranged at the back of the book.

[Vol. I, p. 390] Thomas Allyn & Elizabeth Otis were married 9*th* Oct*or* 1688
Their son James born y*e* 1*st* of July 1691
Their Son Thomas born y*e* 11 of Dec*em* 1693
Their Daughter Hannah Born 13 June 1696
Thomas Allyn Deceas*d* 25 November 1696 Aged In y*e* 32 year of his Age

Sam*ll* Allyn and Sarah Tayler Married 20 Day of Decem*r* 1705 by M*r* Russel
their Son Samuel Allyn was born y*e* 26 of Nov*r* in y*e* year 1706
Samuel Allyn y*e* Father Died 21 Decem*r* 1706 aged in y*e* 39 year of his age

Hannah Allyn y*e* Wife of Sam*ll* Allyn Sen*r* Departed This Life on Tuesday y*e* 23 Oct*or* 1711 About 10 of y*e* Clock in y*e* morning

M*r* Samuel Departed this Life on Fyday 25 Nov*r* 1726

[p. 391] The Records of Anthony Annables Births
Jane his Wife Died About December 1643
he married With Anne Clarck 1*st* of March 1645
his son Samuel borne about 22 of January 1646
his Son Ezekel was Born
his Daughter Desire was born about beginning of Oct*or* 1653

Samuel Annable & Mehitable Allyn Married 1 of June 1667
his Son Samuel born 14 of July 1669
his Daughter Hannah Born March 1672 and buried five Months f.fter
his Son John Born 19 July 1673
his Daughter Anna born 4 of March 1675

Samuel Annable was Married y*e* 11 of April 1695 with Patience Dogged
and Their Daughter Desire was Born on y*e* 3*rd* of January 1696
and Their Daughter Anna was born on y*e* 27 of September 1697
& their Daughter Jane was Born on y*e* 24 of December 1699
& their Son Samuel Born on y*e* 14 of January 1701/2
a Dead Born Child 12 of January 1704
his Daughter patience born 15 of May 1705
his Son Thomas Born 21 of June 1708

John Annable & Experience Tayler Married June 16. 1692
Their son Samuel born 3*rd* Day of September 1693
Their Daughter Mehitable born 28 of September 1695
Their son John Born April 1697 & Deceas*d* a month after
Their Second son John born 31 May 1698
Mary born In December 1701
Cornelius Born 3 of November 1704
Abigail 30*th* of April 1710

Samuel Allyn y*e* Son of M*r* Thomas Allyn born 1 of February 1643
S*d* Samuel Allyn & Hannah Walley Marryed 10 of May 1664
his Son Thomas Born 22 of March 1665
his Son Samuel born 19 of January 1666
his Son Joseph born 7*th* of April 1671
his Daughter Hannah born y*e* 4 of March 167¾
his Daughter Elizabeth born 26 of Novem*r* 1681 & Deceas*d* 23 Decem 1698
Above s*d* Thomas Allyn Deceas*d* In Nov*r* 1696
Samuel y*e* Son Died 21 of Decem 1706

John Allyn & Mary Howland Married
his son John Born 3*rd* of April 1674
his Daughter Mary Born 5 of August 1675 & Died 7 of July 1677
his Son Matthew born 6 of August 1677 & Died Last of Oct*or* 1680
his Son Isaac Born 8 of Nov*r* 1679

[p. 392] Austin Beirse
his Daughter Mary Beirse born In y*e* Year 1640

Martha In yᵉ Year 1642
Priscilla About yᵉ 10 of March 1643
Sarah yᵉ 28 of March 1646
Abigail yᵉ 18 of Decemʳ 1647
Hannah yᵉ 16 of Novʳ 1649
his Son Joseph born 25 of January 1651
his Daughter Hester 2 of Octʳ 1653
Lydia about yᵉ End of Septʳ 1655
Rebekah About Septʳ 1657
his Son James About yᵉ End of July 1660

Joseph Berse and Martha Tayler Married yᵉ 3 of December 1676
Their Daughter Mary born yᵉ 16 of August 1677
Their Son Joseph Born yᵉ 21 of February 1679
Their Son Benjamin Born yᵉ 21 Day of June 1682
Their Daughter Priscilla born yᵉ Last Day of Decemʳ 1683 & Deceased yᵉ 31 of March 1684
Their Son Ebenezer borne yᵉ 20 of January 1685
Their Son John Berse Born May yᵉ 8 1687
Their Son Josiah Berse Born March 10 1690
Their son James Berse Born yᵉ 3 of Octoʳ 1692

Nicholas Bonham & Hannah Fuller Married 1 of January 1658
his Daughter Hannah Born yᵉ 8 of Octʳ 1659
his Daughter Mary yᵉ 4 of Octʳ 1661
his Daughter Sarah born yᵉ 16 of February 1664

Joseph Benjamin & Jemima Lumbard Married 10 of June 1661
Cornelius Briggs & Mehitable Annable Married May 6 1683
Thoˢ Bille & Anna Twining Married yᵉ 3 of Octoʳ 1672
Nathaniel Bacon and Hannah Mayo Married 4 of Decemʳ 1642
Their Daughter Hannah Born yᵉ 4 of September 1643
Their Son Nathaniel Born yᵉ 5ᵗʰ of February 1645
Their Daughter Mary Bon yᵉ 12 of August 1648
Their Son Samuel yᵉ 25 of February 1650
Their Daughter Elizabeth bon yᵉ 28 of January 1653
Their son Jeremiah Born yᵉ 8 of May 1657
Their Daughter Mercy Born 28 of February 1659
Their Son John Born yᵉ Beginning of June 1661

[p. 393] Nathaniel Bacon & Sarah Hinkley Married 27 of March 1673
Their son Nathaniel Born on yᵉ 9 of Septʳ 1674
Their Daughter Mary Born on yᵉ 9 of Octʳ 1677
Their Daughter Elizabeth born on yᵉ 11 of April 1680
Their Son Samuel born on yᵉ 20 of January 1682

Sarah yᵉ wife of yᵉ Above Sᵈ Nathaniel Dyed 16 of February 1686/7
The Above Sᵈ Nathaniel Bacon Senʳ Dyed yᵉ Last of Decemʳ 1691

John Bacon and Mary Hawes Married June 17. 1686
Their Daughter Hannah Born yᵉ 7 of June 1687
Their Daughter Desire Born 15 of March 1688/9
Their Son Nathaniel Born 16 of January 1691/2
Their Daughter Patience Born 15 of June 1694
Their Son John Born 24 of March 1697
Their Son Isaac Born 29 of March 1699
Their Son Solomon Born 3 of April 1701
Their son Jude Born 9 of December 1703

Jeremiah Bacon & Elizabeth Howes Married 10 Decemʳ 1686
Their Daughter Sarah Born 16 of Octoʳ 1687
Their Daughter Anna Born 16 of Novemʳ 1688
Their Daughter Mercy Born 30 of January 1689
Their Son Samuel born 15 of April 1692
Their Son Jeremiah Born 2 of Octoʳ 1694
Their Son Joseph Born 15 of June 1695
Their Son Ebenezer Born 11 of March 1698
Their Son Nathaniel Born 11 of September 1700
Their Son Job born 23 of March 1703
Their Daughter Elizabeth born August 6ᵗʰ 1705

Samˡˡ Bacon & Martha Foxwell Married 9 of May 1659
Their Son Samuel Born 9 of March 1659/60
Their Daughter Martha Midst of 1661*

Nathaniel Bacon & Ruth Dogget were married 11 of Novʳ 1696 by Majʳ Mayhew
Their son Thomas Born 30 of Septʳ 1697
Their Son David Born 11 of Decemʳ 1700
Their Son Jonathan yᵉ 11 of March 1703
Hannah their Daughter born January 15 1704/5
Sarah Born yᵉ 6 of January 1707/8

Samuel Bacon & yᵉ Widdow Sarah Allyn Married pr Mʳ Russel yᵉ 26 of Janry 1706
Their son Ebenezer Born yᵉ 4 of December 1708
Their Daughter Mercy Born yᵉ 22ⁿᵈ of May 1710
Their Son Edward born yᵉ 23 of January 1714/15

(To be continued.)

* This has been altered in a later hand to read "Janry 1671."

BARNSTABLE, MASS., VITAL RECORDS.

(Continued from Vol. II, p. 215.)

[Vol. I, p. 394] William Barden & Deborah Barker Marriel In February 1660
his Daughter Mercy Born 1 November 1662
his Daughter Deborah born 28 of June 1665
his Son John Born 17 of March 1667
his Son Stephen born April 15 1669
his Son Abraham born 14 May 1674
his Son Joseph born Sept 1675
his Daughter Anna born 26 August 1677

Joseph Bolfish and Elizabeth Besse Married In ye Year 1674
his Son John Born 6th of December 1675
his son Joseph born In October 1677
his Daughter Mary born 1 of March 1679–80
his Daughter Hannah born In May 1681
his Son Benjamin born ye 20 of July 1683
his Son Nathan born ye 27 of December 1685
his Son Ebenezer Born ye 10 of March 1687/8
his Daughter Elizabeth born 27 of Aug: 1690
his Daughter Rebecca born 22 of Feb: 1692–3
his Daughter Melatiah born 7 of April 1695
his Son Robert Born ye 10 of Octo^r 1698
his Daughter Sarah born 20th of Feb. 1700

Thomas Bourman & Hannah Annable Married 10 of March 1645
his Daughter Hannah born About ye Latter End of May 1646

his son Thomas Bourman Born About yᵉ Middle of Sep: 1648
his Son Samuel born About yᵉ Latter End of July 1651
his Daughter Desire born About yᵉ Latter End of May 1654
his Daughter Mary About yᵉ Middle of March 1656
Mehitable About yᵉ beginning of September 1658
Tristram About yᵉ Beginning of Aug: 1661

John Barker & Desire Annable Married yᵉ 18 of January 1676
his son John Born yᵉ 4 of May 1678
his Daughter Desire born yᵉ 22 of September 1680
his Daughter Anne born yᵉ 26 of August 1682 & Deceased yᵉ 22 of Novemʳ 1682
his daughter Anne yᵉ 2ⁿᵈ of that Name born yᵉ first of Nov 1683

[p. 395] Abraham Blish his Daughter Sarah born 2ⁿᵈ Decem. 1644
Joseph his Son born 1 of April 1648
Anne yᵉ Wife of yᵉ Sᵈ Abraham Died 16 of May 1651
Abraham Blish & Hannah Barker Married
his Son abraham born About 16 of Octoʳ 1654
Hannah his Wife Died About yᵉ 16 of Feb: or March 1657
yᵉ Sᵈ Abraham Blish Deceased yᵉ 7ᵗʰ of Sep: 1683.

Joseph Blish and Hannah Hull Married yᵉ 15 of Sept 1674
his Son Joseph Born 13 of Sep 1675
his Son John Born 17 of Feb: 1676
his Daughter Anna born yᵉ Latter End of February 1678
his Son Abraham born yᵉ 27 of February 1680
Their Son Reuben born yᵉ 14 of August 1683
Their Daughter Sarah born yᵉ beginning of Aug: 1685 & Died 3ʳᵈ of January 1686
Sarah September 1685
Thankful born In September 1687
John Blish born January 1 1691 & Died Octoʳ 14. 1711 In yᵉ 20ᵗʰ Year of his age
Tristram born In April 1694
Mary In April 1696
Benjamin April 1699
Sarah Blish Deceased 1705
Joseph Blish Deceasᵈ June 14 1730 in yᵉ 83 Year of his Age
Hannah Blish wife of sᵈ Joseph Blish Deceasᵈ Nov 15 1732

Reuben Blish & Elizabeth Bodfish Married by Col Otis 25 Janᵘʳ 1717
Their son John born yᵉ 9 of Septʳ 1717
their son Silas born yᵉ 8 of April 1719
his son Reuben yᵉ 6 of Feb 1721
Elizabeth Born 10 of Feb 1722/3
Daughter Hannah born May 1725
Daughter Thankful born May 30 1727

Joseph Blish and Hannah Child Married See yᵉ Other Book.

John Bursley & Elizabeth Howland Married Decemʳ. 1673
his Daughter Elizabeth born 2 Week In Octoʳ 1674 & buried Latter End of Octoʳ 1675
his Daughter Mercy born Last Week In Octoʳ 1675 & buried In April 1676
his son John born 1 of March 1677/8
his Daughter Mary born 23 of May 1679
his Son Jabez born 21 of August 1681
his Daughter Joanna born 29 Novʳ 1684
his Son Joseph born yᵉ 29 of January 1686
his Daughter Abigail born August 27. 1690
his Daughter Elizabeth born Aug. 5–1692
his Daughter Temperance born January 30–1695

[p. 396] John Bursley & Mary Crocker Married by Mʳ Russel 11 of Feb: 1708/9
Their Daughter Experience born yᵉ Last Day of Novʳ 1706
Another Daughter born 1710 & Died a fortnight After
a Son Born 12 of April 1711 & Deceasᵈ 3 weeks after

Jabez Bursley his Son Benjamin born July 21. 1706
John Born Sept 1ˢᵗ 1708
his Daughter Elizabeth born Feb 1ˢᵗ 1710/11
Abigail born Feb 25 1713 14
Hannah born Novʳ 1715
Joanna born June 1719
Mary born August 1723
Barnabas born 16 Day of January 1724 25

Peter Blossom & Sarah Bodfish Married 21 of June 1663
his Daughter Mercy born yᵉ 9 of April 1664 & Died In yᵉ Year 1670
his Son Thomas born 20 Decemʳ 1667
Sarah Blossom yʳ Daughter was born 1669 & Died 1671
Joseph Blossom their son was born yᵉ 10 of December 1673
Thankful Blossom yʳ Daughter was born 1675
Mercy Blossom yʳ Daughter Was born in Aug: 1678
Jabez yʳ son was born yᵉ 16 of Feb 1680
Peter Blossom Deceasᵈ July 1706

Thomas Blossom & Fear Robinson Married pr Justice Bourn
Their son Peter Blossom was born 28 of August 1698
John Blossom their son born 17 of April 1699
Sarah Blossom born 16 of Decem 1703 & Died Some time after
his Daughter Elizabeth born In Octoʳ 1705
his 2ⁿᵈ Daughter Sarah Born 30 of July 1709

Joseph Blossom & Mary Pinchon Were Married 17 of June 1696 pr Mʳ Laason of Situate
his son Joseph Blossom·born 14 of March 170¾
he had a Child a son born & Died Quickly March 1696/7
Another Son born & Died In May 1702

Another Son born In May 1705 & Dyed In June following
his Wife Mary Died ye 6 of April 1706.
Joseph Blossom his Daughter Mary by a Second Wife born 11 of Decem 1709
Thankful born ye 25 of March 1711

Jabez Blossom and Mary Goodspeed Were Married ye 9th of ye 9th Month 1710 by Mr Russel
his Son Sylvanus Born 20 January 1712

(To be continued.)

BARNSTABLE, MASS., VITAL RECORDS.

(Continued from page 54.)

[Vol. I, p. 397] Sarah Bodfish ye Daughter of Joseph Bodfish Born 20 Feb
Joseph Bodfish Jur & Thankful Blish Married by Mr Basset 11 Octo^r 1712
Their Daughter Elizabeth born 6 Sep^t 1713
Their Daughter Hannah born 18 of July 1716
Their Daughter Mary born 17 of June 1719
Their son Joseph born 8 March 1722
Their Daughter Thankful born In June 1724
Benjamin Bodfish & Lydia Crocker Married 10 of Novr 1709
Their son Sylvanus born ye 2nd of September 1710
his Daughter Hannah born 12 of February 1712
his Daughter Thankful born 19 of February 1714
his Son Solomon born 20 March 1716
his Son Joseph 16 of April 1718
his Son Benjamin born ye 18th of March 1720
his Son Jonathan born ye 10 of August 1727
Benjamin Berse and Sarah Cob Were Married 4 of Feb 1701/2 pr Ma^r Gorham
Their Daughter Martha born 9 of Novr 1702
Augustine Berse born ye 3^d of June 1704
Elizabeth born ye 3rd of May 1707
Joseph Born ye 30 Octo^r 1708
Benjamin ye 26 of March 1710
Jesse born 22 of Octo^r 1712
Priscilla Born 5 of June 1713
David born 17 of March 1716
Peter born 15 of Octo^r 1718
Samuel born December 9th 1720
Sarah July 5th 1722
Thankful Feb^r 4th 1724
Ebenezer Berse & Elizabeth Cob Married 25 of Nov 1708 pr Justice Gorham
his Daughter Bethiah born 6 of August 1709
his Son Samuel ye 26 of Feb 1711

his Wife Died yᵉ 15 of July 1711
by his Second Wife
Elizabeth born March 22 1714
Abigail Novʳ 22 1715
Ebenezer March 1 1717
Daniel July 17 1720
Stephen Octoʳ 1ˢᵗ 1721
Rebecca June 3 1725
Nathaniel Bacon Juʳ & patience Parker Married
Their Son Benjamin born yᵉ 12 of January 1711
Jabez Born April 3 1714
Daniel Born March 17 1717 by his Second Wife Anna Annable
yᵉ son John Born May 21 1722
Mercy born March 23 1724

[p. 398] The Records of Nathaniel Bakers Children
Benney Baker his Son Born August 15 1705 & Deceased June 5ᵗʰ 1706
Mercy Baker Born Feb 4 1706
Sarah Baker Born Octoʳ(illegible) 1708 & Died 19 of Novʳ 1708
his Son Nathaniel Baker born 15 December 1709
his Son Nicholas born 6 of Novʳ 1711
his Daughter Sarah born Novʳ 2 1713
his Daughter Thankful born 28 March 1715
his Son Benney born 28 Septʳ 1716
his Daughter Elizabeth born 9 of March 1718
his Wife Mercy Baker Deceas'd 9 of March 1718
John Berse & Elinor Lewes Married 15 of November 1711 pr Justice Gorham
his Daughter Lydia born 28 Feb 1712
Mrs Grace Baker Deceas'd yᵉ 22 January 1706/7
John Baker and Annah Anable Married yᵉ 14 of Octoʳ 1696 by Just: Lothrop
Their Daughter Annah born yᵉ 8 of Sep 1697
Their Daughter Mercy yᵉ 18 of Aug: 1699
Their son John born yᵉ 14 of June 1701
Rebeckah Baker Septʳ 8 1704
Samˡˡ 7ᵗʰ of Septʳ 1706
his Daughter Mary born 25ᵗʰ of March 1710
his Daughter Mehitable 7ᵗʰ of May 1712
Abigail yᵉ first of Feb 1713/4
Their Son John Baker born Decemʳ 1 1716
Hannah March 24 1718
Thomas Bumpas & Phebe Lovel were Married Novʳ 1679
Their Daughter Hannah born 28 of July 1680
Their Daughter Jean Born Decemʳ 1681
Mary born April 1683
Their Son Samˡˡ January 1685
& Thomas born May 1687
Their Daughter Sarah Born Janʳʸ 1688
Elizabeth Born January 1690

Abigail born Octoʳ 1693
his Son Benjamin Born 27 of March 1703

[p. 399] The births of yᵉ Children of Henry Cob
his son John Born at Plymoth 7 of June 1632
his son James born at Plymoth 14 of January 1634
his Daughter Mary born at Situate 24 of March 1637
his Daughter Hannah born at Situate 5 Octoʳ 1639 at Barnstable
his Daughter Patience born About 15 of March 1641
his Son Gershom born About 10 January 1644
his Son Eleazer born About 30 March 1648
patience his Wife buried 4 of May 1648
Henry Cob & Sarah Hinkley Married 12 of Decem: 1649
his Daughter Mehitable born 1 Sep 1651 & buried 8ᵗʰ of March 1652
his Son Samuel born 12 October 1654 & Died 7 of December 1727 Et:
74.
his Daughter Sarah born 15 January 1658 & buried 25 January 1658
his Son Jonathan born 10 of April 1660
his Daughter Sarah born 10 of March 1662/3
his Son Henry born 3 of Sept: 1665
his Daughter Mehitable 15 Feb: 1667
his Daughter Experience 11 Sept 1671
James Cob & Sarah Lewes Marryed 26 of December 1663
Mary his Daughter born 26 of Novem 1664
his Daughter Sarah born 26 of January 1666
his Daughter Patience born 12 of January 1668
his Daughter Hannah 28 of March 1671
his Son James born 8 of July 1673
his Son Gershom born yᵉ Last of August 1675
his Son John born yᵉ 20 of Decem: 1677
his Daughter Elizabeth born yᵉ 6ᵗʰ of Octoʳ 1680
his Daughter Martha born 6 of February 1682
his Daughter Mercy born yᵉ 9 of April 1685
his Daughter Thankful born yᵉ 10 of June 1687
Samuel Cob & Elizabeth Married 20 of Decemʳ 1680
Sarah yʳ Daughter born 20 of August 1681
Their Son Thomas yᵉ 1 of June 1683
Elizabeth born In Novem 1685
Henry 17 of Feb 1687
Samuel & Mehitable twins born 10 Septʳ 1691
Experience yᵉ 8ᵗʰ of June 1692
Jonathan 25 of Decemʳ 1694
Eleazer 14 of January 1696
Lydia 8 Decembʳ 1699
Henry Cob & Lois Hallet Married 10 of April 1690 pr Justice Thacher
their Son Gideon born 11 of April 1691
their Daughter Eunice 18ᵗʰ of Sep: 1693
their Daughter Lois yᵉ 2 of March 1696

(To be continued.)

BARNSTABLE, MASS., VITAL RECORDS.

(*Continued from page 73.*)

[Vol. I, p. 400] James Cob & Elizabeth Hallet were Joyned In Marriage 18 of Sept 1695 pr John Thacher Justice of ye peace
James born 13 of Sept 1698
Sylvanus 25 of Nov 1700
Elisha 24 of Decem 1702
Jesse 15 of April 1705
Seth 15 of April 1707
Ebenezer 7 of March 1709 Decesed In Sept 1710
Jude 24 of June 1711
Nathan born ye 15 of June 1713
Stephen born ye 27 of January 1716
Elizabeth ye 18 of April 1718
Gershom Cob & Hannah Davis Married 24 of Feb 1702/3 pr Cap Sparrow
Their son John Cob born 22 of May 1704 & Died In April 1706
their Daughter Sarah born 27 of Octor 1705
Gershom born ye 15 of Novr 1707
his Second Son John born ye 17 of Novr 1709
his Daughter Hannah August 29 1711
his Daughter Thankful July 10 1714
his Daughter Anne & Son Josiah Twins born ye 8th of Decem : 1716
his Son Edward born 2 Novemr 1718
Daughter Anne Died 4 Nov 1720
his Daughter Mary born 14 June 1721
Jonathan Cob & Hope Huckens Maried 1 of March 1682/3

Their Son Samuel born 23 of February 1683
Their son Jonathan born 26 of April 1686
Their son Ebenezer born 26 of April 1688
Their son Joseph born 24 of August 1690
their Daughter Lydia born 17 of January 1692

[p. 401] The births of ye Children of William Crocker & Alice his Wife
his son John born May 1st 1637
his Daughter Elizabeth Septr 22 1639
his Son Samuel 3 of July 1642
Job born March 9 1644
Josiah 19 Sept 1647
Eleazer 21 of July 1650
Joseph 1654
Elizabeth Died May 1658
his Son John Crocker Married with Mary Bodfish 1659
his Daughter Elizabeth born octor 7 1660
his Son Jonathan born July 15 1662
Mary his Wife Died In Decem 1662
The Sd John Crocker Married With Mary Bursley 25 April 1663
his Son John Born 17 of Feb 1663
his Daughter Hannah born 10 Octor 1665
his Son Joseph born 10 of March 1667/8
Benjamin Nathaniel Experience Jabez Mary Abigail & Bathshua his Children not entered when Born
John Crocker Senr Deceasd May 1711
Jonathan Son of John Crocker & Hannah Howland Married 20 May 1686
Their Daughter Lydia born 26 of Sepr 1686
Their Daughter Hannah bon 26 of March 1688
Their Daughter Thankful born 6 of March 1690
Their son Isaac born 4 of April 1692
Reliance ye 28 of June 1694
Jonathan Born ye 28 of Aug: 1696
James born Sept 3rd 1699
Ephraim April 1702 & Died 1 of May 1704

Joseph Son of John Crocker & Anne Howland Married 18 Sep: 1691
Their Daughter Deborah born Last Decem: 1691
Their Daughter prudence Born 26 July 1692*
Their son Benjamin born 5th of April 1696

John Son of John Crocker Married with Mary Bacon 5 of Nov 1702 pr Mr Russel
Their Daughter Sarah born 4 of January 1702/3
his son Moses born 5 of April 1705
his Daughter Mary born In July 1707
his son John Born In Sep. 1709
his Daughter Elizabeth born March 1710/11
his Wife Mary Deceased Last March 1710/11

Job Son of William Crocker & Mary Walley Married ye beginning of Novr 1668

* This is evidently an error of the town clerk.

Their first Son born about 18 octor 1669
his Son Samuel born 15 of May 1671
his Son Thomas born 19 of Janua 1674

[p. 402] Sd Job Crocker Son of William Crocker Married With Hannah Tayler July 19 1680
Their Daughter Mary born June 29 1681
his Son John Born February 24th 1683
Their Daughter Hannah born 2 Feb: 1685
Their Daughter Elizabeth born May 15 1688
Their Daughter Sarah born January 19 1690
Their son Job born April 4 1694 Died May 21 1731
Their son David born Septr 5 1697
Their Daughter Thankful born 16 June 1700

10 Dec. 1696 Samuel Son of Job Crocker & Sarah Parker married by Mr Russel
Their son Samuel born 12 of Decem 1697
Their Son Cornelius Crocker born 24 octor 1698
Their Daughter Mary born 8th of April 1700
Their Daughter Patience born 18 of April 1701
Elizabeth born Feb 1702/3
2nd Cornelius Crocker born March 23 1704
Rowland June 18 1705
Gershom December 1706
Ebenezer June 5 1710
Benjamin July 1711
Sarah Rebecca Rachel David not Recorded
Tabitha by a Second Wife

Thomas Son of Job Crocker & Elizabeth Lothrop Wid: Married 23 Decem 1701
Their Son Walley born 30 July 1703 & Dyed 2 octor 1703
Their Son Thomas born 26 of August 1704
Their Son Walley 26 of June 1706

John Crocker Son of Job Crocker Married 11 of November 1704
his Daughter Abigail born 5 octor 1705
his Son Zaccheus 1st of August 1707
his Son John born 27 of July 1710 & Died 30 of May following
his Son Ebenezer born 1 of Nov. 1713
his Son Jabez 16 of June 1720 & Deceasd 10 Decemr 1720
Hannah ye Wife of Sd John Crocker Died 10 of Octor 1720
David Crocker Son of Job Crocker Married With Abigail Loring See ye Other Town Book

[p. 403] Josiah Crocker Son of William Crocker Married with Melatiah Hinkley 23 Octor 1668
his Son John born ye 1 of April 1722
his Son Job born ye 29 of March 1724
his Son Daniel born ye 1 of March 1725/6
his Son Timothy Born 23 of August 1728
his Son Jonathan born November 22. 1731

THE MAYFLOWER DESCENDANT

A Quarterly Magazine

of

Pilgrim Genealogy and History

1902

VOLUME IV

BOSTON
PUBLISHED BY THE
MASSACHUSETTS SOCIETY OF MAYFLOWER DESCENDANTS
1902

---

152   *Barnstable, Mass., Vital Records.*

his Son born 20 August 1699 & Died a Month after
his Son Thomas born 28 of May 1671
his Daughter Mercy born 12 of Feb. 1674
his Daughter Mary born 14 Sept 1677
his Daughter Alice 25 of Decem: 1679
his Daughter Melatiah born 20 Nov 1681
his Son Josiah born y 8 of Feb. 1684
his Son Ebenezer born y 30 May 1687
his Son Seth born 23 of Sept 1689
his Son Benjamin born 26 Sept 1692
Josiah Crocker Sen Deceas'd 2 Feb 1698/9
Melatiah his Widdow Decea'd 2 Feb: 1714/5

Thomas Crocker Son of Josiah Crocker Maried 25 March 1696
Their Daughter Tabitha born 20 Decem 1698
Their son Josiah Born 21 April 1701
one Son Died In June 1706
his Son Seth born 13 of June 1708
his Daughter Hannah born 8 May 1711
Thankful &
Joseph

Ebenezer Son of Josiah Married With Hannah hall See y other Town Book

Joseph Crocker Son of William Crocker & Temperance Bursley married y beginning of Decem 1677
Their Son William born 25 august 1679
Their Son Timothy born 30 of April 1681
Their Son Noah born 8th of Decem 1683
Their Daughter Joanna born 18 Day of July 1687
Their Daughter Martha born 22 Feb: 1689/90
Their Daughter Temperence born 26 Aug: 1694
Their Daughter Remember born 26 Aug: 1699

William son of Joseph Crocker & Mary Daughter of Josiah Crocker Married pr Justice Skiff November 1705
Mercy his Daughter born 22nd Sept 1706
a Son Died 4 July 1708 being a fortnight old
a Daughter Still born Aug 3 1709
his Son William born 9 Sept 1710 1710
his Daughter Alice born In Sept 1712
his Daughter Mary born Aug: 12 1714
Joseph his Son Born In Decem 1718
his Son Benjamin born In March 1720

Timothy Crocker Son of Joseph Maried Melatiah Crocker
Their Daughter Jerusha born 12 December 1711
Daughter Melatiah born March 19 1714
Daughter Bathsheba born April 2 1717
Abigail born April 2 1721
Martha born Decem 21 1724

(*To be continued.*)

BARNSTABLE, MASS., VITAL RECORDS.

(Continued from Vol. III, p. 152.)

[Vol. I, p. 404] Eleazer Crocker and Ruth Chipman Married 7 April 1682

Their Son Benoni Born 13 of May 1682
Their Daughter Bethiah born 23 Sept 1683
Their Son Nathan born y 27 of April 1685
Their Son Daniel born y 23 of March 1686/7
Sarah Born March 23 1689
Theophilus born 11 of March 1691
Eleazer born 3 of August & Ruth also twins 1693
Abel born 15 June 1695
Rebekah his Daughter was born 10 Decem 1697
his Wife Ruth Dyed 8th of April 1698
his Son Benoni Dyed 3 Feb : 1701
Richard Childs & Elizabeth Crocker Married
his son Samuel born 6 of Nov 1679
his Daughter Elizabeth 23 Janry 1681 & Died 5 weeks after
his Son Thomas born Janry 10 1682
his Daughter Hannah born 22 Janry 1684
his Son Timothy was born 22 Sept 1686
his Son Ebenezer born March Latter End 1691 as I think
his Daughter Elizabeth born 6 June 1692
his Son James born 6 Nov 1694
his Daughter Mercy born 7 May 1697
his Son Joseph born 5 March 1699 1700
Thankful 15 August 1702
Deacon Richard Childs Wife Died 1716 ye 15th Day of January
Increase Clap & Elizabeth Goodspeed ye vid: of Nathll Goodspeed Married In Octor 1675
his son John: Clap born In Octor 1676
their Daughter Charity born In March 1677
Their Son Thomas Clap born In January 1681 & Died In January 1683
Their Son Thomas born In Decemr 1684
Isaac Chapman & Rebecca Leonard Married 2 September 1678
their Daughter Lydia born 15 December 1679
Their Son John Born ye 12 of May 1681
their Daughter Hannah born 26 of Decem 1682
Their son James Born 5 August 1685
Their Daughter Abigail born ye 11 of July 1687
Their Daughter Hannah Died 6 of July 1689
Their Daughter Hannah born April 10th 1690
Their son Isaac born 29 Decem 1692
Their Son Ralph Born 19 January 1695
Their Daughter Rebecca born 10 June 1697
Edward Crowel & Mary Lothrop Married ye 16 of January 1673.
their Daughter Mary born of a Lords Day Morning ye 15 of March 1674
their Daughter unnamed born ye 14 of March a Tuesday 1676 & Died of a Lords Day ye 19 of March 1676
Their Son Yelverton born a Saturday Night February ye 17th
their son Joseph born March 1st on ye Lords Day.*
Their Son Benjamin born a Thursday ye 14 of April
Their Daughter Bathshua born Tuesday ye 26 of June & Dyed In ye Spring 1684
their son Edward born 6 of June 1685

[p. 405] The births of ye Children of John Chipman
his Daughter Hope born 31 of August 1652
his Daughter Lydia 25 of Decemr 1654
his Daughter Hannah ye 14 Janry 1658
his Son John ye 2nd of March 1656/7 & Dyed ye 29 May following
his Son Samuel ye 15 of April 1661
Ruth born ye Last of December 1663
Bethiah ye 1 of July 1666
Mercy born ye 6 of Feb 1668
his son John Born 3rd of March 1670
his Daughter Desire born 26 of Feb 1673
his Wife Hope Dyed ye 8 of January 1683
James Claghorn & Abia Lumbard 6 January 1654
his son James born 29 January 1654
his Daughter Mary born 26 Octor 1655
his Daughter Elizabeth born In April 1658
his Daughter Sarah 3 Jany 1659
his son Robert born ye 27 Octor 1661
Shobal not recorded †
Samuel Chipman & Sarah Cob. Married 27 Dececem 1686
Their Son Thomas born 17 Nov 1687
Their Son Samuel born 6 of August 1689
Their son John Born Feb 16 1691
his Daughter Abigail born 15 Septr 1692
his Son Joseph born 10 of January 10 1694
his Son Jacob born 30 August 1695
his Son Seth born 24 of Feb 1697
his Daughter Hannah born 24 Septr 1699
Sarah Born Novr 1 1701
Barnabas born March 24 1702
Robert Claghorn his Daughter Abia born Aug 13 1702

*This is in the margin, opposite the preceding entry.
†This entry is in a different hand.

BARNSTABLE, MASS., VITAL RECORDS.

(Continued from page 122.)

[p. 406] James Coleman his Son Edward born yᵉ 25 of Octoʳ 1695
his Daughter Martha born yᵉ 4 of March 1698
his Daughter Thankful born yᵉ 7ᵗʰ of Feb : 1699
a Son born yᵉ 26 of Febʳʸ & Died that Day 1702
James his Son born yᵉ 11 of April 1704
John yᵉ 26 of Septʳ 1706
Patence Coleman yᵉ 6 of May 1709
Ebenezer yᵉ 15 of August 1711
Nathan Crocker his Son Jabez born 10 June 1709
& Benoni his Son 24 Feb 1711/12
John Clark and Mary Benjamin were Married 16 Aug : 1695
Their son John Born 16 of Novʳ 1697
Elkanah Hamlin and Abigail Hamlin Married pr Justice Gorham
    13 April 1711
his Son Sylvanus Hamlin Born 20 July 1712
his Son Reuben Born 13 March 1714
his Daughter Abigail 27 October 1715
his Son John yᵉ 2 Novʳ 1717
his Daughter Rachel 7 Day of Sep 1720 She Died 1722
patience born 12 June 1721
Tabitha Hamlin Born 14 April 1723
Abigail yᵉ wife of Elkanah Hamlin Deceasᵈ May 29 1733

[p. 407] Shobal Dimock & Joann Bursley Married in April 1653
his Son Thomas born In April 1654
John born In January 1656
Timothy born In March 1658
Shobal born In Feb 1663
Joseph born In Septʳ 1665
Benjamin born In March 1670
Joanna born March 1672
Thankful born Novʳ 1674
These Records perhaps 10 year too old *
Cap Thomas Dimock his Daughter Mehitable born Octoʳ 1686
Temperance born In June 1689
his Son Edward born 5 of July 1692
Thomas 25 of Decem 1694
Desire born In Feb 1696
John Dimock & Elizabeth Lumber Married Nov. 1689

* This entry is on the margin, opposite the preceding family.

his Son Joseph born 25 August 1704
Nathaniel Born 10 of November 1707
Samuel 23 of June 1711
Shobal Claghorn his son James born In August 1689
Thomas 20 of March 1692/3
Shobal 20 of Septemʳ 1696
Robert 18 of July 1699
Benjamin 14 of June 1701
his Daughter Mary born in 1707
his Daughter Jane In 1709
Their son Ebenezer born July 30 1712
his Daughter Thankful born 1690 30ᵗʰ January Dyed 1696 In
    January

(To be continued.)

his Daughter Sarah born In Decem 1690
Anna born In July 1693
Mary June 1695
his son Theophilus In Sept 1696
his Son Timothy born In July 1698
his Son Ebenezer born In Feb 1700
Thankful 5 april 1702
Elizabeth 20 april 1704
Shobal Dimock & Tabitha Lothrop Married
his Son Samuel Dimock born y̨e 17* of May 1702
his Daughter Joannah 24 Decem 1708 & Deceasd about 3 weeks after
his Daughter Mehitable June 20 1711
Joseph Dimock & Lydia Fuller Married 12 of May 1699
Their Son Thomas Dimock born 26 January 1700/1
Bethiah Born 3rd of February 1702
Mehitable Born 22 of March 1707
Ensign Dinmock born 8th Day of March 1709
Ichabod born 8th Day of March 1711
Abigail born 31 June 1714
Pharoh born Septr 2 1717
David born 22 Day Decemr 1721
Daniel North ye Son of Daniel & Hannah North born 21 of Sep 1716
his Daughter Mary born ye 25 of January 1719
James born Feb 10 1720
his Son John North born Janry 10 1722
Hannah Born Sep 3 1725
Winifred yr Daughter born Nov 7th 1727
Dorothy Dun ye Daughter of John & Experience Dun was born ye 5 of January in ye year 1726
Nathan Davis & Elizabeth Phinny were married ye 25 of Nov 1714 pr Justice Parker
his Son Jabez born 7 of Octor 1715
Sarah born August 12 1717 & Deceasd 23 of sd August
his Daughter Elizabeth born 15 Sep 1718
his Son Isaac Born [illegible] January 1720

[p. 408] Robert Davis his Children their Births
his Daughter Deborah Born January 1645
Mary May 1648
his Son Andrew born In May 1650
John 1 of March 1652
Robert In August 1654
Josiah Septemr 1656
Hannah Septr 1658
Sarah In Octor 1660

* Altered in different ink to "07."

Josiah Davis and Ann Tayler Married June 25 1679
Their son John born 2 Sept 1681
Their Daughter Hannah born In April 1683
Their son Josiah born In August 1687
Their Son Seth In Octor 1692
Ruth born In Feb 1694
Sarah born In Feb 1696
Jonathan Davis born About 1698
Stephen 12 of Decemr 1700
Anna 5 of April 1702
Joseph Davis & Hannah Cob Married March 1696/7 pr Mr Thacher
his Son Robert born 7 of March 1696/7
his Son Joseph born 23 of March 1698/9
James July 30 1700
Gershom 5 Sept 1702
Hannah 5 of March 1705
Mary 4 of June 1707
Lydia 12 of Feb 1709
Daniel Born Sept 28 1713
William Dexter & Sarah Vinsen Married In July 1653
his Daghter Mary born In January 1654
Stephen Dexter Born In May 1657
his Son Phillip Dexter born In Sept 1659
James Dexter his Son born In May 1662
his Son Thomas Dexter born In July 1665
his Son John Dexter born In August 1668
his Son Benjamin born In Feb 1670
John Dunham & Mary Smith Married 1 of March 1679 80
Their Son Thomas born ye 25 of Decemr 1680
his Son John Born ye 18 of May 1682
his Son Ebenezer born ye 17 of April 1684
his Daughter Desire born ye 10 of Decem 1685
his Son Elisha born ye 1st of Septr 1687
his Daughter Mercy born 10 of June 1689
his Son Benjamin born 20 June 1691
John Dunham Deceasd 2 January 1696 Aged In his 48th year

[p. 409] John Davis & Hannah Lynnel Married 15 of March 1648
his Son John born About ye Midst January 1649
Samuel Midst Decemr 1651
twins Hannah & Mary 3 of January 1653
twins Joseph & Benjamin June 1656
Simon Midst July 1658
Doler beginning Octor 1660
Jabez
Doller Davis & Hannah Linnel Married 3 of August 1681
Shobal Born 23 of April 1685
Thomas In August 1687

224   Barnstable, Mass., Vital Records.

Hannah In Decem^r 1689
Stephen In Sep^t 1690
Thankful In march 1696
Daniel In July 1698
Job born In July 1700
Noah Born In Sept 1702
Remember Mercy 15 of Octo^r 1704
Joseph Davis & Mary Claghorn Married March 28. 1682
their Son Simon Born 19 January 1683
Mary ye 19 of June 1685
Their Son Joseph born Last of April 1687
Robert Davis 13 June 1689
James Cahoon Son of wid Mary Davis born 25 octo^r 1696
Jabez Davis & Experience Linnel Married 20 Augus 1689
Their Son Nathan born 2 March 1690
Samuel born 25 September 1692
his Daughter Bathsheba born 16 January 1694
his Son Isaac born 23 April 1696
his Daughter Abigail 26 april 1698
his Son Jacob born Last octo^r 1699
Mercy born ye 16 of Feb : 1701
John Davis Ju^r & Ruth Goodspeed Married 2nd Feb in ye year 1674
Their son John Born ye Last of Novr 1675 & Died About ye Middle of August 1681
ye 22 of Feb 1692
Their son Benjamin Born ye 8 of Septem 1679
Their son John Born ye 17 of March 1684
Their son Nathaniel Born ye 17 of July 1686
John Davis Ju^r his Second Wife Mary Hamlin they were Married
his Son Shobal born 10 of July 1694
James born 24 of March 1696
Ebenezer born 13 of May 1697
his Aboves^d Wife Mary Hamlin Deceas^d About ye Last of Nov 1698
John Davis Ju^r & ye Widdow Hannah Bacon Married [*illegible*] 1699
pr Mr Russel
& their Son Nicholas Born 12 March 1699 1700

[p. 410] Stephen Dexter & Anna Sanders Married 27 of April 1696
Their Daughter Mary born 24 August 1696
Their Son Born 22 Decem 1698 & Died ye January following 1698
Their Daughter Abigail born 13 of May 1699
Their Daughter Content born 5 February 1701
Their Daughter Anna born 9 of March 1702/3
Sarah Dexter born ye 1 of June 1705
Stephen born 26 July 1707
Mercy born 5 of July 1709
his Daughter Miriam born 8 of March 1712
his Son Cornelius born 21 of March 1713/14
The Marriage of William Dier & Mary Tayler Decem^r 1686

Barnstable, Mass., Vital Records.   225

Their Daughter Lydia born ye 30 of March 1688
his Son William born ye 30 of Octo 1690
his Son Jonathan Born Feb 1692
Henry Born 1 : of April 1693
Their Daughter Isabel born In July 1695
Ebenezer born 3 of April 1697
Sam^{ll} born 30 October 1698 ———
& Judah his Son born In April 1701
Edward Davis ye Son of Josiah Davis & Mehitable his Wife born ye 19 of June 1713
& their Daughter Mary born ye 8th of August 1714
their Son Josiah Was born 2 Aug 1718

[p. 411] John Ewer and Elizabeth Lumbart Married.
Their Son Shobal born
Their Son Joseph born
Their son Benjamin Ewer Born Septr 5 1721
Shobal Ewer his Daughter Rebekah was born ye 27 April 1715
Shobal Ewer Deceas^d ye 6th of August 1715
Thomas Ewer ye Son of Thomas Ewer born Decem^r 1673
Thomas Ewer Married with Elizabeth Lovell Octo 1684
his Son Thomas born In January 1688
Shobal born 1690
John In Feb 1692
Mehitable born Octo^r 1694 & Died Novr 1694.
Nath^{ll} Born in Novr 1695
Jonathan born July 1696 & Died Novr 1696.
Hezekiah Born Sepr 1697.
thankful born Latter end of Novr 1701.
His Wife Died ye 20 day of May 1717

[p. 412] Edward Fitts Randles Children
his Daughter Hannah born In April 1649
Mary ye Last of May 1651
his Son John ye 7 of Octo^r 1653
his Son Isaac born about ye 7 of Decem^r 1664
Joseph ye first of March 1656
Thos ye 16 of August 1659
Hope ye 2 of April 1661
Nath^{ll} Fittsrandle & Mary Holley Married Novr 1662
his Son John Born ye first of Feb 1662
Mary Daughter of Richard Foxwel born 17 August 1635
Martha ye 24 of March 1638
Ruth ye 25 of March 1641
Dr John Fuller his Daughter Bethiah born Decem 1687
his Son John Fuller born Octo^r 1689
Reliance Fuller born Sepr 8 1691
John Fuller and Thankful Gorham Married June 16 1710 ^r Mr Russel

his Daughter Hannah born 1 of april 1711
his Son John Born 3 of August 1712
Mary & Bethia twins born 1st of Septemb. 1715
his Son Nathaniel born 10 Decem : 1716
Thankful born 19 Sep 1718
Joseph Foster his Son Joseph Born 19 of Sept 1698
his Son Benjamin 16 Nov' 1699
Joseph Fuller Jur his Daughter Rebekah Born Decem 29 1709
his Daughter Bethiah Born March 2 1712

[P. 413] Thos Son of Samll Fuller Senr born 18 of May /50
his Daughter Sarah 14 of December 1654
a Child born 8th of Feb 58 & buried 15 Days after
Thomas Fuller & Elizabeth Lothrop Married 29 of Decemr 1680
Their Daughter Hannah born ye 17 of Novr 1681
Their son Joseph Born ye 12 of July 1683
Their Daughter Mary born ye 6th of Aug : 1685
Their Son Benjamin Born ye 6 of Aug 1690
Their Daughter Elizabeth born ye 3 of Sep. 1692
Their Son Samuel Born ye 12 of april 1694
Their Daughter Abigail born ye 9th of January 1695/6
Jabez Fuller his Son Samuel born 23 Feb : 1687
his Son Jonathan born 10 March 1692
his Daughter Mercy born 1 April 1696
his Daughter 23 Sept 1704 Named Lois born 1704
his Son Ebenezer born 20 Feb 1708
his Daughter Mary Born
Matthew Fuller and Patience Young Married by Justice Skiff 25 Feb 1692
Their Daughter Anne Born in Nov 1693
his Son Jonathan Octor 1696
his Daughter Content born ye 19 of Feb 1698/9
Joan born in ye year 1704 & Died 1708
his Son David born Feb 1706/7 1706/7
his Son Young Born 1708
Cornelius 1710
Barnabas Fuller & Elizabeth Young Married 25 of Feb 1680
Their son Samuel born In Novr 1681
& Isaac born August 1684
& Hannah Born In Sep. 1688
his Son Ebenezer Born Latter End of April 1699
his Son Josiah born February 1709 1709
Samll Fuller his Daughter Sarah was born 16 April 1719
Joseph Fuller his Daughter Remember born 26 of May 1701
his Son Seth Fuller born (*) of Sept 1705

* The original entry was "5." In its present condition it is doubtful whether an attempt was made to change it to "1" or it was blotted accidentally. There are two blots near it.

Thankful 4 of August 1708
Benjamin Fuller his Daugher Temperance born 7 of March 1702
& his Daughter Hannah Born 20 of May 1704
John born 25 Decem 1706
& his Son James born 1 of May 1711

(To be continued.)

THE MAYFLOWER DESCENDANT

An Illustrated Quarterly Magazine

OF

Pilgrim Genealogy, History and Biography

1903

VOLUME V

BOSTON
PUBLISHED BY THE
MASSACHUSETTS SOCIETY OF MAYFLOWER DESCENDANTS
1903

BARNSTABLE, MASS., VITAL RECORDS.

(Continued from Vol. IV, page 227.)

[p. 414] ye Births of ye Children of John Gorham born at Plymoth his Daughter Desire ye 2 of April 1644

At Marshfield
- Temperance ye 5th of May 1646
- Elizabeth ye 2nd of April 1648
- his Son James ye 28 of April 1650
- John ye 20 of Feb 1651

born at Yarmoth his Son Joseph ye 16 of Feb 1653
born at Barnstable Jabez ye 3rd of August 1656
his Daughter Mercy ye 20 of Janay 1658
Lydia ye 11 of Novr 1661
his Daughter Desire Married to John Hawes 7 octor 1661
James Gorham & Hannah Huckens was Married ye 24 Day of Feb 1673
Their Daughter Desire Gorham born ye 9 Day of Feb 1674
Their son James Gorham born ye 6 Day of March 1676/7
Their Daughter Experience Gorham born ye 28 Day of July 1678
Their Son John Gorham born ye 2nd Day of August 1680
Their Daughter Mehitable Gorham was born 20 Day of April 1683
Their Son Thomas Gorham born ye 16 Day of Decemr 1684
Their Daughter Mercy Gorham born ye 22 of Novr 1686
Their son Joseph Gorham born ye 25 of March 1689
Their son Jabez Gorham born ye 6th Day of March 1690/1
Their son Sylvanus Gorham born ye 13 of Octor 1693
Their son Ebenezer Gorham born ye 14 of Feb 1695/6
Their Above sd Daughter Mercy Gorham Departed ye Life 12 of June 1689
Mrs Desire Gorham Relict of Capt John Gorham Senr Late of Barnstable Deceasd Departed this Life ye 13 Day of Octor 1683*

*See Mayflower Descendant, IV: 217.

John Gorham and Mary Otis Married 24 of Feb 1674
his Son John Born ye 18 of January 1675 and Died ye first of April 1679
his Daughter Temperance born ye 2nd of August 1678
his Daughter Mary born ye 18 of Sept 1680
his Son Stephen born ye 23 of June 1683
Shobal his Son Born 2nd of Sept 1686
his Son John Born ye 28 September 1688
his Daughter Thankful Born ye 15 of Feb 1690
his Son Job born ye 30 of August 1692
Mercy his Daughter Born ye 1 Decemr 1695
Col Gorham Deceasd ye 11 of Novem 1716
for ye Births of ye Children of Stephen Shobal John Job See ye Other New Book

[p. 415] Mr Shobal Gorham was Married to Mrs Puelia Hussey May in ye year 1695
his Son George born 29 of January 1696/7
his Daughter Abigail born About ye Latter End of March 1699
his Daughter Lydia born 14 of May 1701
his Daughter Hannah ye 28 of July 1703
& Theodate 18 of July 1705
Daniel born 24 of Septr 1708
& Desire his Daughter born 26 of Septr 1710
their Daughter Ruth born 7 of May 1713
The Children of Thomas son of James Gorham
Thomas Gorham his Son Benjamin born 8 of Sep: 1708
Reuben born Decem 10th 1709
Priscilla his Daughter born Decemr 18 1711
Samuel born 18 of December 1713
Peter born 19 of December 1714
Paul born ye 6th Day of January 1717
Abraham Born ye 10th of July 1720
James born June 23 1723
Gershom Gorham June 22 1725
Abigail May 13 Anno Domini 1729
Mr James Gorham & Mary Joyce Married 29 Sep 1709 pr John Thacher Justice
Their Daughter thankful born 25 May 1711
Roger Goodspeed & Alice Layton married in Decemr 1641
his Son Nathaniel born 6th of Octor 1642
his Son John Born About ye Middle of June 1645
his Daughter Mary born About ye Latter End of July 1647
his Son Benjamin born ye 6 of may 1649
his Daughter Ruth born ye 10 of April 1652
his Son Ebenezer born About ye Latter End of Decem 1655
his Daughter Elizabeth born ye 1 of May 1658
Nathll Goodspeed and Elizabeth Bursley Married Nov 1666

his Daughter Mary born yᵉ 18 of February 1667
Benjⁿ Goodspeed and Mary Davis Married
Their Daughter Mary born 10 of January 1677
John GoodSpeed & Experience Holley Married 9 of January 1668
Their Daughter Mercy born yᵉ 18 of February 1669
Their Son Samuel born yᵉ 23 of June 1670
Their Son John Born yᵉ first of June 1673
Their Daughter Experience born yᵉ 14 of Sept 1676
Their Son Benjamin born yᵉ 31 of March 1679
Their Daughter Rose born yᵉ 20 of Feb : 1680
Their Daughter Bathshua born yᵉ 17 of Feb 1683
John Goodspeed yᵉ Son of John Goodspeed & Rembranc Buck were Married the 16 of Feb 1697
their Daughter Elizabeth born yᵉ 10 Decem 1698
& Temperance was Born yᵉ 17 of February 1699
Their Son Samuel born yᵉ 17 of March 1701
& Cornelius yᵉ 2 of Feb 1703
Their Son John Born yᵉ 16 of Novʳ 1708
Experience June 24ᵗʰ 1710
his Daughter Born 24 april 1712
Benjamin Goodspeed Juʳ & Susannah Allen Married in March 1710
his Son Joseph born 1 January 1711
his Daughter Mary born 12 oct 1713
Their Daughter Mercy Goodspeed born septʳ 26 1725

[p. 416] Ebenezer Goodspeed & Lydia Crowel Married Feb 1677
Their Son Benjamin born yᵉ 31 of October 1678
Their Son born yᵉ 21 of January 1679 & Deceasᵈ yᵉ 20 of December 1680
Their Daughter Mehitable born yᵉ 4 September 1681
Their Daughter Alice born yᵉ 30 of June 1683
Their Son Ebenezer born yᵉ 10ᵗʰ of Septʳ 1685
Their Daughter Mary born yᵉ 2 august 1687
their Daughter Susannah born yᵉ 7 of Novʳ 1689
Their Daughter patience born yᵉ 1 of June 1692
Their Daughter Ruth born yᵉ 12 of July 1694
Their Daughter Lyddia born In Octoʳ yᵉ 14 1696
Their Son Roger born Octoʳ 14ᵗʰ 1698
Their Daughter Reliance born 18 September 1701
Moses Goodspeed born yᵉ 24 of Novʳ 1704
Benjamin Goodspeed & Hope Lumbart married pr Esqʳ Lothrop 1707
Their Son Jabez Goodspeed born 26 January 1707/8
Their Daughter Jane born 7 Sep 1709
James Last June 1711
Their Son David born Novʳ 13 1713
& Nathan born 7 Octoʳ 1715   Nathan Died April 29 1731
Their Daughter Patience born 25 March 1718

his Son Jonathan Born 23 April 1720
Mʳ Samuel Green his Daughter Hannah born yᵉ 28 March 1716

[p. 417] John Howland his Son Isaac born yᵉ 25 of Novʳ 1659
his Daughter Hannah born yᵉ 15 of May 1661
his Daughter Mercy yᵉ 21 of January 1663
his Daughter Lydia born yᵉ 9 of January 1665
his Daughter Experience yᵉ 28 of July 1668
his Daughter Anne born yᵉ 9 of Sept 1670
his Son Shobal born yᵉ 30 of Sept 1672
his Son John born yᵉ 31 of Decemʳ 1674
Isaac Howland and Ann Tayler Married Decemʳ 27 Day 1686
Their son Ebenezer born yᵉ 7 of Sep 1687
Their son Isaac Born yᵉ 3 of July 1689
Their Daughter Mary born In Octoʳ 1691
Their Daughter Ann born In Decemʳ 1694
Their Son John Born yᵉ 2 February 1696
Their Son Joseph Born yᵉ Last of July 1702
Shobal Howland & Mercy Blossom were Married 13 of Decemʳ 1700 pr Mʳ Russel
his Son Jabez born yᵉ 16 of Septᵗ 1701
his Daughter Mercy born 21 of May 1710
his Son Zaccheus Howland
John Howland juʳ his Son George Born 30 Decem 1705
his Daughter Hannah born 2 of Feb 1708
Mary August 11ᵗʰ 1711
Joannah Born yᵉ 8ᵗʰ Day of January 1715
by his 2ⁿᵈ Wife Mary Crocker
his Son John Howland Born 13 Day of Feb 1720 21
his Son Job Howland In June 1726 1726

(To be continued.)

BARNSTABLE, MASS., VITAL RECORDS.

(Continued from page 75.)

John Hadeway & Hannah Hallet Married 1 of July 1656
his Eldest son born About Octr 1657 & Died About 10 Days After
his Son John born About ye 16 of August 1658
his Daughter Hannah born ye Beginning of May 1662
his Son Edward born ye 10 of Feb 1663
Trustram Hull his Daughter Mary born End Sep : 1645
Sarah About ye Latter End of March
Joseph In June 1652
John ye End of March 1654
Hannah In Feb 1656
Joseph Hull and Experience Harper Married Oct^{or} 1676
his Son Tristram born 8 of Octr 1677
Jonathan Hatch & Sarah Rowley Married 11 April 1646
his Daughter Mary born ye 14 of July 1648
his Son Thomas Born ye 1 of January 1649
his Son Jonathan Born ye 17 of May 1652
his Son Joseph Born ye 7 of March 1654
his Son Benjamin 7 of Septr 1655

(To be continued.)

THE MAYFLOWER DESCENDANT

An Illustrated Quarterly Magazine

OF

Pilgrim Genealogy, History and Biography

1904

VOLUME VI

BOSTON
PUBLISHED BY THE
MASSACHUSETTS SOCIETY OF MAYFLOWER DESCENDANTS
1904

BARNSTABLE, MASS., VITAL RECORDS.

(Continued from Vol. V, p. 174.)

his Son Nathaniel ye 5 of June 1657
his Son Sam^{ll} Born ye 11 of Octo^r 1659
his Son Moses ye 4 of March 1662
his Daughter Sarah 21 of March 1664

[p. 418] Samuel Hinkleys Children born at Barnstable
Samuel his Son born ye 24 of July 1642
his Son John Born ye 24 of May 1644
Sarah his Wife Died ye 18 of August 1656

& S^d Samuel Married with Bridget Bodfish vid: About ye 15 of Decem 1657

Samuel Hinkley Senr buried ye End of Octo^r 1662
Thos Hinkley Married with Mary Richards ye 7 of Decem 1641
his Daughter Mary Hinkley was born ye 3rd of Aug. 1644
his Daughter Sarah was born About ye 4 of Nov 1646
his Daughter Melatiah about ye 25 of Novem 1648
his Daughter Hannah About ye 15 of April 1650
his Son Samuel born About ye 14 of Feb 1652
his Son Thos born about ye 5 of Decem 1654
his Daughter Bathshua ye 15 of May 1657
his Daughter Mehitable 24 of March 1659
Mary ye Wife of Thomas Hinkley Died ye 24 of June 1659
Thomas Hinkley Married With Mary Glover ye 16 of March 1659/60
his Daughter Admire born ye 28 of January 1660 & Died 16 Feb 1660
his Son Ebenezer born ye 22 of Feb 1661 & Died about a fortnight after
his Daughter Mercy born ye Last of January 1662
his Daughter Experience born ye Last of Feb 1664
his Son John Born ye 9 of June 1667
his Daughter Abigail born ye 8 April 1669
his Daughter Thankful born ye 20 Aug 1671
his Son Ebenezer born ye 23 Septem^r 1673
his Daughter Reliance born ye 15. Decem 1675
(his) Son Samuel Hinkley and Sarah pope Married 13 of Novr 1676
his Daughter Mary born ye 22 July 1678
his Daughter Mehitable born 28 Decem 1679
his Son Thomas Born ye 19 of March 1680/1
his Son Seth born ye 16 Day of April 1683
his Son Samuel born ye 24 Day of Sep^t 1684.*
Sam^ll Hinkley Son of Mr Thos Hinkley Deceas^d ye 19 of March 1697.†
his Son Elnathan born ye 8 Day of Sep
his Son Job born ye 16 Day of February 1687/8
his Son Shobal born ye 1 of May 1690
his Daughter Mercy born ye 11 Day of January 1693
his Son Josiah born ye 24th Day of January 1694/5
Elnathan Born 29 Decem 1698
Mr John Hinkley Ju^r & Mrs Thankful Trot Married May ye 1st 1691
Their Son John born ye 29 Day of March 1692 & Died 24 Aug 1694
Their Daughter Mary born [illegible] 24 1694
Their Daughter Abiah born ye 24 of March 1696
Their Daughter Thankful born 14 July 1699
Their Second Son John Born Feb 17 1701
his Son James May 9 1704
Ebenezer Hinkley and Mary Stone Married Novr 1706 at Sudbury

their Daughter Rachel born 1 Novr 1707

[P. 419] Samuel Hinkley Married with Mary Goodspeed 14 Decem 1664
his Son Benjamin born 6 of December 1666
Mary his Wife Died 20 Decem 1666
& ye S^d Samuel Married With Mary Fittrandle 15 of January 1668
his Son Samuel born ye 6 of Feb 1669 & Died 3 January 1676
his Son Joseph Born ye 15 of May 1672
his Son Isaac Born ye 20 of Aug: 1674
his Daughter Mary born ult. of May 1677 & Died ye 15 of June 1679
his Daughter Mercy born 9 April 1679
his Son Ebenezer born Aug: 2: 1685
his Son Thomas born January 1 1688/9
Benjamin Hinkley & Sarah Cob Married 27 of Decem^r 1686
5 Children y^t Dyed
Their Son Benjamin born ye 18 of July 1694
Mary born 3 of Octo^r 1696*
Sarah 12 of June 1696*
Nathaniel born June 30 1698
Mercy 1 Sept 1704
Joseph Hinkley & Mary Gorham were married 21 of Sept 1699 p Col Thacher
his Daughter Marcy Was Born 17 Augt 1700
his Son Joseph was born 6 of May 1702
& Mary ye 25 of Feb 1703/4
his Son Samuel ye 24 of Feb 1705/6
Thankful June 9th 1708
Abigail born Octo^r 30 1710
Elizabeth January 4 1712
Hannah Born Jun 10 1715
John born Nov 16 1717
Isaac Born Oct 31 1719

(To be continued.)

* "1684" added in a different hand.   † This entry is on the margin.

BARNSTABLE, MASS., VITAL RECORDS.

(Continued from page 99.)

Ebenezer Hinkley Married with Sarah Lewes
Their Son Ebenezer born 10 Sept 1712
Daniel born 26 July 1714 & Deceas^d 8 of August 1714
Another Son born 24 of Sept : 1715 & Deceas^d 27 of Sept 1715
& their Son Thomas born 27 July 1717
& his Daughter Susannah ye 18 Ap : 1722
their Son Samuel born ye 7th Day of Sept 1727
Their Daughter Mary Hinkley Born April 12 1729
John Hinkley & Bethiah Lothrop Married July 1668
his Daughter Sarah born ye Latter End of May 1669
his Son Samuel 2 February 1670
his Daughter Bethiah born ye Latter End of March 1673
his Daughter Hannah ye Middle of May 1675
his Son Jonathan ye 15 of Feb 1677
his Son Ichabod ye 28 of August 1680
his Son Gershom born ye 2nd of April 1682
Bethiah ye wife of ye above s^d John Hinkley Departed this Life July 10 day 1694
ye Above S^d Mr John Hinkley Deceas^d ye 7th of Decem^r 1709
his Daughter Bethia aboves^d Deceas^d 2nd Day of April 1715
Ichabod Hinkley & Mary Goodspeed Married by M^r [*illegible*] 7 Jan 1701/2
his Daughter Mary born 27 of March 1704
Benjamin 19 [*illegible*] 1707
David ye first of March 1709
John 4 of Jan^{ry} 1710 11 & Decas^d [*illegible*] after
John born 7 of March 1712

Ebenezer his Son Born 7 July 1714
Thankful born 1 August 1716
his Daughter Mary Dyed March 1718
Daughter Mary born 26 September 1718
Mary Hinkley sd Ichabods wife Deceas'd 1 Octo 1719
by his Second wife Mary Bassit yr Daughter Thankful born Decem 1722
Samuel Hinkley Son of Ensign John Hinkley his Son John Hinkley was Born ye 28 July 1700
his Daughter Martha 8 March 1701

[p. 420] The Births of ye Children of James Hamlin
His Son Bartholomew Born ye 11 of April 1642
John ye 26 of June 1644
his Daughter Sarah ye 7 of Nov 1647
Eleazer ye 17 of March 1649
Israel ye 25 of June 1652
James Hamlin Jur and Mary Dunham Married 20 of Novr 1662
Their Daughter Mary born ye 24 Day of July 1664
Their Daughter Elizabeth born ye 13 Day of Feb 1665
Their Son Eleazer & Daughter Experience born 12 April 1668
Their son James born ye 26 of August 1669
Their Son Jonathan born ye 3 of March 1670/1
Their Son Unnamed born ye 28 of March 1672 & Died ye 7 of April 1672
Their Son Ebenezer born ye 29 Day of July 1674
Their Son Elisha born ye 15 of March 1677 & Died ye 20 of Decem 1677
their Daughter Hope born ye 13 of March 1679/80
Their Son Job born ye 15 Day of January 1681
Their Son John Born ye 12 Day of January 1683
Elkanah Not Recorded*
Mary ye wife Died 19 Day of April 1715 aged 73 years*
James Hamlin Jur & Ruth Lewes Married ye 8 of October 1690
his Daughter Mary born 24 of June 1691
Their Daughter Ruth born 25 January 1692
Their Son James born 17 of July 1696
his Son Benjamin ye 8 of November 1702
David Hamlin his Son born In June 1708
Hannah 17 of June 1709
Job Born 25 June 1711
Jonathan Hamlin & Esther Hamlin Were Married 6 of March 1705
⫶ Mr Russel
his Children Born
his Son Solomon Decemr 5th 1705
his Daughter Content Decem 12 1707
Priscilla 13 July 1709

*On the margin.

Zaccheus June ye 17 1711
Elkanah Hamlin In ye Letter C
Ebenezer Hamlin & Sarah Lewes Married 4 of April 1698 by mr Russel
his Son Ebenezer Born 18 March 1698/9
his Daughter Mercy born 10 Sep 1700
his Daughter Hopestil 23 July 1702
his Son Cornelius ye 13 June 1705
his Son Thomas born ye 6 of May 1710
his Son Isaac Born 1 July 1714
his Son Lewes born ye Last Day of January 1718/19
Eleazer Hamlin & Mehitable Jenkins Married About ye Middle of October In ye year 1675
Their Son Isaac born ye 20th Day of August 1676
Their Son Joseph born ye 20 of November 1680
Their Daughter Mehitable born ye 28 March 1682
Their Son Shobal born ye 16 of September 1695*
Isaac Hamlin & Elizabeth Howland Married 14 of Sept 1698 ⫶ Mr Russel
his Son Eleazer born 22 august 1699
his Son Joseph born 4 June 1702
his Daughter Elizabeth born Octor 1705
Joseph Hamlin and Mercy Howland Married ⫶ Mr Russel 27 April in ye year 1704
his Daughter Alice born 4 of February 1705
his Son Seth born In March 1708
Sarah Born April 4 1711
& his Son Joseph Born ye 10 of March 1715
his Son Called Southward born 21 of May 1721

[p. 421] John Hamlin & Sarah Bierse Married In August 1667
his Daughter Melatiah born 1 of July 1668
his Daughter Priscilla born 3 of April 1670
his Daughter Sarah 1 July 1671
his Daughter Martha born ye Middle of Feb 1672
his Daughter Experience born ye Middle of April 1674
his Daughter Hannah born ye Midle of Feb 1675
his Daughter Hester born ye 17 Day of March 1677
Their Daughter Thankful born In Octor 1679 & Died In Octor 1683
his Son John Born ye 10 of march 1680
his Son Ebenezer born ye 12 Day of May 1683
Abigail his Daughter born ye 25 Day of April 1685
his Son Benjamin born ye 11 of Feb 1686
William Hunter & Rebeca Besse Married 17 of Feb 1670
Ebenezer Hamlin & Thankful Hamlin Married 11 of May 1710 ⫶ Mr Russel
his Son Isaac born Latter End of Feb : & Died 7 Weeks after 1711

*This appears to have been changed from "1685."

Barnstable, Mass., Vital Records.

& his Son Gershom born 19 July 1713
their Daughter Thankful born 6 of aug: 1715
Their son Nathan born June 29 in ye year 1717
& Ebenezer born Novr 26 1719
& their Daughter Still born Last of Sep^t 1720
Sam^ll born January 7th 1722
Dorcas June 5th 1727
Timothy Sep^t 3rd 1728
Elizabeth Nov 20 1730
Daniel born April 2 1735
Benjamin Hamlin & Hope Huckens Married May 29 1709 ℞ Mr Russel
Shobal Hamlin his Daughter Jerusha born about ye Middle of May 1722
his Daughter Rebecca born 17 of May 1711
their son Shobal 20 Sep^t 1724
Their Daughter Elenor born ye 18 Octo^r 1726
his Son Joshua born 21 Day of august 1728
Bartholomew Hamlin & Susannah Dunham married ye 20 Day of January 1673
Their Son Samuel born ye 25 Day of Decem 1674
Their Daughter Mercy born ye 1st Day of June 1677
Their Daughter Patience born ye 15 Day of April 1680
Their Daughter Susannah born ye 16 of March 1682
Their Daughter Experience born ye 13 of Feb 1684
Their Son John Born ye 19 of June 1686
Ebenezer born ye 23 of March 1689
Mary born ye 23 of May 1691
Their Daughter Bethiah born 26 of Novem 1693
Their Daughter Reliance born ye 30 Nov 1696
the Above S^d Bartholomew Hamlin Deceas^d in ye 63rd year of his Age In April 24th Day 1704
his Son John Died 26 April 1705 aged 19
Ebenezer Hamlin & Thankful Childs Married by Justice Joseph Lothrop 25 Octo^r 1722
y^r Daughter Elizabeth born 1 Octo^r 1723
Israel Hamlin had a Child that was born & Dyed in ye year 1687
his Daughter Thankful born ye 24 of August 1689
prudence born ye Last of Octo^r 1692 1692
his Son Israel Born 15 of March 1694
his Son Joseph born 12 of September 1697
Jemima 15 of August 1699
his Son Jacob 28 of May 1702
Ann Born ye 10 of April 1706

[p. 422] The Births of ye Children of Thomas Huckens with his Marriage
Thomas Huckens Married With Mary Wells 1642
his Daughter Lydia born About ye 4 of July 1644 & buried ye 28 of ye Same Month July
his Daughter Mary born ye 29 of March 1646
Elizabeth born 27 of Feb 1647 & buried ye 8 of December 1648
Mary his Wife buried ye 28 of July 1648
& Thos Huckens & Rose Hyllier vid : Married 3 Nov 1648
his Son John born About ye 2 of August 1649
his Son Thos ye 25 of April 1651
his Daughter Hannah 14 of Octo^r 1653 Died 13 Feb 1727
his Son Joseph ye 21 Feb 1655
Mr Thomas Huckens was cast away ye 9 of Novemb 1679 & Died in ye 62 year of his age
his Son Joseph Lost with him at ye Same time aged 24 years 1679
John Huckens & Hope Chipman Married 10 of August 1670
his Daughter Elizabeth born ye ult of Octo^r 1671
his Daughter Mary born 3 of April 1673
his Daughter Experience born 4 of June 1675
his Daughter Hope born ye 10 of May 1677
John Huckens Dyed ye 10 of Novr 1678 In ye 29th year of his age
Thomas Huckens & Hannah Chipman Married ye 1 of May 1680
Their Daughter Hannah born ye 6th Day of April 1681
Their Son Joseph born ye 6th Day of Octr 1682
Their Daughter Mary born ye 13 Day of June 1684
Their Son John Born ye 4th Day of May 1686
Their Son Thomas Born ye 15th Day of January 168⅞
Their Daughter Hope born ye 21 Day of September 1689
Their Son James born About ye 20 Day of August 1691
Their Son Samuel born ye 19 Day of August 1693
Their Son Jabez born ye 20th of July 1696
Hannah Huckens Died ye 4 of Novr aged 37 years In ye year 1696
Hannah Huckens ye Daughter of Thomas Huckens Deceas^d 29 octo^r 1698
his Son Jabez Deceas^d In ye month of June 1699
Thomas Huckens & ye Widdow Sarah Hinkley were Joyned In Marriage by Mr Russel 17 of august 1698
his Daughter Hannah Huckens by his second Wife born 22 august 1699
The births of ye Children of Rose Hyllier by her Husband Hugh Hyllier
Deborah Hyllier born at Yarmoth 30th of Octo^r 1643
Samuel Hyllier born at yarmoth About 30 July 1646
Mrs Rose Huckens Dyed being Aged About 71 years In ye year 1687
Abigail Hedge ye Daughter of Mr John Hedge born 16 Novr 1700
Hannah Hinkley ye Daughter of Job Hinkley and Sarah Hinkley born ye 23 Novr 1713
& his Daughter Huldah born 26 Decem 1715

[p. 423] Ralph Jones his Son Shobai Born 27 August 1654

his Son Jedediah 4 of January 1656
John y⁰ 14 of August 1659
his Daughter Mercy Born 14 Nov 1666
his Son Ralp 1 of October 1669
Jeddediah Jones Married With Hannah Davis 18 of March 1681
his Son Shobal born 17 of July 1683
Simon his Son y⁰ 5 of april 1685
Isaac In April 1690
Timothy In May 1692
his Daughter Hannah In Sep⁺ 1694
Matthew Jones Married With Mercy Goodspeed 14 January 1694 *
his Son Benjamin born y⁰ 5 of January 1690
& his Son Ralph 5 of January 1692
his Daughter Experience y⁰ 1 of March 1697
Josiah y⁰ 14 of June 1702
his Son Ebenezer y⁰ 6 of June 1706
Ralp Jones his Daughter Deborah was born in y⁰ year 1696 Ult : March
his Daughter Elizabeth 25 of Nov⁰ 1698
his Daughter Thankful born 12 of April 1701
Bethiah 9 April 1706
his Son Cornelius born y⁰ 30 July 1709
Abigail y⁰ Daughter of John Jones born y⁰ 18 of January 1698/9
Mercy Jones born July 1700
& his Son John Jones born 12 of Feb 1703
John Issum & Jane Parker were Joyned In Marriage In Decem 1677
his Daughter Jane born y⁰ 7 of Octo⁰ In y⁰ year 1679
his Son John Born y⁰ 25 of August 1681
his Son Isaac Born In Feb 1682
his Daughter Sarah born In Decem 1684 †
his Daughter Mary born In June 1687 †
his Daugḣter Hannah
his Daughter Patience
his Son Joseph
his Daughter Thankful
John Issum Sen⁰ Departed this Life 3 Sep⁺ 1713
Joseph Jones Son of Samuel and Mary Jones born y⁰ 9 June 1719
& their Son Benjamin born y⁰ 14 June 1721

(To be continued)

* Sic.

† "10 year too old" is written on the margin opposite these entries.

BARNSTABLE, MASS., VITAL RECORDS.

(Continued from page 140.)

[p. 424] John Jenkins and Mary Ewer Married 2 Feb 1652
Sarah his Daughter born 15 of Nov 1653
Mehitable Born 2 March 1654/5
Samuel his Son Born 12 of Sept 1657
John his Son Born 13 of Nov 1659
his Daughter Mary born 1 Octor 1662
his Son Thomas born 15 July 1666
his Son Joseph Born y Last of March 1669
John Jenkins his Daughter Mehitable born 25 of Sept 1694 N. B. 1694
his Son Samuel born 15 of July 1697
his Son Phillip born 26 July 1699
his Son Joseph born 13 of Aug : 1701
his Daughter Ruth born in y year 1704
s John Jenkins Died July 8th 1736
Joseph Jenkins & Lydia Howland Married by M Russel october 1694
Joseph Jenkins his Daughter Abigail born y Last of July 1695
Bathshuah July 1696
Ann born May 1701
Joseph Born 29 of February 1703
his Daughter Lydia born 30 June 1705
Benjamin Born June 30 1707
his Daughter Reliance born y 6 of Ap : 1709
Thomas Jenkins & Experience Hamlin Married 24 August 1687
Their Daughter Thankful born 19 of May 1691
Experience born 28 March 1693
Mercy 5 of January 1695
Ebenezer 5 of December 1697
Sam 7 of January 1699/1700
Josiah y 16 of April 1702
his Daughter Hope 5 of July 1704
Sarah his Daughter born Decem 1 1706

[p. 426] Mary Daughter of Tho Lothrop born y 4 of Octo 1640
Hannah y 18 of Octo 1642
Tho 7 of July 1644
Melatiah y 2nd of Nov 1646
Bethiah y 23 of July 1649
his Daughter Mary Married * 20 of Nov 1656
Melatiah Lothrop & Sarah Farrar * Married 20 May 1667

* This word is written in a different ink.

his Son Thomas Born 22 of August 1668
his Daughter Tabitha 3 of April 1671
his Son Isaac born 23 of June 1673
his Son Joseph born 15 of Decem 1675
his Daughter Elizabeth born 23 Nov 1677
his Son Ichabod born 20 June 1680
his Son Shobal born 20 April 1682
his Daughter Sarah born 5 March 1683/4
M Melatiah Lothrop Departed this Life y 6 of Feb 1711/12 in y 66 year of his age
his Wife Died May 23 1712 Age 64
Mehitable Lothrop Daughter of Lieut: Joseph Lothrop born 22 Octo 1701
Joseph Lothrop Married with Mary Ansel y 11 of Decem 1650
Still born Maid Child November 19 1651 buried 20 Nov 1651
his Son Joseph born 5 of Decem 1652 and Died at Sea Octo 1676
his Daughter Mary y 22 of March 1654
Benjamin y 25 of July 1657
Elizabeth y 18 of September 1659
John y 28 of November 1661
his Son John Died 30 December 1663
his Son Samuel born 17 of March 1663/4
his Son John born 7 of August 1666
his Son Barnabas born 24 Day of Feb 1668
his Son Hope born 15 Day of July 1671
his Son Thomas born y 6th Day of January 1673
his Daughter Hannah born 23 of July 1675 & Died y first of Feb 1680
Samuel Lothrop & Hannah Crocker Married 1 July 1686
his Daughter Mary born y 19 of Octo 1688
his Daughter Hannah born 11 of Nov 1690
his Daughter Abigail bon 10 Aug : 1693
his Son Benjamin born 16 of April 1696
Joseph 10 Nov 1698
& Sam y 28 of April 1700
Thomas Lothrop & Experience Gorham were Joyned In Marriage 23 April 1697 ☞ Maj : Thacher Justice of y peace
his Son born y 10 of January 1697 Deceas 3 Feb 1697
his Daughter Deborah born 21 of April 1699
& Mary born y 4 of April 1701
& James born y 9 of August 1703
Thomas Born y 8 of July 1705
his Son Ansel Born
Joseph born 8 Day of Decem 1709
his Son Seth born y Last of March 1711/12
17 December 1696 Hope Lothrop & Elizabeth Lothrop were Married by M Russel
their Son Benjamin born 18 Day of Octo 1697
y Son John born 3rd Octo 1699

[p. 427] Barnabas Lothrop & Susannah Clerk Married 1 Decem: 1658
John his Son was born 7th of Octor 1659 & buried In April 1660
Abigail his Daughter born ye 18 of Decemr 1660
his Son Barnabas ye 22 of March 1662/3
his Daughter Susannah born ye Last of Feb 1664
his Son Nathaniel born ye 23 of Nov 1669
his Daughter Bathshua ye 25 of June 1671
his Daughter Anna born ye 10 of August 1673
his Son Thomas born ye 7 of March 1674/5 & Died 13 of Octor 1675
his Daughter Mercy born 27 of June 1676 & Died ye 3 of July 1677
Mrs Ann Lothrop Departed this Life Feb 25 Day 1687/8
Barnabas Lothrop Jur & Elizabeth Hedge were Married ye 14 of Novr 1687
Their Daughter Mercy born 1st of March 1689
Their Daughter Elizabeth ye 15 of Sept 1690
Their Son Barnabas born ye 10 of Novr 1692 & Died About ye 6 of April following
their Son Nathaniel born ye Last of Feb 1693/4
Their Son Lemuel 26 of December 1695
Their Son Barnabas born ye 8 of Feb 1697/8
Susannah October ye 8 1699
Thankful Septr 24 1701
Sarah April 22 1703
Mary born July 15 1705
Kembel Lothrop born ye 21 Day of June 1708
John Lothrop ye Son of Esqr Barnabas Lothrop
his Daughter Elizabeth born 3 Sep 1693
his Daughter Elizabeth Deceasd 9 of Novr 1694
his Son Barnabas was Born 23 Nov 1694
sd John Lothrop Deceasd 23 of Octor 1695
John Lothrop ye Son of Nathaniel & Bethiah Lothrop born ye 28 Day of Octor 1695
John Lothrop & Mary Cole Married ye 3 January 1671
his Son John Born ye 5th of August 1673
his Daughter Mary born ye 27 Day of Octo 1675
his Daughter Martha born ye 11 Day of Nov 1677
his Daughter Elizabeth born ye 16 Day of Sept 1679
his Son James born ye 3 Day of July 1681
his Daughter Hannah born ye 13 Day of March 1682
his Son Jonathan born ye 14 Day of Novr 1684
his Son Barnabas born ye 22 Day of Octor 1686
his Daughter Abigail born ye 23rd of April 1689
his Daughter Experience born ye 7 January 1692
Mr John Lothrop Married with ye Widdow of Dr John Fuller About ye Middle of December 1695
Their Daughter Bathshua born ye 19 of Decemr 1696
Their Daughter Phebe born September in ye year 1701
Their Son Benjamin 8 of April 1704

Barnabas Lothrop Son of Mr John Lothrop
his Son John was Born ye 25 of August 1709
his Daughter Hannah Born 6 of July 1712
his sd wife Died Octor 1714

(To be continued.)

THE MAYFLOWER DESCENDANT

An Illustrated Quarterly Magazine

OF

Pilgrim Genealogy, History and Biography

1908

———

VOLUME X

———

BOSTON
PUBLISHED BY THE
MASSACHUSETTS SOCIETY OF MAYFLOWER DESCENDANTS
1908

BARNSTABLE, MASS., VITAL RECORDS

(*Continued from Vol. VI, p. 239*)

[p. 428] George Lewes Senr his Son John born 2 March 1637 at Situate
his Son Ephraim 23 of July 1641
Sarah ye 2 Feb 1643
James Lewes and Sarah Lane Married Octo^r ye Last 1655
his Son John born About ye Latter End of Octo^r 1656
his Son Samuel ye 10 of April 1659
his Daughter Sarah born 4 of March 1660/1
his Son James born ye 3 of June 1664 *Died June 18 1748* *
The S^d James Lewes Senr Died Octo^r 4 1713 Aged 82 years
James Lewes Elizabeth Lothrop married by Mr Russel Novr 1698
Their Daughter Mary born 16 of August 1700
Elizabeth y^r Daughter born May ye 8th 1702
Their Son James born July 9th 1704
their Son Barnabas born March 17th 1706
Their Son Solomon Born 26 of June 1708
Sam^{ll} Lewes & prudence Leonard Married ye 10 of December 1690†
   by Esqr Lothrop
his Son Samuel born 22 June 1700†
his sons Joseph & David were born 10 of August 1702 S^d David
   Decec^d 3 Jan^{ry} 1706
Ebenezer born 9 of Aug: 1706
Thankful born 22 Jan^{ry} 1708
Hannah Born 1 July 1710

———

* The words in italics are in a different hand.
† Sic.

Thomas Linkhorn and Sarah Lewes Married y⁶ 6 Day of January 1684
Ebenezer Lewes and Anna Lothrop Married In April in y⁶ year 1691
his Daughter Sarah Born 13 Jan⁷⁷ 1691/2
Susanah born 17 April 1694
his Son James born 4 Aug: 1696
Ebenezer born 9 of May 1699
Hannah 14 of Febr⁷ 1701
Lothrop Lewes their Son born 13 of June 1702
George born 5 of April 1704
Nathaniel 12 of January 1707/8
John y⁶ 15 of July 1709
Two twins David & Abigail born 8 November 1711
George Lewes and alice Crocker Married y⁶ 14 of June 1711 ⅌ Col Otis

Sarah Born 5 of April 1712 & Died June 13 1713
his Daughter Mary born 9 of March 1713/14
y⁶ Daughter Anna born 3ʳᵈ Feb. 1715/16
his Son Josiah born 19 Feb: 1617*
His wife Alice Died 23 Feb 1718
Edward Lewes & Hannah Cob Married y⁶ 9 of May 1661
Hannah his Daughter born y⁶ 24 of April 1662
Eleazer his Son Born 26 of June 1664
his Son John Born y⁶ 1 of January 1666
his Son Thomas Born y⁶ Last of March 1669
John Lewes & Elizabeth Huckens married ⅌ Mʳ Russel 4 June 1695
John Lewes Son of Edward Lewes y⁶ birth of his Children
his Son Edward born Sepᵗʳ 6 1697
his Daughter Thankful born y⁶ 6ᵗʰ of December 1698
John Born y⁶ 28 of april 1700
Elizabeth born 28 of august 1701
James Lewes born June 4 1703
Gershom y⁶ 30 of December 1704
Shobal Lewes born y⁶ 29 of Sep 1705
Thomas Lewes (Son of Edward Lewes) & Experience Huckens Married 28 Sept 1698
Their Daughter Experience born 15 of August 1699
Their Son Thomas born 1 of August 1702
his Son Jesse born 11 of March 1705
Their Daughter Desire born 14 of May 1707
Their Son Ephraim born 8 April 1710

(To be continued)

* Sic.

THE MAYFLOWER DESCENDANT

An Illustrated Quarterly Magazine

OF

Pilgrim Genealogy, History and Biography

1909

———

VOLUME XI

———

BOSTON
PUBLISHED BY THE
MASSACHUSETTS SOCIETY OF MAYFLOWER DESCENDANTS
1909

BARNSTABLE, MASS., VITAL RECORDS

(Continued from Vol. X, p. 250)

[p. 429] Thomas Lewes and Mary Davis Married 15 June 1653
his Son James born ye Last of March 1654
his Son Thomas born 15 July 1656
his Daughter Mary 2 of Novr 1659
his Son Samuel born 14 of May 1662
George Lewes Jur Married with Mary Lumbart beginning of Decem 1654
George his Son born ye Latter End of Sept 1655
Mary his Daughter born ye 9 of May 1657
Sarah his Daughter born 12 of January 1659
his Daughter Hannah born In July 1662 and buried In ye Year 1667
Melatiah his Daughter born 13 of January 1664
his Daughter Bathshua born In Octor 1667
his Son Jabez born ye 10 of June 1670
his Son Benjamin ye 22nd November 1671
his Son Jonathan born 25 July 1674
& John born 1 Decemr 1676
& Nathan ye 26 July 1678
George Lewes Senr Departed this Life ye 20th Day of March 1709/10
Jabez Lewes & Experience Hamlin Married 20 Feb 1695
their Son John Born 27 Augt 1696

Page 96

Benjamin Lewes & Margaret Folland were Joyned In Marriage y̆ᵉ 10 of Feb: 1694 ℞ John Thacher Justice of y̆ᵉ peace
his Daughter Mary was born 5 July 1698
his Son Seth born 1 august 1704
his Daughter Elizabeth born 17 January 1711
his Daughter Mercy born 3 March 1712
his Son Benjamin born 14 July 1716
& he had one Son y̆ᵗ Died about 22 april 1701
Jonathan Lewes & Patience Looke Married by Justice Allen of y̆ᵉ Vineyard 25 of octo͞r 1703
his Daughter Thankful born 22 of Nov͞r 1704
his Daughter Jane born April 28 1713
his Son Lot born [illegible] 6 1715
his Son Levi 22 Sept͞r 1718
& Melatiah y̆ᵉ 6 of Feb 1720
Nathan Lewes & Sarah Aery married 24 May by m͞r Russel in y̆ᵉ year 1705
Their Daughter Hannah born y̆ᵉ 13 of Feb 1706
& their Son Daniel born y̆ᵉ 24 of June In y̆ᵉ year 1708
his Daughter Mary born y̆ᵉ 11 of Sept 1710
his Daughter Sarah June 24 1713
his Son Nathan born Oct͞o 29 1715
his Son George born 18 of March 1718/19
David Linnel & Hannah Sherly Married about 15 of March 165¾
his Son Samuel born about 15 December 1655
his Son Elisha y̆ᵉ first of June 1658
his Daughter Hannah About 15 of Decem 1660
John Linnel & Ruth Davis Married
his Daughter Thankful born 12 of Nov 1696
his Son Samuel 16 of Nov͞r 1699
John born June 15 1702
Bethiah y̆ᵉ 14 of May 1704
Joseph born ye 12 of June 1707
Hannah Born 10 July 1709
his Son Jabez born July y̆ᵉ Last 1711
David Loring & Elizabeth Allyn Wid: were Married 30 Jan 1699 ℞ M͞r Russel
his Daughter Abigail born 2 Nov͞r 1699
his Son Solomon Born 19 of March 170½
his Son David born 15 August 1704
his Daughter Elizabeth born y̆ᵉ 1 of June in y̆ᵉ year 1708
his Daughter Lydia born 29 of March 1711
& Mary born y̆ᵉ 19 of April 1714
[p. 430] The births of Bernard Lumbarts Children
his Daughter Martha born about 19 of Sept 1640
his Son Jabez born about y̆ᵉ 1 of July 1642
Jabesh Lumbart & Sarah Derby Married 1 Decem͞r 1660
his first born Son Born y̆ᵉ 18 Feb 1661 & Died y̆ᵉ Same Day

Page 97

The births of y̆ᵉ Children of Jabez Lumbart
his Daughter Elizabeth born In June 1663
his Daughter Mary born In April 1666
his Son Bernard born In April 1668
his Son John Born In April 1670
his Son Matthew born y̆ᵉ 20ᵗʰ of Aug: 1672
his Daughter Mehitable born in Sept 1674
his Daughter Abigail born In april 1677
his Son Nathaniel born y̆ᵉ 1 of August 1679
his Daughter Hepthsibah born In Decem 1681
Bernard Lumbart y̆ᵉ Accompt of his Childrens Age
his Daughter Joanna Born Decem͞r 1692
Mehitable March 18 1693
his Son Matthew Jan͞ry 15 1698
Mariah born Oct͞o 1700
Bethiah born In September in y̆ᵉ Year 1702
his Son John born April 1706
Solomon 1 of march 1710
Nathaniel Luunbart his Daughter Sarah born August 2 1710
Thomas Lumbard & Elizabeth Darby Married y̆ᵉ 23 of Decem͞r 1665
his Daughter Sarah born In y̆ᵉ Month of Decem 1666
Their Son Thomas Lumbart born In March 1667
Their Daughter Elizabeth Lumbart born In Sept 1668
Their Daughter Mary born in y̆ᵉ Month of April 1669
Their Daughter Hannah Lumbart born in y̆ᵉ Month of Decem͞r 1671
Their Daughter Rebecca born in y̆ᵉ Month of May 1676
Their son Jabez Lumbart born In June 1678
Their Daughter Bethiah born In July 1680
Their Daughter Bathshua born In August 1682
Their Daughter patience born In Sept 1684
Their Son Jabez born In Feb 1673 & Died About 8 Days after y̆ᵉ birth y̆ʳof
Thomas Lumbart Jur y̆ᵉ Births of his Children
Mehitable born 27 of Sep: 1690
Elizabeth born 2 Sept 1692
John Born 19 July 1694 & Died In October Ensuing
Thankful born y̆ᵉ 19 of April 1696
Jabez born 11 of Feb 1698
Gershom born 4 of July 1700
Elihu born 20 May 1702
his Son Zaccheus born 9 of April 1704
Hezekiah July 18 1708
Mercy July 30 1706
Abigail April 3 1710
Patience 9 of April 1712
Thos Lumbart Sen͞r his Children Born at Barnstable
his Son Jedediah born y̆ᵉ 20 Sept 1640
Benjamin y̆ᵉ 26 of August 1642

Joshua Lumbart and Abigail Linnel Married yͤ Latter End of May 1650

his Daughter Abigail born yͤ 6 of April 1652
Mercy yͤ 15 of January 1655
Jonathan yͤ 28 of April 1657
Joshua yͤ 16 of January 1660
[p. 431] Jedediah Lumber & Hannah Wing Married 20 May 1668
his Son Jedediah born 25 December 1669
Thomas born June 22 1671 1671
Daughter Hannah born August 1673
Daughter Experience In April 1675
Benjamin Lumbart & Jane Warren Married 19 Sep. 1672
his Daughter Mercy born 2 Novʳ 1673
his Son Benjamin born 22 Septʳ 1675
his Daughter Hope Born 26 March 1679
his Wife Jane Deceasᵈ yͤ 27 of Feb 1682
Sᵈ Benjamin Married to Sarah Walker yͤ 19 of Novʳ 1685
his Daughter Sarah born yͤ 29 of Octoʳ 1686*
his Daughter Bathshua born 4 of May 1687*
his Daughter Mary born 17 of June 1686*
his Son Samuel born yͤ 15 of Sept 1691
his Wife Sarah Deceasᵈ yͤ 6 of Novʳ 1693
Sᵈ Benjamin Married With yͤ Widdow Hannah Whetstone 24 of May 1694
his Daughter Temperance born yͤ 25 of May 1695
his Daughter Martha born yͤ 28 Decemʳ 1704
Benjamin Lumbart Juʳ & Hannah Treddeway Married 23 May 1711 ⅌ Esq Gorham
his Son Jonathan Born 29 March 1712 & Decesᵈ yͤ 22 of May following
his Daughter Hannah Born 8 Sep: 1714
& Sᵈ Hannah his Wife Decesᵈ September 19 1714
Jonathan Lumbart & Elizabeth Edey Married 11 Day of Decem: 1683
Their son Jonathan born yͤ 20 of Novᵉmʳ 1684
Their Daughter Alice born yͤ 19 october 1686
Their Son Ebenezer born yͤ 4ᵗʰ of Febʳʸ 1688
Their Daughter Abigail born at yͤ Vineyard 12 July 1691
Joshua Lumbart & Hopestil Bullock married 6 Novʳ 1682
Their Daughter Mercy born yͤ 16 of March 1684/5
their Daughter Hopestill born yͤ 15 of Novʳ 1686
his Son Joshua Born yͤ 5ᵗʰ of August 1688
Samuel Born yͤ 1 of June 1690
Their Daughter Abigail born 20 January 1692
Their Daughter Mary born 22 Novʳ 1697
Their Daughter Elizabeth Lumbert born 22 April 1700
Jonathan born 16 of April 1703
Thomas Lumber Married With Mary NewCom Octoʳ 4ᵗʰ 1694

* Sic.

his Son John Born yͤ 5 of January 1694
his Son Jededia born yͤ 16 Feb: 1696
his Son Thomas Born 3 aug 1698
Joshua Lumbart and Sarah Parker Married 14 Decem: 1715 ⅌ mʳ Parker
his Daughter Sarah Born 28 Septem 1716
his Son Named Parker born Decem 24 1718
his Wife Sarah Lumbart Died Janʳʸ 6 1718
[p. 432] James Lovel and Mary Lumbart Married In May 1686
Their Daughter Mary born Octoʳ 1686
Their Son Jacob born In August 1688
James Born In August 1692
Mercy In May 1695
Martha In May 1697
Rebeckah In Feb 1698/9
Lazarus Born In Nov 1700
Lydia
John
Sarah
John Lovel & Susannah Lumbart Married In June In yͤ year 1688
Their Daughter Abigail born Octoʳ 25 1688
& Susannah born In Sep: 1692
Their Son Joshua born october 1693
Elizabeth born Novemʳ 1696.
Anna Born Novemʳ 1698
his Son John born 13 of August 1700 & Deceased yͤ Last of Decem 1700
Son John March 15 . 1703
William Lovel Married With Mehitable Lumbart 24 Sep 1693
Their Son Eli born In August 1694
yʳ Daughter Jerusha born Sep: 1696
Their Daughter Elenor born yͤ 10 of Septemʳ 1698
Abia their Daughter born 12 of September 1700
Beulah yʳ Daughter yͤ 7 of Feb: 1704
Elenor yʳ Daughter born about yͤ Middle of May 1707
Mr William Lovell died in his 90ᵗʰ year Apˡ 21ˢᵗ 1753.
Andrew Lovel his Childrens Age
his Daughter Deborah born yͤ 6 of May 1689 at Situate
his Daughter Mary born at Barnstable 17 Novʳ 1693
his Son Jonathan born 27 of March 1697
his Daughter Thankful born 6 octoʳ 1699
his Son Joseph Born yͤ 10 of Octoʳ 1707
his Daughter Jane born yͤ 14 of May 1715
his Son Silas born yͤ 16 of May 1719
Robert Parker Married with Sarah James 28 Janʳ 1656
his Daughter Mary born yͤ 1ˢᵗ of April 1658
his Son Samuel yͤ Latter End of June 1660
his Daughter Alice born 20 Jan 1662
his Daughter Jane born ult March 1664

100

Robert Parker and Patience Cob Married beginning August 1667
His Son Thomas Born 21 of August 1669
his Son Daniel Born 18 of April 1670
his Son Joseph Born ye ult of Feb 1671
his Son Benjamin Born 15 of March 1673/4
his Daughter Hannah born April 1676
his Daughter Sarah Born 1678
his Son Elisha born In april 1680
his Daughter Alice born Sep^tr 15 1681
Elisha Parker and Elizabeth Hinkley married 15 July 1657
his Son Thomas born about ye 15 of May 1658
Elisha About ye Beginning of Novr 1660
his Daughter Sarah Born about ye Latter End of May 1662
See ye upper part over Leaf

(To be continued)

BARNSTABLE, MASS., VITAL RECORDS

(Continued from page 100)

[p. 377] John Manton Married With Martha Lumbart 1 July 1657
John his Son born About ye Midle of June 1658
George his Son Born ye 1st Week In Oct^or 1660
Desire his Daughter Born 1 January 1662
Allin Nicholls and Abigail Berse Married 12 of April 1670
his Son Nathaniel Born 12 of Oct^or 1671
his Daughter Mary born 12 of Feb 1672
his Son [*] Born 1 of January 1674 & Died y^e Last of y^e Same January
his Son Josiah born 23 of April 1676 & Died 1 May 1678
his Son Joseph born 11 of April 1678
his Daughter Abigail born 11 of Feb 1680
his Daughter Priscilla born y^e 28 June 1682 & Died y^e 12 of March 168$\frac{2}{3}$
his Daughter Experience born y^e 8 Day of January 1683
his Son James born y^e 1st Day of April 1689
Mr John Otis & Mrs Mercy Bacon Were Married y^e 18 July 1683
♣ Mr Hinkley Governour
Their Daughter Mary Was Born y^e 10th of December 1685
Their Son John born y^e 14 of January 1687
Their Son Nathaniel was born ye 28th of May 1690
Their Daughter Mercy born ye 15 of Oct^or 1693
Their Son Solomon born ye 13 of Oct^o 1696
Their Son James born ye 14 of June 1702
John Otis Ju^r & Grace Hayman of Bristol Married Decem 13 1711
Their Son John Born April 27th 1713
John ye Eldest Son of John Phinny born at Plimoth 24 of Decem 1638
John Phinny & Abigail Coggin Vid Married 10 June 1650
& his wife abigail buried 6 of May 1653
& his wives Son Thomas Coggin buried 26 Feb 1658
ye S^d John Phinny Married with Elizabeth Bayly 26 June 1654
his Son Jonathan Born ye 14 of August 1655
his Son Robert ye 13 of August 1656
Hannah ye 2nd of Sept 1657
Elizabeth ye 15 of March 1658/9
Josiah ye 11 of January 1660
his Son Jeremiah Born ye 15 of August 1662
Joshua Born ye Last of Decem 1665
John Phinny Ju^r and Mary Rogers Married 10 of August 1664
his Son John Born ye 5 of May 1665
his Daughter Melatiah born about ye middle of Oct^or 1666 & Died in Novr 1667

* A blank was left for the name.

his Son Joseph born 28 Jan^ry 1667
his Son Thomas Born Jan^ry 1671
his Son Ebenezer born 18 Feb^ry 1673
his Son Samuel born 4 Novr 1676
his Mary born 3 Septr 1678
Mercy 10 July 1679
Reliance ye 27 august 1681
Benjamin Born 18 June 1682
Jonathan 30 July 1684
Hannah Born 28 March 1687 & Deceas^d 10 February 1689
See over Leaf ye Under part
Bethiah Phiny ye Daughter of Samuel Phiny & Bethiah Phiny born 9th J[*illegible*]

[p. 378] Sam^ll Parker & Hannah Bumps Married 12 Decem^r 1695
his Daughter Sarah born In Decem^r 1696
his Daughter Mary born ye Last of May 1698
his Daughter Peace born 28 Decem^r 1699
his Son James born 13 of Novr 1701
his Daughter Priscilla born 4 of Sep 1704
his Daughter Prudence born 6 of aug: 1705
Daniel Parker & Mary Lumber were Married 11 Decem^r 1689
Their Daughter Patience born 1690
& Abigail 27th May 1692
Experience 7 of Feb 1693/4 & Deceas^d 24 March 1694
Daniel Parker born 20 Feb: 1694/5   S^d Daniel Deceas^d ye 23 of December 1715
Rebecca Parker born 1 April 1698
& David Parker born 17 Feb 1699 1700
Hannah Born 5 of April 1702 & Died y^e 14 of Oct^or 1715
Sam^ll Parker born 5 of Feb 1703/4
Jonathan Born January 1706
Nehemiah y^e Last Oct^or 1708
Mary Parker 15 of August 1710
Robert Parker Deceas^d y^e Last of September 1680
James Pain & Bethiah Thacher Married 9 Day April 1691
Their Son James born 24 March 169$\frac{1}{2}$
Their Son Thomas Born 9 of April 1694
Their Daughter Bethiah Born 22 Feb 1695/6 In y^e Night & their S^d Daughter Bethiah Died y^e 29 of July 1697
Their Second Daughter Bethiah born y^e 23 of May 1698
Their Daughter Mary Pain born August 13 1700
Experience born March 17 170$\frac{3}{2}$
Rebecca Pain Born April 8 1705 & Deceas^d June 30 1726
James Pain (y^e Son) Deceas^d July 13 1711
John Phinney & Sarah Lumbart Married 30 May 1689
Their Daughter Elizabeth Born 11 of April 1690
Mary born 20 Jan^ry 1692 & Died Jan^ry 1694
Their Son John born 8 of April 1696
Their Son Thomas born 25 May 1697

Their Daughter Hannah born 8 April 1700
Sarah born 8 Octor 1702
& Patience Born 12 Sept 1704
Martha Born 12 July 1706
Jabez born 16 July 1708
Ebenezer Phinny & Susanah Linnel were Married at Barnstable Novr 14 1695 ℞ Jonathan Russel
his Daughter Mehitable born 14 Augt 1696
his Daughter Mary born 23 March 1698
his Daughter Martha born 22 Ap: 1700
his Son Samuel born 1 April : 1702
Ebenezer 26 of May 1708
David born 10 June 1710   The Latter End of ye year 1710
Benjamin Phinny and Martha Crocker Married ult June 1709 ℞ Justice Stephen Skiff
Their Daughter Temperance was born 28 March 1710
Their Daughter Melatiah born 26 July 1712
Their Son Barnabas born 28 March 1715
ye Son Silas was Born 16 June 1718 & Died In May 1720
Their Son Zacheus born 4 August 1720
Seth 27 June 1723
Jonathan Phinny & Elizabeth his Wife their Daught Thankful born ye 24 of December 1713
his Son Joseph Was born 24 January 1716
& his Son Jonathan Was born 22 Sept 1718
Thomas Phinny & ye Widdow Sarah Beettle were Married 25 August 1698 by Mr Russel
See the Birth of their Children 5* pages Onward
[P. 379] Mr John Otis & Mrs Mercy Bacon Were Married ye 18 of July 1683 ℞ Mr Hinkley Governour
Their Daughter Mary was born ye 10 December 1685
Their son John born 14 January 1687
Their Son Nathaniel was born ye 28th of May 1690
Their Daughter Mercy born 15 Octor 1693
Their Son Solomon Born 13 Octor 1696
Their Son James born 14 June 1702
John Otis Jur and Grace Hayman of Bristol Married Dec: 13 1711
Their son John Born April 27th 1713
Mr Nathaniel Otis his Daughter Abigail otis born at Barnstable 19 August 1712 & Died at Sandwich Novr 3 1712
Abigail Otis born at Sandwich Decemr 10 1713
Nathaniel otis born at Sandwich April 16 1716 & Died Sept 6th 1716
Martha Otis born at Sandwich Decemr 11 1717
his Son Nathaniel born at Barnstable Sep 8 1720
Jonathan Otis Born at Barnstable 30 Ap: 1723

(*To be continued*)

* Sic.

THE MAYFLOWER DESCENDANT

An Illustrated Quarterly Magazine

OF

Pilgrim Genealogy, History and Biography

1910

———

VOLUME XII

———

BOSTON
PUBLISHED BY THE
MASSACHUSETTS SOCIETY OF MAYFLOWER DESCENDANTS
1910

BARNSTABLE, MASS., VITAL RECORDS

TRANSCRIBED BY THE EDITOR

(Continued from Vol. XI, p. 192)

[p. 380] Mr Jonathan Russel the births of his Children
his Daughter Rebeckah born at Hadly July 7th 1681
Martha born August 29 1683 at Barnstable & there Died about 3 years after
John born 3 November 1685
Abigail October 2nd 1687
Jonathan born Feb 24 1689/90
Eleazer Apriel 12 1692
Moody August 30th 1694
Martha January 23rd 1696/7
Samuel May 1st 1699
Joseph & Benjamin October 11 1702
Hannah Born 12 September 1707
Revd Mr Russell Died 20th February 1710/11
Mrs Martha Russell ye wife Died 28th Sept 1729
Benjamin died Feby 12, 1712/13
The Revd Mr Jonathan Russel Maried With Mrs Mary otis 1725.
Their son John Born June 30 1730
Sd John Married with Mrs Elizabeth Bridgham 1754
Their son Jonathan Born May 17 1756
Moses Rowley and Elizabeth Fuller Married 22 April. 1652
his Daughter Mary Born 20th March 1653
his Son Moses 10th Novr 1654
a Child yt Died ye 15 august 1656
Shobal & Mehitable 11 Jany 1660
his Daughter Sarah Born 16th Sept 1662
his Son Aaron 1st May 1666
his Son John 22 Octor 1667
John Robinson and Elizabeth Weeks Married about ye middle of May 1667
his Son John born 20th March 1668
his Son Isaac born January 16 1669
his Son Timothy 30 Octor 1671
Daughter Abigail 20th March 1674
his Daughter Fear 16 May 1676
[p. 381] The Births of ye Children of Jobert Shelly
Joseph Shelly born 21 January 1668
Shobal Shelly born 25 April 167-
Benjamin Shelly Born 12 March 679
Benj Shelly his Son Joseph Born   y 1706

his Daughter Thankful born beginning Decemr 1707
his Daughter Lydia Born 8 May 1713
John Passavil his Son James born 5 Decem 1711
his Daughter Elizabeth born 22 Feb 1704*
Thomas Phinny & ye Widdow Sarah Beetle Were Married 25 August 1698 by Mr Russel
Their son Gershom Was born was born 21 March In ye year 1699/1700

his Son Thomas was born 17 February In ye Year 1702/3
his Daughter Abigail born 8 June 1704
his Daughter Mercy born ye 24 August 1708
his Son James born ye 15 of April 1706
John Prince jr ye Son of John Prince was born ye 18 Sept 1716
& his Son Joseph born 10 of May 1718
& his Daughter Rebekah Princ born 9 Sep 1719
and yr Son Samll born April 26 1724
Hannah born 13 Decem 1738
John Serjant & Deborah hillier Married 19 March 1662/3
his Son Joseph Born 18 of April 1663
his Son John Born 16 Feb 1664
Mr William Serjeant Deceasd 16 December 1682
Mrs Sarah Serjeant Deceasd 12 Jan 1688
Samll Stores and Mary Huckens Married 6 December 1666
Daughter Mary born 31 December 1667
Sarah Daughter of Samll Stores born 26 April 1670
his Daughter Hannah born 28 March 1672
his Daughter Elizabeth born 31 May 1675
his Son Samll was Born 17 May 1677
his Daughter Lydia Born June 1679
his Wife Mary Died 24 of Sept 1683
Samuel Stores Married Again With Hester Egard the 14 of Decemr 1685

Their Son Thomas born ye 27 of octr 1686
their Daughter Hester born About ye Middle of October 1688
Their Son Cordiel Born 14 of October 1692
John Smiths Children
his Son Samuel born In April 1644
his Daughter Sarah Born In May 1645
his Daughter Mary Born Novr 1647
his Daughter Dorcas born Augt 1650
his Daughter Shobal Born In March 1653
his Son John Born In Sept 1656
his Son Benjamin Born in Janury 1658
his Son Ichabod born In Janury 1660
his Daughter Elizabeth In Febry 1662
his Son Thomas In Feb 1664
his Son Joseph Born 6 of December 1667

*Sic.

Joseph Smith & Ann Fuller Married April 29 1689
Their Daughter Susannah born 18 January 1689/90
Their Son Joseph born Octo 28th 1691
Their Son James Smith born December 18 1693
their Daughter Ann born Novr 8th 1695
Their Son Matthias born 10 July 1697
Their Son Ebenezer born 31 March 1698/9 & Deceasd 27 of Nov. 1699

Their Son Daniel Born 11 April 1700
yr Son David born 24 May 1703
Their Daughter Elizabeth 19 April 1704
over leaf

[p. 382] The Children of Joseph & ann Smith
Their Son Thomas Born 6th of Feb 1705/6
Their Daughter Mary born 22 December 1707
Their Daughter Jemima Born ye 9 of Novr 1709
Their Son Benjamin born 5 Decemr 1711
Their Son Ebenezer born 26 Sept 1714
Ann ye Wife of ye Abovesd Joseph Smith Departed this Life ye 2 July 1722
his Daughter Mary Deceasd 16 Sept 1728
Joseph Smith & Reliance Crocker were Married ye 5th of Octor 1713 ⅌ Coll: Otis
his Daughter Lydia born 17th August 1714
his Daughter Abigail born ye 21 July 1716
his Son Joseph born 31 July 1718
Mary Smith jr ye Daughter of Samll & Mary Smith his wife born ye 3rd of Septr 1716
Thomas Sturges & Mrs Martha Russel Married Decemr 26 1717 ⅌ Mr Jona Russel
Their Daughter Martha born Novr 19 1718
Elizabeth born June 12 1721 She Died ye 22 Day of August 1721
Thomas Born ye 22 July 1722
Elizabeth born August 26 1725
Rebecca Born Octor 9 1727
Jonathan June 17 1730
Abigail July 22 1732
Hannah August 24 1735
Edward Sturges his Daughter Susannah born 10 of May 1709
his Daughter Abigail Sturgis born ye 9 of Septr 1712
Samll Sturges & Mary Oris Were Married ye 14 Octor 1697 by Capt Gorham
Their Son Nathaniel Sturges born 8th of January 1698/9
John yr Son Born 6th of June 1701
Solomon yr Son Born 25 Septr 1703
Mary Born 14 Feb 1706
Moses born June 18 1708
Jonathan born ye 1st Novr 1711

THE MAYFLOWER DESCENDANT

An Illustrated Quarterly Magazine

OF

Pilgrim Genealogy, History and Biography

1912

VOLUME XIV

BOSTON
PUBLISHED BY THE
MASSACHUSETTS SOCIETY OF MAYFLOWER DESCENDANTS
1912

& Nathll Died ye 20 January 1711
Nathaniel ye 2nd born In Feb 1714/15
Deborah Oris born ye 15 April 1692 } Daughters of sd Mary oris by
& Jane Oris born ye 24 Octor 1696 } her husband Oris;
John Scudder and Elizabeth Hamlin Married Last July 1689
his Son John Born 23 May 1690
his Daughter Experience born 28th April 1692
his Son Ebenezer born 23 april 1696
his Daughter Reliance born 10 Decem 1700
his Daughter Hannah Born June 7 1706
Joseph Stacey was Born ye 22 Sep: 1706

(*To be continued*)

BARNSTABLE, MASS., VITAL RECORDS

TRANSCRIBED BY THE EDITOR

(Continued from Vol. XII, p. 156)

[p. 383] Henry Tayler & Lydia Hatch Married 19 Decemr 1650
his Daughter Lydia Born 21 June 1655
his Son Jonathan 20th Ap: 1658
John Tompsons Daughter Hester born 28 July 1652
Elizabeth ye 28 Janry 1654
Sarah ye 4 April 1657
Lydia ye 5th of Octor (59) *
his Son Jacob born 24 of April 1662
his Son Thomas born ye 19 octor 1664
Edward Tayler & Mary Merll Married 19 Feb: 1663
his Daughter Anne born ye 11 of Decemr 1664
his Daughter Judeth born 12 Decr 1666 and Died About a month after
his Son Isaac Born ye 3 January 1667
his Son Jacob Born 19 April 1670
his Daughter Experience Ult June 1672
his Daughter Mary about 15 Sep 1674
his Daughter Sarah born 6 Octor 1678
his Son John born ye 6 Septr 1680
his Son Abraham born 7 Feb 1683
his Daughter Mehitable born Octor 3 1688
The Above sd Mr Tayler Deceasd 15 of Feb: 1704
& Mrs Tayler his wife Deceasd ye Last of Novr 1701
Isaac Tayler his Childrens Births
his Daughter Mary born 23 July 1711
his Son Isaac Born 28 June 1715
his Son Josiah Born 17 Decemr 1717
his Daughter Experience born 20th aug 1720
his Daughter Thankful born 13 March 1722
Ebenezer Born May 13 1724
Mercy Born March 3rd 1727
William Troop and Mary Chapman Married 14 May 1666
his Daughter Mary Born 6 April 1667
Jasper Tayler & Hannah Fittsrandle Married ye 6th Day of Novr 1668
Their son John Born 28 January 1670 & Died ye 9 of Feb 1670
Their Daughter Mercy born ye 6 of Novr 1671
Their Daughter hope born ye 24 Day of Octor 1674
Their Son Seth born ye 5th Day of Septr 1677
Their Son John Born 21 March 1680

*Sic.

Their Daughter Elenor born 6 Ap: 1682 & Died ye 26th Day of April 1682
Their son Jasper born ye 29th Day of April 1684
Barnstable the 29 of May in ye year 1693 Jacob Tayler & Rebecca Weeks were Married
& their Daughter Hannah was born ye 18 January 1694
& their Daughter Rebeckah was born ye 27 of May 1697
Mr John Thacher & Mrs Desire Dimock Married 10 Nov 1698 ℗ Col Thacher
Mr John Thacher his Daughter Abigail born 2 Novr 1699
Elizabeth 17 June 1701
John Born 25 June 1703
Lot his Son born 23 of May 1705
his Daughter Fear born 28 March 1707
and his Son Rouland ye 28 of August 1710
[p. 384] Capt Jonathan Sparrow Esqr & Mrs Sarah Cob married 23 Novr 1698 ℗ Maj Thacher
Benjamin Parker & Rebekah Lumbart Married 8 Decem 1698 ℗ Major Thacher
Serjant John Hinkley & Mary Goodspeed were Joyned In Marriage 24 Nov 1697 By J. T.
Samll Norman & ye Widdow Casly Married 24 Novr 1697 ℗ Justice Thacher
Joseph Robinson & Bethiah Lumbart Married pr Col Thacher 7 Decem 1704
Juda Rogers & Patience Lumbart Married by Col Thacher 6 April 1704
John Davis & Mehitable Dimock were Married 13 aug: 1705 ℗ Justice Thacher
Paul Widdup & Mary Nichols Married ℗ Justice Thacher 20 May 1708
Benjamin Freeman & Temperance Dimock Married ℗ Justice Thacher 2 June 1709
Jonathan Chase and Sarah Green Married ℗ Justice Done ye 6 Juiv 1709
Benjamin Okilley & Mary Lumbart Married 2 August 1709
Edward Milton & Mercy Hamlin Married Novr 10 1709
John Ring & Hannah Hamlin Married 9 Sepr 1714 ℗ Justice Thacher
John Oldham & Mehitable Gorham Married 12 May 1715 ℗ Justice Thacher
Nathan Tayler & Mehitable Cob Married 30 June 1715 ℗ Justice Thacher
Daniel Hambılton & Desire Springer Married by Col Gorham ye 15 Dec 1715
John Scudder and Ruth Davis Married 19 of May 1715 ℗ Justice Thacher
Edward Coleman & Thankful Lumbart Married ℗ Justice Thacher 16 Sep 1715
John Ring and Hannah Hamlin Married 9 Sept 1714 ℗ Peter Thacher Esqr

Joseph Bodfish and Thankful Blish Married ℗ Justice Basset 30th Octo 1712
Jasper Tayler & Experience Cob were Joyned In Marriage 18 Feb 1713 ℗ Justice Peter Thacher
Elisha Tayler and Sarah Davis Married 24 Octor 1718 By Justice Thacher
[p. 385] Barnstable Novr 12 1695 then Mr Experience Mayhew & Mrs Thankful Hinkley Were Married ℗ Jonathan Russel
Mr Stephen Clap & Mrs Temperance Gorham were Married 24 Decemr 1696 by Mr Russel
Samll Done and Martha Hamblin Were Married 30 Decem 1696
Samll Bangs & Mary Hinkley Were Marrid by Mr Russel 13 Janr 1703/4
Samll Bacon & Mary Huckens Were Married by Mr Russel 30 March 1704
his Son Ebenezer born 15 March 1705 & Deceased 17 July following 1706
Israel Tupper & Elizabeth Bacon Married august 31 1704 ℗ Mr Russel
John Witton & Bethiah Crocker Were Married ye 13 of March 1709/10 by Mr Russel
Samll Howes & Mehitable Goodspeed were Married by Mr Russel 18 Decem 1705
John Morton & Reliance Phinny Married 27 Decemr 1705 by Mr Russel
Nathaniel Baker & ye Widdow Mercy Lewes Married 5 Janry 1718 ℗ Mr Russel
Josiah Howland & yet mercy Shove Married 24 Novr 1709 by Mr Russel
Timothy Crocker & Melatia Crocker Married Octor 27 1709 by mr Russel
Nathaniel Allen & Mary Lovel Married April 26 1710 by Mr Russel
Mr Nathaniel Otis & Mrs Abigail Russel Married 21 Decemr 1710
Abraham Tayler & Mary Beetle Married 1 of March 1709 ℗ Mr Russel
Mr Nathaniel Stone & Mrs Reliance Hinkley were Married Decemr 15 1698
Mr Ebenezer Allen & Mrs Rebecca Russel were Married 14 April 1698*
Mr Joseph Lord and Mrs Abigail Hinkley were married 2 June 1698 *
Joseph Parker & Mercy Whetstone were married by mr Russel 30 June 1698
Ebenezerr Burge & Mercy Lumbart Married 20 March 1701 by mr Russel
Israel Luce and Grace Baker were Married 16 Decem 1701 ℗ mr Russel

*These two entries are bracketed and "by Mr Russel" is written opposite them.

Mr James Lewes & Mrs Mercy Sturges Were Married 15 Dec: 1720 *
Mr John Bourn & Mrs Mercy Hinkley were Married 16 March 1721 *
Samll Jenkins and Mary Hinkley Married Novr 9 1721 *
Ebenezer Jenkins & Judith White Married Nov 9 1721 *
Phillip Jenkins & Elizabeth Clark Married Decem 13 1721 *
Eleazer Hamlin & Mary Phinny Married 25 Feb 1721 *
Jonathan Crocker & Elizabeth Bursley Married Nov 28 1723 *
Samll Lumbart and Mary Coomer 10 April 1717 †
Mr John Russel & Mrs Mehitable Lothrop Ap: 12 1722 †
Robert Claghorn & Thankful Coleman Janry 16 1722 †
Andrew Allen and Abia Lovel Augt 1722 †
Theophilus Dimock & Sarah Hinkley 1 Octo 1722 †
Ebad Negro & Martha Negro 27 of April 1721 were Married ℗ Mr Russel
Ebenezer Crocker & Hannah Hall Married by Mr GreenLeaf Nov 22 1715
Benjamin Crocker & Priscilla Hall were Married by mr Greenleaf 17 Sep: 1719

(*To be continued*)

BARNSTABLE, MASS., VITAL RECORDS

(Continued from page 89)

[p. 386] John Rogers & Elizabeth Williams Married June 24 1696 by Justice Lothrop

Barnabas Lothrop & Bethiah Fuller 20 Feb 1706 *

John Cob & Hannah Lothrop 25 Dec 1707 *

Benjn Lewes & Hannah Hinkley 2 June 1708 *

John Jenkins & Abigail Whetstone 3 Sep 1708 *

John Trap & Sarah Huckens 14 of Octo 1708 *

Ebenezer Hinkley & Sarah Lewes Married 17 June 1711 *

Jonathan Crocker & Thankful Hinkley 1 Feb 1710 *

Ebenezer Goodspeed & Mary Stacy 7 Nov 1711 *

Job Hinkley & Sarah Lumbart 15 Nov 1711 *

Henry March & Elizabeth Lothrop 14 Decem 1711 *

James Chapman & Mehitable Tharp Married by Capt Joseph Lothrop 14 August 1723

John Hedge & Thankful Lothrop ye 25 January 1699/1700 †

Seth Tayler & Susannah Sturges ye 20th May 1701 †

Robert Claghorn & Bethiah Lothrop 6th of Novr 1701. †

Thomas Crocker & Elizabeth Lothrop 23 December 1701 †

Joseph Blish & Hannah Child 30 July 1702 †

Elisha hedge & Sarah Lothrop ye first Sep^t 1702 †

Joseph Huckens & Sarah Lothrop 28 Sep^t 1702 †

Shobal Lewes & Mercy Lumbart 8 Decem 1703 †

Sam^{ll} Look & Thankful Lewes 19 Octo^r 1704 †

Benjamin Shelly and Alice Goodspeed 8th Aug: 1705 †

Adam Jones & Mary Baker 26 Octo^r 1699 †

Thomas Lewes and Experience Huckens 28 Sep 1699 †

Shobal Dimock and Tabitha Lothrop 4 May 1699 †

James Howland & Mary Lothrop 8 Sep 1697 †

John Baker and Anna Anable 14 Octo 1696 †

Joseph Lothrop and Abigail Child 14 January 1695 †

John Lothrop & ye Widdow Hannah Fuller 9th Decem 1695 †

[p. 387] John Clark & Mary Benjamin was Married 16 august 1695 ⅌ Capt Gorham

Their Son John Born 16 Novr 1697

John Gorham and Ann Brown Was Married 14 Feb: 1705/6 ⅌ Col John Gorham

Stephen Will and Mary his wife Married 25 Sep^t 1712 ⅌ Justice Gorham

Elisha Hopkins & Experience Scudder Married ye 9 of octo^r 1712 ⅌ Justice Gorham

---

* "⅌ Esqr Lothrop" at the right of these entries probably refers to all.

† These are bracketed, with "Married by Esqr Lothrop" in the margin.

Barnstable, Mass., Vital Records

James Lovel and Abigail Gorham Married 25 Octo 1716 by Col John Gorham
Benjamin Hatch & Experience Davis Married 13 Feb ⅌ Justice Gorham 171½
Mr Benjamin Allen & Mrs Elizabeth Crocker Married ⅌ Justice Gorham April 5 1712
John Page & Sarah Haddeway Married 11 octor 1710 ⅌ Esqr Gorham
Lot Conant & Deborah Lovel Married 1 Feb ⅌ Justice Basset 1710/11
Benjamin Bump of Rochester & Susannah Lovel of Barnstable Married 11 July 1711 ⅌ Major Basset
Jedediah Lumbart and Hannah Lewes were Married ye 8 Nov: 1699 By Major Gorham
William Case & Hope Hamlin Married 9 May 1712
John Holden of Warwick & Hannah Carder Married 3 July 1712 *
Ebenezer Berse & Joana Lumbart Married 4 Sept 1712 *
Thomas Ewer & ye Widow Sarah Warren Married 18 Sept 1712 *
Thomas Ewer Deceasd June 1722
Shobal Fuller & Hannah Crocker Married 10th 7th 1708
Joseph Fuller & Joanna Crocker Married Feb 9th 1708/9
Nathan Crocker & Joanna Barsley Married March 10 1708/9
Ebenezer Morton & Hannah Bacon Married 25 March 1709
William Green & Desire Bacon Married 25 March 1709
Abraham Tayler & Mary Beetle Married March 31 1709
[p. 388] Mr James Whippo & Mrs Abigail Greene were Married at Boston by Capt Sewal 25 Feb 1692

his Son James was born ye 27 of Novr following 1692
his Son Lawrence Was born June 16 1694
his Daughter Jane Was Born May 12 1696
his son George Born 12 April 1698
his Sd Son George Deceasd 2 Octor 1698
his Daughter Margaret born 12 Aug 1699
Elizabeth Born February 6th 1700/1
his Son George born 22 Feb 1703
his Son Benjamin Born 22 July 1705 & Died 6 weeks after
his Daughter Martha born 10 September 1706
Lieut Caleb Williamson and Mary Cob were Married 3 May 1687
his Daughter Mary born 25 June 1688
his Son Timothy Born 29 Septr 1692
his Daughter Sarah Born 2 January 1695
his Son Ebenezer born 4th April 1697
his Daughter Martha born 13 Feb 1699/1700
James White ye Son of Immanuel & Martha White born ye 20th of Novr 1719
Their Daughter Hannah born ye 10 of June 1721
Their Daughter Mary born 24 Feb: 1722
Samuel White born 23 Sep 1724

[p. 389] Esqr Parker   Baset &c.
a Marriage between John Trowbridge & Temperance Goodspeed was Solemnized at Barnstable 27 July 1717 before William Baset Justice of ye peace
Mr Sylvanus Bourne & Mrs Mercy Gorham Married 20 March 1717 ⅌ Col: Baset
Samll Jones & Mary Blish Married 26 June 1718 ⅌ Esqr Parker
Abel Crocker & Mary Isum Married 16 of April 1718 ⅌ Esqr Parker
Joseph Hacd of Diton and Patience Goodspeed Married 12 May 1718 ⅌ Esqr Parker
Thomas Joyce & Mercy Bacon were Married 19 of March 1719 as also James Berse & Mercy Fuller Married ye Same Day ⅌ Justice Bacon
Benjamin Fuller & Rebekah Bodfish 25 March 1714 *
Thomas Lumbart & ye Widdow Patience Coleman 10 Sept 1715 *
John Jenkins & Patience Pain vid 23 Novr 1715 *
Samll Chipman & Abia Hinkley Decemr 8 1715 *
Eleazer Crocker and Mercy Phinny 26 January 1715 *
Benjamin Marston & Lydia Goodspeed April 26 1716 *
John Ewer & Elizabeth Lumbart July 5 1716 *
Benjamin Hinkley & Abigail Jenkins Nov 2nd 1716 *
Isaac Isham & Thankful Lumbart 8 of May 1717 * Joanna †
Samll Bumpas & Sarah Warren 1 of Augt 1717 *
Joshua Lovel & Sarah Crook January 23 1717 *
Isaac & Elizabeth Crook January 23 1717 *
Samll Higgins of Eastham & Mehitable Phinny of Barnstable octor 9 1718 *
John White & Marcy Jenkins Married Decemr 23 1718 *
Michael Wilson & Jane Issum April 3rd *
Samll White & Susannah Goodspeed May 14 1719 *
May 28th Samuel Annable & Remember Crocker *

(To be continued)

---

* These are bracketed, with "By Justice Gorham" in the margin.

THE MAYFLOWER DESCENDANT

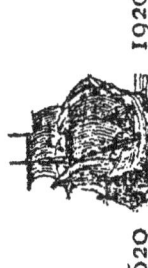

1620　1920

A QUARTERLY MAGAZINE OF
PILGRIM GENEALOGY AND HISTORY

VOLUME XIX

1917

PUBLISHED BY THE
MASSACHUSETTS SOCIETY OF
MAYFLOWER DESCENDANTS
BOSTON

BARNSTABLE, MASS., VITAL RECORDS

TRANSCRIBED BY THE EDITOR

(Continued from Vol. XIV, p. 227)

[Vol. I, p. 194] Marriages sollemnized by the Revd Enoch Pratt.

Micajah Handy to Betsey Holmes of Barnstable Nov^{mr} 27th 1807
David H. Eldridge to Polly Snow of D^o Novr 27th
Asa Conant to Anna Smith of D^o Dec^{mr} 24th
Alpeus Hinckley to Sylvia Lovell of D^o January 14th 1808
Thomas Phinney to Mary Carsley of D^o February 28th
James Howland to Patty Hopkins . March 31st
Barnabas Crocker to Joanna Crocker . April 7th
Isaac Bodfish to Betsy Bodfish . May 6th
Josiah Ames to Chloe Lovell . June 18th
Stephen Southwick of Newport to Lydia Backus Septr 19th
Peter Howes to Rebecca Backus . Octr 20th
Eben^r C. Shermon of Newbedford to Content Tabor, Octr 22^d
Benjn Gifford to Sally Allen, both of Sandwich Septr 29th
Peter Cammet to Anna Goodspeed . March 7th 1809
Allen Fuller to Betsy Smith . March 20th
William Holway to Mary Fish . D^o 30th
Nathan Thomas, to Jane Goodspeed . D^o 30th
Bartlet Hilliard to Sally Ames . July 15th
Cornelius Jones to Abigail Bursley . July 23^d
Heman Backus to Mahitable Crocker . July 23^d
Edmond Hinckley to Betsey Crocker . July 23^d
Ellis Jenkins to Susanna Goodspeed . Nov^{mr} 30th
Josiah Bodfish to Mahitable Parker . Nov^{mr} 30th
Nye Jones to Betsey Jones . D^o 30th
Lot Crocker to Betsey Chipman . Jan^{ry} 1st 1810
John Goodspeed to Phebe Ford of Wellfleet . D^o 25th
Almon Goodspeed to Rebecca Parker . Feby 25th
Thomas Goodspeed to Patty Goodspeed . D^o 28th
David Bodfish to Betsey Nye—May.
James Fuller to Rosanna Jones . July 28th
Marsena Jones to Mercy Bursley . Septr 14th
Thomas Isham to Sophia Hinckley . Octr 17th
Reuben Backus to Patience Marston . D^o 2^d

[p. 195] Marriages sollemnised by the Revd Enoch Pratt.
Richard Cowet to Leah Redner, of Couler march 26th 1811
Eliphalet Hatch of Falmouth to Eunice Lovell. Feby 15th
Alvin Hinckley to Polly Isham . Septr
Barnabas Ryder to Mercy Adams . Octr
Thomas Backus to Polly Bates . Decemr
Crocker Backus to Betsey Crocker . April 1812
Benjamin Jones to Betsey Crocker . June
John Ames to Maria Hilliard . Augst
William Crosby to Lorinza Hinckley . Do
Luther Hinckley to Polly Marston . Octr
Enos Aames to Polly Coombs . Octr
Benjamin Bacon to Sophia Crosby . Octr
Job Howland to Anna Lovell . Novr
Anselm Parker of Falmouth to Charlotte Jenkins – Do
Ezra Crocker to Lydia Nye of Sandwich . Novr
Joseph Nye of Sandwich to Betsey H. Wood . Feby 3d 1813
Silas Goodspeed to Rachel Goodspeed . Feby 11th
Samuel Crocker to Thankful Percival of Sandh Do
Zenas Lovell to Lydia Marston . March
Zenas Fish to Lydia Nye . Augst 13th
William Lumbard of Sandwich to Eunice Crosby Novr 30th
Joshua Parker to Deborah Black . Decmr 17th
Samuel Blackwell of Sandwich to Jane Whelden . Decmr
David Lovell to Patty Crocker . January 5th 1814
Moses Sturgis to Hannah Cottelle . Feby 9th
James P. Crocker to Serena Lovell . March 11th
Ezekiel Crocker Jr to Deborah Jones . May 14th
Cornelius Jones to Mariah Jones . June 19th
Samuel Crosby to Martha Bodfish . Do 30th
Samuel Pitcher to Chloe Ames . July 12th
Thomas Jones to Polly Jones . Do 21th
Jesse Bradford of Plymouth to Maria Lovell . Octr 30th
James Childs of Lee . to Betsey Goodspeed . Novr 10th
Jedediah Jones Jr to Hannah Bodfish . Decr 1st
Isaac Fish of Barnstable to Cyntha Launders, of Sandh March 8th 1815
Nathan Jones to Rhoda Atwood – Do 26th
David Green to Hannah Bates – April 13th
David Parker of Boston to Olive Garrett – Do 22d
Josiah Hinckley to Mercy C. Easterbrook – July 9th
Richard Derrick to Eunice Bursley, both of Sandwich . Do 27th

[p. 196] Marriages Solemnised by Revd Enoch Pratt, as follows . viz.
Elijah Loring to Hannah Hinckley, of Barnstable July 19th 1815
John Thacher Jr to Eliza Hewett . Do Augst 13th
Timothy Horsfield of Yarmouth to Eliza Doane . Do* . Do 20th
Ansel D. Annable to Lucretia Crocker . Do* . Novr 12th
Ebenezer Bacon to Phebe Davis . Do* . Octr 8th
Eliphalet Jones to Chloe Hilliard . Do* . Jany 28th 1816
Lot Wing of Sandwich to Clarissa Hallet . Do* . Feby 1st
Jonathan Eldridge, to Melinda Bearse, both of Barnstable Febry 29th Do
George Crocker, of Barnstable to Alice Hoxie of Sandwich . May 5th Do
William Tupper to Ruth Crosby . both of Barnstable . June 5th Do
Nathan Goodspeed of Barnstable to Thankful Holway of Sandwich June 13th
Crocker Marchant to Amelia Lovell of Barnstable July 28th
Micajah Handy, to Aurela Gage – of Barnstable . Septr 19th
Henry Lovell, to Lydia Marchant of Do – Novmr 7th
Alvan Coleman to Lydia Robbins of Do – Novmr 28th
Joshua Lovell Jr to Lydia Scudder – Do – Novmr 28th
Ezra Lovell to Chloe Hinckley – both of Do – April 13th 1817
Ezra Goodspeed, to Liticier Wiley of Do – . May 28th
William Hinckley to Rebecca Allyn – Do – June 1st
Oliver Hinckley to Louisa Crocker – Do – August 14th
Seth Carsley to Temperance Bradley – Do – August 25th
Nathaniel A. Crosby to Eliza Lovell Do – Octr 2d
James Percivell of Sandwich to Mary Crocker, of Barnstable Octr 9th
Alfred Gifford of Hudson N. Y. to Clarissa Crocker Do* Octr 14th
Ausmon Bursley to Huldah Fish, both of Do* . Octr 19th
Oliver Scudder to Chalana Lumbard of Do* . Octr 21th
Freeman Percivell of Sandwich to Maria E. Wood of Do* . Octr 29th
Daniel Lovell to Sarah Jenkins both of Barnstable Novr 6th
John Lewis to Sarah Parker – of Do – Decmr 4th
Joseph Goodspeed, to Zilpha Jones – Do – Decmr 6th
Harcules Hodges, to Ester Parker – Do Dcemr 23d
Philip Colby of Middelborough to Maria Otis of Barnstable January 1st 1818

* Barnstable.

Benjamin Berry to Lucy Bearse, both of Barnstable – January 29th
Zenas Jones to Martha Jones – of D⁰ – March 4th
Andrew Crosby to Thirsa Lovell . of D⁰ – July 2d
Silvanus Hatch, of Falmouth to Sarah F. Stewart, of Barnstable Sep^tr 9th
Barachiah Bourne, D⁰ – to Eliza Young – D⁰ – Sep^tr 9th
Abraham Hinckley to Betsy Jones both of D⁰ – 1819
Freeman Crosby to Caroline Parker – of D⁰ – 1819

[p. 197] Marriages Solenized by the Revd Enoch Pratt as follows viz
Chipman Hinckley to Abigail Hamlen both of Barnstable April 25th 1819
Warren Hinckley to Lucy Russell – D⁰†
Allen G. Drody to Priscilla Clark – D⁰†
Stephen Coombs to Lucretia Isham – D⁰†
Charles Man of Scituate to Mary D. Lothrop of D⁰†
Seth Goodspeed to Clarissa Robbins – D⁰*†
Stephen Baley of Raymond N. H. to Sally Whitman of Barnstable Nov^mr 2d
Seth Meiggs of Sandwich to Rebecca Fuller of D⁰* – Novr 2d
Arthur B. Marston, to Hannah Jones, both of Barnstable January 2d 1820
Harvey Hinckley to Caroline C. Smith of D⁰ January 20th D⁰
Thomas S. Nye, of Sandwich to Betsy Whitman of D⁰* – February 15th D⁰
Daniel Parker to Rachel Nye both of D⁰* March 14th D⁰
John Hamlin to Chloe Chamberlin of D⁰* April – D⁰
John Goodspeed, to Lydia Meiggs – of D⁰* April – D⁰
Joseph Huckins, to Rebecca Hawes – of D⁰* Sep^tr 7th D⁰
Silvester Baxter, of Yarmouth, to Mercy B. Parker of D⁰* Sep^tr 10th D⁰
Holbrook Lovell, to Sarah Allen, both of Barnstable Sep^tr 14th D⁰
James Childs, to Elizabeth Crocker of D⁰* Sep^tr 28th
Noah Bradford, to Caroline Parker, of D⁰* Octr 5th
David Phinney, to Joanna Smith of D⁰* Octr 8th
Joseph Bodfish, to Tabitha Hatch, of D⁰* Nov^m 23d
Charles Marston, to Nancy Goodspeed, of D⁰* Febr^y 11th‡ 1821

* Barnstable.
† No date was entered.
‡ "Febr^y 11th" has been crossed out in pencil, and "January 18th" interlined, in pencil, in a different hand. This pencil interlineation has been used in the copied volume, and no mention made of the original date recorded.

Daniel H. Sturgis to Betsy B. Crocker – of D⁰* – June 16th
Robert H. Cammet, to Cynthia Baker of D⁰* – July 17th
Isaac Phinney, to Mehitable Ames – of D⁰* – Sep^tr 11th
Samuel Childs, to Sarah Goodspeed – of D⁰* – Octr 11th
Charles B. Tobey of Nantucket to Mary Goodspeed of D⁰* Nov^mr 15th
Ira Hinckley, to Hannah Robbins of Barnstable – Nov^mr 22d
Arthur B. Crocker, to Eliza Whelden of D⁰* Dcem^r 5th
James Robbins, to Sally Bearse – of D⁰* Dcem^r 26th
Silas F Jones to Ollive Lovel both of Barnstable Jan. 29th 1822
Thomas Vinson of Dennis to Mary Smith of D⁰* March 19th
George Blish to Rebeckah P Fish both of D⁰* April 11th
Lot Gage to Hannah Chipman both of D⁰* June 13th
Josiah Clark to Rachel Berry – of D⁰* August 8th
Abram Fuller to Lucy Wheldren – of D⁰* September
Isaih Rider of Chatham to Martha Crocker of D⁰* December 4th
Noble Everet of Wareham to Mercy Nye of D⁰* December 5th
David Lothrop of Yarmouth to Sally Swenton of D⁰* Dec 26th
Aaron Nickerson Martha Phinny both of D⁰* Dec 17th
Alaxander Pinkam of Nantucket to Celio Fuller of D⁰* [†] .

[p. 198] Marriages Sollemnized by the Rev. Enoch Pratt 1823
January the 2d Albert Hinkley to Eliza Goodspeed both of Barnstable
19th Jason Howland to Anna F Jones both of Barnstable
26th David Parker of Boston to Sophia Marston of Barnstable
Feb 7th Isaac Ewer to Mercy Parker both of Barnstable
March 18th Stephen C Nye to Rachel Huckins both of Barnstable
April 6th William W Stirgis to Ruth D Childs both of Barnstable
May 20th Reuben Jones of Fairfield to Sally Jenkins of Barnstable
June 12th Bela Wheldren to Clarisa Crocker both of Barnstable
& Thomas Smith to Susanna Howes both of Barnstable
Sept 1 Thomas Gray of Boston to Mary S Gorham of Barnstable
Oct 26 Samuel Burbank of Nantucket to Loisa Crocker of Barnstable
Nov 4th Enoch T Cobb to Abiah Crocker both of Barnstable
19th Henry Cobb to Patience M Jones both of Barnstable
Nov 27th James N Howland to Lurana Bursley both of Barnstable
Dec 18th John Crocker of Sandwich to Ruth Fuller of Barnstable

* Barnstable.
† The date was not entered.

A D 1824
Jan. 1. David Snow of Orleans to Betsy Fish of Barnstable
" Warren Freeman of Sandwich to Sarah G Harris of Barnstable
22d Prince Bodfish to Clarisa Fish both of Barnstable
Feb 3d Charles H Bursley to Joanna Chipman both of Barnstable
4th Doct. Frederick N Thayr to Augusta M Dewy of Barnstable
5th Daniel Bassett to Sarah Linnel both of Barnstable
" Charles Goodspeed to Sophrona Marston both of Barnstable
16th James Lumbard to Betsy Isham both of Barnstable
17th Oliver Crosby to Freelove Lumbard both of Barnstable
18th Oliver Hinkley Jun to Eliza Tupper both of Barnstable
19th John Colman to Dorcas S Childs both of Barnstable
March 4 Jonathan Parker to Maria Phinney both of Barnstable
22d Bradford B Williams to Jula Ann Hallet both of Barnstable
August 5 Obed Clark 3d of Nantucket to Mary Ann Wing of Barnstable
Sept 12th Thomas Isham to Lucy Crocker both of Barnstable
Oct 3d Benjaman Hinckley to Rebeckah E Lewis both of Barnstable
Nov 11th William Crocker Jur to Sarah Nye Howland both of Do
28th Clement Kelley to Polly Roggers both of Barnstable by Rev. P Fish
Dec 2d James H Fuller to Abigail Chipman both of Barnstable
Dec David Pratt of Carver to Sally Barrows of Barnstable
1825
Jan 13th Wilson Crosby to Mary Ann Hinckley both of Barnstable
18th Calvan Fish of Sandwich to Martha Adams of Barnstable
Feb 1st Elijah Phinney to Temperence Harlow both of Barnstable
3d Allen Tupper to Abigail H Lovell both of Barnstable
" Josiah Ames to Abigail H Parker both of Barnstable

[p. 209] Marriages solemised by the Revd Josiah Sturtevant as Returned by him viz
Benjamin Lewis Jr to Mehitable Pinney* both of Barnstable, May 9th 1819
Harvey Hallet, to Nancy Linnell of Do Oct 7th Do
Eli Hinckley, to Caroline Gage of Do July 25th Do
Silvanus Simmons Jr to Hannah Hadaway of Do Novmr 3d Do
Benjamin Eldridge, of Chatham, to Eliza Phinney, of Barnstable May 7th 1820
Thomas Linnell, to Sophia Case, both of Barnstable, May 16th Do

*Sic.

George Hinckley, to Puella* Scudder, both of Barnstable, August 13th Do
Watson Crosby, to Olive Bassett, both of Barnstable. Octr 10th Do
Lot Case, to Eliza Cahoon, both of Barnstable, Novmr 22d Do
Asa Stephens, to Caroline Crosby, both of Barnstable, Novmr 23d Do
Simeon Coombs, to Sarah Hinckley, both of Barnstable Sept 11th 1821
Ansel Hamles†, to Asenath H. Crosby, both of Barnstable Octr 28th Do
Freeman Phinney, to Harriet Crosby, both of Barnstable Novmr 11th Do
Thomas Bearse, of Nantucket to Jemima Norris of Barnstable Novmr 25th Do
Reuben Hilman of Do‡, to Betsy Chase, of Barnstable Dcemr 13th Do
Charles Phinney, to Lucy Scudder, both of Barnstable January 27th 1822
Almond Bearse, of Barnstable to Mary T. Thayer, of Taunton March 5th Do
Judah Bacon to Mahala Bearse, both of Barnstable April 11th Do
Josiah Scudder Jun to Sophrona Hawes both of Barnstable Feb 16th 1823
Elijah Lewis to Jane Phinney both of Barnstable April 22d Do
Seth Hallet to Sophia Bassett both of Barnstable May 25th Do
Lemuel Holway to Melissa Hallet both of Barnstable May 22d Do
Ira Bearse to Melintha Crowel both of Barnstable May 28th Do
George Savory to Catharine B Baxter both of Barnstable June 8th Do

[END OF VOLUME I OF ORIGINAL RECORDS.—Editor.]

BARNSTABLE, MASS., VITAL RECORDS

(Continued from page 83)

In our last article we completed the vital records in the oldest volume of the Barnstable town records. We now begin printing the births, marriages, etc., in the second volume. There are no vital records in the first one hundred and forty-seven pages of that volume.

In the following transcript, the number of the original page is printed in brackets, at the beginning of each new page. Pages which do not contain vital records are not mentioned in the transcript.

[Volume II]

[2 : 148] Seth Goodspeed Married Abigail Linnell. Their children viz:

Anna	Born Sept 29 1753	Died Feby 15 1821.
Temperance	" Novr 7 1755.	Died
Patience	" Oct 10 1757.	
Abigail	" Apl 4 1760.	
Hannah	" Sept 19 1762.	
Eunice	" Oct 5 1764	
Olive	" Sept 21 1766	Died Novr 21 1814.
Allen	" Jany 5 1769.	" Jany 7 1831.
Sophia	" June 13 1771.	
Temperance	" Jany 14 1774.	

Mrs Abigail Goodspeed Died July 7 1805 Ag^d 75 years
Mr Seth Goodspeed Died March 26 1810 " 82 "

[p. 201] Marriages Solemnized by ye Rever^d m^r Joseph Green
Ebenezer Claghorn & Elizabeth Hamblin Sep^t 8 : 1763
Joseph Davis & Lucretia Thacher Novr 17 1763
John Gray & Abigail Thacher Novr 24 1763
David Howland & Mary Coleman Decem^r 15 1763
Edward Bacon ju^r & Lydia Gorham Janu^y 26 : 1764
John Coleman of Granville & Abigail Delap Feb: 9 : 1764

marriages Solemnised By David Gorham Esqr
Luke Butler and Remember Blachford oct^r 9th 1760
Transmitted To the Cle^r of ye Sessions Jany 28th 1766

marriages Solomnised By the Rev^d m^r oakes Shaw
Viz m^r John Smith & miss Abigail Hamblen both of Barnstable Jany 18th 1764
m^r Joseph Smith & m^rs mary Basset both of this Town Novr 22^d 1765
Bezaleel Waste of Dartmouth & Joanna Cannon of this Town Novr 28th 1765
m^r Joseph Palmer of falmouth & miss Thankfull Davis of this Town Decr 6th 1765
m^r Lemuel Howland of Sandwich & Abigail Hamblin of this Town Decr 11th 1765
Joseph Barnabas Indian man of this Town and Ruth Ralph of Eastham Decr 24th 1765
Transmitted To ye Cle^r of ye Sessions Jany 28th 1766 Pr Edwd Bacon Town Cle^r

marriages Solomnised By the Rev^ed m^r Joseph Green 1764 & 1765
Viz m^r mathew Wood & miss martha Davis Jn^r both of this Town July 26th 1764
m^r Sturgis Gorham & miss Phebe Taylor Septr 13th 1764
m^r Nathaniel Allen & miss Patience Cobb Septr 18th 1764
m^r William Crocker Jn^r & miss mary Cobb Jn^r Septr 30th 1764
Samuel Bearse & Sarah Bearse Novr 15th 1764
Elpalet Loring & Abigail Gillman Novr 15th 1764
Thomas Stetson of Sandwich & Susanna Gray of this Town Novr 22^d 1764
oris Cobb & Theodate Lewis Decr 6th 1764
David Rumsey of fairfield & Anna Lovell of this Town Decr 26th 1764

Jonathan Sturgis & Temperance Gorham Feby 7th 1765
Joseph Linnel & Sussanna Cobb Jn^r march 21st 1765
m^r Josiah Crocker & miss Deborah Davis Octr 6th 1765
m^r Otis Loring and miss Sarah Hinckley Decr 5th 1765
Zacheus Allen of falmouth & Thankfull Thacher of this Town Decr 30th 1765
Transmitted To the Cle^r of the Sessions Jany 28th 1766 Pr Edwd Bacon Town Cle^r

[p. 202] Persons Entered & Published In order for Marriage
Nathan Cannon and Thanckfull Basset feb: 26 : 1763
Benjamin Howland and Anna Crocker Feb: 26 : 1763
Isaac Phinney and Anna Thomas of Windham March 12 : 1763
Joseph Howland & Elizabeth Lovell march 19th 1763
Andrew Allyn j^r of Barnstable & Dorcas Hawes of Dartmouth april 16th 1763
Lemuel Crocker & Sarah Backhouse of Sandwich may 7th 1763
Thomas Palmer of Falmouth & Elizebeth Thacher May 7th 1763
James Colman ju^r and Anna Lumber may 7th 1763
Thomas Allyn and Hannah Gorham of yarmouth may 14th 1763
Shobael Lovell and Mary Fuller June 4th 1763
David Howland & mary coleman June 18 : 1763
Seth Lothrop & mary Fuller of Sandwich august 6th 1763
Ebenezer Foster & Martha Snow august 13 : 1763
Joseph Davis & Lucretia Thacher august 20th 1763
Ebenezer Claghorn & Elizebeth Hamblin aug^t 27 : 1763
Richard Sparrow of Haddam in Connecticut and Deborah Howland of Barnstable octo : 1st 1763
John Gray & Abigail Thacher octo^r 8th 1763
John Green and Elizebath Baxter of yarmouth nov^r 19th 1763
John Smith and Abigail Hamblin Decr 3 : 1763
the Rev^d m^r Oakes Shaw of Barnstable and m^rs Elisabeth Weld of Attlebourough Decr 7th 1763
David Loring & Philippi Dexter of yarmouth Decr 17th 1763
Edward Bacon Jn^r & Lydia Gorham Decr 17th 1763
John Coleman of Granville & Abigail Delap Decr 31 : 1763
Jabez Hinckley and Deborah Wing of Harwich Janu^y 14 : 1764

A List of Persons names Entered In order for Publication and marriage by Edwd Bacon Town Cler
Viz Rowland Cobb of Barnstable and Thankfull Garritt of Sandwich march 24th 1764
Josiah Goodspeed and Jemima Blossom april ye 7th 1764

David Rumsey of fairfield in Conecticut and Anna Lovell may ye 4th 1764
Nathaniel Allen and Patience Cobb : June 8th 1764
Thomas Stetson of Sandwich and Susanna Gray Jn^r of Barnstable June ye 9th 1764
mathew wood and martha Davis Jn^r both of Barnstable July 6th 1764
Sturgis Gorham and Phebe Taylor both of Barnstable July 25th 1764
Abner Coffen Servant To David Gorham Esqr of Barnstable and peggy Cyprus of Harwich Septr 14th 1764
william Crocker Ju^r and mary Cobb both of Barnstable Septr 15th 1764

(To be continued)

BARNSTABLE, MASS., VITAL RECORDS

(Continued from page 128)

[p. 207] The names of Persons Entered with the Town Clerk In order for Publishing their Intentions of marriage &c from this Date and onwards Viz

Mr Elpalet Loring & mrs Abigail Gillman both of Barnstable Sept 22d 1764

Nicholas Cobb of this Town & Ann Perry of Sandwich Octr ye 6th 1764

Jesse Couet of Barnstable & Prissilla Elis of Nantucket now Resident in Barnsbl octr 20th 1764

Samuel Bearse & Sarah Bearse Both of Barnstable octr 27th 1764

Ebenezer Gorham of Barnstable & Hope Carver of Plymouth Novr 17th 1764

oris Cobb and Theodate Lewis both of Barnstable Novr 17th 1764

Jonathan Sturgis & Temperance Gorham both of Barnstable Jany 5th 1765

Joseph Smith & mary Basset both of Barnstable Jany 26 1765

Joseph Linnel & Susanna Cobb Jnr both of Barnstable Feby ye 2d 1765

Hezekiah Jackson of Plymouth & Elizabeth Thacher of Barnstable Feby 23d 1765

Barnabas Crocker & Ann Smith both of Barnstable march 2d 1765

John Bates Jnr & Hannah Cammet both of Barnstable march ye 8th 1765

Nye Jones & Deborah Crocker Both of Barnstable march ye 30th 1765

Nathan Bacon of Barnstable & nary Taylor of yarmouth April ye 6th 1765

John Parcefull of Barnstable & mary Snow of Harwich April ye 27th 1765

Bezaleel Waste of Dartmouth & Joanna Cannon of Barnsb Sept 16th 1765

David Blachford of Barnstable & Elizabeth Ellis of province Town Sept ye 21st 1765

Josiah Crocker & Deborah Davis Septr 21st 1765 both of Barnstable

James Lothrop & Rebecca Paine both of Barnstable Octr 19th 1765

Lemuel Howland of Sandwich & Abigail Hamblen of Barnstable Oct 26th 1765

Joseph Palmer of falmouth & Thankfull Davis of Barnstable Novr 6th 1765

Joseph Barnabas Indian man of Barnstable & Ruth Ralph Indian woman of Eastham Novr 23d 1765

Zacheus Allen of falmouth & Thankfull Thacher of Barnstable Decr 7th 1765

Thomas Gorham Jnr of Barnstable & Rebecca Jones of yarmouth Decr 14th 1765

Edward Bacon Esqr of Barnstable & mrs Rachel Doane of wellfleet Decr 21 1765

Mr Matthias fuller & miss Lydia Blossom both of Barnstable Decr 26 1765

Mr Nathaniel Crocker & miss Catherine Bridgham both of Barnsble Jany 25th 1766

Joshua Ralph & Rachel Ralph Indians of Barnstable Jany 25th 1766

Nathan foster & mercy Smith both of Barnstable february 21st 1766

Joseph Goodspeed ye 3d & Hannah Bodfish both of Barnstable march 26th 1766

Edmund Hawes of this Town & Hannah Snow of Eastham march 30th 1766

John Bursley and mary Howland Both of this Town april 11th 1766

Benjamin Goodspeed & Susanna Smith Both of this Town April 26th 1766

Asa Crocker & Thankfull Cobb Jnr both of this Town April 26th 1766

Timothy Hinckley & mary Goodspeed (may ye 17th 1766) Both of this Town

Benjamin Hamblen & mehetable Childs both of this Town may 31th 1766

Samll Scudder & Rachel Lewes both of this Town July 2d 1766

[p. 209] The Children of Joshua Lumbart (Son To m^r Saml Lumbart) and Jane his first wife
Their Son Timothy Born may ye 10 1757*
Their Daughter Sarah Born January 10th 1758*
His Children by his Second wife Hannah
a Daughter mary born feb^y 7th 1764
Southworth Hamblin, Tabitha his Wife Their Children
their Daughter Bethiah Born July 3^d 1758
their Son Eleazer Born march 25th 1760
their Son Southworth Born April 12th 1762

[p. 212] Marriages Solennized By the Revd Oakes Shaw . viz
Benjamin Hamblen j^r & Jerusha Hamblen . octo^r 9th 1760
Jabez Claghorn & Eunice Davis . Novr 21 . 1760
Jesse Crosby & Ruth Goodspeed . Novr 27 . 1760
Benjamin Hamlen 3^d & Drusilla Dexter . Novr 27 . 1760
Christopher Tayler & Hannah Howland . Jany 15 1761
Jeremiah Jo and Hannah Tunegin . Feby 18 . 1761
John Gray & Mary Otis . May : 14 . 1761
Isaac Hinckly J^r Town Cler, Transmitted to the County Clerk July 20 1761

Jabez Goodspeed & Margarett Basset august 4th 1761
James Coleman j^r & Zeruiah Thomas Sep^t 24 : 1761
Lot Jankins & Mary Howland oct^r 22 1761
John Marston & mary Crocker J^n [†] 1762
Levi Chase of Sandwich & Hannah Blossom Sep^t 23 1762
James Lovell & Martha Fuller Decr 9 : 1761
Benjn Howland & Anna Crocker March 15 : 1763
Nathan Cannon & Thankfull Basset March 23 1763
TransMitted to the Clerk of the Sessions Jan^{ry} 1 : 1764
Joseph Howland & Elizebath Lovell March 1763
Jabez Bursley & Susanna Crocker april 1763
Shobael Lovell & mary Fuller august 11 : 1763
Ebenezer Foster and Martha Snow octo^r 1763
Richard Sparrow of East Haddam & Deborah Howland Novr 1763

(*To be continued*)

---

* Sic.

† The day and month were not recorded.

THE MAYFLOWER DESCENDANT

1620　1920

A QUARTERLY MAGAZINE OF
PILGRIM GENEALOGY AND HISTORY

VOLUME XX

1918

PUBLISHED BY THE
MASSACHUSETTS SOCIETY OF
MAYFLOWER DESCENDANTS
BOSTON

BARNSTABLE, MASS., VITAL RECORDS

Transcribed by the Editor

(*Continued from Vol. XIX, p. 156*)

[p. 213] Marriages Solemnized By the Revd Joseph Green
George Lewis Ju^r & Mary Davis Octo^r 12th 1760
Benjamin Lumbert & Mercy Bacon Sept 4th 1760.
Nath^{ll} Allen & Deborah Linnell Novr 6th 1760
David Baker & Lydia Phiney Decem^r 25th 1760
John Crocker 4th and Thankful Hallet Jany 8 . 1761
Timothy Parker & Rachel Gorham Feb^{ry} 12 . 1761
John Hinckly & Thankful Lumbert Feb^r 19 . 1761
Jabez Bearse & Hannah Bearse March 26 . 1761
Lemuel Bears & Patience Phiney April 30 1761
Samuel Baker & Martha Lothrop April 30 1761
Isaac Hinckly J^r Town Cler, Transmitted to the County Clerk
July: 20: 1761

*This is another error, in the records, of "Mary" for "Marah". It occurs several times in records relating to this woman; but the numerous cases in which the name is plainly given as "Marah" are conclusive evidence that "Marah" is correct.

Daniel Davis & Mehetable Sturges July 7 : 1761
Nathaniel Hinckly & Joanna Lewis Oct 13. 1761
Jabez Wilder of Hyngham & Sarah Crocker Oct 22 1761
Timothy Hamblen & Mary Hallet Nov: 22. 1761
Ambrose Carsley & Mercy Lewis . Dec 3. 1761
Eleazer Scudder & Mary Lewis March 18 : 1762
Simeon Jankens & Hodiah Hinckley March 25 : 1762
Moses Shaw & Anna Phinney March 25 : 1762
John Carsley & Rebecca Page May 13 : 1762
Jonathan Lothrop & Eunice Cobb June 27 : 1762
Isaac Bacon & Alice Taylor oct 29 : 1762
Joseph Jankens & Remember Stewart Dec 9 : 1762
Nathan Jankens & Rachel Howland Dec 9 : 1762
Adino Hinckley & Mercy Otis Dec 16 : 1762
Nero Negro & Pegg Mingo Jan 27 : 1763
Micah Humfrey & Elizebath Davis april 22 . 1763
Thomas Palmer & Elizebath Thacher may 26 : 1763
James Coleman jr & Anna Lumber June 28 : 1763
Transmitted to the Clerk of the Sessions Jan 1 : 1764

Marriages Solemnized By Judah Thatcher Justice of the Peace
Josiah Smith & Deliverance Howes June 29 . 1761
Isaac Ham & Elisabeth Arnos Indians Mach 16 1761

[p. 214] Marriages Solemnized By Nymphas Marston Esq
Silas Lovell and Charity Fuller August 7th 1760.
Prince Lothrop and Martha Bassett Oct 23d 1760
Elijah Blish and Sarah Stewart January 25th 1761
Samuel Isham & Lydia Goodspeed Feb 8 . 1761
Isaac Hinckly, Town Clerk, Transmitted to the County Clerk July 20 1761.
Nathanael Adams & Thankful Chadwick of falmouth April 9 . 1761
Shoble Hamblen & Sarah Crocker July 16 : 1761
Ruben Fish and Mary Meigs Both of sandwich Dec 3 . 1761
William Goodspeed of Barnstable & Mercy Meigs of Sandwich March 25th 1762
Mathias Smith of Barnstable & Hannah Fuller of Sandwich may 23 : 1762
Joshua Lumbert jur & Hannah Fuller Dec 23 : 1762
Transmitted to the Clerk of the Sessions January 1 : 1764

marriages By Nymphas marston Esq
Benjamin Smith & martha Bursley y 4th of Nov 1762
Josiah Goodspeed and Jemima Blossom the 30th of april 1764
Jesse Covet & Priscilla Ellis the 29th of Nov 1764
Barnabas Crocker & Ann Smith both of Barnstable march 24th 1765
Nye Jones and Deborah Crocker both of Barnstable may y 2d 1765
Transmitted To y Cler of y Sessions Jan y 28th 1766 Pr Edw Bacon Town Cler

The Children of Benjamin Smith and martha His wife
their Son Joseph Smith Born August y 10th 1763
their Son Benjamin Smith Born march y 2d 1765
their Son Timothy born January 15th 1767
their Daughter Susannah born July : 14th 1769
Daniel Davis & Mehitable his Second Wife their Children Born
their Son Dani Born May 8th 1762

[p. 215] James Smith and Hannah his wife their Children
Their Son Elisha Born y 24th of Sept 1759
Daughter Elizabeth Born April y 10th 1762
their Son Ebenezer Born July y 4th 1764
their Son John born august y 20th 1766
their Daughter Jemimah born april y 5th 1769
their Son Peter Born July : 2d 1771
their Daughter Rebecah born Feburary y 9th 1774
Nathaniel Jenkins and Mariah his Wife their Children Born
their Daughter Olive Born May 24th 1752
their Son Elis Born March y 2d 1755
their Son Nathaniel Born oct 22 : 1758
their Son Alvin Born February 27 : 1761
their Daughter Temperance Born February y 7th 1763 a Still Born Son may 13th 1769
The Births of the Children of Thomas Dimock & Elizabeth his wife
Charles Dimock their Son Born December y 10th 1756
their Daughter Hannah born July y 21st 1758
their Son John born June 16th 1764
Benjamin Childs Rebecca his wife their Children Born
their Son Thomas Born Sep 25th 1752
their Son Isaac Born February 10th 1755
their Daughter Rebecca Born March 9th 1759

(To be continued)

THE MAYFLOWER DESCENDANT

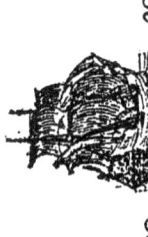

1620   2020

A QUARTERLY MAGAZINE OF
PILGRIM GENEALOGY AND HISTORY

VOLUME XXIII

1921

PUBLISHED BY THE
MASSACHUSETTS SOCIETY OF
MAYFLOWER DESCENDANTS
BOSTON

BARNSTABLE, MASS., VITAL RECORDS

TRANSCRIBED BY THE EDITOR

(Continued from Vol. XX, p. 43)

[p. 217] Persons Entered and Published in Order for marriage By
  Isaac Hinckly Ju' Town Clerk
Jesse Crosbey & Ruth Goodspeed Octo' 4th 1760
Benjamin Hamlen & Drusilla Dexter Nov' 1: 1760
Timothy Parker of Falmoth & Rachel Gorham Dec: 4: 1760
David Baker and Lydia Phiney . Dece': 6: 1760
Christopher Tayler and Hanah Howland Dec' 6 1760
London Negro man Servant to James Otis Esq' and Bathsheba
  Towardy an Indian Dece': 19 , 1760
Samuel Isham & Lydia. Goodspeed Jan: 9: 1761
Lemuel Bearse & Patience Phiney Janu' 10. 1761.
John Hinckly & Thankful Lumbert j' Jan': 31 . 1761
Josiah Smith of Yarmoth & Deliverance Howes Febr: 11: 1761
Jeremy Jo an Indian & Rachel dic [*]12 . 1761
Nathanael Adams & Thankful Chadwick of Falmoth Feb' 14 1761
Jabez Bearse and Hannah Bearse Feb': 20: 1761
Timothy Hamblen & Mary Hallet Feb' 21 . 1761
James Coleman j' & Zurviah Thomas march 21 1761
John Gray of Boston and Mary Otis . April 4 . 1761
Samuel Baker & Martha Lothrop April 11: 1761
Daniel Davis and Mehetable Sturges June 13: 1761
Shoble Hamlen and Sarah Crocker June 13 . 1761
Jabez Goodspeed and Margarett Bassett . July 4 . 1761
George Conant & Lydia Freeman of Harwich aug' 22 . 1761

* The month was not entered.

Joseph Lovell and Elisabeth Harlow of Plymoth aug. 29 1761
Ebener Cannon jr and Experience Tupper of Dartmoth aug. 29 1761
Ambrose Carsly and Mercy Lewis aug. 29 . 1761
Jabez Wilder of Hingham & Sarah Crocker Sept: 12: 1761
Nathanael Hinckly & Joanna Lewis Sept 26 1761
Lot Jenkins & Mary Howland Sept 26 1761
James Lovell and Martha Fuller Octor 7: 1761
Eleazer Scudder & Mary Lewis Novr 28 . 1761
Simeon Jenkins & Hodiah Hinckly Decr 5 1761
Moses Shaw of Middleborough & Anna Phiney Jany 20 1762
William Goodspeed & Mercy Meigs Sandwch march 6 1762
Nathaniel Lothrop & susanna Taylor of yarmouth march 27: 1762
Benjamin Blachford & Sarah Godfrey of yarmouth march 27: 1762
John marston and mary Crocker april 9th 1762
James Fuller and Rachel Fish of Sandwich april 24: 1762
John Carsley and Rebeccah Page april 24: 1762
Benjamin Smith and Martha Bursley april 24: 1762
[p. 218] Persons Entered and Published in order for marriage
Matthias Smith jr and Hannah Fuller of Sandwich may 7th 1762
Timothy Jones of Sandwich and Rebecca Fuller June 12 1762
Jonathan Lothrop and Eunice Cobb June 12 . 1762
Nathan Jankens and Rachel Howland July 3d: 1762
Levi Chace of Sandwich & Hannah Blossom of Barnstable July 17th 1762
Micah Jones of Barnstable & Jane Toby of Sandh august 7: 1762
Isaac Bacon and Alice Taylor august 14th 1762
Seth Ewer and Lydia Holmes of Plymouth august 14th 1762
Joseph Jankins and Remember Stewart Sept 11th 1762
adino Hinckley and Mercy Otis Sept 25th 1762
Nathaniel Howland and Martha Thacher of Wharham Octor 2d: 1762
Nathaniel Backhouse & Kezia Price of Falmouth Octr 16th 1762
Micah Humfrey of Hingham & Elizebath Davis of Barnstable Novr 6th 1762
Jabez Bursley & Susanna Crocker Novr [*]7th 1762
Joshua Lumber jr & Hannah Fuller Decemr 4: 1762
Nero Negro and Pegg Mingo January 8th 1763
[p. 219] Prince Marston and Sarah his Wife their Children
their Son Isaiah Born augst 27 . 1758.
their Son Nymphus Born July 24th 1760
their Son Winslow Born June 1st 1764
their Son John Born april 6th 1766
their Son Benjamin Born Feby 9th 1768
their Daughter Lydia Born Feby 12th 1770
their son Prince, born 1773
Jonathan Bodfish & Desire his wife their Children
their Son Silvanus Born Novr 15: 1754
their Son Benjamin Born April 14: 1756   Died 14 Jany 1827

*The first figure appears to be "2" altered into "1".

their Son Johnn Born March 16th 1761
their Son Isaac Born July 22d 1763
their Son Josiah born Novr 8th 1765
their Daughter Deborah born June: 11th 1768
their Son Simeon born Feby 10th 1771
Daniel Hamlen and Deliverance his wife their Children
Their Daughter Abigail Born July 2d 1761.
[p. 220] James Parcivall and Anna his wife their Children
Daugr Mary Born octor 18: 1738.
Son John Born Oct 2: 1740.
Daug: Hannah: Novr 5 1743.
Daugt Sarah Decer 27 . 1748.
Daugt Jemima Octor 29 . 1750.
Thomas Hinckly & Phebe his wife their Children
Son Daniel Bora March 20th 1754
Daugt Phebe Born Augt 8th 1755
Daugt Patience Born July 16th 1757
Joseph Lothrop & Deborah his wife their Children viz
Daugt Rebecca Born Decemr 20th 1758
Elisha Gray & Susannah his wife their Children Born viz
their Son John Born July the second day 1740
their Son Elisha: Born the Twenty Second day of June 1744
Eli Fuller and Mercy His wife their Children Born viz
Martha Fuller Born Novr 17: 1747
Jedidah Fuller Born March 28 . 1749
David Fuller Born June 21: 1751
William Fuller Born Sept. 28 . 1753
Jerusha Fuller Born May 2: 1756
[p. 221] James Blossom and Bithiah his wife their Children
their Son James Born February 3: 1760.
their Daughter Temperance Born octr 1761
their Son mathias Born Sept 12th 1765
their Daughter Lucretia Born octr 8th 1768
their Daughter Asenath Born August 30th 1770
Isaac Goodspeed and Ann his wife their Children
Daughter Sarah Born Octor 25th 1755
Son Isaac Born april 29th 1758.
Daughter Hannah Born May 17th 1760.
Son Luther Born Novr 1st 1762
Son Eljijah & Daniel Born January 17th 1765
Son Henan Born Feby 14th 1767
Son Charles Born July 20th 1769
Francis Wood & Elisabeth his wife their Children Born viz
Jabez Born July 8th 1758   Died October 22d 1826
David Born febr: 27 . 1761
Tilson wood their Son born march 13th 1763
their Son Ansel born may ye 8th 1765

Barnstable, Mass., Vital Records

their Daughter Elizebeth Born June 5th 1768
their Son Francis Born July ye 4th 1770
their Son Zenas born October 4th 1772
Ebenezer Scudder and Roose his wife Their Children Born viz
their Son Ebenezer Born august the 13th 1761 Died Augt 28 1847
their Son James Born march ye 14th 1764 Died
their Son thomas Born September ye 10th 1766
their Son Isaiah Born June ye 8th 1768
their Son Asa July 26th 1771 Died May 25th 1822.
their Daughter Elizabeth born October 12th 1773
Their Son Josiah born November 30th 1775
"   " James D. "   Oct 27th 1779.
"   " Thomas D. "   Jany 25 1782.
"   " Rose "   April 24 . 1784.
Mrs Rose D. Scudder Died Apl 17 1812. Agd 72 years
Mr Ebenezer Scudder " June 8th 1818. " 85. "

[p. 222] Marriages Solemnized by the Rev Joseph Green
Benjamin Davis and Patience Bacon May 19 . 1757
Ephraim Burges of harwich and Sarah Bacon aug: 17 1757
Joseph Nye of Sandwich & Thankful Goodspeed Octo 20 . 1757
Elisha Holmes of Plymoth and Sarah Ewer Octor 23 : 1757
Saml Davis and Mary Gorham Decem 22 . 1757
Joseph Crocker and Elisabeth Davis Januy 12 : 1758
Jonathan Pitcher and Ruth Bearse Febr: 9 . 1758
Southworth Samson and Jedidah Pain Febry 23 . 1758
Isaac Hinckly Jr Town Clr Transmitted to the County Clerk
James Huckins & Lydia Scudder march 30 : 1758
David Childs & Hannah Davis April 4 . 1758
Lott Thatcher & Martha Tayler Octor 23 . 1758
Ebenezer Scudder & Rose Delap Jany 11 . 1759
Josiah Davis & Thankful Gorham May 3 . 1759
Isaac Hinckly Jr Town Clr. Transmitted to the County Clerk
Barnabas Downes & Mary Cobb Septr 3 : 1759
Seth Fuller & Deliverance Jones Octo 15 1759
Elisha Kent of Goodfield & Annah Hallet Novr 1 : 1759
Joseph Crocker & Relief Lovell Jany 3 : 1760
Thomas Goodspeed & Puelia Lovell Febry 7 . 1760
Timothy Davis of Falmoth & Tabitha Crocker Febry 7 . 1760
Edward Adams & Rebecca Crocker March 20 : 1760
Joseph Lawrence and Thankful Childs March 27 . 1760
Saml Sturges the 3d and Lydia Crocker April 3 . 1760
Andrew Garrett & Lucy Davis April 17 1760
Ephraim Berry & Mercy Baker May 8 . 1760
Lazarus Lovell & Mercy Ewer May 29 . 1760
Samuel Crocker & Anna Lumbert May 29. 1760
Saml Winslow of Hardwick & Martha Goodspeed June 12 . 1760
William Baker of Harwich & Sarah Cummins July . 17 . 1760

Isaac Hinckly Jr Town Clerk Transmitted to the County Clerk
[p. 223] Samuel Sturges jr and Abigail his Second wife
their Son John Born Octor 13 : 1757
Their Daughter Lucretia Born Novr ye 11th 1758
Samuel Gilbert & Thankful his wife their Children
Seth Gilbert Born February 4 : 1759.
their Daughter Abigail Born January ye 17th 1762
their Son Benjamin. Born June ye 21st 1764
Benjamin Cobb & Anna his wife their Children Born
Reliance Cobb Born May 9th 1750
Eleazer Cobb Born augt 7th 1752
Lucy Cobb Born June 3d 1756
Benjamin Cobb Born Jany 28 . 1759
Joseph Cobb Born february 19th 1763
Samuel Cobb Born April ye 22d 1765
John Easterbrook & Abigail his wife thier Children
Rachel Born aug: 10th 1750.
Gorham Born July 7th 1756
Elisabeth Born July 2 : 1759
Samuel Born Jan 28th 1765

(*To be continued*)

THE MAYFLOWER DESCENDANT

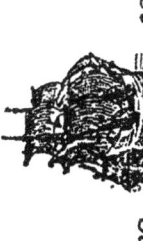

1620   2020

A QUARTERLY MAGAZINE OF
PILGRIM GENEALOGY AND HISTORY

VOLUME XXV

1923

PUBLISHED BY THE
MASSACHUSETTS SOCIETY OF
MAYFLOWER DESCENDANTS

BARNSTABLE, MASS., VITAL RECORDS

TRANSCRIBED BY THE EDITOR

(*Continued from Vol. XXIII, p. 129*)

[On pages 224 and 225, of the original, the months and days were entered in ruled columns, and frequently the month was omitted. In such cases we have supplied the month, printing it in italics and between brackets.—*Editor*.]

[p. 224] 1757 Persons Entered in Order for Marriage Isaac Hinckley Jr

Benjamin Nye jr of sandwich & Susannah Phiney March 19
Benjamin Davis & Patience Bacon } April 2
Joseph Blish jr & Sarah Crocker }
Daniel Hamlen & Deliverance Childs
Elisha Holmes of Plymouth & Sarah Ewer [*April*] 8
Jonathan Childs & Thankful Howland [*April*] 23
Lemuel Nye jr of Sandwich & Rebecca Crocker [*April*] 29
Joseph Nye jr of Sandwich & Thankful Goodspeed May 28
Robert Lawrence of Sandwich & Elisabeth Lambert June 4
Samuel Davis & mary Gorham jr July 30
Joseph Holway of sandwich Mary Parcivall Sept 3
Joseph Crocker & Elisabeth Davis } [*Sept*] 10
Seth Ewer and Elisabeth Rich of Truro }
David Childs and Hannah Davis Sept 17
James Huckins & Lydia Sendler Octo 15
George Conant & Elisabeth Crocker [*Octo*] 22
Abel Cushing of hingham & Hannah Crocker [*Octo*] 31
Benjamin Bayley of Scituate & Desire Russell Nov 2
Levi Lovell susannah Bates†
Jabez Bursley and Anna Crocker [*Nov*] 5
Thomas Hatheway & Huldah Smith [*Nov*] 19
Thomas Allen and Esther Truet of Boston [*Nov*] 26
Samuel Hinckly & Keziah Stone of Harwich } Dec 19
Southworth Samson & Jedidah Pain }
William Haskell & Hannah Butler . [*Dec*] 24
Jonathan Pitcher & Ruth Bearse } [*Dec*] 31
James Blossom & Bethiah Smith }
Joseph Blossom & mercy Ellis of Harwich Janr 7 1758
Joseph Childs & Meribah Dexter of Rochester Febr 11
Lemuel Keen & mehetable Tobey [*Febr*] 18

† See introductory note.

* See introductory note.

Ebenezer Jenkins & Elisabeth Clark Harwich† [Febr*] 18
Gershom Davis & Thankfull Skiff of sandwich } march 25
Barzilla Weeks & Sarah Hamlen
Samuel Gilbert of Connecticut & Thankful Fuller; of this Town April 1
Thomas Allen and mary Hawes of Sandwich [April*] 15
Caleb Perry of sandwich & Thankful Blish } [April*] 22
Lot Thatcher & Martha Tayler
Thomas Churchell of Plymoth & Mary Ewer May 6
Joseph Tobey & Hannah Job Sept 23
Isaac Ham & Elisabeth Amos [Sept*] 30
[p. 225] James Crocker & Abigail Sturges Octo 17: 1758
Nathanael Hinckly & Elisabeth Chipman [Octo*] 14 . 1758
Ebenezer Scudder and Rose delap Novr. 11 . 1758
Ebenezer Bacor & Elisabeth Crocker Decr 3: 1758
Micah Negro man Sert to Seth Blossom Bathsheba Towardy Feb 10: 1759
Daniel Carpenter & Temperance Crocker 17 of february 1759
Ebenezer Foster & Miriam Egerton 24 febru'y 1759
Thomas Goodspeed & Puelia Lovell march 7 . 1759
Josiah Davis and thankful Gorham march 24 . 1759
Ebenezer Fish of Falmoth & Elisabeth Handy march 31 . 1759
Seth Fuller and Deliverance Jones . April 21: 1759
Mr Gideon Hawley of marshpee & Lucy Fessenden of Sandwich May 18th 1759
Ebenezer Nye and Melatiah Sturges June 16 1759
Barnabas Downes & Mary Cobb July 14 . 1759
Joseph Crocker & Relief Lovell Augt: 25: 1759
Timothy Davis of Falmoth & Tabitha Crocker Oct: 6: 1759
Elisha Kent of Goodfield & Annah Hallet Octo: 13: 1759
Joseph Lawrence of Sandwich & Thankful Childs oct 27 . 1759
Benjamin Crocker & Anna Handy of Sandwich Novr 24: 1759
Ephraim Berry and Mercy Baker Dec 1: 1759
Samuel Sturges 3d & Lidia Crocker jr Febr'y 16: 1760
Thomas Chipman & Bethiah Fuller of Colchester Feb: 23d 1760
Edward Adams & Rebecca Crocker march 1t 1760
George Lewis Jur & Mary Davis jr march 8 . 1760
Jabez Claghorn & Eunice Davis march 15 1760.
Nathanael Allen & Deborah Linnell marth 15 1760
Samuel Winslow of Hardwick & Martha Goodspeed marh 18 . 1760
Benjamin Lumbert & Mercy Bacon March 22 . 1760
Andrew Garrett and Lucy Davis march 22 1760
Samuel Crocker and Anna Lumbert April 5 1760
Joseph Hallet & Thankful Baxter of Yarmoth April 12: 1760
Lazarus Lovell & Mercy Ewer April 19 . 1760

*See introductory note.
†Of Harwich.

John Crocker 4th and Thankful Hallet June 7: 1760
William Baker of Harwich & Sarah Cummins June 21: 1760
Prince Lothrop & Martha Bassett June 21: 1760
Silas Lovell and Charity Fuller July: 19: 1760
Elijah Blish & Sarah Stewart July 26 1760
Dublin Negro & Thankful Will Aug: 30: 1760
Luke Butler of Nantucket & Remember Blatchford Sept 18 1760
Benjamin Hamlen & Jerusha Hamlen Sept 27 1760
Job Hamlen & Abigail Gifford of Sandwich Sept 27 1760
[p. 226] Nathan Foster and Mary his wife their Children
Abigail Foster Born September 24 . 1756
John Bursley Foster Born June: 11th 1758
Mary Foster Born octr 4: 1765
by His Second wife Mercy
James Foster born Feby ye 8th 1767
Mercy Foster born march: 7th 1768
Thomas Foster Born march 4th 1771
Caryed to page (257)*
The Children of Lemuel Fuller & his wife
Their Son Joseph fuller Born January 30th 1761
Their Son Benjamin Born Sept 18th 1763
Their Son Samuel Born november 27th 1765
Joseph Cobb & Desire his wife Their Children Born
Daugr Thankful Born Novr 14: 1757
Daugr Remember Mercy Born Jany 13 . 1760
their Son Joseph Born August 18th 1762
Otis Loring & Sarah his wife their Children
Son david Born may 1t 1756
Son George Born march 23: 1758
Sarah Loring Born may 29: 1762
By His Second wife Sarah
their Son Eliphelet born march 13th 1767
their Son otis born February 18th 1769
their Daughter Mehitable Born June 27th 1771
Ebenezer Cobb and Lydia his wife their Children born viz
Son James Born January 12 . 1756
Son Ebenezer Born March 17 . 1759.
[p. 227] Joseph Otis Esqr & Rebekah his wife
Their Daughter Rebekah Otis Born Aug: 25 1754
Their Son James Otis Born Sep 20 1755
Their Daughter Elisabeth Born Janu'y 12 . 1760
Joseph Born 1762 . Died in infancy
A Daughter
By his second wife Mariah Walter
Joseph Born Sept 1771.

*On this page "(257)", now numbered 264, six more children of Nathan and Mary Foster were recorded.

Nathaniel Walter Jany 1773 . Died in N. Orleans 1841
John Ap^l 1774
Thomas Novr 1775 Died Ag^t 14 1803
Charles July 1777 " Ag^t 14 1794
A Son Feby 1779 " Same day
William Feby 1783 " Ap^l 7 1837.
Arthur Decr 1784 " July 24 1801
Mariah 1788
Mary A Mar 7 1780
George Conneat* & Susannah his Wife
y^r Son George Conneat* born July 22 1756
George Conant & Elisabeth his third wife
their Son Crocker Born June 23: 1759.
Said wife Elisabeth Died: Septr 17: 1759.
James Childs Jur & Mary his Wife
their Daughter Elizabeth Born May 6 1756
The Children of Nathaniel Baker born as followeth
Isaac April 2 1734
Mercy May 6 1738
Binney Octo^r 2 1751
anna Jany 18 1754
[p. 228] Married: Joshua Ralph & Martha Will March 5th† 1756
Ephraim Peter & Margaret Pognut† may 9 1756
Jonathan Bacon & Sarah Davis May 13th 1756†
Sam^ll Jones and Ann Jones of Sandwich Married March 3 1757
David Crocker Justice of ye peace
Married by ye Rev^rd Mr Jonathan Russel
Mr Samuel Sturgis Jur & Mrs Abigail Carpenter Jur Jan^ry 24 . 1757
David Crocker Esqr & Mrs Mary Stuart 27 Jan^ry 1757
Ichabud Nye & Remember Backus march: 1757
Benjamin Nye & Susannah Phiney April . 7 . 1757
Jonathan Childs & Thankful Howland may 19 1757
Isaac Phiney & Desire Steward May 16 . 1757
Joseph Blish j^r & Sarah Crocker [‡] 19th 1757
Lemuel Nye & Rebecca Crocker octo 25 1757
John Goodspeed j^r & Mercy Bursley may 29 . 1757
Daniel Hamlen & Deliverance Childs Novr 3 . 1757
Robert Lawrence & Elisabeth Lumber Nov: 17 . 1757
Jabez Bursley & Anna Crocker Decr 15 . 1757
Thomas Hatheway & Huldah Smith . Dec^er 18 . 1757
James Blossom & Bethiah Smith Jan^uy 19 . 1758

*Conant. "gorge Conant Susanea Crocker", intention of marriage 5 January. 1755 [page 238 of original]; children of "George Conant" (by two wives) including George born 1756, were recorded on page 239 of original.

† See duplicate entry, on original page 232.

‡ The month was not entered.

Abel Cushing & Hannah Crocker Jan^u 19 . 1758
Levi Lovell & Susannah Bates Jan . 26 . 1758
Isaac Hinckly Jr Town Clerk Transmitted to the County Clerk
William Haskell & Hannah Butler march: 20: 1758
Sam^ll Gilbert of Conneticut & Thankful Fuller . April 23: 1758
Caleb Perry of Sandwich & Thankful Blish Octo^r 22 : 1758
Thomas Churchell of Plymoth & Mary Ewer octo 26 . 1758
Nathanael Hinckly Jr & Elisabeth Chipman Novr 23 . 1758
Barzilla Weeks & Sarah Hamlen Decr 7 . 1758
James Crocker & Abigail Sturges Decr 14 . 1758
Ebenezer Baker & Elisabeth Crocker Febru^y 25: 1759
Isaac Hinckly Jr Tow Clr Transmitted to the County Clerk
Micah a Negro man & Bathsheba an Indian march 27 . 1759
Daniel Carpenter & Temperance Crocker April 5 . 1759
Ebenezer Foster & Miriam Egerton April 5 1759
Ebenezer Nye & Melatiah Sturges July 8 . 1759
Isaac Hinckly Jr Tow Cl Transmitted to the County Clerk

(To be continued)

BARNSTABLE, MASS., VITAL RECORDS

(Continued from page 133)

[p. 229] Andrew Lovel & Jemima his Wife
y⁽ʳ⁾ Son Zelotes bourn Nov⁽ʳ⁾ 24 1753
their Daughter Sebra born Sept⁽ʳ⁾ 26th 1756
Jemima Born January 15th 1768
Releif Born march 12th 1770
Their Daughter Martha born†
Samuel Crocker Jur & Elizabeth his Wife
Their Daughter Abigail Born 1ˢᵗ July 1753
Their Son Elijah born 27 octo⁽ʳ⁾ 1755
by his Second wife anna
Daughter Elizabeth born Feby 24: 1764
Daughter anna born april 7th 1766
Son Elisha born august 30th 176: Elisha Died May 15th 1817
Son Ezekiel born Jan⁽ʸ⁾ 20th 177\

* "the" is crossed out, in the original.
† The date was not entered.

Daughter Susanna born July the 7th 1773
The Children of Ebenezer Baker and Elizabeth his wife
Their Daughter Dorcas born December ye 3d 1760
Their Son Nathaniel Baker born ye 7th of December 1761
Their Daugter Lydia Born february 19th 1763
their Son Stephen baker born february 29th 1764
their Son David Baker born September 2d 1765
Thomas Gorham jr & Hannah his wife
Their Son Job Bourn Decemr 12 1754
Their Son Isaac Born April 29 1756
Daughter Desire Born Octor 16 1757
Son Ezekiel Born December 3 1758
Son John Born March 7 1760
Daughter Elisabeth Born June 10 1761
By his Second wife Rebeckah
their Daughter mary Born Septr 11th 1766
Cornelius Davis and Annah his Wife
Their Daughter Mercy born March 22 1751
Their Daughter Annah born July 4: 1754
[p. 230] Eli Phinney and Mary his wife married march 14th 1754
their Son Richard Phinney born 2nd Day of Febry 1755 Died August ye 23d 1765
Their Daughter Susanna Born Septr 29th 1757 Died August 20th 1765
Their Daughter Deborah Born April 28th 1760
Their Son Solomon born may 18th 1762
Their Son paul born June 17th 1764
Their Son William Born December 25th 1766 } Twins
Their Son Edward Born the Same 25th of Decr 1766 }
Edward died march ye 6th 1769
their Daughter Jane Born June 10th 1769
born Their Son Robert March the 18th 1773
Samuel Childs and Mary his Wife
yr Son Saml born July 7 1753
James Childs and Mary his wife*
Jeremiah Bacon and Hannah
yr Daughter olive Born Aug 3 1755
Barnabas Chipman Jur and Mary
yr Daughter Martha born Sep 4 1752
Elizabeth 8 of Feb - 1755
their Son Joseph Born May 14th 1758
their Daughter Hannah born June 6th 1760
their Son Barnabas born Novr 20th 1763
Ignatius Smith and Susannah
their son Abner born April 2nd 1755
Son Enoch Born may 2: 1757

* Nothing more was entered.

Churchel Blossom Son to Seth Blossom By his first wife Sarah Born Octor 15 1749.
[p. 231] William Crocker Jur and Lydia his Wife
Their Daughter Abigail Crocker born March 15 1754
Their Son David Crocker born Aug 23 1755
their Daughter Temperance born Jany 2 1763
By his Second wife Mary
their Daughter Sarah born June 26th 1765
their Daughter Mary born Novr 2d 1766
their Son William born Novr 19th 1768
their Son Mathias born July 26th 1770
Seth Blossom and Abigail Crocker Married
Their Son David Blossom born Jany 12 1755
Their Son Peter Blossom born Decemr 4 1756
Their Daughter Abigail Blossom Born May 10th 1760
their Son Seth Blossom Born Decr 11th 1763
their Daughter Hannah Born august: 15th 1766
Levi Born April 15th 1772
James Howland & Rebeckah his Wife
Their Daughter Abigail Howland born Decem 31 1754
Rebecca Born 26 . march 1757.
Elisabeth aug: 11 . 1759
Joseph & Jabez Howland twins Born Jany 29: 1762
their Daughter Mercy Born august 5th 1767
their Son James born august 7th 1771
The Children of David Baker & Lydia His wife
their Son David Baker Born June ye 16th 1763
Shobal Hamblin Jur and Martha his Wife
Their Son Joshua Born July 2 1752 . Old Stile
Susannah April 15 1754 New Stile
Timothy Feb 2nd 1756
Sarah Febr 10th 1759
the other Children See page 238*
The Children of Job Howland & Hannah his Wife
Their Daughter mary born July 21st 1755
Their Son John Born march 31st 1757
their Son Shove Born Decr 28th 1759
their Daughter Hannah born may 20 1762
their Son Job born July 24th 1764
Daugher Joanna born July 28th 1766
their Son Benjamin born August 7th 1768
Second Son Benjamin born June 18 1770
Mehitable born June 23d 1773
Son Southward born march 29th 1775
Son Timothy born Sepr 17th 1777

*Children by a second wife, Sarah, and a third wife, Ruth, were recorded on original page 238, now numbered 245.

Barnstable, Mass., Vital Records

[p. 232] Marriages

Oct⁰ʳ 10 1754 Sam⁽ˡˡ⁾ Whitney & Mehitable* Robin Married ᵇʸ John Thacher Jus⁽ᵗ⁾ of yᵉ peace

March 4† 1756 Joshua Ralph Martha Will married pʳ David Crocker Justice of y peace

Joshua Lumbart juʳ & Jean Claghorn Maried Sept⁽ʳ⁾ 1755 ᵇʸ David Crocker Justice of yᵉ peace

Jonathan Bacon & Sarah Davis May 1756†

Ephraim Peter and Margaret pogmot† May 1756

Andrew Garritt & Temperance his wife

theire Son Andrew Born feb⁽ʳ⁾ 25ᵗʰ 1755

The Children of the Said Andrew Garritt and Lucy his Second wife

their Son Jesse born feb⁽ʳ⁾ yᵉ 20ᵗʰ 1761

their Son Isaac born may 17ᵗʰ 1763

their Daughter Temperance born august yᵉ 19ᵗʰ 1765

their Daughter Susannah Born october 7: 1768

Barnabas Lothrop & Thankful his wife their Children born

Hannah 4 of March 1745 Monday

Mary 12 of March 1747 Thursday

Barnabas 27 of Jan⁽ʳʸ⁾ 1749 . Fryday

Abigail 8 of April 1752 . Sabbath day

Isaac Born 8 of Feb 1754 N S. Thursday

John 23 Nov⁽ʳ⁾ 1755 N Stile

Isaac Sept⁽ʳ⁾ 6ᵗʰ 1757.

Jonathan Lothrop and Mary his Wife

their Son Joseph born 9 oct⁽ʳ⁾ 1752

Rebekah born 29 oct⁽ʳ⁾ 1755 . New Stile

the Children of Jonathan Lothrop By unis his Second wife

their Son Thomas Born april 9ᵗʰ 1763

their Son Jonathan Born february 13ᵗʰ 1766

their Daughter mercy Born July 10ᵗʰ 1758 by His first wife

Their Son David born June 20ᵗʰ 1770

Joseph Linnel & Dorcas Smith married

Their Son Levi Born Feb⁽ʳʸ⁾ 1749 } old Stile
Dorcas 27 "   1752

Lydia 21 Feb⁽ʳʸ⁾ 1754 } New Stile
Heman 28 January 1756

(To be continued)

---

* Evidently a mistake of the town clerk, for "Mehitable".

† See duplicate entry on original page 228.

THE MAYFLOWER DESCENDANT

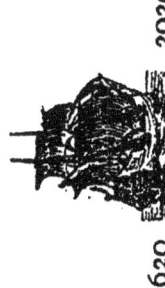

1620   2020

A QUARTERLY MAGAZINE OF
PILGRIM GENEALOGY AND HISTORY

VOLUME XXVII

1925

PUBLISHED BY THE
MASSACHUSETTS SOCIETY OF
MAYFLOWER DESCENDANTS
BOSTON

BARNSTABLE, MASS., VITAL RECORDS

Transcribed by the Editor

(Continued from Vol. XXV, p. 150)

[p. 234] Marriages Solemnized by ye Rev^r Mr Joseph Green Viz

Amos Hatch & Elisabeth Lumber Novr 15 1753
Mordecai Tupper and Abigail Cob Jan^ry 8 1754
Jonathan Lumber and Susannah Lewes Jan^r 24 1754
Henry Cob & Bethiah Hinkley Jan^ry 31 1754
Eli Phinny & Mary Phinney March 14 1754
Kenelm Winslow and Abigail Bourn Ditt* 14 1754
Sam^ll Linnel & Mary Sturges April 11 1754
Jonathan Crocker & Sarah Childs May 2 1754
John Sturgis Esqr & Mrs Mehitable Russel May 9 1754
Thos Gorham and Hannah Gorham May 16 . 1754
Thomas Crowel Junr & Martha Coleman Oct^o 3 . 1754
Isaac Baker & Rebekah Lewes Octo^r 6 1754
Isaac Godspeed and Anne Jenkins Octo^r 17 1754
Mr Sam^ll Sturgis & Mrs Olive Allen Novr 28 1754
Otis Loring & Sara Lewes Feb 20 1755
Lemuel Bacon & Deborah Lumbart March 13 1755
John Whitmarsh & Susannah Lambert May 29 1755

*Probably intended for "Ditto".

Mr John Gallison & Mrs Eunice Bourn June 19 1755
Thomas Young & Mary Davis June 26 1755
Seth Davis & Sarah Sturgis Sept 29 1755
Thomas Dimock & Elizabeth Bacon Octor 6 . 1755
Josiah Gorham & Hannah Hallet Octor 9 1755
Mr George Clap & Mary Gorham Novr 13 1755
Mr Justin Hubbard of Hingham & Sarah allyn Decem 14 1755
John Loggee & Eleanor Berse Janry 13 1756
Barnabas Howes & Martha Hinkley Janry 15 1756
David Hallet & Sarah Butler Feb 12 1756
Thos Annis & Lydia Berse Feb 17 1756
Isaac Case & Martha Phinny March 4 1756
prince Gorham & Abigail Gorham April 22 . 1756
James Haddeway & Mary Lumbart Decer 9 . 1756
Sylvanus Stuart & Lydia Lovel Decemr 16 1756
James Churchil & Mary Gorham Sylvanus Bourn Hannah Sturgis both Feb 3rd 1757
Joseph Cob Desire Lumbart Feb 10 1757
[p. 235] Timothy Chipman and Elizabeth Basset Maried Janry 23 1752

Their Daughter Abigail Born Decemr 9 1752 Decd august 6th 1757
Their Son Saml Born 8th of May 1754
Their Daughter Mary born Novr 1 1755
Their Daughter Abigail Born Janry 31: 1758 . Decd Septr 10 1759
Their Son William Born Febr 4: 1760
their Son John Born June 24: 1762
Their Son Timothy born may ye 6th 1764
Their Daughter Elizabeth Born January 27th 1767 Decd Septr 16 1768
Deacon Timothy Chipman Deceased august 24th 1770 aged 47 years
Benjamin Lumbert Mary his wife
Their Son Joseph born June 19 of March O. S. 1755
Their Daughter Martha 12 of March 1754
Isaac Jones Jur and Mercy his wife
Their Son Timothy Borin* 16 Sep 1752
Their Daughter Patience born 18 Sep 1754
Susannah born Febr 22d 1759
abner born march 20 1761
Their Son Goodspeed Jones June 15th 1763
Lydia born octr 10th 1765
Thos Sturgis Jur and Sarah Pain of Eastham were Married Janry 24 1745. Their Children Born as followeth
Martha Sturgis was Born Novr 6 1745 Died Decemr 29 1745
William Sturgis Born Feb 19 1748
Russel Sturgis Born August 28 1750
Abigail Sturgis was Born Aug. 3 1752

*Sic.

Thomas Sturgis April 5 1755
John Sturgis Born August 15th 1757
Elizabeth Sturgis Born Decemr 13th 1759
Samuel Sturgis born Sept 28th 1762
Josiah Sturgis born Sept 19th 1767
Mr Saml Sturgis Jur and Olive Allen Married
Their Daughter Abigail Sturgis born Octor 13 1755.
Olive Sturgis ye Wife Dyed May 14 1756
[p. 236] Persons published In order for Marriage 1755 ⅌ David Crocker Town Clerk

Josiah Gorham of Yarmouth & Hannah Hallet } March
Joseph Lothrop and Deborah Perkins of Plympton } 22
Joshua Lumbart Jur & Jean Claghorn Ap: 19
Capt John Gallison of Marblehead & Mrs Eunice Bourn May 17
Thomas Young & Mary Davis Jur May 24
Mr George Clap of Situate & Mrs Mary Gorham May 31
Mr Barnabas Howes & Mrs Martha Hinkley Sept 6
Seth Davis & Sarah Sturgis Sept 13th
Joseph Goodspeed Jur & Sarah Adams Jur Octor 17 1755
Mr Justin Hubbard of Hingham & Mrs Sarah Allyn 17 octor
Ebenezer Hamlin & Joanna Hamlin Octor 25
Isaac Simon Jur & Alice Cain Novr 1 1755
Jabez Lumber & Orange Farris Nov 21 . 1755
Jonathan Nye Sandwich Remember Annable } Decem 12 1755
David Hallet Jur & Sarah Butler }
John Loggee & Eleanor Berse } Janry 10 1756
Isaac Case and Martha Phinney }
Thomas Annis & Lydia Berse Janry 22 1756
Joshua Ralph and Martha Will Febry 14 1756
Thomas Crocker Jur & Mercy Hamblin Feb 21 1756
Jonathan Bacon Jur and Sarah Davis Feb 28 1756
Gamaliel Ewer & Martha Fuller March 13 1756
Ephraim Peter & Margaret Pognut April 22 1756
Joshua Nye & Lydia Jenkins . May 7 . 1756
Ebenezer Childs and Abigail Freeman May . 15 1756
Sylvenus Stuart & Lydia Lovel July 3 1756
James Hatheway & Mary Lumbart August 21 . 1756
Seth Stuart & Mary Downs . Yarmoth Octor 2 . 1756
Elisha Thacher Abigail Webb of Brantree*
Christopher Tayler & Bethiah Atkins Chatham*
Isaac Phinny & Desire Stuart both of ye Town*
Eleazer Fuller and Elizabeth Hatch*
David Crocker Esqr & Mrs Mary Stuart Octor 30 1756
Seth Cushman of Dartmoth & Abia Allen Novr 6 1756
Thom Negro and Mary Clap Novr 6 1756

*These four intentions are bracketed, and "Octor 23 1756" entered at the right.

Mr Sylvanus Bourn Jur & Mrs Hannah Sturgis Decem 5 1756
Joseph Cob & Desire Lumbart Decem 24
Mr Sam^ll Sturgis Jur & Mrs Abigail Carpenter Jur Decem^r 25 1756
Peter Pognut & Hannah tuncagain Decem^r 25 1756
James Churchil & Mary Gorham } Jan^ry 15 1757
Sam^ll Jones and Ann Jones of Sandwich
Ichabod Nye Remember Backouse Jan^ry 21 1757
Remington Gosnold Chilmark* & Desire Lewes Feb 1 1757
Southworth Hamblin Tabitha Atkins Feb 26 1757
Nathan Thomas & Susannah Goodspeed Feb^ry 18 1757
James Smith and Hannah Barlow of Sandwich Feb 26 1757
prince Marston Sarah Winslow }
Samuel Fuller Abigail Jones } 5 March 1757
Ephraim Burgis Sarah Bacon
[p. 237] Sylvanus Hinkley & Sarah his Wife.
Their Son Zaccheus Hinkley born 19 of March 1754
Silvanus Hinckly born aug^t 25th 1756:
Prince Hinckly born Decr 27. 1758
Daughter Lydia Born June 8th 1761
their Son Levi Born may ye 17th 1764
Daughter Elizabeth Born September 23^d 1766
Daughter Reliance Born march 26th 1769
Benjamin Hinkley & Lydia his wife
their Son Nymphas born Sept 13 . 1753.
Silas Lovell & mary his first wife their children
their Son Joseph Born Novr 12th 1750
& Thomas June ye 12th 1753
Daughter Lydia January 16th 1756
martha ye 1st of oct^r 1758
and: by Charrity his 2^d wife
their Son Owen Born Sept 17th 1764 } Born & Recorded
their Daughter Relief Born Jany 22^d 1767 } Plymoth
Eunice Born June 26th 1769
Silas born — 1744
Andrew " May 3^d 1748.
Mrs Charity Lovell died Jany 1812.
Thomas Ewer Jur & Lydia Harlow Married Sept^9 1753
Their Son Thomas Feby 22^d 1750
Their Son Eleazer august 26: 1752
Their Son Ansel Born at Barnstable Sept^9 1753
Their Son Seth born 5th of July 1755
their Daughter Lydia Born Septr 16th 1758
their Secon Son Ansel Born Septr 21st 1760
Ebenezer Cobb & Mary his wife their Children
Rachel Cobb was Born august 23: 1751

* Of Chilmark, Mass.— Editor.

Hannah Cobb Born March 11: 1753
Eunice & Huldy twins Born april 4: 1755
Lydia Cobb Born march 2: 1758
Benjamin Childs & Mehitable Hamlin Married
Their Son Lewes Childs born august 29 1752
Their Daughter Hannah Childs born Sept 6 1754
their Daughter Mehitable Decem^r 27th 1756
[p. 238] persons published in order for mariag by Robert Davis town Clerk
1754 mr John Sturgis Esqr and m^rs mehitable Russel April 14 1754
Samuell whitne and mehitable Roben may 5
Ebenezer Cobb of this town and Lyda Churchel of midelbery may 12
1754 Isaac goodsped and anne Jenkins June 9
Ebenezer Bearse Jur of this town and marey Barrey* of yarmoth august 11
mr Jams warin of plymoth and mrs marcy otis of this town September 1
Thomas Croel Jur of yarmoth and martha Colmon of this town September 15
Isaac Baker and Rebakah Leuis Both of this town September 22
1754 mr Samul Sturges Jur and mrs olive allyn Both of this town November 3
Thomas Dimock and Elisabath Bacon Both of this town novmbr 10
mr John whitmarsh of wamoth and Susannah Lumbert novmbr 17
Otis Loring and Sarih Leuis Both of this town novmbr 17
1754 gorge meffrech and Abigail pochnat Both of this town novmbr 17
1754 Lamuill Bacon and Debarah Lumbert Both of this town Decemr 8
mr Danial Crocker and ms phebe winslow of harwech decmbr ye 28
1755 gorge Conant Susanea Crocker Both of this town Janury ye 5
Nath^ll goodspeed of this town and Elisabeth fuller of Bolton Janury ye 5
mr John Russel Jur of this town and mrs Elisabeth Brigen of plimtown Janury ye 12
mr James Childs Jur and marey parcker Both of this town febuary ye 9
princ gorham and abigail gorham Both of this Town febru 23
Annos a Sarvent molata to mr peter Blosam and Elisabeth Rafe februry 23
Isaac Baker and Rebacker his wife thir Children
Their Dafter Rebacker Born Janeure y^e 5 1755
Their Son James Baker Born June 15th 1756
Their Son Lewis Baker Born December 28th 1761
Their Son Ezekiel Baker Born September 24 1764

* Probably for "Berry."— Editor.

THE MAYFLOWER DESCENDANT

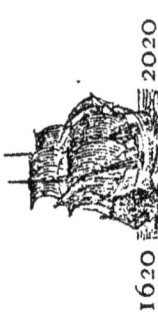

1620 2020

A QUARTERLY MAGAZINE OF PILGRIM GENEALOGY AND HISTORY

VOLUME XXXI

1933

PUBLISHED BY THE
MASSACHUSETTS SOCIETY OF
MAYFLOWER DESCENDANTS
BOSTON

Their Son Nathaniel Baker born may 12th 1766
Their Son John Baker born July 30th 1768
Ther Son Isaac Baker born may 28th 1771
Ebenezer Crocker & Zerviah his Wife Their Children born
Their Son Alvan Fryday 6 Novr 1747
Achsah Monday July 24 1749
Zerviaah Wednesday July 17 1751
Ebenr Thirsday July 26 1753 died Febry 17th 1817
Joshua Fryday July 4 1755
Knelm Lords Day aug 14 1757
George Monday Febry 18. 1760
Zenas Friday Decer 25 1761
Ebenezer Crocker Died February 17th 1817
[p. 239] George Conant & Sarah his Wife.
Son George Conant Febr: 15. 1754.
George Conants Children by His: 4th:wife Lydia
George Conant Born July 27th 1762
Thacher Conant Born August 13th 1763
said son Decased November 16th 1763
Second Son thacher Born march 2d 1767
Thomas Dean jr and Abigail his wife thir Child
Daughter Hannah Dean Jany 20: 1753
Their Son Archelaus Dean born June 26 1755
John Lewis and Deborah his wife their Children Born
David Lewis August 10: 1753
Son Peter Born June 7: 1756:
Son Ebenezer Born march 30: 1759
their Son John Lewis Born august 4th 1763
their Daughter Deborah Born June 4th 1766
their Son Elijah Phiney Lewis Born march 23d 1769
Nathll gorham and annar his wife ther Children Born
Lewis gorham ther Son Novemr 11th 1753
their Son George Lewis Born october ye 3d 1763
Josiah Scudder & Sarah his Wife their Children
their Daughter Hannah Born august 1st 1752
their Son James Born Novr 17th 1754
their Daughter Betty Born august 28: 1757

(To be continued)

BARNSTABLE, MASS., VITAL RECORDS

Transcribed by George Ernest Bowman

(Continued from Vol. XXVII, p. 10)

[2:240*] 1753 Persons published in Order for Marriage
Ichabod Negro Servant to John Hinckly Jur and Patience Quoy Augt 4
Amos Hatch of falmoth & Elisabeth Lumbert 13
Andrew Garret of Sandwich & Temperance Parker 14
Job Howland & Hannah Jenkins 18
Barnabas Chipman & Alice Howland 21
Ignatius Smith & Susannah Howland Septr 1
Joshua Menasseh & Bethiah Cook Indians 22
Eli Phiney & Mary Phiney Octob: 12
Sam^{ll} porridge & Lidia Ned 12
Henery Cobb & Bethiah Hinckly 31
Seth Blossom & Abigail Crocker 31
Mordecai Tupper & Abigaill Cobb Nov 24
Knelm Winslow jur of marshfield & Abigaill Bourn } Decem^r 1
Jonathan Lumber jur & Susannah Lewis
Barnabas Bursley & thankful Smith 8
1754 Samuel Bacon & Mary Howland jur Janu: 12
Samuel Linnell jur & Mary Sturges 12
Nathanael Ryder & Bathsheba Hinckly 12
Prince Bearse & Desire Downes of Yarmoth 12
James Tobey & Eunice Claghorn 19
Jonathan Crocker & Sarah Chiles 26
John Bacon & Joanna Foster of Plymoth Feb. 16
John Goodspeed jur & Mercy Bursley Mach 4
Thomas goriham Jur and Hannah gorham March 22
Jabes Crocker and Remember fuller march 25
Isaac fuller of this town and Susanah wardsworth of pembrook march 31
Thomas Annable and ann his wif thir Children Born
Bachelder Annable may the 24: 1741 and Died
Thankfull Annable Born Sept the 25: 1743
Ann Annable Born August ye 21: 1745 and Died
Thomas Annable Born october ye 17: 1747 and Died thes By abigil Dimock
Abigil Annable april 21: 1749 and Died
Abigail Annable Born Janeury ye 19: 1753
Joseph Annable Born Septe^r ye 1: 1754
[p. 241] Simon Jones jur & Hannah his wife their Children

Son Joseph March 2. 1752
Daughter Mariah April 2. 1755
Jedidiah Born Sept 5th 1760
Simon Born Septr 17th 1763
Asa Born may 24th 1766
Daughter Hannah Born april 24th 1770
Seth Phiney & Bethiah his Wife their Children
Zilpah Phiney Novr 30th 1749
Two Sons at a Birth mach 10: 1753 Dyed In about two hours after
Nathan Bassett & Thankfull his wife their Children
Nathan Bassett Decem^r 30: 1750
Cornelius Bassett Jany 20. 1753.
Timothy Hope & Abigail his wife their Children
Sarah Hope July 12. 1753
by his second wife Thankfull
Timothy born Octr 30th 1772
[p. 242] Marriages by the Reve^d Joseph Green
Joseph Bacon Meriam Coleman } Decem^r 13 1750
Samuel Hamlen Ju^r Temperance Lewis
James Churchel Mercy Cobb Janu: 10
Nymphas Mastin Mary Allen 17
John Richards Hannah Chehu Indians 31
Shoble Hamlen ju^r Martha Lumbert March 7
Jabez Parker of Yarmoth Sarah Hallet [March] 28 1751
Samuel Jordan of Biddeford . Mercy Bourn ju^r April 10
Benjamin Lumbert ju^r Mary Davis May 23
Lemuel Fish of Falmoth Martha Coleman Septr 19
Jabez Linnell Sarah Sturges 26
Ebenezer Lumbert Bethiah Smith 26
Nathanael Gorham Annah Lewis Octo^r 31
Benjamin Blossom of Sandwich Elisabeth Linnell 31
Benjamin Chiles Ju^r Rebeca Davis Novr 6
Jonathan Lothrop Mary Thatcher Decem^r 12
Isaac Davis Hannah Davis Janua: 16 1752
Gershom Cobb Mehetable Davis Febr: 6
Josiah Gorham Nantucket Deborah Lovell 26
Thomas Buck Yarmoth Mercy Bearse 20
Samuel Chiles mary Hinckley 20
Thomas Allyn Elisabeth Sturges April 19
Shoble Davis Thankful Lewis Ju^r 30
Committed to County Clerk April 30 1752
Josiah Scudder & Sarah Phiney July 21 1752
John Lewis & Deborah Phiney Octo^r 19 1752
Timothy Hope & Abigail Pitcher Decem^r 14
Ebenezer Gorham ju^r & Mary Thatcher 21
Jabez Merchant Yarmoth & Remember Hallet Janu: 4 1753
Nath^{ll} Bassett of Rochester & Elisabeth Bearse March 1
Seth Goodspeed & Abigail Linnell 15

---

* These page numbers were added in pencil, when the book was rebound, and were used in the modern copy and its index.

Barnstable, Mass., Vital Records

Silvanus Hinckly & Sarah Phiney May 31
George Conant & Sarah Goodspeed June 20
David Hallet jur & Sarah Lewis July 19
Barnabas Downs of Yarmoth & Mercy Lumbert Sept 20
Lemuel Lumbert & Thankful Bearse Nov 1
Joseph Otis & Rebeca Sturges Nov 1
[p. 243] Zacheus Fuller & Sarah Jones Married Febry 22 1752
Jonathan Lewis & Elisabeth his wife their Children
James January 25. 1740.
Barnabas Oct 7: 1743.
Joshua Jany 9: 1748.
Jonathan May 25: 1750.
Thomas Agry & Annah his Wife their Children
Son John January 2: 1752
Thomas Ames & Mehetable his wife their Children
Elizabeth Ames: Oct 19. 1747
Thomas Ames Febry 10. 1749
Zephorn Ames Jany 30. 1752
Jerusha Ames June 30 1754
their Son Isaac Mach 20 1757
their Son Enos Sept 2: 1759
[p. 244] 1752 Persons Published In order for Marriage Pr Isaac Hinckley Jur

Entred in order for marriag
Thomas Allyn & Elisabeth Sturges. 1752 March 7
Nathanael Jenkins & Meriah Ellis of Rochester 7
Shoble Davis & Thankful Lewis Jur 7
John Lewis & Deborah Phiney 21
Timothy Robbins yarmoth mary Sturges Barnstable May 2 and on may the Eigth the Bans of matrimony were forbidden Between Said Robbins & said mary By the father in Law the Mother & Said mary herself accordingly I Gave Publick Notice thereof on may the Ninth 9 Isaac Hinckley Ju Town Clerk
Benjamin Lovell Susannah Lovell May 23
Ebenezer Gorham jur Mary Thatcher June 13
Josiah Scudder and Sarah Phiney June 27.
Benjamin Bacon & Thankful Downs of Yarmoth July 11.
Thomas Hinckly & Phebe Homes of Plymoth Augt 22
Jabez Merchant of Yarmoth & Remember Hallet 29
Nathanael Bassett of Rochester & Elisabeth Bearse Sept 29
Timothy Hope & Abigail Pitcher Octor 14
Thomas Weeden of Newport on Rhode island and Mary Howse of Barnstable Octo 20
William Crocker ju: & Lydia Knowles of Eastham Decer 23
1753 Jonathan Bodfish & Desire Howland 1753 Jany 13
Andrew Lovell & Jemima Landers of Sandwich 20
Silvanus Hinckly & Sarah Phiney Febr: 3
Thomas Job & Jerusha Gundy Febr [3]

Samuel Crocker ju & Elizabeth Lumbert Febr. 16
Peter Negro Servant to John Thatcher jur and Alice Pease Febr. 17
Seth Goodspeed & Abigail Linnell 17
Lemuel Lombart & Thankfull Bearse march 10
David Freeman & Abigail Davis 17
Cornelius Lovell & Rebeca Tobey 24
David Hallet jr & Sarah Lewis 30
Nathan Foster & Mary Lothrop 31
George Conant & Sarah Goodspeed April 28
Barnabas Downs of Yarmoth & Mercy Lumbert May 18
Lemuel Bacon & Mary Johnson 26
Daniel Fuller & Martha Hinckly June 16
Ebenezer Cannon & Patience Goodspeed July 14
Joseph Otis & Rebecah Sturges 28
[p. 245] Samuel Hamlen Jur & Joanna Bumpas marrd Nov 16. 1749 pr D. C. Esq.
Rebeca Hamlen Sept 13: 1750.
Shobal Hamlen Jur his Children by his Second wife Sarah*
Martha born May 31st 1762
Susannah born Febr 15th 1765
Shobal born July 18th 1766
By his third wife Ruth
Ruth born Nov 21st 1768
Mercy born April 16th 1771
Hope born Nov ye 11th 1773
Nathanael Sturges & Abigail his Wife their Children
James Sturges . Apr: 27: 1735.
Elisabeth Sturges Decemr 3: 1736.
Nathanall Sturges . octo: 28. 1739.
Jonathan Sturges augt 9. 1743.
David Sturges . may 11: 1745.
Joseph Sturges may 4: 1748.
Abigail Sturges July 22d 1752
Ebenezer Born Jany 28: 1756
William Davis & Martha his wife their Children
Mehitable Davis March 4th 1746
William Davis Januy 18: 1748
Catharine Davis april 29: 1751
Elizebath Davis april 13: 1755
Martha Davis august 19: 1758
Ruth Davis January 24: 1763
Samuel Jenkins Jur & Mary Chipman Married Marh 11. 1749
Son Josiah Sept 30: 1750
Daughter Deborah Feb 2d 1752
Abiah Jany 21 1754
Saml Novr 23 1755

*Children of Shobal Hamlen, Jr., and his wife Martha are recorded on original page 231. See Mayflower Descendant, 25: 149.

Mary Born Janu^y 16. 1758
Joseph Born June 6th 1760
[p. 246] Marriages by ye Revd Jonathan Russel
Sam^ll Jenkins Mary Chipman March 11 1749
James Lewes Joanna Howland April 12 1750
Jeremiah Bacon & Hannah Tayler April 26. 1750
Ebenezer Cob Mary Smith Novr 15. 1750
Joseph Thomas Mary Lothrop Decem^r 5 1750
Cuffee Sarah Job Decem 28 1750
John Crocker 3rd & Mary Bursly Feb 14 1750
1752 Zacheus Fuller & Sarah Jones of Barnstable married By Ezra Boufn Justice of the Peace Febr: 22. 1752
1751 Marriages By Reverend Jonathan Russell.
Jedidiah Winslow of Rochester & Elisabeth Goodspeed march 7
Seth Steward of Sandwich & Mary Tayler may 16
Joseph Hamblin Hopestill Davis Sept. 5
1752. James Allen & Lydia Marston Jan: 7
Bruce Steward of Sandwich Deborah Taylor April 3
Returned to the County Clerk April 30
1753 Benjamin Lovell & Susannah Lovell Jany 30
Jonathan Bodfish & Desire Howland may 3
Nathan Foster & Mary Lothrop may 21
Ebenezer Cannon & Patience Goodspeed July 30
Ichabod Servant to John Hinckly ju^r & Patience Quoy Augt 19
Barnabas Chipman & Alice Howland Septr 13
Joshua Menasses & Bethiah Cook Octo^r 18
Daniel Fuller & Martha Hinckly Novem 1
Ignatius Smith & Susannah Howland Novr 21 } Feb 21
Cornelius Lovell & Rebeccah Tobey Decem^r 6
Job Howland & Hannah Jenkins Decem^r 6
Andrew Garret & Temperance Parker Decem^r 20
1754 Seth Blossom & Abigail Crocker Janua 10
Married p̃ Mr Russel 1754
James Tobey Eunice Claghorn
Cap Sam^ll Bacon and Mary Howland March 7
Nathan^ll Rider and Bathsheba Hinkly March 7
Barnabas Bursly and Thankful Smith May 16
Mr James Warren & Mrs Mercy Otis Novr 14
1755 George Conneat Susanna Crocker Jan^ry 30
Jabez Crocker Remember Fuller March 27
Amos Chin Elizabeth Ralph April 6
James Childs Ju^r & Mary Parker June 5
Ebenezer Hamblin Joanna Hamblin Decem 3
1756 Joseph Goodspeed Sarah Adams Jan^ry 29
Thomas Negro & Mary Clap Novr 25
Francis Wood & Elizabeth Howland Decem 15
[p. 247] Published
James Churchel and Mercy Cob November 10 1750

Sam^ll Hamlin Ju^r Temperance Lewes Novr 10 1750
Mr Nymphas Marston Mrs Mary Allyn Novr 17 1750
William Allen & Jane Spooner Novr 24 1750
Jedediah Winslow Rochester* & Elizabeth Goodspeed [Novr 24 1750]
Mr Samuel Jordan of Biddeford & Mrs Mercy bourn 1 Decem^r 1750
Col Otis † Cuffee & Sarah Job 1 Decem^r 1750
Matthew Cob & Mary Garret 8 Decem^r 1750
David Lumbart Abigail Issum [8 Decem^r 1750]
John Crocker 3 Mary Bursly Ju^r Decem 22 1750
Benj^a Blossom, Sandwich Elizabeth Linnell [Decem 22 1750]
John Richards & Hannah Chehu Jan^ry 12 1750
Jabez Parker of Yarmoth & Sarah Hallet } Jan^ry 19th 1750
Benjamin Lumbart and Mary Davis
Lemuel Fish of Falmoth & Martha Coleman } Jan^ry 26 1750.
Shobal Hamlin Martha Lumbart
Mr Enoch Taylor & Mrs Thankful Howes Yarmoth
Barnabas Chipman Ju^r & Mary Blackwel Sandwich } Feb^ry 9 1750
Joseph Hinkley Ju^r & Mary Davis Sandwich
Ebenezer Lumbart and Bethiah Smith March 2 1750
Mr Seth Stuart and Mrs Mary Tayler Ju^r March 15 1750
Persons Published Pr Isaac Hinckley Ju^r Town Cler
Mr Benjamin Blossom & m^rs Bathsheba Passival Apr: 6. 1751
Mr Jabez Linnell and m^rs Sarah Sturges widow may 9. 1751
Mr Joseph Hamlen and m^rs Hopestill Davis } July 13: 1751
Mr James Allen and Mrs Lydia Marston
Mr Nathanael Gorham mrs Annah Lewis
Isaac Jones Ju^r and Mercy Goodspeed Augt 10: 1751
Zacheus Fuller and Sarah Jones Augt 24: 1751
Benjamin Chiles Ju^r & Rebeca Davis Sept. 14: 1751
John Green of Falmoth & Jerusha Fuller Sept 18: 1751
Samuel Chiles and Mary Hinckley Octo 26: 1751
Bruce Steward of Sandwich & Deborah Tayler Jan 18: 1752
Timothy Chipman & Elisabeth Bassett of Sandwich Nov 2. 1751
Jonathan Lothrop & Mary Thatcher Nov 16 1751
Gersham Cobb & Mehetable Davis Nov. 30. 1751
Thomas Buck of yarmoth & Mercy Bearse Decr 5 1751
Isaac Davis & Hannah Davis Decr 5. 1751
Josiah Gorham of Nantucket & Deborah Lovell Nov 2: 1751
Thomas Jenkins & Thankful wing of Harwich Feb 1 1752
Benjamin Chiles & Mehetable Hamlen Feb 8: 1752
Thomas Dean & Abigail Horten of Eastham Feb 29. 1752
[p. 248] Daniel Davis & Mehitable his Wife their Children Born
Their Daughter Mary Davis Born April 29 1740
Their son Daniel Davis born Octo^r 10 1741
Their son Robert Davis born March 27 1743

*Of Rochester.
†Col. Otis's Cuffee, etc.— *Editor*.

Their son John Davis born Oct'r 7 1744
Their Daughter Deborah Davis born Aug 13 1746
Their son Thomas Davis born Aug 24 1748
their Daughter Desire Born march 27. 1750
their Son Ansel Born march 13. 1752
their Daughter Experience Born January 11. 1754
their Daughter Mehetable Born July 11. 1756
their Son Lothrop Davis Born*
D'r Abner Hersey & Hannah his wife
Their Daughter Mary Hersey born Jan'y 19 1749
John Berse Jur & Lydia his wife their
Daughter Olive Berse was Born Jan'y 31 1746
Their son Gersham Berse was Born Oct'r 5th 1748
Their son Enoch Berse was Born July 24 1750
Ebenezer Son of Deacon John Crocker & Elizabeth his wife
their son James Born Feb 19 1739
Their Daughter Mary Born Nov'r 7 1744
[p. 249] Benjamin Crocker Ju'r BathSheba his Wife
Their son Joseph Crocker born April 15th 1748
Their son Benjamin Crocker born Sept'r 17th 1749
Timothy born oct'r 3d 1751
Abigail born Nov'r 9th 1753
Bathsheba Nov'r 11th 1755
Peter born Jan'y 11th 1758
Josiah Born april 17th 1760
David Childs & Hannah his Wife
Their Son David Childs Born Feb 7. 1735
Jonathan born Decem'r 25. 1737
Anna born Aug: 18. 1740
Assenath born Feb 28. 1741
Josiah their son born 7 Sep't 1745
Edward Their son born 13 Sep: 1749.
Jonathan Hallet & Mercy Bacon Married &c
Their son John Hallet born 4 of Octo'r 1745
Their Son Jonathan Hallet born 9 of Decem'r 1749
Nathaniel Hallet Born nov'r 28th 1752
their Daugter Anner Hallet Born march 20th 1755
their Son Samuel † Hallet Born March 26th 1758
their Son Benjamin Hallet Born Janu'r 18th 1760
ther Son Edward Hallet Born april 6th 1762
[p. 250] Seth Lothrop and Mary his Wife
Their son Nathaniel Lothrop was Born Decem'r 27 1739
Joseph Lothrop May 1 1742
John Lothrop April 5 1745

* The date was not entered.
† "Abner" was first written, but was crossed out, and "Samuel" interlined in a different hand and ink.

y'r Daugter Thankful Lothrop Feb'ry 18 1746
Mary Lothrop March 24 1748
Solomon Lumbart and Sarah Lumbert His wife
Their Son Daniel Lumbart Born Aug 6 1741
Lemuel Lumbert Sep't'r 6 1743
Ichabod Lumbert Nov'r 10 1746
James Churchil & Martha his Wife
their Daughter Sarah Churchil born Sept'r 23 1749
M'r John Otis Ju'r & Temperance his wife
Their Son John Otis Born Decem'r 17 1742 Died Jan'ry 6 1742*
Their son John Otis Born February 19 1743*
Their son Heyman Otis born Oct'r 27 1747 Died Nov'r 18 1747
Their Second Son Heyman Otis born March. 1 1748

[There are no vital records on pages 251-253 inclusive.]

[p. 254] Marriages by y'e Rev'd Joseph Green
Isaac Lewes & Martha Berse Feb'ry 19 1747
Prince Tayler & Hannah Childs March 6 1747
Daniel Crocker & Elizabeth Childs May 19 1748
Edward Crosby & M'rs Hannah Gorham July 24 1748
Thomas Phinny 3 and Abigail Lumbart Nov'r 24 1748
M'r Isaac Hinkley Ju'r & M'rs Hannah Bourn Decem'r 18 1748
M'r Jonathan Bourn & M'rs Susannah Mendal † Decem'r 22 1748
Benjamin Cob and Ann Davis May 29 1749
John Easterbrook Abigail Gorham Aug 23 1749
Joseph Berse and Lydia Dean Octo'r 12. 1749
Jonathan Ellis & Thankful Lewes Octo'r 16 1749
John Nye & Hannah Allen Octo'r 26 1749
Sam'll Annable Ju'r & Desire Dimock Dec'r 7 1749
Cornelius Davis and Anna Lumbart Dec'r 28 1749
Prince Davis and Sarah Coleman Feb 15 1749
Cesar Serv't to John Gorham Esq'r & Rheta Serv't to David Gorham Esq'r Married March 1. 1749
Lemuel Lewes Temperance Berse March 7 1749
Thomas Egred and Anna Dimock March 7 1749
Benjamin Hinkley & Lydia Phinny Nov'r 22 1750
Nathan Noyes & Mehitable Bangs wid: Sep't 20 1750 y'e Bride Setting in y'e Bed y'e Bridegroom Declared before y'e Witnesses present that he took her in her Shift as She was having Never Received anything of her former Husbands Estate Nor Expecting to Receive Any and that he would not pay any of y'e Debts of it — This Returned on y'e Back of y'e Certificate Pr M'r Green Attest David Crocker Town Clerk
Persons Joynen in marriage By David Gorham Esq'r

* The death would be 17 January, 1743, in new style dating. The birth of the second son John would be 1 March, 1744, in new style. — Editor.
† The surname has been marked over in pencil. The intention, on page 257, gives the name as "Mendall". — Editor.

David Freeman & Abigail Davis Aprill 8th 1753
Samuel Crocker jr & Elisabeth Lumber Apr: 8. 1753
Samuel Porridge & Lydia Ned Nov. 1: 1753
[p. 255] Silas Blish and Mercy his wife
Their Daughter Rebekah Blish born January 4 1748
their Daughter Abigail Blish Born April 30: 1751
their Daughter marcy Blish born August 17: 1753
Their Son Silas Born July 25: 1756:
Elisha Born December 3d 1758:
their Second Daughter mercy Born march ye 14th 1762
Reuben Jones and Sarah Passaval Married
Their Daughter Deliverance Jones born Octor 6 1739
Their son Ephraim Jones born June 20 1745
The Children of James Allyn & Lydia His wife
Son James Born Novr 6th 1752
Son Benjn Born August 5th 1754
Son marston Born Octr 25th 1756 Died August 20th 1757
Son marston ye 2d Born Octr 11th 1759 Died July 22d 1766
Son Thomas born november 17th 1760
Son Nymphas Born July 28th 1764 Died Septr 25th 1766
Son John Born march 21st 1767
Daniel Crocker & Elizabeth Childs Maried May 6 1749
Their son Job Crocker born May 6 1749
by His Second wife Phebe:
winslow Crocker born Decmr 31st 1755
Elisebeth Born march 14th 1760
Daniel Born march 8th 1762
by His third wife Bathsheba
Daughter Mary born July 11th 1767
Daughter Abigail Born Novr 6th 1769
their Son Joseph Born January: 27th 1771
Son Prince born Septr 6th 1772
their Daughter Temperence born July 28th 1776
David born Feby 21th 1779.
Josiah Born Augt 24th 1781
Daniel Lovel and Sarah his wife
yr Daughter Desire born Septr 24 1746
Their Son Daniel Lovel born April 17 1748
Their Son Christopher Lovel born April 30 1750
Their Daughter Abigail Lovel Born Novr 17 1753
Their Daughter Sarah Lovel Born January ye 7th 1758
Their Son Nehemiah Lovel Born July ye 18th 1764
their Son Gorham Lovel Born August ye 4th 1767
their Son Shobal Born March 6th 1770
Desire died Oct 12th 1826.
Sarah " Jany 11th 1836.
Mr Daniel Lovell died Augt 9th 1785.
Mrs Sarah B. Lovell " Jany 9th 1808.

[p. 256] Thomas Fuller and Elizabeth his wife
Their Daughter Elizabeth born Jany 21 1743
Their son Thomas Fuller born Aug: 14 1745
Their son Jacob Fuller born March 6 1746
Their Daughter Hannah Fuller born April 2 1749
Abijah Fuller & Hester his wife
Their Daughter Melatiah born Feb 8 1747
Moses Sturges and Eleanor his wife their Children Born
Daughter Fear Born November 27th 1745
Ezekiel their Son Born October 30th 1747.
Son John Born Jany 20th 1750
Their Daughter Mercy Born January 15 1751
Their Daughter Mary Born January 30 1758
John Sanderson & Tabitha his wife Their Children Born
Rebekah Sanderson Born June 27. 1748
Edmond Hinkly & Sarah his Wife
Their son Edmond born Novr 10 1745
Their son Abner born March 25 1747
their Daughter Mary Born July 11th 1749
their Son Enock born March 27th 1751
their Son Heman born January: 27th 1754
their Daughter anna born December 6: 1757
their Son Benjamin born December 24: 1761

(To be continued)

BARNSTABLE, MASS., VITAL RECORDS

(*Continued from page 15*)

[p. 257] Persons published In order for Marriage 1748
M'r' Edward Crosby & M'rs' Hannah Gorham July 10 1748
Seth Phinny and Bethia Bump Aug: 11 1748
M'r' Isaac Hinkly & M'rs' Hannah Bourn Sep 7 1748
Thomas Phinny 3'rd' & Abigail Lumbart Octo'r' 29 1748
M'r' Jonathan Bourn of Sandwich M'rs' Susannah Mendall Nov 1748
Peter Molatto Serv't' to M'r' Annable & Betty alias Elizabeth Quason Decem' 24 1748
Simon Jones Ju'r' & Hannah Linnel 3'rd' Decem'r' 31 1748
Thomas Ewer Ju'r' and Lydia Harlow of Plymoth Jan'ry' 20 1748
James Molatto Serv't' to Deacon Davis & Mary Twekit Jan'ry' 21 1748
Primus and Amaritta Servants to Col Otis March 4 1748
Ebenezer Lumbart and Thankful Davis April 15 1749
Benjamin Cob & Ann Davis April 22 1749
John Nye of Sandwich and Hannah Allen May 13 1749
John Easterbrook and Abigail Gorham May 13 1749
M'r' Jonathan Russel of This Town M'rs' Desire Bourn of Situate Aug 22 1749
Joseph Berse & Lydia Dean 26 of Aug 1749*
Jonathan Ellis of Nantucket & Thankful Lewes [26 of Aug 1749*]
Cornelius Davis and Annah Lumbert Sept'r' 15 1749
Moses Cognihu & Thankful Moses Sep't' 15 1749
Jeremiah Bacon and Hannah Tayler Sep 23 1749†
Sam'll' Annable Ju'r' & Desire Dimock [Sep 23 1749]†
Nath'll' Lumbart and Abigail Lumbert [Sep 23 1749]†

* These two entries are bracketed, with one date.

† These three entries are bracketed, with one date.

John Dun and Desire Gallop Chatham Octo^r 7 1749*
Sam^ll Hamlin Ju^r & Joanna Bumpas [Octo^r 7 1749]*
Jabez Goodspeed & Elizabeth Adams Octo^r 21 1749
Sam^ll Jenkins Mary Chapman Octo^r 28 1749†
Joseph Bodfish Mehitable Goodspeed [Octo^r 28 1749]†
Thomas Egred & Anna Dimock Nov 24 1749
Lemuel Lewes & Temperance Berse Decem^r 23 1749
Prince Davis & Sarah Coleman Decem^r 30 1749
Cesar and Rheta Negroes Feb 3 1749
Benjamin Hinkly & Lydia Phiny Feb 22 1749
Joseph Bacon Ju^r and Miriam Coleman March 3 — 1749
Mr James Lewes & Mrs Joannah Howland March 17 1749
Joseph Thomas & Mary Lothrop March 31 1750
Nathan Noyes of Falmoth and Mehitable Bangs June 5 1750
Nathaniel Ewer ju^r & Drusilla Covel Chatham July July 14 1750
Eben^r Cob & Mary Smith July 27 1750
John Lovel and Elizabeth Dimock of Falmoth Sep 1 1750
Jabez Gorham Mary Burbank Sep 1750
[p. 258] Mr John Russel and Mehitable his Wife
  "   Son Silas Born August 10th 1752
Their Son Lothrop Russel born Decem^r 8 1747
Silas Ewer and Lydia his Wife
their Daughter Mehitable born May 1 1747
Their Daughter Abigail Ewer born March 2 1748
Their Daughter Susannah Born Decem^r 5 — 1750
Their Daughter Elizabeth Decem^r 14. 1754
Son Prince Born Febru^y 5th 1757
David Crocker Ju^r & Dorcas his Wife
Their Daughter Anna born Decem^r 26 1742
Their Daughter Rachel Feb 1744
Their son Samuel Crocker Born Feb 1747
Beniman Blosom and Elisabeth‡ his wife
Their son Beniman Born august 18: 1753
Eben^r Childs Ju^r & Hannah his Wife their son
Ebenez^r Childs born Novr 3rd 1747
Their son Josiah Childs born 8 Aug 1749
Hannah born Sept 10 1751
David March 2 1754
Hannah ye wife Died Feb 23 1755
Deacon Ebenezer Childs Died Jan^r 17 1756 S^d Deacon being Father
    of ye first named Ebenezer
Ebenezer Childs Children by his Second wife Abigail
their Son Jonathan Born may 13 1757

* These two entries are bracketed, with one date.
† These two entries are bracketed, with one date.
‡ "Abigail" was first written, but was crossed out and "Elisabeth" interlined, in different ink.

Daughter Abigail Born Decem^r 26. 1758
Hope Born Jany 21. 1761
[p. 259] Capt Simon Davis and Priscilla his Wife
Their Daughter Mary Davis born Febr^y 28 1741
Their Daughter Content Davis born March 23 1743
Their Daughter Priscilla Davis born Feb 17 1745
The Children of Joseph Peirce and Mary his Wife
Their Daughter Mary Peirce born Octo^r 14 1739
Their son Benjamin Peirce born April 3 1743
Their son Joseph Peirce born April 3 1745
Their son Samuel Peirce born Decem^r 10 1746
Samu^el Peirce Died February 16th 1818
Jonathan Hamlin & Thankful his wife
Their Daughter Thankful born 18 April 1747
Son Jonathan march 22^d 1749
Daughter Tabitha Janua: 14 1751
Content Their Daughter Born may the 6th 1753
Peter Berse and Deborah his Wife
Their son Sam^ll Berse born 10 Sepr 1742
Their son Jesse Berse born 2 Novr 1743
Their son David Berse born 20 Novr 1745
Edward born June 12th 1750
[p. 260] Joseph Goodspeed and Abigail his Wife
Their son Benjamin Goodspeed born Feb 8 1739
Their son William Goodspeed born July 15 1741
Their son Josiah Goodspeed born April 20 1744
Their Daughter Abigail Goodspeed born Decem^r 16 1746
Their son Timothy Goodspeed born April 22 1749
Their Son Joseph born Febu^y 26th 1756
Cornelius Goodspeed and Mary his Wife
Their son Cornelius Goodspeed born April 27 1747
Zaccheus Phinny and Susannah his wife
Their son Benjamin Phinny born June 10 1744
Their son Timothy Phinny born April 5 1746
Their son Barnabas Born March 31 1748
Benjamin Jones Ju^r & Grace his Wife
Their Son Saul Jones born January 10 1743
Their Daughter Mary Jones born June 19 1745
Their Son David Jones born Aug 6 1747
Son Joseph Born July 15 1752
[p. 261] Barnabas Phinny Mehitable his wife
Their son Ichabod Phinny Born April 25. 1746
Nath^ll Hinkly & Desire his Wife
their son Benjamin Hinkly born 23 of May 1747.
Their son Nathaniel Hinkly born March 15 1748
Daughter Sarah Born June 29th 1751.
Ebenez^er Tayler Ju^r & Phebe his Wife
Their Daughter Annah born Agust 5 1747

Christopher Tayler & Bithiah his wife their Children
their Son Abraham Born Nov‍r 25‍th 1757
Reuben Blish & Ruth his Wife
their Son Reuben born 20‍th of Octo‍r 1747
Their son David Blish born May 11 1749
Their son Thomas Born 21 July 1751
Elizabeth born Octo‍r 19 1755
Joseph Bodfish and Mehitable his wife
their Dafter marey Born June the 30: 1751
thear Dafter Hannah Born apriel the 11: 1753
Daug‍t: Thankful Born march 14. 1755
Twins Lydia & Ruth: Born July 7. 1757
their Second Daughter Thankfull Born July 9‍th 1761
their Daughter Elisebeth Born June 27‍th 1765
their son Joseph Born July 28‍th 1768
[p. 262] William Basset and Margaret his wife
Their Daughter Martha Basset born January 1. 1741
Their son William Basset born March 9 1743
Their Daughter Thankful Basset born Aug: 19 1746
Sam‍ll Basset & Susannah his Wife
Their Son Nehemiah born Sep‍t 22 1743
Their Son Ebenezer born Decem 27 1744
Tupper Mordecai* & Abigail his wife their Children
their Daughter Rebecca Born July 5‍th 1755
their Son Lothrop Born December 18‍th 1756
their Daughter Abigail Born Feb‍r 19‍th 1761
their Daughter Elizebath Born april 3‍d 1763
their Daughter Susanna Born February 26‍th 1765
Melatiah Lewes & Abigail his wife
Their Children born as followeth
Theodate Lewes the 16 of March 1743
Miraim Lewes 18 of Septem‍r 1745
Levi Lewes 27 of Novem‍r 1746
Meltiah Lewis 27‍th of July 1752
[p. 263] Persons published by David Crocker Town Clerk
Eben‍r Childs & Hannah Crocker Ju‍r Aug 16 1746
Eli Fuller & Mercy Rogers of Harwich Aug 29 1746
Seth Blossom & Sarah Churchil of Sandwich Octo‍r 11, 1746
M‍r Nathaniel Gilman of Exeter and M‍rs Abigail Russel Nov‍r 8 1746
Ebenezer Crocker 3‍rd & Zerviah Winslow of Harwich Nov‍r 15 1746
James Claghorn & Temperance Goodspeed Decem 6 1746
Cesar Serv‍t to John Gorham Esq‍r & Mercy Daniel Jan‍r 17 1746
Shobal Baxter of Yarmoth & Mehitable Hallet Feb 14 1746

*This is an error of the record. It should read "Mordecai Tupper". The marriage intention of "Mordecai Tupper & Abigaill Cobb" entered 24 November, 1753, was printed in our last issue [Mfr. Desc. 31:6]; and the marriage of "Mordecai Tupper and Abigail Cob Jan‍ry 8 1754" by Rev. Joseph Green, at Barnstable, was printed in our twenty-seventh volume, page 5. — *Editor.*

Sussex Negro and Experience Peter March 21 1746
John Sanderson & Tabitha Hamlin April 3 1747
Benjamin Ewer & Hannah Lawrence of Sandwich Ap 13 1747
Benjamin Crocker Ju‍r & Bathsheba Hall Yarmoth Ap 13
Reuben Blish and Ruth Childs April 13
Benjamin Berse and Anna Nickerson of Chatham July 25 1747
Paul Crowel Ju‍r of Chatham & Reliance Cob of th‍s Town Aug 6 1747
Silas Blish of this town and Mercy Toby of Falmoth Aug 14: 1747
Thomas Bumpas of Plymoth and Mercy Stuart of this Town Aug 15 1747
M‍r Cornelius Sampson of Kingston & M‍rs Desire Crocker August 29 1747
Timothy Goodspeed & Anne Smith Sep 12 1747
Benjamin Phinny & Elizabeth Ames Sep 19 1747
Jabez Berse & Elizebeth Hallet Sep‍t 26 1747*
Shobal Hamlin & rebekah Smith [Sep‍t 26 1747*]
Joseph Linnet & Dorcas Smith Octo‍r 3 1747.
Joseph Baxter Yarmoth Hannah North Octo‍r 24
Prince Taylor of Lebanon & Hannah Childs Dec. 16 1747
Cap‍t Sam‍ll Lumbart & M‍rs Thankful Thacher of Yarmoth January 9 1747
M‍r Nath‍ll Crosman of Taunton & M‍rs Jean Otis Jan‍ry 15 1747
Isaac Lewes & Martha Berse Jan‍ry 27 1747
Stephen Berse and Hannah Coleman Feb 6 1747
Daniel Crocker & Elizabeth Childs Feb 6 1747
Thomas Annable and Abigail Dimock March 26 1748
Ichabod Serv‍t to Cap‍t Hinkly & Mehtable Job April 9 1748
[p. 264] Married ℗ David Crocker Justice of the peace
Jacob Lovel Ju‍r and Hannah Lumbart 24 July 1746
Thomas Hatheway Berkley† & Bethiah Allen aug 14 1746
Seth Blossom & Sarah Churchil at Sandwich Jan‍ry [‡] 1746
Benjamin Ewer & Hannah Lawrence Octo 22 1747.
Thomas Bump of Plymoth & Mercy Stuart Nov‍r 2 1747
Thomas Annable & Abigail Dimock April 11§ 1748
M‍r Nathaniel Crosman & M‍rs Jean Otis May 26 1748
Stephen Berse & Hannah Coleman June 9‍th 1748
Benjamin Casly and Elizabeth Dun July 26 1748
Peter Molatto Serv‍t to M‍r Sam‍ll Annable & Betty Quason Jan‍ry 13 1748
James Molatto Serv‍t to Deacon Davis & Mary twekit Feb 17 1748
Simon Jones Ju‍r & Hannah Linnel April 6 1749
Nathaniel Lumbart and Abigail Lumbart Octo‍r 12 1749

*These two entries are bracketed, with one date.
†Of Berkley, Mass. — *Editor.*
‡The day of the month is blotted and illegible.
§This may have been intended for "1" as the second figure is faint. The date certainly is not "2" as given in the town copy.

Samuel Hamlin Jur & Joanna Bumpas Nov 16 1749
William Allen & Jean Spooner Decem 27. 1750
Jan 24. 1750 Matthew Cob and Mary Garret Married ꝑ Stephen Skiff Esqr
David Lumbart and Abigail Isham Febry 21 1750
The Children of Nathan Foster & Mercy his wife Continued and brought forward from page 219*
Nathan, born March 19th 1773
Abigail born January 4th 1775
Joseph born July 16th 1776
John born July 15th 1778
Abigail born May 6th 1780
Elizabeth February 16th 1783
[p. 265] The Births of the Children of John & Bethiah Hinkley
Their son Joseph born Novr 10 1745
Their Daughter Bethiah born August 25 1747
Their Daughter Mary Hinkly Aug 9 1749
Daughter Elizabeth Born April 9th 1752
Son John Born Octor 15 1754
Son Freeman Born June 27th 1757
Son James Born April 2d 1760
Sarah born oct 28: 1763
the above said Mary Hinkly Died April 2d 1820
James Davis & Jean his wife
thr Daughter Elizabeth Davis born July 2nd 1746 & Died
Their Second Daughter Elizabeth Davis born March 25 1748
Their Daughter Jean born 24 of April 1750
Their Daughter patience born June 13: 1752
Their Daughter Desire Born october 22: 1754
Their Son Joseph Born September 13th 1757
Their Son Robert Born June 30th 1760
Their Daughter Hannah Born Decemr 19th 1762
Their Son James Born January 19th 1767
Benjn Bursly & Joanna his Wife
thr son Jabez Bursly was Born 26 of July 1735
thr Daughter Martha was Born 25 of August 1740 by his Second Wife Mary.
thr Daughter Elizabeth Bursly was Born December 23 1744
his Daughter Sarah Bursly born 3 Feb 1747
Son Benjamin born march 27. 1752
Son Lemuel Bursley born June 17 1755
Isaac Tayler & Mary his Wife
Their Daughter Ann Tayler born June 10 1746
Nathan Bodfish and Patience his wife
Their Daughter abigail Born July 10th 1756
Their Daughter Patience Born Decr 10th 1761

*Printed in Mayflower Descendant, 25:131.

[p. 266. *There are no family records on this page.*]
[p. 267] John Thacher and Content Norton Married Novr 28 1734
Their Daughter Elizabeth Thacher born Feb 29 1735/6
Their Daughter Abigail Thacher born March 20 1738
Their Daughter Content Thacher born Sept 6 1740
Their Daughter Rebekah Thacher Born Aug 7. 1742
Their Daughter Desire Thacher born July 18 1745
Jethro born Janry 16th 1747*
Fear born Febry 1st 1748 Died March 26th 1829*
John born Decr 29th 1751 Died July 4 — 1833*
James born Feby 14th 1754*
Mary born March 16th 1757*
Samuel born May 29th 1759 Died aged 2 years & 24 days*
Lewes Hamlin & Experience his wife
Their Daughter Sarah Hamlin born Janry 3rd 1739
Their Son Nathaniel Hamlin born Novr 29 1741 } these two
Their Son Lewes Hamlin born Decemr 19 1743 } born at Lebanon In the Colony of Connecticut
Their Daughter Sarah Hamlin born Decemr 17 1745
Their Daughter Mary Hamlin born Decemr 16 1747
Son Philemon Born April 2: 1751
Daughter born Mercy March 25 1753
Son Perez Born Sept 26 1755
Charles Conneat & Joanna his wife
Their Son Asa Conneat born Feb 6 1744
Their Daughter Mary Conneat born March 18 1745
Their Son Charles Conneat Born May 14 1747
Their son John Conneat born 17 of Aug 1748
Their son Benjamin Conneat born 22 of Octor 1749
Their Son Barnabas Born 2d of march 1750
Their Son Thomas Born April 8. 1752
Their Daughter Elisabeth Born april 14: 1753
Their Daughter Sarah Born June 7. 1754
Their Daughter Hannah Born octo. 20: 1755
Their Son Lemuel Born January 28. 1757
Their Daughter Olive Born Sept 11. 1758
Their Daughter Martha Born Augt 19. 1760

(*To be continued*)

*These six entries are in a modern hand.—*Editor.*

BARNSTABLE, MASS., VITAL RECORDS

(Continued from page 87)

[p. 268] Eben^r Hinkley & Mehetable Sturgis Married
Their Daughter Sarah Hinkley born April 19 1744
Their Daughter Temprence Hinkley born Janeury 20 1748
Their Son Ebenezer Hinkley Born September 23: 1754
The Children of Thomas Chipman and Bethiah His Wife
Their Son Timothy Fuller Chipman born feb^y ye 1st 1761
their Son Isaac Born Septr ye 12th 1762
their Daughter Rebecca born January ye 26th 1764
Solomon Hamlin & Rebecca his Wife
Their Daughter Hannah Hamlin born July 31 1737
Joseph Bursley Ju^r & Bethiah his wife
Their Son John Bursley born Novr 1 1741
Their Daughter Bethiah born March 2 1743
Their Son Lemuel bursley born March 2 1745
Their Daughter Sarah Bursly born octo 14 1748
Their Daughter Abigail Bursly born Octo 23 1750
Their Son Joseph Bursley Born March 27 . 1757
[p. 269. *There are no family records on this page.*]
[p. 270] Benny Baker & Patience his Wife
Their Son John Baker born Janry 3 1743
Their Daughter Thankful June 29 1745
Jeremiah Bacon & Hannah Tayler married April 26 . 1750 P^r m^r Russell
Daughter Abigail born Apr: 16 . 1751
Daughter Deborah Feby 20: 1753.
Daughter olive Aug: 3 . 1755
Son Prince Born may 12: 1759
Son Lot Born July: 7: 1761
Son Eliphalet Born January 21st 1764
Son Jeremiah Born at wareham June 15th 1767
Son Daniel Decem^r 15th 1769
Asa Doctor born Feby 16th 1773 at Sandwich
Sam^{ll} Blossom & Hannah his Wife
their Daughter Thankful Blossom born Septr 8 1745

Their Son Joseph Blossom Born Octor 28th 1747
Their Sun Samule and Hannah Born January 24th 1752 and Died
Ther Daughter mehetable Born June 23: 1753
John Blish & Mary his wife
their Son John Blish Born Novr 14 1745
Their Daughter Mary Blish born Febry 27 1748
Their Son Stacy Born March 26 . 1751
Their Daughter Sarah Born Febry 15 1753
their Daughter Rebecakah Born october ye 14th 1756
their Grand Child Mary Crocker Born of their Daughter mary agust 20th 1765 Enock Crocker the Reputed father of Said Child
William Crocker & Hannah his wife
Their Daughter Mary Crocker Born March 25 1744/5
Their Son William Crocker born Febry 6 1746
Their Daughter Martha Born Novr 28 1748
Their Daughter Temperance Janry 22 1749
Mr William Crocker Died May 3d 1819
[p. 271] Peter Camet & Thankful his Wife
Their Daughter Hannah born march 26 1742
Their Son David Born Sept 25 1744
Nathan Bangs & Mehitable his wife
Their Daughter Susannah born Decemr 27 1742
Jedediah Jones & Meriah his Wife
Their Son Nye Jones born Feb 20 1741
Shobal Jones & Mary his Wife
their Daughter Catharine Jones born May 19 1744
[p. 272] Augustin Berse & Bethiah his Wife
Their Son Prince Bearss born March 12 1730/1
Their Daughter Temperance Berse born March 17 1732/3
Their Daughter Mercy Bearss born March 9 1734/5
Their Daughter Lydia Bearss born Decemr 25 . 1736
Their Son Simeon Berse born June 27 . 1739
Bethiah ye Wife Deceasd 7 Octor 1743
Edward Bacon & Patience his wife
Their Son Edward Bacon born Octor 19 1742
Their Daughter Lydia born Feb 5 1744
their Son Nymphas Bacon born June ye 2d 1746
Their Son James Bacon born Octor 30 1748
Their Daughter Susannah Bacon Born Decemr 13 1750
Their Son Samuel Bacon Born octor ye 17th 1747
Their Daughter Sarah Bacon Born Decembr ye 25th 1752
their Daughter Susannah ye 2d was Born Feb: ye 14th 1755
Their Son Ebenezer Bacon was Born Augus ye 30th 1756
their Daughter Lydia Died april 28th 1745
Son Nymphas Died December 6th 1746
Son Samuel Died Nov: 7th 1747
Daughter Susanna Died March 24th 1753
their 2d Daughter Susanna Died april 20th 1755

Mrs Patience Bacon Departed this Life Octr 21st 1764 In the 44th year of her age
John Fuller & Temperance his Wife
Their Daughter Desire Fuller born August 1st 1742
Their Son John Fuller born June 23 1744
Their Son Edward Fuller born Decemr 28 1746
Son Francis Born March 10 . 1749
Son Job Born Novr 25 1751
[p. 273] Stephen Cob & Abigail his Wife
their Daughter Mary Cob born Feb: 20 1742/3
Their Son Judah Cob born Aug 24th 1744
Their Son James Cob born July 4 1746 & Died January 28 1747
Their Daughter Abigail born April 28 1748
Their Son Stephen Cob born March 31 1750
Joseph Howland and Rachel his wife
Their Daughter Hannah Howland born Aug 8 1739
Their Daughter Mary Howland born Septr ye 9th 1740
Their Daughter Rachel Howland born May 2 . 1742
Rachel ye Wife of ye Abovesd Joseph Howland Died May 9 1742
he Married with Marrah Fuller
Their Daughter Ann born Septemr 19 1747
Thomas Young and Mary His Wife
Their Son Bangs Young Born July ye 18th 1756
Their Daughter Rebecca Born april ye 8th 1759
their Daughter mary Born may ye 29th 1761
their Daughter Elizabeth young Born Septr ye 21st 1763
Joseph Hamlin and Hannah his Wife
Their Son Micah Hamlin born 11 Novr 1741
Isaac Lewis Junr & Martha his wife
their Daughter Lydia born August 14 1748
Son Solomon Born April 10: 1750:
Son Lothrop Born Decemr 21 . 1751 :
Son Isaac Born April 4: 1758
Daughter Martha Born July 13: 1761
Daughter Rebecca Born April ye 5th 1763
[p. 274] James Goodspeed & Elizabeth his Wife
Their Daughter Martha Goodspeed born July 31 1741
Their Daughter Mary Goodspeed born June 14 1743
Their Son David Goodspeed born August 20th 1745
Their Daughter Hannah Goodspeed born 14 March 1747
Ebenezer Claghorn & Sarah Lumbart Married
Their Son Joseph Claghorn born Octr 9 1743
By his Secound wife Elizebeth
their Daughter Sarah born July ye 27th 1764
their Daughter Jane born october ye 1st 1765
Ephraim Lewis and Sarah his wife
their Daughter Thankful born June 5 1739
Rebekah Lewes born Octr 13 1741

Their Son Jacob Lewes born Janry 4th 1743/4
Isaac Hinckley Jur & Hannah Bourn married Decr 18: 1748
Son Richard Born Octo 29: 1749.
Daugr Hannah marh 25: 1751.
Abigail Hinckly Febru 13: 1753
Joseph Hinckly march 6: 1755
Elisabeth Hinckly Aprill 30: 1757.
Isaac Hinckly June 18. 1760
Charles Hinckley Novr 1st 1762
Eunice Hinckley July 14. 1765

(*To be continued*)

BARNSTABLE, MASS., VITAL RECORDS

(*Continued from page 142*)

[p. 275] Benjamin Lothrop (Son of Samll) & Experience his Wife
Their Daughter Mary Lothrop born April 30 1731
Their Son Benjamin Lothrop born July 1 1741
Reuben Hamlin & Hope his Wife
Their Son Elkanah Hamlin born June 1 1740
Their Son Benjamin Born May 7. 1742
Their Daughter Abigail Hamlin born Febry 21. 1743
Their Son Lemuel born April 4. 1746
Their Son Thomas born Septr 26 1748
ye Above Sd Elkanah born June 1 1740 Died 19 of April 1750 In his 10 Year
Their Daughter Hannah Born August 4th 1753
John Hamlin & Jerusha his Wife
Their Son John Hamlin born June 16 1743
Their Daughter Lydia Hamlin born Octor 21. 1746
Benjamin Gorham (Son of Thomas Gorham) & Sarah his Wife
Their Son Samuel Gorham born Septr 2nd 1740
Isaac Gorham Son of Remember Backouse by Isaac Gorham ye Reputed Father born August 19 1746
[p. 276] Mr Benjamin Gorham & Mary his wife
Their Son Sturges Gorham born June 28 1742
Their Daughter Deborah Gorham born July 6 1744 & Died Octor 1745
Their Son Benjamin Gorham born March 26 1746
Their Daughter Mary Gorham born Octor 8 1748
Their Daughter Mehitable born Fryday Novr 28 1755 N S*
their Daughter Olive Born March 12. 1759
their Son Edward Born February 15th 1762
David Phinny & Mary his Wife
Their Daughter Deborah Phinny Born Sept 6 1735
Their Son Elijah Phinny Octor 4 1738 Died 17 July 1741

*"N S" is for "New Style".— *Editor.*

148 Barnstable, Mass., Vital Records

Their Daughter Elizabeth Phinny born May 10 1741 & Died Nov 15 1743
Their Daughter Mary Phinny born 6 of Decem 1749
Reuben Claghorn & Eleanor his Wife
Their Daughter Jean Claghorn born April 12 1733
Their Son Seth Claghorn born Nov 1 1737
Their Daughter Joanna Claghorn born 12 Janu 1742
Their Daughter Lois born February 8 1747
[p. 277] Jesse Lewes & Mercy Crosby Married
Their Daughter Mary born Decem 23rd 1736
Their Daughter Anna born March 13 . 1738
Their Daughter Naomi born Janu 12 . 1740
Jabez Crocker & Mary his Wife their Children born
y Daughter Anna Crocker born March 6 1738
Their Daughter Deliverance Crocker born May y 7 . 1740
Their Son Asa Crocker born Sept 4 1741
Their Daughter Ruth Crocker born August 25 1743
David Childs & Hannah his Wife Their Children
Their Daughter Susannah Born July 30th 1762
Asenah born Sept y 22d 1765
Job born Sept 8th 1767
Hannah born Nov 17th 1769
Anna born Nov 4th 1771
Josiah born December 14th 1773
David born July 8th 1775
Shubael Davis born Dec 16th 1777
Benjamin Born Aug 11th 1779
Edward Born March 9th 1783
Reuben Maggs & Rebekah his Wife Their Children born
y Daughter Mary Maggs 24 Sept 1733
y Daughter Hannah Maggs 25 March 1735
y Daughter Mercy Maggs born 29 January 1736
y Son Josiah Maggs 3 Sept 1739
y Son Matthew Mags 18 July 1742 Died June 7th 1824
[p. 278] John Casely & Dorcas his Wife
Their Son John Casley born Feb 14th 1740
Their Son Ebenezer Casely born Aug: 12 1744
Mary born May 23d 1749
Seth born Feb 21st 1751
Isaac born July 10th 1753
Dorcas born July 8th 1755
Eunice born Sept 19th 1759
Benjamin Caseley Jur & Huldah (*Hinckley**) his Wife (*Nov 29 . 1739 by Mr Green**)
Their Son Ambrose Casely Born y 19 of June 1741

* The additions in italics are in pencil, in a modern hand. The marriage, by Rev. Joseph Green, is recorded on original page 340.— *Editor.*

Barnstable, Mass., Vital Records 149

Their Son Benjamin Casly born 9 March 1743
Their Son Thomas Casely born Feb 14 1745
Their Son Lemuel Casly born Nov 17 1747
Their Son Samuel Casly born Decem 3rd 1749
Their Daughter Hannah Casly born Decem 2nd 1750
Their Daughter Mehetible Born June 8th 1758
Their Son David Born March y 15th *
Nathan Crocker Jur & Mehitable his Wife
Their Son Enoch Crocker Born 1 of June 1741
Their Daughter Susannah Crocker born April 9 1743
Their Daughter Deborah Crocker born March 30 1745
Their Daughter Azubah Crocker born August 14 1747
Their Son Elijach Crocker Born Febru: 11 . 1749
Their Son Nathan Crocker Born August 10 . 1753
Their Son Jonathan Crocker Born March 23 . 1756
their Son David Born March 15th 1761
their Daughter Mehitable Born June 8 1758
Solomon Bodfish and Hannah his wife
Their Son Benjamin Bodfish Born April 28 1743
Their Son Solomon Bodfish Born March 28th 1744
Daughter Hannah Born Decem 2 . 1747
Lydia Born Febru: 27 1749
Son Nathan Born march 19 1751
Daughter Rachel Born July 25th 1754
their Son Solomon Born march 20th 1756
[p. 279] David Hallet & Mary Annable Maried y 19th Day of August 1719
Their Children born as followeth
Their Daughter Abigail born 22 June 1720
Their Son Jonathan born 1 Decem 1722
Their Son David born 12 Decem 1724
Their Daughter Elizabeth 9 Jan: 1726
Their Daughter Mehitable 21 April 1729
Their Daughter Remember 12 May 1731
Their Daughter Sarah 28 May 1733
Their Daughter Annah 14 May 1737
Their Daughter Mary 11 May 1739
Their Son Abner 19 May 1741
John Crocker (Son of John Crocker) & Lydia his Wife
Their Daughter Elizabeth born Feb 28 1738
Their Son Stephen born Decem 8 . 1740
Their Son Joseph Born y 6th of Feb. 1742
Their Son Allyn Crocker born Feb 18 1744/5
Their Daughter Bathsheba Crocker Born January y 23rd 1746.
Lydia May 12 1749
David born

*The year was not entered.

Hannah born March 13th 1753
John born May 12th 1755
Abigail born February 1758
Lazarus Son of Lazarus Lovel & Mary his Wife born Decem 10 1736
    About 2 Minutes before Sun Rise
Their Daughter Rebeckah Lovel born May 23 1743
Their Son Simeon Lovel born Aug: 8 1748
[Children by] his Second wife Mercy Ewer.*
Mrs Mary Lovell died Janry " Apl 5th 1813. Agd 91 Years*
[p. 280. *There are no family records on this page.*]
[p. 281] Isaac Crocker & Elizabeth his Wife Married March 22 1738
Their Son Ansel Born August 27 1739
Rebekah March 24 1740
Their Son Thomas Crocker born Sep 19 1743
Josiah Crocker Octr 14th 1762
Ansel Crocker Jany 22d 1767
Benjamin Hamlin & Mehitable his Wife
Their Daughter Mary Born July 16 1741
Their Son Benjamin Hamlin Born Feb 25 1742
Their Son Nathll born Feb 21 1744
Their Daughter Jean born March 23 1746
Their Son Ichabud Born June 28 . 1749
    By his Second wife
their Daughter Mary born april 12th 1767
their Son Lewis born Decemr 24th 1768
their Son Benjamin born Septr 30th 1770
Ebenezer Tayler Son of Ebenezer Tayler & Mary his Wife born ye 28
    Day of Sept 1737
Their Daughter Alice born ye 18 of April 1740
Their Son Josiah Tayler born 24 January 1742
Their Daughter Susannah Decemr 2 1744
Their Son Seth Tayler born Octor 19 1746
Their Son Jasper Tayler born Septr 7th 1748
Their Daut Sarah Born octor 12 . 1750
Their Daughter Ann april 9 . 1753
John Ewer & Jean his Wife
Their Son Ebenezer Ewer born Decemr 20 1741
Their Son John Ewer born Decemr 25th 1744
Their Son David Ewer born April 15th 1747
their Son Jonathan Ewer Born June 7th 1754
their Daughter Reliance Ewer Born June: 16th 1756
their Son Ebenezer Ewer Born December 31st 1758
their Son John Ewer Born october 31st 1763
[p. 282. *There are no family records on this page.*]

* The words in brackets have been crossed out, apparently in the same ink as the rest of the last three entries, which are in a later hand than the first three Lovell entries. — *Editor.*

[p. 283.] James Berse & Mary Fuller Married
Their Son Jabez born Feb 20 . 1720
by his Second Wife Thankful Linnel
Their Son James born Feb 3 1728 & Decesd Sep 29 1739
Lemuel Berse yr Son born May 3 1731
Their Daughter Thankful Berse born Aug: 1 1736
Ebenezer Fuller & Mariah Jones Married Their Children born
David 6 of February 1725
Jonathan 9 of April 1729
Daniel 16 of Septr 1731
John Fuller born 3 of June 1734
William 27 of Septr 1736
Jean 12 of January 1739
Ebenezer Cannon & Mercy yr Children born
Ebenezer Cannon yr Son born March 19 1736/7
Ruth Cannon born January 18 1738/9
Nathan Cannon born April 10 1741
Joanna Cannon born 4 of Sep 1743
Joseph Cannon Born 14 of Decem 1745
Ebenezer Thomas & Thankful Blossom his wife
Their Son William Thomas born August 29 1737
their Daughter Ann Thomas born June 23 . 1739
Their Son Elijah Thomas Born June 6th 1741
Their Son Elisha Thomas born May 13 . 1745
[p. 284. *There are no family records on this page.*]
[p. 285] John Bacon Born march 24 1796/7–1696/7 his wife July 1698*
John Bacon & Elizabeth Freeman Married May 5 1726
Their Daughter Mary born March 24 1727 Died July 17 . 1727
Their Son John Bacon Ap: 22 1728
Barnabas April 18 1729 Died July 15 1729
our * 4 Child a Daughter born & Died in ¼ hour Jan: 3 1729/30
Elizabeth born May 8 1731
Isaac 25 Decemr 1732
Mark January 27 . 1734
Simeon July 26 1736 Died March 21 1739/40
Daughter Desire born May 20 . 1738
Daughter Mary born Aug: 23 1740
Nicholas Baker and Darcas his Wife
Their Son Nathaniel Baker Born March 23 1733/4
Their Son Ebenezer Baker born June 7 . 1736
David Octor 18 1739
ye Above Sd Nicholas Died January Last . 1739/4†

* The "1696/7" was added in a different hand and ink, evidently to correct the error in the record. These two births were interlined at the top of the page. The record of the fourth child indicates that this family was recorded by John Bacon — or was copied into the town records from a copy of his own family record. — *Editor.*

† Evidently an error, in the record, for 1739/40.

152   Barnstable, Mass., Vital Records

Lewes Hamlin & Experience his Wife
Their Daughter Sarah born January 3rd 1739/40
Thomas Childs & Mary his Wife
Their Son David born July 20 1711
Jonathan Novr 27 1713
Silas March 10 1715
Hannah July 29 1720
Thomas Sept 10 1725
Benjamin Decem 4 1727
Mary April 1 1733
[p. 286] Elisha Thacher & Phebe his wife
their Daughter Lucretia Thacher born April 20 1737
their Son Samuel Sturges Thacher born Novr 4 1741 & Died Febr^y 14 1741*

Their Son Anthony Thacher born June 28 1744
Barnabas Bursley and Thankful his wife their Children Born viz
Daughter hannah Born: Februy 3^d 1756
Daughter Thankful Born March 29 . 1759.
Their Son Barnabas Born April 24: 1761
Deacon John Baker & Annah his Wife
y^r Daughter Annah Baker born Sept 8 1697
Daughter Mercy Baker born August 18 1699
Daughter Rebekah Baker born Sept 8 1704
Son Samuel Baker born Sept 7 1706
Daughter Mary Baker Born March 25 1710
Daughter Mehitable Baker born May 7 . 1712
Daughter Abigail Baker born 1 Feb: 1713/14
Son John Baker Born Decem^r 1 1716
Daughter Hannah Baker born March 24 1718/9
The Children of James & Bethiah Haddeway
Their Daughter Lois born 17 of April 1732
James born Novem^r 13 1733
Mrs Mary Hathaway wife of James Hathaway Died Feruary 12th 1821†
Isaac Fuller & Jerusha his Wife ye Children born
Eli 11 of April 1720
Mehitable 10 of March 1722/23
Jerusha 19 of January 1725/26
Zaccheus Fuller born 15 of Octo^r 1727
Charity 11 December 1729
Isaac 9 Sept 1731
Seth 29 May 1734
Hannah 9 April 1736

(*To be continued*)

* This death would be 1742 in new style dating.
† This entry, in a different hand and ink, was interlined between the births of Lois and James.

THE MAYFLOWER DESCENDANT

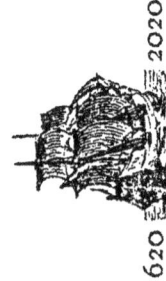

1620　2020

A QUARTERLY MAGAZINE OF
PILGRIM GENEALOGY AND HISTORY

VOLUME XXXII

1934

PUBLISHED BY THE
MASSACHUSETTS SOCIETY OF
MAYFLOWER DESCENDANTS
BOSTON

BARNSTABLE, MASS, VITAL RECORDS

TRANSCRIBED BY GEORGE ERNEST BOWMAN

(*Continued from Vol. XXXI, p. 152*)

[Vol. 2, p. 287] John Bates & Abigail his wife
Their Daughter Susannah Bates born July 15 1739
Their son Samuel Bates born December 7: 1741 & Died march 28 . 1742
Their son John Bates born January 10 1742
Their son Job Bates born Feb 3rd 1745
Their Daughter Mehitable Born 19 Feb 1748
Thomas Born march 17 : 1750
Samuel Born Sept 27 . 1754
Seth Born march 7 . 1758
The Births of the Children of Seth & Mary Hallet Their Daughters &c
Temperance Hallet Born April 18 1729
Hannah Hallet born Decemr 4 . 1731
Deborah Hallet was Born April 14 . 1734
Joseph & Thankful hallet twins born Sept: 21 . 1736
Abigail Hallet was Born August 8. 1738
The Children of Ebenezer Case & Elizabeth his Wife
Their son Barnabas Case Octor 24 1729
Isaac Case March 25 1732
Sarah Case July . 1 . 1735
Lot Case 1737
Betty Case born Octor 7 1739
Their Daughter Mary Case born March 14, 1741
James Delap & Mary his Wife
Their Daughter Rose born Feb 25 . 1739
Their Daughter Abigail Delap born Novr 6 1741
Their Daughter Catharine Delap born Sept 3 1743
Their Son Thomas Delap born April 14 1745
Mary born Novr 3 1747
Sarah born April 11 . 1750
Jean Born Aug: 13 1752
Hannah July 14 1755 New Stile
[p. 288] Dr James Hersey & Lydia his Wife
Their son James Hersey born Novr 9 1738
by his Second wife Mehitable
their Son Ezekiel Hersey was Born January 15 1741.*

---

* Following this entry, in a different hand, and in pencil, we find:
"Mehitable Davis was married four times, & had one Son by each husband.
1st to James Hersey — Ezekiel
2　"　John Russell — Lothrop
3　"　John Sturgis
4　"　Davis — Daniel"

Gershom Hamlin & Hannah his Wife
Martha th^r Daughter born May 11 1740
Their son Enoch Hamlin born January 23 1742/3
Their Son Gershom Hamlin born Sep 16 1745
Their Son George born 3rd Feb 1749
Jabez Linnel & Sarah his Wife
Their Daughter Mary Linnel born Feb 20 1737
Their Daughter Deborah 8 April 1739
Their son Elisha Linnel Octo^r 20 1740
Their Son Joseph Linnel born Nov 6 . 1743
Their Daughter Jean born March 16 1744
Their son John Linnel born January 28 1748
Solomon Sturges & Abigail his wife
Their Daughter Mercy Sturges 3 Sep : 1735
Son Sam^{ll} Sturges 7 Sep: 1737
Daughter Abigail May 22 . 1739
Their Son Solomon Sturges born March 13 1742
Mathew Lumbart & Mercy Davis Their Children born viz
Desire May the 28 1729 & Died June 20 1729
Gershom July 8 1730
Remember May 6 1734 & Died August 27 . 1734
Desire December 19 1736
[p. 289] The Births of the Children of Mr John Gorham ju^r & of Elizabeth his Wife
Susannah Gorham th^r Daughter born Novr 21 1732
Mary Gorham th^r Daughter born Decem^r 3 . 1733
Annah Gorham th^r Daughter born July 23 1735
John Gorham th^r Son born Decem: 26 . 1736
Christopher Gorham th^r Son born Jan: 10 1737/8
Thomas Bacon & Desere his Wife their Children Born
their Son Oris Bacon Born Decem^r 19th 1762
The Children of Thomas Adams & Sarah his wife
Martha born July 20 1725
Thomas Nov. 27 1726
Elizabeth Octo 10 1728
Walley July 26 . 1730
Sarah March 30 1732
Nath^{ll} April 1 . 1734
Edward April 15 1736
Hannah March 11 1737/8
The Children of Nathaniel Bacon Son of Jeremiah Bacon & Sarah his Wife . Viz
Rebekah Bacon born Decem 17 1726
Jeremiah Bacon born June 25 1732
Elizabeth Bacon born May 1 1734
Sarah Bacon born May 9 1736
Nath^{ll} Bacon born March 3 1737

[p. 290] The Births of the Children of Mr Jonathan Davis & Susannah his Wife
Their Daughter Susannah born July 29 . 1738
David Cobb & Thankfull his wife their Children Born
their Daughter Thankfull Born oct^r 28th 1745
their Son David Born January 19: 1750
Elisebath Cobb Born august 7: 1753 & Died June 10th 1821
Jonathan Cobb Born July 18: 1756
The Children of Sam^{ll} Fuller ju^r & Melatiah his wife
They Married January 20 1725
Their son Ahijah born December 19 1726
a Still Born Son Decem 7 1728
Twins Jan: 26 1730 a Son and Daughter The Son Died 4 weeks old the Daughter is Abigail
The Children of John Goodspeed & Rebecca his Wife
th^r Daughter Susannah Goodspeed born 22 April 1736
th^r Daughter Lydia Goodspeed born 21 January 1738
th^r Son Philemon Goodspeed Born 25 of April 1742
th^r Son John Goodsped born 15 of Novem^r 1745
James Coleman & Martha His wife
their Daughter Martha Coleman born March 19 1732
Their son James Coleman born August 8 . 1735
Their son John Coleman born May 14 . 1737
Their Daughter Mary Coleman born March 27 . 1739
The Children of Lemuel Bacon & Deborah his Wife
viz Jabez born July 2^d 1757
[p. 291] James Lothrop & Patience his Wife th^r Children born viz.
their Daughter Deborah born Ap: 15 . 1733
Their Daughter Mary born Ap: 6 . 1735
Their son James Lothrop born March 15 . 1737*
Ebenezer Lewes & Mary Cory of Long Island Married . Nov. 1736.
their Daughter Mary born Novr 22 1737
Their son David Lewes born Jan^{ry} 19 1739/40
Their son Ebenezer Lewes born Jan^{ry} 5th 1742/3
Their Daughter Martha born Octo^r 21 . 1745
James Fuller and Temperance his Wife
Their Daughter Martha born June 21 1734
Their son John born Feb 6 1735
Their Daughter Mary Fuller born Novr 5 1741
Their son James Fuller born Feb^{ry} 21 1743
Their son Joseph Fuller born March 3 1745
Their son Benjamin Fuller Born Sept 21 1748
William Blatchford & Elizabeth his Wife
Their son Peter born May 10 . 1729

*Following this entry we find, in pencil, in a different hand:
"Martha bap. June 21, 1741
Ebenezer   "   May 15, 1743
David   "   Oct 7 1774"

their Daughter Lydia born April 5 . 1734
Their Son Benjamin born June 11 . 1738
Their Daughter Remember March 3 1739
Their Daughter Mercy April 13 1742
Their Son David Blatchford born June 17 1744
Their Daughter Lydia Born May 22 . 1746.
their Son william Born June 25 . 1750 Died August 30th 1816
David Blackford* Died November 16th 1822
[p. 292] James Hamlin Ju r his Children born
his Son Silas Hamlin born April 15th 1722
his Son Caleb Hamlin born Feb: 8th 1723/4
his Daughter Deborah Hamlin born Jan ry 19 1726/7
Benjamin Hamlin his Son born Jan ry 1 1730
David Hamlin his Son born Jan ry 11 1732
Hannah Hamlin his Daughter born Aug: 30 1735
Oct or 9 1735 Seth Hamlin & Sarah Blish Married
Their Daughter Mercy Hamlin born Nov r 15 1737
Their Daughter Sarah Hamlin born Aug: 18 1739
Their Daughter Abigail born August 14 1741
Their son Seth Hamlin born August 20 1744
Their Daughter Alice† born August 12 1747
Abraham Blish & Temperance his wife
Their Son Abraham born Oct or 20th 1739
Their Son Elijah born March 5 1738/9
Their Daughter Rebekah born Nov: 14 1740
Their Son Benjamin Blish born May 9 1743
Their Son Elisha Blish born April 23 1745 & Died 17 November following.
Their Second Son Elisha born March 1 . 1746
Their Daughter Martha Blish born . 14 of July 1749.
Temperance Born Nov r 21 . 1751.
Timothy Blish Aug 3 1756
[p. 293] James Cobb Ju r & Hannah Rich Married by M r Avery of Truro May 14 1724
Their Son James born June 16 1725 & Died the 8th of Oct or 1725
Elizabeth born Oct or 29 1726 Saturday
Lois born June 27 1729 Fryday night
Isaac born Decem r 21 1731 Tuesday night
Ezekel born August 31 1734 Saturday
Hannah born April 20 1737 Wednesday
Jesse Cob & Thankful his Wife
Ther son Joseph born 22 Sep. 1734
Ebenezer Gorham & Temperance his wife Their Children born Viz
Ebenezer 7 Aug 1729

* So recorded.
† "Abigail" was first written, but was crossed out and "Alice" interlined above.

Prince 14 March 1730/1
Hannah 16 April 1733
Mary 16 June 1735
Sam ll Jenkins & Mary his Wife their Children born
Experience 4 Decem r 1722
Mary 7 Sept: 1725 & Died 7 June 1727
Sam ll 20 Oct or 1727
Nathaniel 6 Decem r 1729
Simeon 18 Sept 1733 . Died Aug t 19th 1808
Lot born March 13 1737
Ebenezer Jenkins & Judith his wife
th r son Thomas born March 8 . 1725/6
Judith his Wife Died April 27 . 1729
his Children born of his 2 nd Wife Elizabeth Viz
Ebenezer July 6 1733
Nathan Oct r 21 . 1734
Martha born Nov r 4 . 1737 Fryday
Elizabeth born May 9, 1740 Fryday
[p. 294] Stephen Freeman & Hannah his Wife
their Daughter Keziah born Sept r 24 1737
Gershom Hamlin & Hannah his Wife
th r Daughter Martha Born May 11 1740
Silvanus Stuard and Lydia His Wife their Children
Puella Their Daughter was Born Dec r the 26th 1757
Their Son Solomon was born Oct r the 7th 1759
Their Daughter Remember was born feb y the 6th 1762
Ebenezer Crocker & Ann his Wife
their Son Rouland Crocker born June 8th 1736
Their Daughter Joanna Crocker born Decem r 8 1737
Their Son Ezekiel born Nov r 24 1739
Their Daughter Tabitha born Feb 20th 1741
Their Daughter Bethiah born June 8th 1744
Their Son Gershom Born Oct or 8 1746
Seth Crocker & Joanna his wife
th r Daughter Hannah born July 18 . 1732
by His Second Wife Temperance Thacher
his Son Thomas born June 8th 1735
James Childs & Elizabeth his Wife th r Children born Viz
Samuel July 15 . 1723
James Ap: 22 1725
Elizabeth Decem 20 . 1730
Sarah Ap: 9 . 1736
Thankfull Aug: 4 1741
Their Son Richard Childs born March 22 1743/4
John Lothrop & Hannah his wife th r Children born viz
Hannah April 18 . 1728
Mary June 20 . 1730
Nath ll Sept 22 . 1732

Joseph July 10th 1735
Lot born 17 of Novem 1737
Barnabas October 17 . 1740
Hannah the Wife of the Above S^d John Lothrop Deceas^d August 2nd 1741
Sam^ll Annable 3rd & Bethiah his wife th^r Children viz
Sam^ll May 5 1728
Mehitable July 9 1730
Thomas Decem 3 . 1734
Barnabas born Novr 13 1737
[p. 295] The Children of David Parker & Mary his Wife
their Daughter Mary born Feb: 18th 1733/4
Their son Daniel Born March 25th 1734/5
Samuel Lumbart Jur & Anna his Wife their Children born Viz
Daughter Sarah Septr 3 . 1718
son John Jan^ry 9th 1719/20
son Joseph Jan^ry 8th 1722
Daughter Anna March 26th 1724
son Benjamin Decem^r 4th 1726
Daughter Elizabeth Feb: 25 . 1729/30
Daughter Mercy Jan^ry 30 1732/3
Israel Butler & Elizabeth Blossom Married July 1 1725
Their Son Nath^ll Butler born 9 at Night on the 11 Ap: 1726
Son Benjamin Butler born Decem: 18 1727 Sun Set
th^r Daughter Elizabeth Butler born June 6 1730 about 12 at Noon
th^r Daughter Sarah Butler born Octr 31 1732 P M
Elizabeth the Wife Died Jan^ry 7th 1734/5
S^d Israel Butler Married to Mary Parker Oct^or 29 1735
th^r Son James Butler was born Decem 15 1736. 6 at Night
th^r Daughter Hannah Buttler born May 11 1738
th^r Daughter Mary Buttler born Sept 26 1739
th^r Son Daniel Butler Born Feb 23 1740
his Wife Mary Died 1745
[p. 296] The Children of George Howland & Abigail his wife
Daughter Hannah Born August 4th 1732 & Died 5th Day of September following
son Seth born March 17 . 1734/5
son John born June 2 1738
son Shove Howland born June 15 1741
Their Son George Howland born April 25th 1743
The Children of Benjamin Hinkley Ju^r and Abigail his Wife born as followeth Viz
Abigail 30 July 1718
Edmond 30 January 1719/20
Samuel 16 Oct^or 1721
Joseph 23 oct^or 1723
Benjamin 28 April 1727
Sylvanus 7 April 1729

Nath^ll 7, April 1732
Martha 24 April 1734
Bathsheba 14 April 1736
Timothy April 16 1738
Zaccheus October 6th 1740
The Children of Sam^ll Crocker Ju^r & Ruth his wife
their Son Noah Crocker Born Sep 12 1724
their Daughter Sarah Crocker born Jan^ry 5 . 1726
their Daughter Hannah Crocker born May 16 . 1729
their Daughter Anna Crocker born March 8 . 1731
their Daughter Joanna Crocker born June 4 . 1735
their Daughter Joanna Crocker Died August 7 . 1735
John Lothrop by his Second Wife Thankful
Their Daughter Bethiah Lothrop born Oct^or 2^d 1745
[p. 297] The Children of Jacob Lovel & Content his Wife
son Jacob Lovel born May 29th 1724
Joseph 3rd Oct^or 1725
Benjamin 28th March 1723
Cornelius March 14 1730/1
The Children of Samuel Lumbart Son of Joshua Lumbart by Mary his wife
Mary born 1 Feb: 1717/8
Abigail April 23 . 1720
Joshua March 18th 1721/2
Sam^ll August 18th 1726
Benjamin March 4th 1728/9
Isaac Jones & Patience his Wife
their Daughter Lyddy born Feb 24 . 1711/12
Jedediah April 1. 1714
Patience Feb: 10 . 1717/8
Isaac June 16th 1720
Sarah Oct^o 1st 1724
Simon April 11th 1728
Micah Aug: 30th 1732
The Children of Thomas Phinny & Reliance his Wife
Eli born Jan^ry 16 1726/7
Lydy August 21 . 1729
Sarah Feb^ry 17 . 1731/2
Isaac August 26 . 1734
Patience Feb 27 . 1736
Abigail Nov 3rd 1740
Elizabeth March 1 . 1742
Children of Sam^ll Bump, & Joanna his Wife
Sarah born Ap: 5 1718
Joanna May 15 1719
Jabez 28 June 1721
Thomas 20 March 1722/3
John May 17 1725

Warren 28 June 1727
Bethiah Aug 23 1729
Mary 1 Jan: 1731/2
Phebe April 21 1734
[p. 298] The Children of Stephen Davis & Desire
Mary & Martha twins born April 23d 1731
[*Their Son Simeon born Oct'r 18 1744*]
Their Son Stephen Davis born July 6 . 1746
The Children of Jacob Lovel, by his first wife Mary Shaw.
his Daughter Mary born†
his Daughter Hannah born March 8th 1716/17
his Daughter Elizabeth†
his Daughter Mercy†
The Children of David Loring jur & Sarah his Wife
th'r son David born at Hingham 5th Day of April 1730
son Otis born at Barnstable 15 of June 1732
Daughter Sarah born January 26th 1734
Their Son Eliphalet Loring born November 4th 1736
Their Daughter Desire Loring born October 15 1738
Their son Elpalet Loring born Sept 4th 1740
Their son Joshua Loring born October 17th 1741
Their son Abner Loring born April 5 1743
Their Son Elijah Loring born Aug. 20 1744
The Children of Elpalet Loring & Abigail His Wife
their Son Elpalet Born Sept'r the 15th 1765
The Children of Abraham Tayler and Mary his Wife
Jean th'r Daughter born Oct'o 15th 1709
Sarah born May 21 . 1712
Christopher August 12th 1716
Mary Feb 17th 1718
Hannah born Octo'r 12th 1730
Deborah January 30 . 1733
Shobal Lewes & Mary his Wife Their Children
Their Daughter Elizabeth born Feb 2 . 1739
Their Daughter Sarah Lewes born Decem'r 8th 1744
[*There are no family records on pages 299 and 300.*]
[p. 301] Col: John Otis Departed this Life The 23d day of Sep'br 1721.
About Ten of the A.M. Aged About 70 years
Mr John Lothrop Died the 27th day of Sep'br‡ About Eliven a Clock
A M Aged About 85 years
Martha Barse the wife of Joseph Barse Died the 27th of January 1727/8
Aged About Seventy Seven
Daniel Parker Esq'r Departed this Life the 23d of Dec'br 1728 Aged 59.
Job Crocker Son of Decon Job Crocker Departed This Life May 21
1731 Etatis 38

* This entry was been crossed out.
† No dates were entered.
‡ The year was not recorded.

Experience Hatch Widdow Deceas'd Decem: ult 1736
Deacon John Lewes Deceasd March 5 1738
M'rs Hannah Crocker the Widdow of Deacon Job Crocker Deceased
May the 14 1743 In the 85th Year of her Age
the Afores'd Deacon Job Crocker Deceasd In March 1718/19 Etat: 75
John Linnel Died Feb 7 1747
M'r Joseph Smith Deceas'd March 14 1746
M'rs Elizabeth Loring Deceas'd June 17 1748
Benny Baker Son of Nathaniel Baker Died 29 Decem 1747
Patience his wife Died 28 Decem'r 1748
Nathaniel Son of Nicholas the Grandson of the Above Nathaniel Died
7 of Decem'r 1748
Isaac Howland Deceas'd 8 of Nov'r 1751 Etatis 63
Barnabus Downes & Mercy his wife their Children
their Son James Born May 12th 1754
their Son Barnabus Born Oct'r 2: 1756
their Son Prince Born Decem'r 5: 1758
by his Second wife
Mercy born Oct'o 8 1765*
Rachel born Sept 7th 1766*
Mary born April 11th 1767*
Elisabeth born July 25th 1768
David born Decem'r 20th 1769
Samuel born June 7th 1771
Edward born Sep't 13th 1773
Abigail born Oct'r 7th 1798*
M'r Barnabas Dowens Died April 18th 1820.
[p. 302] M'r Thomas Cobb and Rachel his wife th'r Children
Abigail Born the 29th of March 1711
Nathaniel Born the 15th of October 1713
Elizabeth Born the 14th of Feb'r'y 1715
Samuel Born the 20th of March 1717
Mathew Born the 15th of April 1719
David Born the 28th of Fer'y 1721
Henery Born the 16th of April 1724
Twins { Thomas Born the 29th of April 1726 he Died In August
       { Eber Born the 30th of April 1726
Jonathan And Martha Lovel
their Son Andrew born Sep'br 19th 1725
Hannah Born April 18th 1727 Dyed Sep'tbr 23d 1727
Daughter Lusana born April 15th 1729
Daughter Relief Ap: 5 . 1732
Daughter Jean March 5 . 1734
The Children of Benjamin Fuler jur And Rebacca his wife
Mary Born July 15th 1714 [*14 year old†*]

* So recorded. — *Editor.*
† These words in italics seem to be in the same hand and ink as the birth record.

Lidia Born March 23ᵈ 1716.
Thomas Born June 18ᵗʰ 1718.
Elizabeth Born Sepᵇʳ 30ᵗʰ 1720.
Benjamin Born Oᶜᵇʳ 28ᵗʰ 1723.
Abigail Died Decᵇʳ 29ᵗʰ 1726 . aged 13 months
Rebacca his wife died the 10ᵗʰ day of March 1727/8
Lieuᵗ Benjamin Fuller Deceᵈ Janʸ 2ᵈ 1748
Benjamin Fuller by a Second Wife had a
Son Joseph Born Octoʳ 18ᵗʰ 1730 & Died May 30 1732
Thankful Fuller 26 of April 1733
Rebecca June 1 1735
Seth March 14 1736/7
[p. 303] Thomas Foster of Plymouth and Lois Fuller of Barnstable were Married by the Revᵈ Mʳ Joseph Green On the 25ᵗʰ Day of Novᵇʳ 1725
Zacheus Crocker & Eliizabeth his Wife
their son Joshua Crocker born Aug : 6 1735
Their son Zaccheus Crocker born Decemʳ 19 1737
Their son Sylvanus Crocker born
Their Daughter Hannah Crocker born June 21 1743
Shobal Hamlin & Elenor his Wife thʳ Children Born
Jerusha May 4 . 1722
Shobal born Sep . 20 . 1724
Joshua Augus 21 . 1728
Mehitable Decem 4 . 1730
Eleanor April . 15 . 1733
Lydia Novem 15 . 1735
Moses Crocker & Mary Fish of Sandwich Married May 15 1735
Their son Nathaniel born May 7 . 1736
Their son John Crocker March 8 1737/8
Their Daughter Sarah Crocker born Aug : 6 : 1740
Their Son Moodey Crocker born 14 Feb 1742.
Their Son Edmond Crocker born August 16 1745
Benoni Crocker & Abigail his wife
their Son Lemuel born March 1 1737
Their Son [*] Crocker Born
Their Daughter Abigail Crocker born 22 May 1745
Their Son Abner Crocker born 18 Aug : 1747

(To be continued)

*The baptismal name and the date were not entered.

BARNSTABLE, MASS., VITAL RECORDS

(*Continued from page 60*)

[Vol. 2, p. 304] Persons Married by Daniel Parker Esq[r] as followeth
Benjamin Lothrop and Mercy Baker Married May 26th 1720
Elisha Parker and Mary Goreham . May 26th 1720
Roger Goodspeed and Hannah Phiney . Oc[br] 6th 1720
John Crocker and Mary Hinckly . June 22[d] 1721
Ralph Jones and Abigail Linnel . March 27th 1720/21
James Childs and Elizabeth Crocker . Sep[br] 27th 1722
Jerimiah Bumpus of Rochister & Jane Lovel . No[br] 15th 1722
Joseph Jankens & Dorcas Paine January 30th 1722/3
William Basset and Sarah Jankens Janry 30th 1722/3.
No[br] 25th 1723 Samuel Crocker and Ruth Hamlin Married
Thomas Crosbee of Harwich & Elizabeth Lewis Married 1724
De[cbr] 2[d] 1724 Joshua Edwards and Peace Parker.
De[cbr] 22[d] 1724 Job Davis and Mary Phinney Maried.
[p. 307] William Waldron, Eldest Son to the Rev[d] William Waldron of Boston . Born at Barnstable the 7th day of February 1723/4
Jabez Snow of Harwich, and Elizabeth Lewis of Harwich were Married by Joseph Lothrop Esq[r] the Second Day of April Anno Domini 1724
William Hodgdon and Margeret Ames . Married, at Dorchister . In the Year : 1713.
Mehitabe Hodgdon born At Barnstable June . 3[d] 1714
Hannah Hodgdon Born December, 28th . 1717.
David Hodgdon Bourn Aug[t] the Last . 1723.
Joseph Childs . and Deliverance Hamlin Married by the Rev[d] M[r] Jonathan Russell, April 23[d] 1724.
their son Joseph Born 17th Day of Aug[st] 1724.
their Son James Born March 4th 1742
Noah Davis; and Hannah Fuller . Married by the Rev[d] M[r] Jonathan Russell, May . 7th 1724.
Louis Aug[st] 26th 1724.
Thankfull born the March 27th day . 1728.
Unis 20th April 1734.
Jacob Chipman and Abigail Fuller . were Married the 25th october 17[21] by Col. John Otis:
Daughter Sarah born November 23[d] 1722
Daughter Abigail* born June 26th 1724
his wife Abigail Died Oc[br] 5th 1724

* "Elizabeth" was first written, but was crossed out and "Abigail" interlined in the same hand and ink.

Benjamin Lothrop . and Mercy Baker were Married by Daniel Parker Esq[r] may . 1720.
his son Nathaniel . Lothrop born the 8th day of April 1723 . 1723.
his son Elijah born No[vbr] 18th 1724
[p. 308] John Cob . and Hannah Lothrop . Married the 22 day of December . 1707 . by Barnabas Lothrop Esq[r]
Ephraim Cob . Born the fifth Day of De[cbr] 1708.
John Cob . Born the first day of July 1711 he died March the first 1713.
John Cob . Born the Second Day of October . 1719.
David Hallet . and Mary Anible Married the 19th Day of Aug[st] Annoque Domini 1719 . 1719.
their Son Jonathan Hallet born the first of December 1722.
son David born 12th December 1724
their Daughter Elizabeth . born the . 9th of Janury . 1726/7
Joseph Bacon and Patience Anible Married by Jn[o] Bacon Esq[r]
their son Joseph born the 11th day of April of AD . 1723.
Daughter Desier born December 3[d] AD . 1724.
thr Daugher Jean 28 Feb. 1727/8
Samuel Bacon 26 of March 1731
Patience Bacon 9 June 1734
Annah Bacon 29 July 1737
Mercy Bacon 17 April 1740
Roger Goodspeed, and Hannah Phiney, married the [*] Day of [*] by Daniel Parker Esq[r]
their Son Thomas Goodspeed Born the 27th day of October Anno Domini 1721.
Isaac Goodspeed Born the 23[d] day of Sep[br] 1723.
their Daughter Sarah born 5th day of Dec[ber] 1727
Elizabeth 14 November 1731.
their son Joseph Goodspeed born Sep[t] 17 . 1736
Mary Pitcher Daughter to Joseph Pitcher . born the first of August 1720.
his Son Samuel Born the 27th No[br] 1722
William born 11th June . 1726.
Reuben 23 of Feb. 1728
Abigail Aug 10 1731
Jonathan August 12 1723
Mary July 15 1734
Joseph Feb 23 1736
Lydia Feb: 5 1738
Elizabeth Phiney Daughter to John Phiney jur & Martha his Wife born the 15th July 1721.
his Son Edmond born the 27th July . 1723
their son Stephen born De[cber] 16th 1725.
their Daughter Martha born the 18th. Oc[br] 1727
[p. 309] Edward Dillingham jur and Elizabeth Goodspeed, were Married by Col. Melatiah Bourne Oc[br] 10th 1723
* The day, month and year were not filled in.

Job Goreham's Daughter Temperance born July 23d 1721
their son Thomas Born Augst 13th 1723.
Their Son Edward Born September 2nd Day 1725
Daughter Desire Born March 17th 1727/8
Son Job Born November 6th 1730
Isaac Isum . his son Isaac Born March 21st 1718.
His Son Samuel Born October 26th 1719.
his son John Born August . 6th 1721.
His son Ebenezer Born August . 25th 1723.
Timothy born 30th may 1725
Joshua Born April 14th 1727.
Daniel April 13 1729
Abigail Feb 17th 1731.
Thomas Ewer, his son John born the 28th April 1719
Daughter Mercy Ocbr 7th 1721.
Daughter Sarah Born March first 1723/4.
Thomas Born the 3d of October 1726.
Seth Born the 14th of March 1728/9
his Daugter Sarah born Feb 23 1731/2
his Son Sylvanus born 18 Day of March 1741/42
Ebenezer Childs, his Daughter Elizabeth Born the 18th of July 1720 . She died the 18th of Sepber following
his son Ebenezer Born the 10th day of April 1723
the Last not recorded.*
Benjamin Crockers Daughter, Deborah born June 22d 1721
his Daughter Desire Born the 9th of August 1727.
Martha June 6th 1732
Mr Moody Russell and Mrs Dinah Sturges were Married . Ocbr 8th 1724 . by Mr Jonathan Russell.
their Daughter . Abigail Born the 23d June 1725
[p. 310] Joshua Lovel's Daughter Zerviah . born the 28th May 1718.
Daughter . Sarah born 13th October 1719.
Abigail . born August . 27th 1727.
Remember born Septr 11th 1729
son John born January 8th 1731/2
Mercy September 9 1735
The above Joshua married Sarah Ischam†
Ocbr 22d 1724 Then Seth Lewis and Sarah Revis ware Married by Joseph Doane Esqr
Ebenezer Goodspeed jur, his Daughter Rebecca Born October 28th 1714.
his Son Ebenezer Born 7th February . 1715/16
his Daughter Mary Born the 2d August . 1721.
Samuel Bacon jur . his Daughter Sarah born the 24th fery 1713/14
his Son Orrice born 7th may: 1715.
Thomas Born the 23d of October . 1716.
Daughter Susanah December 24th 1718

* This line is in a different hand and ink.
† This line is in a modern hand.

Deborah Born the 4th December 1720.
his wife Dyed the 24th may 1721 . viz Deborah;
December 10th 1724 . Eleazar Hamlin jur And Alice Phinney, were Married by the Revd Mr Jonathan Russell.
Jemima Smith Daughter of the Below Named James-Smith & Thankfull his Wife Born March 13 1745 Died January 6 1746
Decb 31st 1724 James Smith and Thankfull Hinckly married by the Revd Mr Jonathan Russell
their Daughter Sarah Born the 4th November 1725
a Daughter born the 11th of June & Died the 23d of Sd Month 1727.
Sarah Died the 26th Sepber 1726.
Anne Born April 21st 1728 . and Died July. 26th 1729
Their son James Born May 2nd 1730.
Daughter Thankful born May 13 1732
Elizabeth born November 14 1734
Abia born Octor 2 1737
John March 14 1739/40
Mercy May 8 1742
[p. 311] Marriages Consummated, By John Otis Esqr viz
Nob 9th 1711 . Timothy Cannon . and Elizabeth Hamlin . were Married
June 26th 1712 . Ebenr Howland, and Elizabeth . Justice were Married
July 10th 1712 George Brimhorne and Anna Bacon were Married
July 10th 1712 . Josiah Davis and Mehitable Taylor were Married
July 25th 1712 . James Allen and Susanah Lewis were Married
Ocbr 2d 1712 John Goreham and Prudence Crocker were Married
Novbr 7th 1712 Joseph Bursley and Sarah Crocker were Married
March 10th 1713 . Nathaniel Jackson and Abigail Chipman were Married
March 10th 1713 . Nathan Crocker and Abigail Bursley were Married
July . 23 . 1713 Andrew halt* of Yarmouth & Mehitable Anible were Married
Ocbr 5th 1713 . Joseph Smith and Relience Crocker were Married
Novr 1st 1714 . John Attchehoo and Sarah Joel were Married
Novbr 8th 1714 John Sanderson and Mehitable Hamlin were Married
Decbr 6th 1716 . Indian Robin, and Dinah Daniel were Married
May 16 . 1717 . Then Ebenr Lincoln and Hannah Allen were Married
Sepbr 1717 . Joseph Hamlin and Abigail Davis were Married
Ocbr 17 . 1717 Samuel Lumbert and Anna Baker were Married
Feby 20th 1717/18 Samuel Sanderson & Barshaba Whetstone were Married
Sepbr 25th 1718 John Phinney jur and Martha Coleman were Married
Decbr 25th 1718 . Barnabas Lothrop jur and Hannah Chipman were Married
January 18 . 1719 Robin Will and Unice Fish were Married
March 12th 1720 Peter Tobie and Hannah Pocknut were Married
May 2d 1720 Then Mr Samuel Spear of Cape Codd & Thankfull Nickols were Maried
June 9th 1720 . Timothy Jones and Elizabeth Jones were Married

* "Hallet".— Editor.

Barnstable, Mass., Vital Records

June 9th 1720 Peter Blosom and Hannah Isum were Married
August 19th 1720 . David Hallet and Mary Anible were Married
Augt 19th 1720 Nathll Bacon and Anna Anible were Married
Ocbr 17 . 1717 Ruben Blush and Ann Fuller were Married
March 6th 1717/18 Samuel Chard and Mary Dexter were Married
Ocbr 21st 1718 . Then Tom Will & Martha Pees were Married
Ocbr 22d 1718 Jeduthan Robins of Plimtown & Rebacca Robins were Married
Fery 21st 1718/9 Saml Wequash and Mercy Ned were Married
June 18th 1719 John Howland and Mary Crocker were Married
[p. 312] July 9th 1719 Isaac Fuller and Jerusha Lovell were Married
ocbr 8th 1719 Robert Davis and Jean Anible were Married
Sepbr 15th 1720 Shubal Davis and Hopestill Lumbert were Married
August 1720 . Thomas Newcomb and Hipziba Wood were Married
March 9th 1720/21 Eleazer Tobie and Martha Lovel were Married
Augst 31st 1721 Benjamin Jones and Hannah Giford were Married
Ocbr 25th 1721 Jacob Chipman and Abigail Fuller were Married
Ocbr 19th 1721 Joseph Lothrop and Ann Jaukens were Married
 their son Jno Born Nobr 1st 1722 . Died 8th march 1724/5
Nobr 23d 1721 William Smith and Mary Draper were Married
Novbr 12th 1724 Then Mr David Crocker & Abigail Loriing were Married
 all these married by Col: Otis
Nobr 11th 1724 John Fish and Phebe Bunpus were Married p Col. Otis
Joseph Jenkins Jur & Mercy his Wife
thr Daughter Mercy born May . 25 . 1737
Son Joseph Jenkins born May 3 1739
Their Daughter Bathsheba born Octor 22 1741
Their Daughter Mary Jenkins born March 13 . 1743
Their Daughter Abigail born September 6 1745
Their Son Zaccheus Jenkins born 8 of Feb 1748
Sd Jenkins the Father Dyed January 15 1749
Benjamin Jenkins and Mehitable his Wife
Their Daughter Ann born Octor 3rd 1731
Their Daughter Hannah Born Janry 25 . 1733/4
Their Daughter Lydia born Born March 16 . 1735
Their Daughter Mehitable born Feb 24 . 1737
Their son Benjamin Jenkins born April 12 . 1740
Their Son Southworth Jenkins born Nov 29 1742
Their Daughter Bethiah Jenkins born June 4 . 1747
Their Daughter Sarah March 1 : 1750
Samuel Parker & Desire his Wife thr Children
Their Daughter Temperance born May 11th 1733
thr Daughter Hannah born March 31 . 1735
their Daughter Desire born March 14 . 1736/7
Patience the 11 of May 1739

Barnstable, Mass., Vital Records

Their Son Samuel Parker born July 13 1741 & Died
Their Second Son Samuel born August 8 . 1742
Their Daughter Abigail born Aug: 31 1744
Their son Freman Parker born Aug 31 1747
Their son Freman Parker born Octor 15 1749
[p. 313] Isaac Howland jur Children, born . viz
Ann Sepbr 4th 1721
Sarah Born July 23d 1722.
Son Joseph born the tenth of May 1726.
Benjamin Nov: 22 . 1729
twins Born Decemb 22 1734 one Died the others Name is Rachel
Their Son Samuel Howland born January 30 1740/1
Hannah Parker Daughter To Elisha Parker, and Mary Parker . born at Barnstable The 30th Day of March 1721.
Samll Chipman & Abiah Chipman Married Decemr 8th 1715 and had a Son Born 10th of aug: 1717 & died August 25th 1717.
The Children of Samuel and Abiah Chipman . Born as followeth viz.
Hannah . July . 1st 1719.
Samuel Nobr 21st 1721.
Timothy April 30th 1723.
Ebenezer Septr 9th 1726;
John June 30th 1728
Mary . May 2nd 1731
Nathaniel born January 31 1732/3
Abiah Chpman the Wife of the Sd Samuel Chipman Deceased July 15 1736
Deacon Samll Chipman & Mary his Second Wife
their Son Joseph Chipman born May 26 & Died July 4 1740
Nathl Ewer and Mary Stuward of Sandwich Married by Mr Benja Fesenden Novbr 8th 1723.
his Son Silas born 27th day of November 1724.
Son Nathaniel born April 17th 1726
their Daughter Desire born Novemr 26th 1727.
Son Gamaliel born June 19th 1733
their Daughter Mary Ewer born Aug: 7th 1737.
Joseph Jenkins & Dorcas Pain Maried by Esqr Parker January 31 1722
Joseph & Darkis Jankens their Son Joseph Born at Barnstable the 4th day of November 1724
Their Daughter Mary born June 11th 1729
Daughter Dorcas April 10 1731
Keziah 30 March 1733
Rebekah born August 27 . 1735 . Died In Octor following
Experience born March 11 1738/9
2nd Rebekah born September 19 1740
thr Daughter Patience Jenkins born Sept 1 1742
Edward Lewis and Rebecca Lothrop Married the 14th day of May 1719
Mehitable their Daughter born the 4th of March 1720/21
Solomon their son born the 22d December 1722.

Isaac Born 27th Sepbr 1724
The Children of James Davis & Thankful his Wife
Their Daughter Hannah born May 31st 1731
[p. 314] Simon Davis and Elizabeth Lumbert Married by Joseph Lothrop Esqr the 12th may 1725
Josiah Barse and Zerviah his wife, their Childeren born viz.
Anna . 11th July 1719.
Josiah . 5th February 1720/21
Unis born 2d day January 1722/3.
Jonathan Born 22d November . 1724
Lois born the 17th day of July 1726.
Unis Died the 6th day of April 1727.
Jonathan Died December 2nd 1731.
Son Thomas born March 10 1728/9
Unis born February 13th 1731/2
Samuel Goodspeed . and Rebekah . his wife.
their Daughter Temperance born the 20th May 1725.
their Son John born the 31st day of august 1728.
Eunice Goodspeed April 6 1731
Anne Goodspeed April 24 1734
Abigail Goodspeed July 11 1736
Remember Goodspeed May 18 1739
Their Son Samuel Goodspeed born March 1 . 1741
Their Son Abner Goodspeed born June the 17th 1743
Their Son Anthony Goodspeed born April 18th 1746
The Childeren of Joseph Smith jur and Relience his wife . viz
Epharim born August 16th 1720.
Ann Smith born May 15th 1722
Manasseth Smith borne February 26th 1723/4
In the Old book.*
his Daughter Lydia born the 17th August 1714.
his Daughter Abigail born 21st July 1716.
his son Joseph Born 31st July . 1718.
his wife relience Died 4th may 1724 . aged 30th years.
his Daughter Sarah Born of Sarah his Second wife . January 22d 1727/8
Joseph Smith Departed this Life the 20th Spebr 1728.
James Otis and Mary Allyn Marred by Mr Elisha Williams of Wethersfeild+ . May the 14th 1724.
Their Son James Born 5th Fery 1724/5
thr son Joseph born March 6th 1725/6
Mercy t4 Septr 1728
Mary 9 Sept 1730

Hannah 31 July 1732
Nathaniel 9 July 1734 and Died 13 January following
Martha Otis born 9 of Octor 1736 Died Novr 25 following
Abigail Otis born 30 of June 1738 & Died 31 of July 1738
their Daughter Elizabeth Otis born 1 Sep 1739
thr Son Samll Allen Otis born Novr 24 1740
Sarah Otis born the 11 of April 1742 & Dyed 5 of May 1742
Nathll Otis born the 9 of April 1743 & Died the 30 of April 1743
The Childeren of Samuel Dimuck and Hannah his wife
their Daughter Mehitable born the 25th Day of April 1725 Sabbath
Samuel Octor 17 1726 Monday
Hannah Novr 26 1728 Tuesday
Shobal Jan 31 1731 Sabbath
Joseph Feb: 19 1733 Monday
Their 2nd Daughter Mehitable born Monday Septr 29 1735
Their Son Daniel Dimuck born Sabbath Day May 28 1738
[p. 315] James Allin and Susanah Lewes Married by Col: John Otis July 24th* 1712
Their Children born
Their Daughter Elizabeth Bourn+ 8th day of June 1713
Their Daughter Susanah Born 18th Day of Sepber 1715
Their Daughter Anna Born 1st Day of Januty 1717/18
Their Son Thomas Born 8th Day of Novbr 1719
Their Daughter Hannah Born 13th Day of Decbr 1721
Their Daughter Rebakah Born 24th Day of Novbr 1723
Their Daughter Abigail Born 7th Day of June 1725
Their Daughter Mary Born 26 Day of March 1727
Their Son James Born 1st day of March 1728/9
Their Daughter Sarah Born 21 Day of December 1730
Their Daughter Martha born April 24th 1733
their Daughter Olive born 18th of Decemr 1735
their Daughter Martha Died In her 4th Year June 21 1736
The Childeren of Jerimiah Bacon, and Abigail his wife, born . viz
Prince born 15th June 1720
Jerimiah Bourn+ the 14th January 1723/4
William Green and Desier Green their Children Born viz.
his Son Warren born June 9th 1712.
Desier born October the 24th 1718.
Son William Born July 17th 1721
Daughter Sarah Born December 27th 1723.
his son: Jno born April 12th 1726,
their son James born Septr 19 1728
James Crocker and Alice his wife.
his Son Simeon born March 22d 1722.
Abigail Born Septbr 19th 1724.
Ebenezer Phinney & Rebekah his Wife

---

* Joseph Smith's children by his first wife. Ann, her death, his second marriage, on 5 October, 1713, to Reliance Crocker, and the births of Lydia, Abigail, and Joseph, all entered in Volume I, page 382, of the original records, were printed on page 155 of our twelfth volume.
+ Connecticut. — Editor.

* "25th" was altered to "24th" in the same ink.
+ This is an error for "Born".

156

their Daughter Sarah born May 11th 1732
Their Son Jonathan born September 14 1733
Martha July 16 . 1735
their Son Lemuel Ap: 24 1737
Their Son Seth Phinny born June 9th 1743
Their Daughter Rebekah Phinny born March 16 1747

(To be continued)

THE MAYFLOWER DESCENDANT

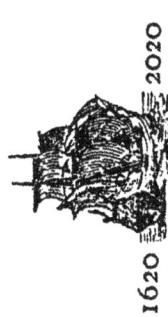

1620 2020

A QUARTERLY MAGAZINE OF
PILGRIM GENEALOGY AND HISTORY

VOLUME XXXIII

1935

PUBLISHED BY THE
MASSACHUSETTS SOCIETY OF
MAYFLOWER DESCENDANTS
BOSTON

BARNSTABLE, MASS., VITAL RECORDS

TRANSCRIBED BY THE EDITOR

(*Continued from Vol. XXXII, p. 156*)

[Vol. 2, p. 316] May 27th 1725 Benjamin Lumbert jur and Sarah Crocker married by Mr Jonathan Russell.

July 1st 1725 Israel Buttler and Elizabeth Blosom Married by Mr Jonathan Russell.

The births of the Children of Jabez Phiney & Jane his Wife
Their son Joseph Born the 6th Day of September 1733
Daughter Mary Decemr 3rd 1735
Their Daughter Anne Phinny born Feb 16 1738
Their Daughter Hannah Phinny born Janry 21 1741
Their son Joseph Phinny born Octor 12 1744
their son John Phinny born Decemr 2 1748
Nathan Crocker and Joanna* his wife.
their son Jabez born the 10th Day of June 1709.
their son Benoni born 24 February 1711/12
Nathan Born 7th March 1713/4
Isaac Born the 6th May 1719.
John Born . 11 January 1721/2,

* "Barsheba" was first written, but was crossed out and "Joanna" interlined above. The marriage of Nathan Crocker and "Joanna Barsley", on 10 March, 1708/9, was printed in our fourteenth volume, page 226. — *Editor.*

Temperance born the 3ᵈ of October . 1724.
Jonathan Crocker jur And Elizabeth his wife.
their son Ephriam born October 2ᵈ 1724.
Jonathan Crocker Died Sepᵇ 21ˢᵗ 1725 . and his son Ephriam Died Ocᵇʳ 7ᵗʰ 1725.
Trustrum Blush and Ann his wife.
their son Benjᵃ Born June 16ᵗʰ 1718
Anna born Novʳ 19ᵗʰ 1719.
Silanus Born Ocᵇʳ 13ᵗʰ 1721.
Samuel Fuller and Ruth his Wife Their Children
Daughter Sarah born April 16 1719
Barnabas born April 1ˢᵗ 1721
Eliezer born February 9ᵗʰ 1722/23
his Children by his 2ⁿᵈ Wife Lidia
Son Joshua born Octoʳ 3ʳᵈ 1727
Elizabeth born January 24: 1728/29
Rebekah born April 3ʳᵈ 1731
Lot Fuller their son born September 18 1733
[p. 317] Mʳ John Gorham and Mʳˢ Prudence Crocker were Marred by Col. John Otis the 2 day of October In the year: 1712.
his son Joseph born the 26ᵗʰ of Augˢᵗ 1713.
his son Benjamin born the 18ᵗʰ of June 1715
his Daughter Ann Born the 13ᵗʰ of Janry 1716/17
his Daughter Deborah Born the 13ᵗʰ of Novᵇᵉʳ 1718.
his son John Born the 10ᵗʰ of Novᵇᵉʳ 1720.
his Daughter Thankfull born the 10ᵗʰ of Feʳʸ 1721/22
his Daughter Mary born the 1ˢᵗ of January 1723/4
Nathaniel born Sep 30 1726
Experience June 23 1728 Died July 5 . 1728
Mercy born July 5 1729
Naomi born June 16 1731 Died June 21 1731
Abigail June 1 . 1732
Prudence August 16 1734
Thomas Haddeway And his wife Sarah, their Childeren Born In Barnstable viz
Son lot born 6ᵗʰ may 1717.
Sarah born 24ᵗʰ June 1718.
Temperance born the 23ᵈ Day of May 1720.
Patience born the 27ᵗʰ of February 1724/5.
Susannah, born Sepᵗ 3ʳᵈ 1726.
Their son Thomas born December the third 1730
Samuel Gilbert and Thankfull his wife there Children
Abigall Born January the 17ᵗʰ 1762
Jonathan Rusell son of Mʳ Jonathan Rusell and Mercy his wife born March 4ᵗʰ 1725/6.
Daughter Mercy born the 20ᵗʰ Decᵇʳ 1727.
Mʳ John Russel & Elizebeth his wife their Children born
their Daughter Abigail born September 13ᵗʰ 1757.

son Jonathan born March 30ᵗʰ 1762
son Otis born october 6ᵗʰ 1763
Jabez Goodspeed & Reliance his Wife
their son Jabez Goodspeed born the 31ˢᵗ of July 1737
Their Daughter Jane born March 21 1739
Their son Heman Goodspeed born Sepᵗ 4 1743
Their son Benjᵃ Goodspeed born 26 of May 1745
[p. 318] Nathˡ Freeman and Mary Paine Married the 11 October 1723 by Peter Thacher Esqʳ
their Daughter Bethiah born the 4ᵗʰ July 1725
their son James born the 11ᵗʰ of October 1726
Mʳ Nathaniel Freeman dyed the Second day of December 1727
his son Nathˡ Born the 30ᵗʰ of March 1728 & Dy'd the 17ᵗʰ of April 1728
The Children of Edmond Hawes & Mary his Wife
Sarah Hawes born March 26 1733
Mary Hawes born August 11 . 1735
Edmond Hawes born July 26 1738
The Revᵈ Mʳ Joseph Green and Mʳˢ Hannah Russell were Married by the Revᵈ Mʳ Jonathan Russell Novᵇᵉʳ the 18ᵗʰ 1725
thʳ son Joseph Green born the 12ᵗʰ day of Sepᵇʳ 1727
thʳ Daughter Martha born Novemʳ 17ᵗʰ 1730
Their Daughter Hannah Green born June 6 1745 & Died July 7 1745
Madam Hannah Green wife of the Revᵈ Mʳ Joseph Green Died June 6 1745
Mʳ Silvanus Bourne and his wife Mercy their Children Born viz
Desier born Barnstable Janry 19ᵗʰ 1718
Mary born Falmouth April 22ᵈ 1720
Melatiah born Barnstable Novᵇᵉʳ 14ᵗʰ 1722
William born February 27ᵗʰ 1723/4
Hannah born Barnstable Decᵇʳ 8ᵗʰ 1725
Mercy born August 22ᵈ on Munday 1727.
Abigail Born June 21ˢᵗ on Saterday 1729
Son Silvanus born Novʳ 21 . 1731
Eunice Febʳʸ 16 1732
Richard Bourn born Novʳ 1 1739
Ebenezer Bacon and Lydia his wife
Their Daughter Martha born November 6ᵗʰ 1734
Their Son Barnabas November 26 1735
Their Daughter Mary Bacon Born April 12 1738
Their Son William April 6 1741
Their Daughter Mercy Bacon born July 24 1744
Mʳ Joseph Green juʳ and Hannah his wife
there Son Isaiah Lewis Born Decemʳ 28ᵗʰ 1761
[p. 319] Jonathan Lewis and Patience his wife, their Daughter Thankfull born Novᵇʳ 22ᵈ 1704
Jane Born April 28ᵗʰ 1713
their Son Lot born May 6ᵗʰ 1715
May 16ᵗʰ one died 1717.

Lois born Sep^br 22^d 1718
Melatiah Born Fery 6th 1720
Patience born May 23^d 1723
Lemuel born April 28th 1725
Jeremiah Howes & Sarah His Wife
th^r Son Barnabas born July 6 . 1730
th^r Daughter Abigail born July 16 . 1737
Andrew Allen And Abiah his wife
Their Daughter Bethiah born the 9th of January 1723/4.
their Son Elisha Born March 23^d 1726.
Son William Bourn the 28th day of October 1728.
Daughter Abiah born September 16th 1733
Nath^ll Allen born June 20 1736
Andrew Allen their son born March 10 1737
Mehitable Allen born Octo^r 22 1740
Their Daugter Beulah Lovel born Feb: 6 1742
James Lovel jur and Abigail [*] his wife
their Daughter Ruth born march 20th 1718.
Abigail born October 14th 1719
their Son Daniel born June 20th 1722.
Desier† Lovel Born May 9th 1726
Susannah July 18th 1728
Deborah Nov 13 1730
James April 22 . 1732
Lydia Lovel their Daughter Born May 19 1735
Puelia Lovel July 12 1738
Shobal Lovel Son of the above s^d James Lovel born Octo^r 16 1740
Their Daughter Anna Lovel Born July 9 1743
Mr James Lovell died about 1761 his wife died June 28 1778‡
Peleg Lawrence & Mary his Wife their Children bourn
viz Their son John Born Jan: 22nd 1727/8
Hannah born May 12th 1730
John Lovel & Bethia his Wife
their son John Born October 17th 1733
Elizabeth Aug: 9 1736
Patience born Feb 6 1739
Martha born May 2 1741
Their Daug Mary Lovel Born 19 Decem^r 1744
th^r Daughter Sarah Lovel born June 21st 1747
John Lovell the Son Died Oct 15th 1754.
[p. 320] Phillip Jankins and his wife Elizabeth
their Son David born Sep^br 25th 1722

* "G" has been interlined in a modern hand. The marriage of James Lovel and Abigail Gorham, on 25 October, 1716, was printed in our fourteenth volume, page 226.— *Editor*.

† Before this name some one has written in pencil "2d wife".

‡ This entry is in a later hand and different ink.— *Editor*.

Reuben Claghorn & Elinor
their Daughter Jean born 12 April 1733
their son Nathaniel born born 22 Aug: 1735
Robert Claghorn & Thankful his wife
his son James born Decem: 8th 1723
his Son Nehemiah born 30th January 1725/6
Eunice May 4th 1728
Benjamin Decem 17th 1733
son Jabez Claghorn born 9th May 1736 Died June 20 1821,
Mrs Thankful Claghorn Died Ap^l 1st 1770.
Mr Robert Claghorn " July 11th 1750.
Prince Davis Son of Stephen Davis and Rebekah his wife bourne No^br 17th 1724.
Ann Davis their Daughter born the 13th of Dec^hr 1726.
their son Isaac born Sep 14 1729
Rebecca Feb 26 1731
Susannah May 14 1734
Sarah January 21 1737
Solomon Otis and Jean his wife
their Daughter Jean born the Tenth December 1725
Daughter Mary August 29 1727 Mary Died Oct^o 15 1738
son John 24th of Sep^tr 1729
Mercy on the 18th of January 1731 & Died March 17th 1731
Solomon Otis Born January 1st 1732
Amos Otis born June 14 1737.
Peter Blosoms Son Seth born 15th day of March 1721/2
Ignatius The Son of Daniel and Abigail Smith born Octo^br 5th 1726.
Their Daughter Susanna born February 8th 1727/8
Polycarpus born September 16 1733
Abigail born June 19 1737
Their son Ebenezer Smith born January 8th 1739/40
Their Second Daughter Susannah born May 11 1745
[p. 321] Gershom Lumbert, And Thankfull Lewis were Married by the Revd Mr Joseph Green the 17th Day of March 1725/6
Their Daughter Hannah born 25th Janu^ry 1726/7
June the 9th 1726 Then Daniel Stuwart And Prudence Parker were Married by the Revd Mr Jonathan Russell
Sep^br 8th 1726 Then Daniel Smith And Abigail Jones were Married by the Revd Mr Jonathan Russell
Oc^br 27th 1726 . Then Pharoah Negro & Hannah Samson ware Married by the Revd Mr Jonathan Russell
Oc^br 31st 1726 Isaac Crocker and Elizabeth Fuller were Married by the Revd Mr Jonathan Russell
Decr 20th 1726 Samuel Fuller and Lydia Lovel were Married by the Revd Mr Jonathan Russell
24th Jan^ry 1726/7 Peleg Larrance And Mary Parsevel were Married by the Revd Mr Jonathan Russell

Thomas Phinney And Reliance Goodspeed were Married the 31st of March 1726 by the Rev'd Mr Jonathan Russell
Moses Goodspeed And Hannah Allen were Married by the Rev'd Mr Jonathan Russell March 31st 1726
Eben'r Wood and Lida Lovel Maried Mariad Mach 9th 1726 by Mr Rusel
Joseph Smith And Sarah Bodfish March 8th 1726 by Mr Russell
Joseph Blosom jur & Temperance Fuller 30th * 1726/7
Thomas White And Hope Jankens April 19th 1727 by Mr Rusel
James Oaker and Marcey Caine Aug't 10th 1727 by Mr Rusel
Edward Morse, Margerent White Sep'br 19th 1727 by Mr Rusel
Cornelius Crocker & Lydia Jankens No'br 9th 1727 by the Re'd Mr Jn'tn Russel
[p. 322] Nov'br 17th 1726 Then Thomas Davis & Susanah Sturges were Married by the Rev'd Mr Joseph Green
Jabez Howland And Elisabeth Pasifull Dec'br 22d 1727 by the Rev'd Mr Jonath Russel
James Davis, And Thankfull Hinckly Married by the Rev'd Mr Jonathan Rusel the 4th day of Jan'ry 1727/8
their son Joseph Born August 15 1733
Benjamin Davis born June 27 . 1735
Eunice Davis August 8th 1737
Thankful Davis the 7 of Nov'em 1739
James Davis march 4: 1741
David Davis Janu'y 4: 1743
Moses Goodspeed And Hannah his wife
their son Nath'l born the 18th of March 1726/7.
son Seth born Feb: 2nd 1728/9
Mehitable August 17 1731
Lyddy January 6th 1733/4
their son Nathan born March 7 1735
their Daughter Ruth born August 20 1739
Thomas Crocker and Mehitable his wife
Their son Walley born the 28th of Febry 1727/8 Walley died the Aug'st 23d 1729
His wife Mehitable Departed this Life the 13th Day of March 1728/9
His Daughter Elizabeth by his Second Wife Rebekah was Born December 5th 1731
Sarah born Feb'ry 26th 1733/4
Rebekah born Nov'r 30 1735
Their Daughter hope born March 6 1738
Their Son Thomas Crocker born January 23rd 1740
Their Daughter Esther Crocker born August 28 1743
Their Son Barnabas born Oct'r 26 1746
Son Huckins Born march 15 . 1748.
Daughter Mary Born aug't 31: 1753
[p. 323] Eleazer Cobb and Relience his wife
their son Benjamin Born 20th of November 1725

Joseph Born 28th day of March 1727
Their Daughter Reliance born Septem'br 30 1728
Joseph Cob Above S'd Deceased the 11th Day of Octo'r 1737
Joseph Bursley And his wife Sarah
their Son Joseph Born 8th March 1713/4
Lamuel born Sep'br 8th 1718
Mercy born July 10th 1721
David Crocker Son of David Crocker & Abigail his wife born the 14th day of April 1726
Their Daughter Abigail born May 30th 1728
A Son born Jan 9th 1725 Died Feb 19 1725
Son William Born December 8th 1730
his Daughter Alice born April 16th 1733
David Crocker Above S'd born April 14 1726 . Deceased June 28th 1734.
their Daughter Hannah born Wednesday; Sept 24 1735
their Daughter Sarah Born Tuesday Oct'or 24 1738
Their Daughter Lydia Crocker born Feb 28 1742 & Died Sep 24 1743
Ebenezer Scuder And his wife Lydia
their son David Born 23d Day of July A D. 1726
their Daughter Elizabeth born the 9th of January 1727/8
Samuel born June 19 1729
Rebekah born May 26 1731
Ebenezer born May 25 1733
Lydia born July 15 1735
their son Eliezer born Feb: 12 . 1736/7
the abov's'd Ebenezer Scudder Deceas'd April 6th 1737
Silvanus the Son of James & Sarah Stuart born the 9th of August 1729
th'r son Solomon born January 27th 1731
th'r Daughter Desire born May 13 1734
th'r Daughter Sarah born Feb 27 1736/7
th'r Daughter Remember Oct'o'r 14 1739
th'r Daughter Mehitable born June 10 1742
th'r Daughter Mary Stuart born Oct'o'r 7 1745
th'r son James Stuart born September 11 1748
their Son Levi Stewart born Aug't 25 1753

(To be continued)

* The month was not entered.

BARNSTABLE, MASS., VITAL RECORDS

(Continued from page 29)

[Original Vol. 2, p. 324]
Thomas Davis son to Thomas And Susanah Davis born the 25th day of Augst on fryday 1727.
Their Son Isaac born March 16 1731/2
Lucy April 16th 1737
their son Jesse born January 14 1733/4
S^d Thomas the Father Died April 9 1738
John Hinckly And Bethiah
their Daughter Thankfull born 7th day of October 1727 on a Sabath day
Bethiah Feb 1 . 1730
John Septr 13 1732
Martha April 28th 1734
Adino December 12th 1735
Their Daughter Hodiah born Octo^r 6 1738
Their Son Jabez Hinkley born Octo^r 27 1741 died Feby 20th 1817
Abiah their Daughter born October 13th 1746
The Children of Steph. Gorham . And Elizabeth his wife. See the Old book* his Other Children
Barnabas Gorham born 20th mach 1715
Zacheus Gorham born 20th April 1717.
Elizabeth Gorham born 6th July 1718.
Eunice Gorham born 29th March 1720.
Stephen Gorham born 20th Fery 1722.
Josiah Gorham born 2d June 1723.
Lowis Gorham born 5th Nob^r 1727.
Ensign John Annable & Elizabeth his Wife
Their son John Born April 29th 1729
Their Daughter Abigail born Feb: 1731
Their son Abishai born Sep^{tr} 19th 1733
Their son William born Octo^r 17 1735
Their son Isaac Born July 5th 1738
[p. 325] The Age of the Children of Thomas, and Rachel Huckings
1 Samuel their Son born Sep^{br} 29th 1718
2. Thomas born Nob^r 30th 1719.
3. John Huckens born May 12th 1721
4. Jabez Huckens and
Snow Huckens born Twins March 12th day 1722/3
5 Joseph Huckens born June 24th 1726.
one Child son 7th day of Fery 1727/8

*No other children have been found on the original Barnstable records. — *Editor.*

6 James Huckens born April 11 1730 Died June 25th 1818
7 Daughter Elizabeth born July 9th 1732
The Children of Jonathan Lumbart Ju^r and Susana His wife
Their Son Jonathan Born the 24th of august 1757
John Bacon jur and his wife Elizabeth.
their son John [b]orn the 22d day of april 1728
Barnabas Bacon born April 17th 1729.
Mary their Eldest Child, born 24th March 1725/6 it Died the 17th Day of July following
James Coleman and Patience Phinney Married by the Revd Mr Joseph Green . March 12th 1727/8
their Daughter Martha born the Last day of Jan^{ry} 1728/9.
Ann Daughter to Richard & Hannah Thomas born June 15 1715
Son Joseph born August 24 1721
[p. 326] The Children of Barnabas Lothrop Son of Mr John Lothrop . viz
his son John by his wife Bethiah born Augst 25th 1709.
Jonathan by his wife Hannah born Sep^{br} 28th 1719
son Barnabas Born In the Month of June 29th 1721.
their Son Samuel Born 5th of October 1728 . he died May the 25th 1729
Mary by his wife Thankful Born March 12th 1747.
Silvanus Cob and Mercy Baker Married by the Revd Mr Joseph Green Nov^{br} 7th 1728
Daug^r Mercy born Octo^r 13 1729
Son Ebenezer born Aug: 13 . 1731
Son Sylvanus Feb 18 1734 & Deceasd May 10 1737
Their son Benniy born January 23 1736/7
Their Daughter Rebecca April 2 1739
Son Sylvanus July 21 1744
Jonathan Lumbart, and Martha Phiney Maried by the Revd Mr Joseph Green March 12th 1727/8
th^r Son Jonathan born Octo^r 30th 1729
Martha Octo^r 24th 1731
Mercy March 5th 1733/4
Hopestill April 30 : 1737
Sarah born April 11 1739
Their Daughter Susannah born Jan^{ry} 9th 1741
Their Son Simeon Lumbart born Octo^r 18 1744
Susanna Lumbart Died September 9th 1817
Mercy Daughter to Ichabod & Mary Hinkley born Novem^{br} 22 1726
The Children of Joshua Lumbart & Hannah his Wife
Son Sam^{ll} April 25 1721. Died August 16 1721
Daughter July 9 1722 Died August 6 1722
Joseph Jan^{ry} 10 1723/4
Daughter Jan^{ry} 28 1724/5 Died Feb 20 1724/5
Hannah July 31 1726

Ebenezer April 1 1728
Lemuel Feb 15 1730/1
Hopestil Octo̅r̅ 17 1733
Mrs Hannah Lumbert Died May 9 1796
Mr Joshua Lumbert " Decr 20 1807
[p. 327] William Blackford and Elizabeth Lewis Married by the Revd Mr Joseph Green Nobr 12th 1728.
Nathan Thomas & Susanna his wife Their Children
their Daughter Thankfull Born February 5th 1759
their Son Elijah Born may 4th 1761
Their Daughter Rebecca Born August 8th 1763
their Daughter Remember Born July 11th 1766
their Daughter Zilphah Born Decemr 10th 1768
their Daughter Lydia Born July 19th 1771
Joseph Russell and Anna Vassall Married by the Revd Mr Joseph Green January 2d 1728/9
Their Son Leonard born January 21 1729/30 & Died 5th Feb: following
Anna the Wife of the Sd Joseph Russel Departed this Life 5th Feb 1729/30
Mr John Sturgis & Abigail* his wife
their Son Samuel Born March 18 1729/30
son John Born Feb: 18th 1731 & Dyed March 25: 1735
Daughter Rebekah born May 12th 1735
Daughter Abigail Sturges born Octor 1 . 1737 Dyed Octor 21 . 1737
their Son Ebenezer Sturges born Feb: 3rd 1738
their Second Daughter Abigail Born Sept 4 1740 Dyed Sep 23 1740
Their Son Ebenezer Died January 12 1740
Their Daughter Hannah Sturges born the 9th of March A D 1741
Their Daughter Abigail Born Nov 28 . 1752
abigail Sturges the wife of the above Said John Sturges Dyed Decr 10 1752
Anne Daughter to Cornelius & Experience Annable born Febry 23rd 1729/30
Mehitable Sept 4 1731
Susanah Sept 15 1733
Cornelius April 27 1736
Ansel Jan 29 1737/8
Elijah Annable their Son Born June 10 1741
Their Son John Annable born 18 of April 1744
[p. 328] Mr John Russell and Mrs Mehitable Lothrop Marid by the Revd Mr Jonathan Russell April 12th 1722
their son John Bourn† the 28th of Sepber 1723
their son Lothrop born the 12th of Janry 1724/5

their Daughter Abigail born the 17th of March 1727
their son Jonathan born the 28th of November 1728
Their son Joseph born the 4th of April 1731
Their Daughter Rebekah born June 10 1737
Their son Joseph Died Feb 23 1737
Jonathan Bacon jr and Sarah his wife Their Children
Son David Born Novemr 21: 1757
Their Daughter Ruth Born Octor 5th 1759
Son 'Stephen Born Novr 25th 1761
Daughter Rebekah born March the 9th 1764
Son Ezekiel born the 29th of August 1776*
Daughter Sarah born July 8th 1769
Daughter Abigail born January 8th 1772
Daughter Polly born August 28th 1774
Shobal Gorham jur And Mary Thacher Married On Thirsday the 23d day of December 1708
Their son John bourn 12 day of December 1709
their son David born 6 Day of April 1712
their Daughtr Mary born 7 Fery 1714
their son William born 6 May 1716
their Daughter Lydia born 28 June 1718
their Daughter Hannah born 22d may & Dyed June the 18th following 1720
their Daughter Hannah born 1st day of May 1721
their son Shubal born 27th day of June 1723
their son Joseph bourn 29th day of May 1725
their son Benja bourn 5 June 1726
Thomas Hinkley & Temperance his Wife
Son Seth Born August 17 1720 & Died Septr 20 1720
thr Daughter Mercy Born Feb 11th 1721
thr Daughter Temperance January 20th 1723
thr Son Elijah December the first Day 1725
thr Daughter Mary Septr 30th 1727
Isaac Born April the 18th & Died the 20th of october following 1729
[p. 329] The Barths and Deaths of the Childeren of Capt John Davis, And Mehitable† his wife
1 Thomas his son born October the 1st 1706.
2 John his son born Sepbr the 8th 1708.
3 Solomon his son born April the 5th 1711 . he died July the 18th .1712
4 William Davis born April 10th 1713 he died July the 4th 1714
5 Solomon Davis Bourn June 24th 1715
6 Mehitable Davis Born Augt 10th 1717.

* So recorded.— Editor.

* "Allin" has been interlined, in pencil, in a modern hand.
† Born.— Editor.

* "Dimmock" has been interlined, in pencil, in a modern hand. In the Barnstable records printed in our fourteenth volume, page 87, is: "John Davis & Mehitable Dimock were Married 13 aug: 1705 ℗ Justice Thacher".— Editor.

7 William Davis Bourn Augᵗ 29ᵗʰ 1719
8 Josiah Davis bourn Fery. the 19ᵗʰ 1722
10 Isaac And
   Jesse . Twins born Augᵗ the 3ᵈ 1724 Jesse Died Augᵗ 23ᵈ 1724
   And Isaac October the 28ᵗʰ 1724
11 Isaac Davis born March the first 1726. And Died November the second 1727.

Jabez Howland and Elizabeth his Wife
Their son James born June 30ᵗʰ 1729
Jabez Janʳʸ 27ᵗʰ 1730/1
Elizabeth Octoʳ 26 1732
Mercy August 15 1734
Nathaniel Howland Octoʳ 9 1736
Ansel Howland born December 3 1738
Their Daughter Mary Howland born Janʳʸ 31 1741
Mr John Sturges & Melatiah* his wife
Their son Josiah born Octoʳ 17 1737
Their Daughter Melatiah Octo 11 1739
Their Son Timothy Crocker Sturges born March 30 1742
Their Daughter Lucretia Sturges born Octo 14 1743

[p. 330] John Lewis Juʳ of Barnstable the Births & Deaths of his Children

October the 13ᵗʰ day Lydia Lewis Died 1724
October the 23ᵈ Experience Died 1724
October the 27ᵗʰ Temperance died 1724 these born At Yarmouth†
August 30ᵗʰ 1725 their Son Jabez Born 1725
March 18ᵗʰ 1727 Thankfull Lewis 1727
Feby 19ᵗʰ 1728/9 Deborah born 1729
Daniel Smalley & his Wife Ruth
Their Daughter Martha born July 10ᵗʰ 1735
Their son Daniel Smalley born Octo 28 1740
the Children of Joseph Crocker Son to Cornelius Crocker & Elizebeth his wife
their son Joseph born November 15ᵗʰ 1760
their Daughter Mary born December 20ᵗʰ 1763
Cornelius Crocker and Lydia his wife
their son Elijah born April the 12ᵗʰ 1729
Elisha born Septemʳ 14 1730
Samuel born July 29 1732
Joseph born April 12 1734
Lydia 14 April 1739
Cornelius Crocker their son born Aug - 20 . 1740

* "Crocker" has been interlined, in pencil, in a modern hand. On page 357 of this original volume is recorded, under marriages in 1734: "March 21 John Sturges Melatiah Crocker".—Editor.

† Apparently this refers to the preceding children.—Editor.

Josiah Crocker their Son born Decemʳ 30ᵗʰ 1744
Cornelius the son of Mʳ Cornelius & Mʳˢ Ruth Bennet born Septembᵉʳ 30ᵗʰ 1732
John Howland & Mary Crocker Maried June 1719
Their son John Born Feb 13 1720/1
Job June 18ᵗʰ 1726
[p. 331] Benjᵃ Mastain and Lydia his wife
their son John Born Decᵇʳ 25ᵗʰ 1716
their Daughter Patience Bourn January 1ˢᵗ 1720
their son Benjamin Bourn January 2ᵈ 1725
Nimphas Born the 12ᵗʰ February 1727
Their Daughter Lidia Born the Latter end of March 1731
Their son Prince born March 24 1735/6
Their second Son John Born December 3 1738 John Marston died February 22ᵈ 1817
Gershom Davis And Elizabeth Sturges Married the 29ᵗʰ Day of February 1725/6
their son James born 2ᵈ June 1727
their son Robert Davis Born Juley the 12 : 1732 and Died
their Son Samuel Davis Born Sepᵗ the 13 : 1734
their Dafter Elisabeth Davis Born August : 12 : 1736
their Dafter Marey Davis Born Decmbʳ 5 : 1740
their Dafter Abegail Davis Born Septembr 12 1744 and Died
their Dafter Abegail Davis Born July 12 1746
their Dafter Marcy Davis Born febury 4 1748 and Did
Barnabas Chipman And Elisabeth Hamlin Married the 20ᵗʰ day of February 1727/8 by the Revᵈ Mʳ Jonathan Russell
their son Barnabas Born the 28ᵗʰ of December 1728
Joseph Decem 22 1731
Elizabeth May 12 1734
Thomas March 5 1735/6
Hannah Feb 20 1737/8
The Children of Job Davis & Mary his Wife
Daughter Mary born June 21 1725 & Died Jan 24 1725/6
Son Thomas Born October 16 1726
Shobal the Son of Job & Mary Davis born March 19 1729
Mary thʳ Daughter born July 18 1731
Mehitable March 19ᵗʰ 1733/4
Their Son Seth Decemʳ 27 1736
their Daughter Hannah Sepᵗ 6 1739
their Son Ebenezer born December the 17 1742
Ebenezer son to Ebenezer and Mary Chipman born 18 Novʳ 1738
[p. 332] Daniel Davis & Mary His Wife their Children
Their Son Daniel born April 1ˢᵗ 1724
Son Samuel born May 8ᵗʰ 1727
Son Joseph born May 28ᵗʰ 1729
Son Joseph Deceased June 30ᵗʰ 1729

Son Jonathan born Septr 21st 1733
The Children of Joseph Fuller Ju^r & Joanna his Wife
Rebekah Born Decem 29 1709 Died July 30th 1732
Bethiah March 2nd 1712
Temperance April 23 1716
Timothy April 3rd 1719
Matthias Septe^r 6th 1723
Bathsheba Aug: 10 1726
Lemuel Feb: 10 1732
Mr Thomas Foster & Lois his Wife
Their Son Gershom born September 23rd 1733
The Birth of the Children of Mr David Parker & Mary his Wife
Daughter Mary Born 18 Day of Feb^ry 1733/4
their Son Daniel Parker born March 25 . 1735
Their Daughter Patience Parker born March 3rd 1736 Patience Died Octo^r 27 1737
his Wife Mary Died the 12 Day of February 1737
The Births of the Children of David Parker by his Second Wife Mercy
Their Son David Parker Born A^ugust 31 1740
Their son Ebenezer Parker Born March 6th 1741
Their son Elisha Parker born January 30 1743
Their son James Parker born July 28 1747
[p. 333] Samuel Annable & Remember Crocker Married by Daniel Parker Esqr May 28 1719
Their Son Joseph Born March 19 1720
Their son Anthony born Decem^r 1 1721
Their son David Annable Born March 11 1724
Their Dau^ghter Anna born August 14: 1726 & S^d Anna Deceased Nov: 26 1727
Their Daughter Temperance born Decem^r 11 1728
Their son Benjamin born Feb 26 1730/1
Martha born Nov: 29 1734
their Daughter Mary born Sep 9th 1740 and Died March 8th 1743
The Children of Edward Dimock & Hannah
Anna Dimock born Novem^r 23 1721
Thomas Dimock born March 16 1727
Desire Dimock born August 6 1730
George Lewis ju^r And Mary his wife their Children Born
their Daughter Mehitable Born July 21 . 1762
their Son Lothrop Born February 13 . 1764
their Daughter Sarah Born January the 13th 1766
their Daughter Annah Born March 21th 1768
Their Son James born August 21th 1770
Their Son Ansel born February 2^d 1773
Their Son George born march 28th 1775
Son Daniel Davis born July 22^d 1777

Daughter Mary born September 29th 1779
Major Lewis Twins their Son Robert and their Daughter Abigail Born Jany 12th 1782*
The Children of Walley Crocker & Abigail his wife
Their Daughter Abigail born Novr 2nd 1731
Their Daughter Temperance born Decem^r 18th 1733
Their Son Walley Crocker born April 18 1737
David Freeman and Abigail his wife their Children
their Son Thomas Davis Freeman Born March 25: 1757
[p. 334] The Children of Thomas Dean & Lydia his Wife
Daughter Lydia born 7th of July 1728
Son Thomas born April 19th 1730
Jonas Dean born Octo^r 27 1732
Ephraim born Octo^r 17 1734
William born May 27 1736
Eunice born Nov. 4 1737
Levi the Son of Samuel Bump Ju^r & Sarah his Wife born March 17 1734/5
Sarah the Wife of s^d Samuel Deceased April 10th 1736
The Children of Ensign Dimock & Abigail his Wife
son Thomas Born Octo^r 29th 1732
Mehitable April 12 1735
his son Joseph Dimock born July 12 . 1740
The children of Matthias Smith & Hannah his Wife
Their Daughter Mary born March 26th 1731
Hannah Born Octo^r 4th 1732
Bethiah Born Aug 10 1734
Huldah born August 9 1736
their Son Matthias born 28 Decem 1738
Their Daughter Anne born Octo^r 15 1740
Their Son Samuel Smith born Novr 14 1743
Their Daughter Lydia Smith Aug: 13 1745
Their Daughter Abigail Smith born July 16 1747
Their son Benjamin Smith born June 5 1750
[p. 335] Persons Married By The Revd Joseph Green
Mr John Davis & Mrs Abigail Otis Feb: 5 1729/30
Stephen Davis & Desire Lewes March 12 1729/30
Thomas Hawes of Yarmoth Thankful Gorham of Barnstable July 2nd 1730
Antipas Lewes of Yarmoth & Martha Bearse of this Town Married by Esqr Shobal Baxter Octo^r 15 . 1730
John Lumbert & Thankfull Revis both of This Town married 11th of March AD 1730/31 by Esqr Shobal Baxter
Dr Cornelius Bennet & Mrs Ruth Gorham Jan 12 1731/2 by Esqr Baxter

---

* This entry is on the inner margin of the page, opposite the children of George and Mary Lewis. — *Editor.*

Jonathan Pitcher and Ruth his wife
their Son Abner Born Decemr the 25th 1761
Their Son Jonathan Born September the 10th 1764
Their Son Stephen Born August the 21st 1767
Their Daughter Ruth born April the 29 1771
By his Second wife Hannah
Mary born Janry 4 1778
their Son Reuben Born December 31st 1781
Isaac Davis & Hannah his wife
their Son Isaac Born the 29th of Decr 1764
Mr Jonathan Pitcher and Hannah his Second Wife
their Son Joseph born March 29th 1780
Their Son Abner born August the 22d 1783
Their Son Ezra born March 20th 1786
their Son Samuel born March 23d 1789
their Daughter Mercy born June 9th 1791
Samuel Phinny Jur & Hannah his Wife
Their Daughter Susannah born Jan. 15 . 1730/1
Their Son Nathaniel born Decemr 10 1733
Their Son Peter May 31 1737
Their Son William Phinny Born May 14 : 1740
Their Daughter Hannah born Novr 29 1745
[p. 336] Josiah Morton Jur of Plymoth & Melatiah Phiney of Barnstable were Maried May 18 1732 ℙ Ezra Bourn Justice of Peace Recorded
& July 25 1743 Mr Joseph Bourn & Hannah Fuller of Barnstable Were Married by Ezra Bourn Esqr
It: Joseph Howland & Mariah Fuller May 16 1745 ℙ Ezra Bourn Esqr Recorded
Thomas Ames & Mehitable Fuller Octor 30 1746
Elnathan Lewes of Yarmoth & Priscilla Bearse of this Town Married Octor 16 1735 ℙ Shobal Baxter Justice of the Peace
Southworth Samson & Jedida his wife their Children
their Son William Born January the 24th 1759
their Daughter Mary Born Decr 20th 1761
Sally born . . . . . Died January 31st 1835*
Martha born*
Jemima born. . . . . & Died April 27th 1820*
Shobal Nickerson of Harwich and Thankful Bearse Published Janry 23 1745
Thomas Bacon & Desire Hallet Feb 1 1745
Joseph Cohannet & Hester Lawrence Indians Janry 31 1745
Ananias Porrige and Mary Woes Feb 14 1745
Isaac Gorham Yarmoth & Sarah Smith March 21 1745
Israel Butler and Mary Woodcock March 21 1745
Ebenr Tayler and Phebe Fuller March 14 1745

* These three entries are in a much later hand. — *Editor*.

1746
Hezekiah Gorham & Anna Davis March 28
James Swift & Elizabeth Loring March 28
Samll Hinkley & Alice Howland April 5 1746
Thomas Hatheway Berkley* & Bethiah Allen May 17 1746
Josiah Hamlin & Deborah Parker May 24 1746
Mr Nathaniel Hinkley and Desire Green } June 27 1746
Jacob Lovel Jur and Hannah Lumbart
Mr Jacob Lovel & Mrs Abigail Sturges } July 17 1746
Abijah Fuller & Hester Arnold
Silas Ewer & Lydia Garret of Sandwich Aug: 1
Thomas Ames & Mehitable Fuller aug 2nd 1746
[p. 337] Joseph Blish Son of Joseph Blish jur & Mercy his wife Born July 20th 1731
Their Daughter Hannah born October 28 1732
Their Son William born December 22nd 1733
Their Daughter Mercy Blish born Octor 20 1740
Their Son Ebenezer Blish Born April 1 1744
Their Son Timothy Born February 16 1745
Lot Thacher & Rebekah his Wife
Their Daughter Mary Born May 29 1731
December 16th 1732 the Above Sd Lot Thacher Was Drowned Coming from Cape Cod
Feb. 19 1732/33 Lot Son to the Above Sd Lot, born at Barnstable
Samuel Baker & Prudence his Wife
their Daughter Martha Born January 24th 1732/3
Anna born May 12 1735
Bethiah born June 12 1737
Their son Samuel Baker born Sep 30 1740
Their Daughter Mercy Baker born May 30 1743
George Lewes jr & Sarah His Wife their Children Born
Daughter Annah Decemr 9th 1728
Thankful Janry 10th 1729 Died the 16th of March following
John Born Octor 5th 1731
Their Daughter Thankful born 6th of April 1734
Their Daughter Sarah July 31 . 1737
Their Daughter Temperance 25 Aug 1739 Died Sepr 4 1739
Their Son George Lewes born 9 of April 1741
Their Daughter Temperance Lewes born 13 of June 1743 & Died the 4 of January 1744
Their Son Josiah Lewes born the 29 of April 1745
Temperance Lewes thr Daughter born Octor 20 1747
Their Daughter Susannah born Sept 15 1749
Ther Son James Lewis Born Augt the 6: 1753 Drowed Oct 1773
[p. 338] Joseph Blish & Hannah Child Married ℙ Esqr Lothrop the Last of July 1702

*Of Berkley, Mass. — *Editor*.

His Son Joseph Born the 2nd of February 1704
His Daughter Abigail born the 29th of Novemr 1705
His Daughter Sarah Born the 1st of Octor 1707
His Daughter Mehittable born the 14 of June 1711
Abraham his Son born Septr 29th 1712
His Daughter Hannah born June 10th 1715 Sd Hannah Died February 8th 1723/4
Hannah the wife of Sd Joseph Blish Deceased Novemr 11 1732
Sylvanus Cob & Mercy his Wife
their Daughter Mercy Born Octor 13 1729
Their Son Ebenezer Born August 13 1731.
Sylvanus born Feb. 18 1734/5
Their Son Benny born January 23 . 1736/7
Their Daughter Rebecca born April 2 1739
Their son Sylvanus July 21 1741
Samuel Linnel & Hannah his Wife their Children born viz
Elizabeth Octor 8th 1726
Hannah Febry 1st 1728
Abigail January 14th 1730
Samuel April 9th 1733
John Linnel born Nov: 10 . 1735
Daughter Bethiah Linnel born April 27 1744
John Howland Jur and Alice his Wife
their Daughter Desire Born June 15 1732
Susannah 22 Decemr 1734
David & } Twins . born August 8th 1737.
Jonathan }
their Daughter Deborah born October 25 1739
The Children of David Smith & Sarah his Wife
thr Son Benjamin Smith born Octor 7 1736
Their Son Ebenezer Born May 9 1739 thr son Ebenezer Deceasd Sept 30 1739
Their Son Joseph Smith born 16 July 1740
Their Daughter Susannah Smith born Novr 23 1743
[339] Persons Married by the Revd Mr Joseph Green
Sackfield West of Yarmouth & Ruth Jenkins May 7th 1729
John Barlow of Sandwich & Abigail Hamlin Aug: 27 . 1730
James Haddeway & Bethiah Lumbart Octor 8th 1730
John Sturges & Susannah Lothrop Novr 12 1730
Lot Grey of Harwich & Jane Oris Jan 7th 1730/1
Paul Abraham & Amy Moses Indians Jan 20th 1730/1
Jacob Hamlin & Content Hamlin Aug: 18th 1731
Thomas Phinney & Mariah Lumbart Novr 1731
Mr John Gorham jur & Mrs Elizabeth Allyn March 9th 1731/2
James Lothrop & Patience Coleman July 20th 1732
Isaac Lewes & Experience Hamlin Septr 13th 1732
Jonathan Sturges & Sarah Baker Octor 26th 1732

John Lovel & Bethiah Bearse Novr 14 1732
Mr David Gorham & Mrs Abigail Sturges August 2nd 1733
Ebenezer Tayler & Mary Lewes August 16th 1733
Matthias Gorham of Yarmoth & Mary Davis Nor 1st 1733
John Stephens & Sarah Attaquin of Marshpee No 8th 1733
Jesse Cob & Thankful Baker Jan 1st 1733/4
Theophilus Pain & Hannah Bacon Jan: 15 . 1733/4
Ebenezer Bacon & Lydia Lothrop Jan 17th 1733/4
Shobal Harry & Mary Cowet Jan: 17th 1733/4
Joseph Studley of Yarmoth & Experience Pain Sep 26 1734
Mr Stephen Clap of Situate & Mrs Mary Gorham Octr 24 1734
John Linnel Jur & Mercy Phinny Novr 28th 1734
John Cullio & Lydia Bearse Janry 1st 1734/5
Recorded in the County*
Benjamin Thacher of Yarmoth & Hannah Lumbart Janry 30 1734
Guinney Toby & Desire Attaquin Indians &c July 22 1735
Joseph Bangs Harwich & Thankful Hamlin Sep: 18 1735
Saml Russel & Bethiah Pain Decemr 11th 1735
Luke Linkhorn of Situate & Lydia Loring March 18 . 1735/6
John Davis jur & Anna Allen March 25 . 1735/6
Zaccheus Hamlin and Mary Lumbart July 29 1736
John Coleman & Reliance Cob Aug 5 1736
Thomas Lothrop & Mary Parker. Septr 16 1736
Edmond Freeman Harwich & Martha Otis Septr 30 1736
Ephraim Lewes & Sarah Hamlin Octor 7 . 1736
Jabez Linnel & Sarah Bacon Novr 11 1736
Hezekiah Lumbarrt & Jemima Lumbart Nov 25. 1736
Aaron Keneway & Patience Joel Decemr 10 1736
David Hawes Elizabeth Cob March 10 1736
John Hall Yarmoth & Thankful Lewes April 14 . 1737
the 16 Last Entred County Record July 1737
[p. 340] By the Revd Mr Josephl Green
Solomon Lumbart & Sarah Lumbart Married July 7 1737
Jonathan Lewes & Elizabeth Cob Octor 13 1737
Francis Beniah & Desire Pocknut March 30 1738
Recorded In the County
Married by the Revd Mr Joseph Green
James Delap and Mary Okilley June 22 1738
Thomas Witherel of Plymouth & Elizabeth Lothrop Aug 24 1738
Mr Saml Barker of Situate & Mrs Deborah Gorham Nor 16 1738
Oris Bacon and Hannah Lewes Novr 23: 1738
Nathaniel Cob & Susannah Bacon Decemr 14 1738
John Miller of Yarmoth & Hannah Parker } January 25 1738/9
Thomas Hedge of Yarmoth & Mary Gorham }
Paul Abraham & Sarah Robins March 8 1738/9
John Casly & Dorcas Hamlin May 17th 1739
Prince Howes Yarmoth & Abigail Hallet August 2 . 1739

*This refers to the preceding marriages on original page 339. — *Editor.*

Daniel Davis & Mehitable Lothrop Aug 2 1739
Gershom Hamlin & Hannah Almony August 9 1739
Elisha Grey & Susannah Davis Aug 16 1739
Solomon Barber Weymoth & Temperance Haddeway Sep 20 1739
Benjamin Casly & Huldah Hinkley Nov⁺ 29 1739
Nathaniel March & Anne Scudder March 27 1740
Lieu⁺ Simon Davis Priscilla Hamlin June 5 1740
James Goodspeed Elizabeth Fuller Nov 13 1740
Nathan Hamlin Elizabeth Trick March 12 1740/1
D⁺ James Hersey & Mehitable Davis April 9 1741
Nathan Bangs & Mehitable Davis May 27 1741
John Fuller & Temperance Gorham Octo 29 1741
Peter Berse & Deborah Bacon Nov⁺ 12 1741
Benney Baker & Patience Lumbart Nov⁺ 19 1741
John Robinson & Exsperience Hatch Dec: 24 1741
Timothy Right & Patience Keneway March 18 1741
James Lewes 3 & Bethiah Haddeway April 20 1742
Peter Molatto & Sarah Job June 24 1742

(*To be continued*)

BARNSTABLE, MASS., VITAL RECORDS

(Continued from page 128)

[Original Vol. 2, p. 341]
The Children of Samuel Lewes & Reliance his Wife
Susannah, born, Jan 19 1722
Nehemiah July 4 1724
Samuel April 13 1726
Leonard Octo^r 25 1728
Solomon May 31 1730
Barnabas April 12 1734
The Children of James Lewes Son of Ebenezer Lewes Esqr
his Daughter Rebekah born August 5 . 1734
The Children of Thomas Dimmock and Elizabeth his wife
Their Son Charles Dimock born Decr 10th 1756
Their Daughter Hannah Born July 21st 1758
Samuel Jones & Mary his Wife Their Children born
Joseph born June 9th 1719.
Benjamin July 14th 1721
Samuel 4 April 1723
Mary April 13th 1727
The Children of John son of Deacon John Lewes Born
Timothy July 25 1727
Hannah April 17 1729
John May 29 1731
Mehitable Septr 13 1733
Bethiah Decem^r 25 1735
The Children of Lemuel Lewis & Temperance his wife viz
Richard born Novr 26th 1750
George born Sep^t 12th 1754
The rest of the family of Lem^l Lewis is in Book 6 page 158
Joseph Hinkley (Son of Joseph Hinkley ju^r Deces^d in Sep: 1738 and
Mary his wife) Born October 4th 1738* being born after the Death
of his father Entered March 1st 1738* ℈David Crocker Clerk
[p. 342] John Scudder Ju^r & Ruth his Wife Their Children born &c
Ann born Feb 4th 1715
Elisabeth Octo^r 3 1717 & Died the 6th of Novr Following
James Novr 2 1718
John Aug: 22 1720
Mehitable Aug: 2 1722 & Died Aug 23 1723
Ebenezer born June 17 1724
Josiah born March 28 1726

*This is in old style. In new style it would be 12 March, 1739.—*Editor.*

David Feb 5 1727
Hannah May 9th 1730 & Died 9 August following
Jonathan July 1 1731
Nathaniel Sept. 17 1733
Benjamin July 29 1736
The Children of William Basset & Sarah his Wife
th^r Son Samuel born August 31 1724
Daughter Experience born May 15 1727
Mary born May 18 1729
Nathaniel born Sep^t 4 1732
Chillingsworth Foster & Mercy Foster
th^r Daughter Mercy born May 2 . 1735
his Son Chillingsworth July 17 1737
Solomon Sturges & Abigail his Wife
their Daughter Mercy Sturges born Sep^t 3 1735*
Their son Sam^{ll} Sturges born. Sep^t 7 1737*
Their Daughter Abigail Sturges born May 22 1739*
Jonathan Sturges Sarah his Wife
Daughter Mary born Sep^t 7 . 1733
son Sam^{ll} born May 27. 1736
Nath^{ll} Claghorn son to Samuel Claghorn Born April: 29: 1743
[p. 343] Mr David Gorham & Abigail his Wife
Their son David born August 24 1735
Their Daughter Elizabeth August 22 1737
Their son Edward Gorham born Ap 23 1739
Their Daughter Lydia born May 30 1741
Their son William Gorham born July 12th 1743
Their son Shobal Gorham born Feb^{ry} 3rd 1745 Dec^d Decem^r 22 1748
Their son Benjamin Gorham born Feb^{ry} 23rd 1747
Abigail Gorham th^r Daughter born March 5 1749
Their Son Shobal born feb^y the 18th 1751/2
Their Daughter Mary born May the 21st 1754
David Smith &^c Sarah his wife
th^r Son Benjamin born Octo^r 7th 1736
th^r Son Ebenezer born May 9 1739 Died 20 Sep following
th^r son Joseph July 16 1740
Nath^{ll} Lewes & Fear his wife
Their Daughter Elizabeth born July 31 . 1737
Their Daughter Abigail born Decem^r 24 . 1740 & Died April 29 1741
Their second Daughter Abigail born Sep^{tr} 2 . 1742
Their Daughter Hannah born Octo^r 16 1744
Their son Nathaniel Lewes born June 5 1747
Nathaniel Cob & Susannah his Wife
Their Son Thomas Cob born December 1 1739
Their Son Oris Cob born Novr 9 1741

*These three children, with a fourth, Solomon, born 13 March, 1742, were also recorded on original page 288 — printed in our thirty-second volume, page 52. —*Editor.*

Their Son Sam^ll Cob born Novr 30 1744
Nathaniel Cobb & Susannah Bacon Married Decr 14 . 1738
[p. 344] The Children of Joseph Blossom ju^r
his Daughter Lydia Blossom born March 19 1729
Son James Blossom born Feb 9 1731
Sarah Blossom Born Octr 14 1734
Mary Blossom Born Sep^t 14 1736
Ebenezer Goodspeed 3rd & Elizabeth his Wife
Their Daughter Thankful born March 10 1736
Martha 7 Feb 1738
Their son Edward June 5th 1741
their Son Joseph Born oct^r 15th 1743
their Son Rufus Born January 15th 1749
their Son Silas Born January 27th 1751
their Daughter Hannah August 9th 1755
the Daughter Elizabeth Born Feby 7th 1757
their Daughter Mary Born May 29th 1759
Robert Bodfish & Eliizabeth hadeway Married
Their Daughter Elizabeth Bodfish born 11 of Sep^tr 1741
Their Son Ebenezer Bodfish Born Feb^r 15th 1743/4
Isaac Bacon was married To Alice Taylor by the Rev^d m^r Joseph Green Octr the 29th 1762
the Births of their Children Viz
their Son Isaac Bacon Born Novr 1th A D: 1763
Their Daughter Alice Bacon Born Octr the 6th 1765
Their Son John Bacon was Born Octr 19th 1767
their Son Josiah Born Feby 24th 1770
Mr Isaac Bacon Died June 24th 1819.
[p. 345] Marriages by the Revd Mr Joseph Green
Mr Josiah Crocker of Taunton & Mrs Rebekah Allyn July 27 1742
Isaac Gorham & Mary Cob 21 Sep^tr 1742
Melatiah Lewes & Abigaill Berse Octo^r 1 1742
George Servt to Cap: Hedge & Besse Servt of Mr Eben^r Hinkley Married Octo^r 7th 1742
Sam^ll Claghorn & Hannah Hinkley Octo^r 12 1742
Barnabas Lothrop & Thankful Gorham Feb 3 1742
Eleazer Nickerson & Sarah Berse Feb 17 1742
William Tayler and Desire Thacher June 2 1743
Dr Abner Hersey & Mrs Hannah Allen Octo^r 3 1743
John Manning of Wendham* & Sarah Lumbart June 10 1744
Bayes Hawes & Jean Lewes July 1 . 1744
Pompey S^t† to m^r Seth Hallet & Tamar S^t† to Mr Thos Sturges July 19 1744
Augustin Berse & thankful Bacon Sep 7 1744
Mr John Russel & Mrs Mehitable Hersey Octo^r 21 1744
David Dunham & Hannah Lumbart Octo^r 29 1744

*Windham, Conn.— Editor.
† Servant.

Jonathan Hallet & Mercy Bacon Novr 22 1744
Jonathan Hamlin & thankful Bumpas Decr 12 1744
Isaac Tayler & Mary Loring Decem^r 28 1744
John Hinkley & Bethiah Freeman Jan^ry 24 1744
James Lewes & Dorcas Baker Sep^t 30 1745
James Davis & Jean Bacon Octo^r 3rd 1745
John Berse Ju^r & Lydia Lumbart Feb 12 1745
Shobal Nickerson and Thankful Berse March 6 1745
Hezekiah Gorham and Anna Davis May 12 1746
Nath^ll Hinkly & Desire Green July 24 1746
Jacob Lovel and Abigail Sturges Sep 1 1746
Ebenezer Tayler & Phebe Fuller Octo^r 9 1746
David Dimock & Thankful Cob Oco^r 14 1746
[p. 346] Marriages by the Rev^rd Mr Jonathan Russel
Benjn Bursley & Mary Goodspeed Feb^ry 2 1743
Sam^ll Blossom & Hannah Bodfish Octo^r 28 1744
Edmond Hinkley & Sarah Howland Decr 6 1744
Southworth Hamlin & Martha Howland Decr 13 1744
Zachariah Perry & Hannah Blish 7 Feb^ry 1744
William Davis & Martha Crocker Feb^ry 25 1744
Lieut John Annable & Mrs Mary Blush March 5 . 1744
Joseph Annable & temperance Crocker Decr 31 . 1744
William Green & Mary Conant Octo^r 1745
Joseph Lumbart Ann Howland Feb 6 . 1745
Abijah Fuller and Hester Arnold August 7 1746
Isaac Gorham and Sarah Smith Sep^t 11 1746
Eben^r Childs & Hannah Crocker Jan^ry 15 1746
Reuben Blish & Ruth Childs May 21 1747
Cornelius Sampson Desire Crocker Octo^r 3 1747
John Sanderson & Tabitha Hamlin Oct 15 1747
Benj^a Phinny Elizabeth Ames Novr 5 1747
Ichabod Servt to Capt Hinkly Mehitable Job Ap: 22 1748
Sam^ll Hinkly Alice Howland May 12 1748
Seth Phinny and Bethiah Bump Octo^r 26 1748
Primus and Amaritta August 31 1749

Married by the rev^d Joseph Green
Josiah Hamlin & Deborah Parker Novr 27 1746
Mr Nath^ll Gilman of Exeter & Mrs Abigail Russel Decem 25 1746
Shobal Baxter Yarmoth & Mehitable Hallet March 5 1746
Sussex Negro Servt to Nathan Bodfish & Experience Peter April 14 1747
Paul Crowel of Chatham & Experience Cob Aug 27 1747
Joseph Baxter Yarmoth & Hannah North Nov 15 1747
Joseph Linnel & Dorcas Smith Novr 26 1747
Jabez Berse & Elizabeth Hallet Novr 26 1747
Cesar Negro & Mercy Daniel Indian, Serv^ts to John Gorham Esqr Feb 11 . 1746

Barnstable, Mass., Vital Records

[p. 347] 1742 Persons published In Order for Marrige
Bernard Lumbart & Sarah White of Yarmoth March 18. 1741
Seth Fish of Sandwich & Patience Hamlin of this Town April 16 1742*
Seth Phinny & Lydia Ames of Plymoth [April 16 1742]*
Jonathan Bacon & Mary Hall Yarmoth April 22 1742
Peter Molato & Sarah Job May 15
Melatiah Lewes & Abigail Berse May 22 1742
Stephen Cob & Abigail Chipman June 4 1742
Mr Josiah Crocker Taunton Mrs Rebekah Allen June 11 1742
Mr Seth Crocker & Mrs Abigail Blish June 18 1742
Mr Nathaniel Stone Jur of Harwich & Mrs Mary Bourn June 26 1742
Moses Sturges & Eleanor Robins August 21 1742
Isaac Gorham & Mary Cob August 28 1742
Samll Claghorn & Hannah Hinkley Sept 11 1742
George of Yarmoth & Besse of this Town Sept 11 1742
Zaccheus Phinney & Susannah Davis Octor 2 1742
James Robin and Hannah Capee Octor 9 1742
John Passavil & Lydia Fuller Novr 10 1742
Zaccheus Cain & Mary Bryant Novr 20 1742
Mr Barnabas Lothrop & Mrs Thankful Gorham Janry 13 1742
Eleazer Nickerson of Yarmoth & Sarah Berse 14 Janry 1742
Ebenezer Hinkley Jur & Mehitable Sturges of Yarmoth Feb 12th 1742
Joseph Bates Middleborough & Mary Blossom April 16 1743
Mr Joseph Bourn and Mrs Hannah Fuller Ap 20 1743
Mr William Tayler of Yarmoth & Mrs Desire Thacher of this Town 1743 In the Spring
Charles Conneat & Joanna Bursley July 2 1743
John Coleman & Mary Hamlin Aug 6 1743
Josiah Smith of Yarmoth Resident at Plymoth & Dorothy Dun Aug 20 1743
Mr William Crocker & Mrs Hannah Baker Aug 27 1743
Mr Abner Hersey & Mrs Hannah Allen Sep 14, 1743
Benjamin Jones of this Town & Grace Hauxey of Sandwich Octor 29
Shobal Jones of Sandwich & Mary Allen of ths town Octor 29 1743
Benjamin Bursley and Mary Goodspeed Nov 23 1743
Peter and Melle Negro Servants to Mr John Thacher Ju Decem 24 1743
Mr John Bursley of this Town & Mrs Hannah Landers of Sandwich 4 Feb 1743
John Pocknut & Elizabeth Richards Feb 18 1743
[p. 348] Persons published 1744
John Manning of Wendham† and Sarah Lumbart 7 of April
Thomas Amos & Mary Wois April 14
Bayes Hawes of Yarmoth & Jean Lewes June 2 1744
Pompey Servt to mr Seth Hallet Tanar St to mr Thomas Sturges June 9 1744
Edmond Hinkley & Sarah Howland July 6 1744

Augustin Berse & Thankful Bacon July 28 1744
Jonathan Hallet & Mercy Bacon Aug: 4 1744
Mr John Russel Jur & Mrs Mehitable Hersey 11 Aug 1744
Southward Hamlin and Martha Howland Septr 8 1744
John Lothrop & Thankful Sanders Septr 15 1744
David Dunham of Boston & Hannah Lumbart Sep 20 1744
Samll Blossom & Hannah Bodfish Septr 21 1744
Jonathan Hamlin & Thankful Bunpas Octor 27 1744
Thomas Sturges & Sarah Pain of Eastham } Novr 29 1744
Zechariah Perry of Sandwich & Hannah Blish
Isaac Tayler & Mary Loring } Decemr 1 1744
Joseph Annable & Temperance Crocker
Decem 29 1744 Mr John Hinkley Jur & Mrs Bethiah Freeman
Cornelius Goodspeed & Mary Lovel Janry 12 1744
Lieut John Annable & Mrs Mary Blish Feb 8 1744
Mr William Davis & Mrs Martha Crocker Feb 9 1744
Barnabas Phinney & Mehitable Morton plympton* March 16 1744
Joseph Lumbart & Anne Howland April 6 1745
Timothy Hallet & Thankful Jones April 12 1745
Joseph Howland & Mariah Fuller April 20 1745
Daniel Lovel & Sarah Beetle of Edgartown May 10 1745
Josiah Davis & Thankful Matthews July 17 1745
David Cob and Thankful Hinkley August 10 1745
James Lewes and Dorcas Baker } Sept 17 1745
James Davis Jur & Jean Bacon
William Green and Mary Conant Septr 26 1745
David Dimock & Thankful Cob Nov 1745
John Berse Jur & Lydia Lumbart January 18 1745
[p. 349] Psons Published by David Crocker T Clerk 1739
Viz Ebenezer Crocker & Elizabeth Lovell March 17th
Deacon Samuel Chipman & Mrs Mary Green Boston Ap: 14
Benjamin Gorham Sarah Cob Yarmoth Ap: 21 1739
Reuben Hamlin & Hope Hamlin A. 21
John Pepeno Jur & Bethiah Pocknut Ap. 14. 1739
John Daniel & Mary Peter Ap: 14
Solomon Barber of Weymouth & Temperance Haddeway May 5
Gershom Hamlin & Hannah Almony May 11
Joseph Goodspeed & Abigail Smith May 11
Abraham Netompom & Mercy Richards May 14
Nathan Basset Jur of Middleborrough & Thankful Fuller jur June 2
Daniel Davis & Mehitable Lothrop June 8
Reuben Jones of this Town & Sarah Passavil now of Sandwich June 29
Mr Ebenezer Hinkley Mrs Thankful Miller of Yarmoth July 13
Nathll Clark j† of Harwich & Mary North of this Town July 13
Isaac Bacon of this Town Hannah Severns Chatham July 13
Mr Elisha Grey of Harwich & Mrs Susannah Davis July 26

*Of Plympton, Mass. — Editor.
† Junior. — Editor.

*These two entries are bracketed, with a single date.—Editor.
† Windham, Conn. -- Editor.

John Blish & Mary Goodspeed Daughter of Ebenezer Goodspeed jur Aug 18 1739
John Hamlin & Jerusha Hamlin August 25 1739
Mr David Parker & Mrs Mercy Crosby Yarmouth Sepr 6 1739
Robert Bodfish & Elizabeth Haddeway Octo 26 1739
Jacob Keneway & Hannah Wampom Barnstable Township Novr 3 1739
Benjamin Casly Jur Huldah Hinkley this Town Novr 10 1739
Sylvanus Hamlin of This Town Dorcas Fish Falmoth F. 23
Nathaniel March & Anne Scudder March 1st 1739
Samll Pain of Eastham & Desire Green of This Town March 8
James Goodspeed & Elizabeth Fuller of This Town March 8
Lieut Simon Davis & Priscilla Hamlin March 15
Benjamin Hamlin & Mehitable Black Sandwich M 15
Edward Bacon & Patience Marston April 19 1740
Joseph Thorp & Dorcas White April 26 1740
Jacob Paul & Mercy Richards Indians May 24 1740
Revd Rowland Thacher Warham* & Mrs Abigail Crocker } May 31, 1740
Thomas Annable & Anne Gorham
John Ewer & Jean Toby Falnouth
Josiah Fuller of this Town and Ann Rowley Falmoth June 13 1740
Samuel Lothrop and Sarah Burnpas June 20 1740
Barnabas March & Elizabeth Trick June 27 1740
Zaccheus Cain and Almy Simon Novr 3 1740
[p. 350] Persons published In order for Marriage 1740
Timothy Fuller & Jean Lovel both of Barnstable Janr 3 1740
John Daniel of This Town Mercy Molosses Eastham Ind Janry 11 1740 } January 24 1740
Nathan Bangs of Falmoth Mehitable Davis of ths Town & Nathan Hamlin & Elizabeth Trick
Mr Elijah Dean of Raynham & Mrs Jerusha Crocker Janry 28 1740
William Basset Jur & Margaret Merryfield Jan 31 1740
Mr Benjamin Gorham & Mrs Mary Sturges of Yarmoth Feb 7 1740
Peter Camet & Thankful Bodfish March 13 1740
1741 Dr James Hersey & Mrs Mehitable Davis March 26
John Robinson Experience Hinkley April 10
Mr John Otis Mrs Temperance Hinkley April 17 1741
Nathan Bodfish & Patience Haddeway April 17 1741
Silas Lovel & Mary Chaddock of Falmoth June 3rd
Peter Berse & Deborah Bacon Sept 11 1741
Thomas Thomas† Cambridge & Elizabeth Dunn Sept 18
Bernard Lumbart & Abigail Rider Yarmoth Sept 25
Solomon Bodfish & Hannah Bursley Jur Octo 17
David Crocker & Dorcas Davis of Falmoth Octor 24
Samuel Lumbart & Beulah Lovel Octor 1741
Zaccheus Cain & Hannah Porrige Octor 28 1741
Mr John Dillingham Harwich & Mrs Abigail Hinkley Novr 13 1741
Mr Joseph Nye Sandwich & Mrs Mary Bodfish Novr 13 1741

*Wareham, Mass.— Editor.
† So recorded.— Editor.

Timothy Right & Patience Keneway Decem 12 1741
Bernard Lunbart & Sarah White of Yarmoth March 18 1741
[p. 351] Marriages by the Revd Jonathan Russel*
Joseph Jenkins Mercy Howland July 15 1736
Stephen Beels Hingham Alice Crocker Sep 16 } 1736
James Case Sarah Blossom Sep 23
Abraham Blish Temperance Fuller Novr 12
Aug: 11 1737 Seth Lothrop & Mary Fuller
Nov 24 James Percival & Anna Thomas
Decem 8th Joseph Gorham & Abigail Lovel
Decem 22 Nathaniel Clap Desire Bourn
Feb 9th Jabez Crocker & Mary Baker

Sylvanus Barrow Ruth Blossom June 8 1738
Mr Samll Toby & Bathsheba Crocker Sept 6 1738
Benjamin Nye Elizabeth Baker Sept 28 1738
Nathll Fuller and Abigail Hinkley Feb. 22 1738
Moses Mendal Susannah Sturges April 5 1739
Lewes Hamblin & Experience Jenkins April 12 1739
Nathan Basset & Thankful Fuller Octor 25 1739
Robert Bodfish and Elizabeth Hadeway Decem 10 1739
Joseph Bursley & Bethiah Fuller Decem 20 1739
Nathan Crocker & Mehitable Crocker Decemr 27 1739
Thomas Annable Anne Gorham Aug 7 1740
Edward Bacon and Patience Marston Sep 2 1740
Rowland Thacher and Abigail Crocker Sep 24 1740
Peter Cammet & Thankful Bodfish May 4th 1741
William Basset & Margaret Maryfield May 8 1741
Elijah Dean and Jerusha Crocker May 19 1741
Joseph Nye and Mary Bodfish Decem 10 1741
John Otis & Temperence Hinkley Decem 31 1741
John Dillingham & Abigail Hinkley Jan 3 1741
Zaccheus Cain & Almy Simon Married by John Otis Esqr March 12 1740
[p. 352] Persons Married by David Crocker Justice peace
Thomas Winslow of Rochester & Rebekah Ewer June 27 173[5]
Benjamin Bursley & Joanna Cannon July 7th 1735
Cornelius Jones of Sandwich & Hannah Pasavil of This Town July 1736
Ebenezer Goodspeed Jur & Elizabeth Bodfish Sepr 29 1736
Stephen Freeman & Hannah Jenkins Octor 22 1736
Ebenezer Thomas & Thankful Blossom 8 Decem 1736
Joseph Shelly Raynham & Thankful Bodfish Feb 23 . 1736
Jedediah Jones & Mary Fuller of Sandwich at Sandwich Ap: 14 1737
Recorded In the County

Michael Hammet & Hannah Jones Decem 1 1737
Decem: 8: 1737. Joseph Hanlin & Hannah Lovel
Joseph Rogers of Harwich & Fear Basset Octor 19 1738

*This refers only to the nine records following.— Editor.

Sylvanus Bodfish & Mary Smith December 20th 1738
Joseph Howland and Rachel Crocker Janry 18 1738
Isaac Crocker & Elizabeth Fuller March 22 1738
Jabez Bllossom jur & Hannah Backous at Sandwich May 17 1739
Joseph Goodspeed & Abigail Smith June 28 1739
Ebenezer Crocker & Elizabeth Lovel Jur July 26 1739
Reuben Jones & Sarah Passavil July 26 1739
John Blish and Mary Goodspeed Nov 15 1739
Reuben Hamlin & Hope Hamlin Nov 29 1739
John Hamlin & Jerusha Hamlin January 24 1739
Ebenezer Jones & Rebekah Crocker March 20 1739
Samll Lothrop and Sarah Bumpas July 17 1740
Timothy Fuller & Jean Lovel Jan: 22 1740
Samll Lumbart & Beulah Lovel Novr 12 1741
Solomon Bodfish & Hannah Bursley Decem 17 1741
James Robin & Hannah Cappee Novr 11 1742
John Passavil & Lydia Fuller Decemr 2 1742
Benjamin Jones & Grace Hauxay Novr 17 1743
Shobal Jones Jur & Mary Allen Janry 12 1743
Levi Chase and Mary Pike of Sandwich } Feb 19 1744
Cornelius Goodspeed & Mary Lovel
Timothy Hallet Yarmoth & Thankful Jones May 23 1745
David Cob & Thankful Hinkley Aug 12 1745
Ananias Porridge and Mary Woes March 5 1745
James Swift & Elizabeth Loring May 1 1746
[p. 353] John Hall of Yarmoth & Thankful Lewes Barnstable Published March 2nd Day 1736
Joab Owet & Jerusha Sampson March 4 1736
Seth Lothrop & Mary Fuller published March 19 1736
Persons Published 1737
Jedidiah Jones & Mariah Fuller of Sandwich March 30 1737
Solomon Lumbart & Sarah Lumbart May 14
Mr Nathll Clap of Situate Mrs Desire Bourn May 20th
Joseph Hamlin and Hannah Lovel June 24
Dr James Hersey & Mrs Lydia Gorham July 16th
James Passavil & Ann Thomas Sept 16 1737
Joseph Gorham & Abigail Lovel Octor 22 } 1737
Francis Beniah & Desire Pocknut Octor 22
Josiah Jenkins & Mary Ellis of Midleborrow Sept 4 1737
Tony and Amariah Negroes Servants to James Lovel Junr Decr 3 1737
Jabez Crocker and Mary Baker Janry 13 1737
Benjamin Crocker Jur & Abigail Jenkins Falmoth Jan 21 1737
Sylvanus Barrow Middleborroug & Ruth Blossom Feb. 2nd 1737
Persons Published 1738
Joseph Rogers of Harwich & Fear Basset March 21 1738
Mr Thomas Witherel Plymoth & Mrs Elizabeth Lothrop May 10
James Delap . Mary O Killey May 12
Benjamin Nye jur Falmoth Elizabeth Baker May 19
Mr Samll Toby of Berkley & Bathsheba Crocker May 20th
Joseph Bursley and Bethiah Fuller July 5th
Samuel Barker jur of Situate & Deborah Gorham July 5 1738
Prince Howes Yarmoth & Abigail Hallet Sept 26 1738
Nathaniel Cob & Susannah Bacon } Octor 8th 1738
Orren Bacon & Hannah Lewes
John Miller of Yarmoth & Hannah Parker } Nov 4 1738
Thomas Hedge of Yarmoth & Mary Gorham
James Gorham and Mary Hallet Jur of Yarmoth } Nor 11 1738
Sylvanus Bodfish and Mary Smith
Lewes Hamblin & Experience Jenkins Novr 24 1738
John Casly & Dorcas Hamlin Decem 1 1738
Joseph Howland & Rachel Crocker Decem 30 1738
Moses Mendal Dartmoth Susannah Sturges } Feb 3 1738
Nathl Fuller & Abigail Hinkley
Paul Abraham Sarah Robins Feb 3 1738
Nathan Crocker & Mehitable Crocker Feb 24
Isaac Crocker Elizabeth Fuller 3 March

(To be continued)

THE MAYFLOWER DESCENDANT

1620 2020

A QUARTERLY MAGAZINE OF
PILGRIM GENEALOGY AND HISTORY

VOLUME XXXIV

1937

PUBLISHED BY THE
MASSACHUSETTS SOCIETY OF
MAYFLOWER DESCENDANTS
BOSTON

BARNSTABLE, MASS., VITAL RECORDS

TRANSCRIBED BY THE EDITOR

(Continued from Vol. 33, p. 170)

[Vol. 2, p. 354] Persons published by David Crocker Town Clark 1735
Cap[t] Jonathan Davis & Susannah Allen April 6th
Shobal Lewes Wid Mary Snow Harwich* Ap: 19
Ebenezer Cannon & Mercy Blossom May 31 . 1735
Benjamin Burley† & Joanna Cannon June 21 1735
Joseph Bangs of Harwich Thankful Hamlin July 5 . 173[5]
Ebenezer Claghorn & Sarah Lumbart } July 12 1735
Benoni Crocker & Abigail Bursley
Elnathan Lewes of Yarmoth & Priscilla Bearse Sep[t] 10th
Timothy Bourn of Sandwich & Elizabeth Loring } Sept 28 1735
Israel Butler & Mary Parker
Job Gorham & Bethiah freeman fairfield‡ } Octo 19, 1735
Lazarus Lovel & Mary Lumbart ju[r]
Benjamin Nye of Sandwich & Bethiah Fuller Octo 25 . 1735
Joseph Shelly of Raynham & Elizabeth Bodfish Nov 1 . 1735
Sam[ll] Russel . & Bethiah Pain Nov 12 173[5]
Zaccheus Hamlin & Mary Lumbart Nov[r] 29 1735
Jonathan Lewes 3rd & Elizabeth Cory of Southole Long Island. Decem 13 1735
Luke Linkhorn of Situate & Lydia Loring } Jan[ry] 4 1735
James Case of Lebanon & Sarah Blossom
Nathaniel Lewes & Fear Thacher
Jesse Lewes & Mercy Crosby Harwich* } Jan. 30th 1735
David Smith & Sarah Hamlin
Stephen Dexter And Abigail Collier } Feb 27 1735
M[r] John Davis and Anna Allen
James Claghorn & Elizabeth Ryng Kingston§ } March 6 1735
Cornelius Jones Sandwich‖ & Hannah Passavil of this Town Ap 24 1736
Joseph Jenkins & Mercy Howland May 2 1736
Stephen Beels Hingham¶ & Alice Crocker May 15 1736
Ephraim Lewes & Sarah Hamlin June 15th 1736
John Coleman & Reliance Cob July 9th 1736

* Of Harwich, Mass.
† So recorded.
‡ Of Fairfield.
§ Of Kingston, Mass.
‖ Of Sandwich, Mass.
¶ Of Hingham, Mass.

Aaron Keneway & Patience Joel July 24th 1736
Edmond Freeman Harwich* & Martha Otis } Aug 7.†
Abraham Blish & Temperance Fuller
Thomas Lothrop & Mary Parker Augt: 21†
Jabez Linnel & Sarah Bacon 3rd Sept 3rd†
Hezekiah Lumbart & Jemima Lumbart Aug 14th†
Ebenezer Goodspeed Jur & Elizabeth Bodfish Sept 14 1736
Stephen Freeman & Hannah Jenkins octor 3d 1736
Ebenezer Thomas & Thankful Blosson Octor 31 1736
Samll Cain & Sarah Will Indians Decemr 17 1736
Joseph Shelly Raynham‡ & Thankful Bodfish Janry 27 1736
David Hawes Yarmoth§ Elizabeth Cob Junr Feb 17 . 1736
Jonathan Lewes jur & Elizabeth Cob Feb 26 1736
[p. 355] Persons Published in Order for Marriag by David Crocker Town Clark 1731
Mr Eliphalet Carpenter of Woodstock & Mrs Abigail Bacon Sep 26
Caleb Nye of Sandwich & Hannah Bodfish Sep. 26
Ensign Dimock & Abigail Toby of Sandwich September 26
Jeremiah Robin & Sarah Wicknot Octo 3 . 1731
Dr Cornelius Bennet & Mrs Ruth Gorham Novemr 7 1731
James Fuller & Hannah Howland of ths town N 21 1731
Jesse Lewes & Naomi Lewes of Yarmouth Decem 26 1731
John Gorham jur & Elizabeth Allen Jan 23 1731 32
Saml Baker & Prudence Jenkins Feb 6th 1731/2
James Lothrop & Patience Colman Feb: 13 1731/2
Ebenezer Jones & Hannah Jones Feb 20 1731/2
Samuel Parker & Desire Freeman of Harwich } March 12th 1731/2
Jabez Phinney & Jane Tyler
Jabez Crocker & Deliverance Jones
Nathaniel Baker Jur of this town Ann Lumbart of Newton } May 21 1732
John Goodspeed & Rebecka Goodspeed
Ebad — Negro — Fench Betty‖
Ebenezer Jenkins & Elizabeth Tupper June 18 1732
Reuben Maggs & Rebecca Jones June 25 . 1732
Solomon Sturges & Abigail Lewes of this Town July 23 1732
Jonathan Sturges & Sarah Baker of this Town Aug 20 1732
Isaac Lewis & Experience Hamlin August 27 1732
Thomas Annable & Thankful Hawes of Yarmouth Aug 27 . 1732
John Lovel & Bethiah Bearse Septem 1st 1732
Joseph Bearse & Phebe Fish Sept. 10 1732

*Of Harwich, Mass.
†These five entries are bracketed, with "1736" in the margin.
‡Of Raynham, Mass.
§Of Yarmouth, Mass.
‖Probably intended for "French Betty".

Ichabod Lothrop of Tolon* & Abigail Baker Sep 17 . 1732
David Parker & Mary Hawes of Yarmoth Sept 24 . 1732
Nicolas Baker & Dorcas Bachouse of Sandwich Octo 22 1732
John Allen of Hingham & Hannah Howland of This Town Nr 12 1732
Nathan Nye 3tius of Sandwich & Patience Passavil F. 24 1732/3
James Lewes Jur of this Town & Rebekah Hatch of Falmoth March 4th 1732/3
Ebenezer Tayler & Mary Lewes of this Town March 18th 1732/3
Samuel Bumpas & Sarah Rogers of Plymoth March 29 1733
David Phinney & Mary Pope of Sandwich April 1 . 1733
Mr Joseph Russel of This Town & Mrs Sarah Pain of Bristol May 13 1733
William Kent & Hannah Crocker both of this Town June 3 1733
James Fuller & Temperance Phinny June 17 1733
[p. 356] Mr David Gorham & Mrs Abigail Sturgis published ⅌ David Crocker Town Clark July 7th 1733
Jabez Goodspeed & Reliance Toby of Sandwich July 7 173[3]
Josph Blish & Remember Bachouse July 29 1733
Reuben Blish & Mary Thomas Sept 29 1733
Matthias Gorham of Yarmoth & Mary Davis Octor 6 1733
John Jones & Thankful Jones of Sandwich } Octor 20 173[3]
Lemuel Hedge of Yarmoth & Mary Baker
Theophilus Pain of Eastham & Hannah Bacon of This Town } Nov: 10 1733
Ebenezer Crosby of Yarmoth & Mehitable Baker of this Town
Zecheriah Cain & Desire Will Nov: 10 1733
Ebenezer Bacon & Lydia Lothrop Nov: 24th 1733
Jesse Cob & Thankful Baker Decemr 1st 1733
Shobal Hary Marshpee† Mary Cowet . December 23 1733
Mr John Sturges & Melatiah Crocker January 12 1733/4
Joseph Studdley of Yarmoth & Experience Pain March 2nd 1734
Jabez Robinson of Falmoth & Hannah Crocker } March 21 1734
Zacheus Crocker & Elizabeth Beels of Hingham
Mr Stephen Clapp of Situate & Mrs Mary Gorhan April 14 1734
Seth Crocker & Temperance Thacher of Yarmoth June 2nd 1734
Elkanah Hamlin & Margaret Bates of Plymoth June 9 1734
Thomas Winslow of Rochester & Rebekah Ewer June 9 1734
Benjamin Thacher of Yarmoth & Hannah Lumbart July 14 1734
Joshua Backouse of Sandwich & Sarah Crocker July 27 1734
David Childs & Hannah Cob } Aug: 23 1734
Ebenezer Crocker & Ann Eldredge of Falmoth
Peter Thacher of Yarmoth & Anna Lewes Aug: 30 1734
John Linnel Jur & Mercy Phinny Octor 5th 1734
Mr John Thacher Jur & Content Norton of Chilmark No 2nd 1734

*Probably Tolland, Conn. — Editor.
†Of Mashpee, Mass.

John Cullio & Lydia Bearse Nov 10th 1734
Moses Crocker & Mary Fish of Sandwich Decemr 28th 1734
Nathan Cob & Bethiah Harden of Eastham Jan 17 } 1734/5
Dr Simon Jones & Hannah Atkins Jan 17
James Robin Patience Peter Sandwich* Jan 17 1734/5
Moses Barnabas Experience Job Feb 1 1734
Nathaniel Sturges & Abigail Cob Feb: 1 1734
Guinny Toby & Desire Attaquin Feb 1 1734
Solomon Hamlin Rebecca Taylor of Yarmouth } March 1 173[4]
Seth Hamlin Sarah Blish

[p. 357] Persons Married by The Revd Mr Jonathan Russell 1730
Seth Crocker & Joanna Levet April 16
Benjamin Lothrop & Experience Bursley April 30
Matthias Smith & Hannah Fuller Sept 3
Thomas Crocker & Rebekah Hamlin Octr 20
Walley Crocker Abigail Annable Octr 22
Joseph Blish Mercy Crocker Octr 28
Benjamin Jenkins Mehitable Blish Octr 29

Persons Married by the Revd Mr Jonahan Russel in the year 1731
Jan. 27 Phillip Symons Priscilla Parker
Sept 1. William Green Mary Fuller
Sept 23 Gershom Davis Mary Hinkley.
Octo 28 George Howland Abigail Crocker
Oct 28 Caleb Nye Hannah Bodfish
Novemr 10 Eliphalet Carpenter Abigail Bacon

1732
May 30 Samuel Baker Prudence Jenkins
June 15 John Goodspeed Rebecca Goodspeed
July 6 Jabez Crocker Deliverance Jones
July 25 Ebenezer Jenkins Elizabeth Tupper
Octo. 5. Jabez Phinny Jane Tayler
Octr 10 Reuben Maggs Rebecca Jones
Nov 9 Ichabod Lothrop of Tolon† Abigail Baker
Decem 28th John Allen Hingham‡ Hannah Howland

1733
March 1. Eben Jones Hannah Jones
Sept 22 James Fuller Temperance Phinney
           Nathan Nye Patience Passavill
Octr 25 Reuben Blish Mary Thomas

* Of Sandwich, Mass.
† Tolland, Conn.
‡ Of Hingham, Mass.

1734.
Jan 10 Ebenezer Crosby Yarmoth* Mehitable Baker
May 16. Joseph Hatch Tolon† Rebeckah Lothrop
March 21 John Sturges Melatiah Crocker
May 30 Wm Kent Hannah Crocker
July 25. Jabez Robinson Hannah Crocker
Novr 7. Joshua Backhouse Sarah Crocker
Octo 9 1735 Seth Hamlin Sarah Blish
Octo 30 { Israel Butler & Mary Parker .
         { Ebenezer Claghorn & Sarah Lumbart
Janry 22 Lazarus Lovel & Mary Lumbart
Feb 19 Benoni Crocker Abigail Bursley
April 8 1736 David Smith & Sarah Hamlin

[p. 358] Persons Married By John Thacher Esqr 1732‡
Solomon Sturges & Abigail Lewes both of Barnstable Aug: 2nd 173[5]§

David Childs & Hannah Cob both of Barnstable Janry 29 1734
Nathaniel Sturges & Abigail Cob Feb 20 1734
Jonathan Davis & Susannah Allen April 24 1735
Nathll Lewes & Fear Thacher Feb: 19 1735/6
Dr Thomas Hersey & Mrs Lydia Gorham July 27 1737
Simon Porridge and Mary Crook July 7. 1738
Joseph Smith of Eastham & Rebekah Thacher of Barnstable Octor 18 .
1738
Stephen Cob & Abigail Chipman July 8 . 1742
Moses Sturges & Eleanor Robins Sept 22 1742
John Colman and Mary Hamlin Married Aug : 25 1743

Peter Thacher of Yarmoth & Annah Lewes of Barnstable Joyned in
  Marriage on the 24th of Octr 1735 . ℔ Peter Thacher Justice of
  the peace

[There are no family records on page 359.]

(To be continued)

* Of Yarmouth, Mass.
† Tolland, Conn.
‡ The year plainly reads "1732". — Editor.
§ The last figure is uncertain — probably "2". Four children of Solomon and
Abigail Sturges, 1735-1742, were recorded on original page 283, and three were
also recorded on original page 342 — printed in our thirty-second and thirty-third
volumes. — Editor.

BARNSTABLE, MASS., VITAL RECORDS

(Continued from page 21)

[p. 360] Persons Published by David Crocker Town Clark 1729/30
Richard Smith & Abigail Collier Jany 11 . 1729/30
Mr John Davis & Mrs Abigail Otis Jany 18th 1729/30
John Neal & Mary Green Jany 25th 1729/30
Stephen Davis & Desire Lewes Febr^y 1 1729/30
Ebenezer Clark of Rochester & Mary Claghorn Feb 8th 1729
Limus & Jenny Colonel Gorhams Servants F. 8th 1729/30
Isaac Simon & Susannah Nye alias Pocknut F 15 1729/30
Seth Crocker & Joanna Levet March 15 1729/30
Reuben Claghorn & Elinor Lovel March 22_ 1729/30
Benjamin Jenkins & Mehitable blish Ap: 12 1730
Thomas Hawes of Yarmoth Thankful Gorham Barnstable May 31 1730
James Haddeway & Bethiah Lumbard of Barnstable July 19 1730
Ebenezer Phinny Rebecca Burn of Plymouth Aug 2 . 1730
John Barlow of Sandwich & Abigail Hamlin Aug 2 1730
Mr Matthias Smith & Mrs Hannah Fuller Aug: 16 1730
Mr Joseph Blish & Mrs Mercy Crocker Aug: 23 . 1730
Mr Lot Thacher & Mrs Rebekah Keen of Pembroke A. 30 1730
Mr Nathaniel Bacon & Mrs Thankful Lombart Sep 6 173[0]
Mr Walley Crocker & Mrs Abigail Annable Sepr 13 173[0]
Mr John Sturgis & Mrs Susannah Lothrop Sep^tr 27
Mr Antipas Lewes of Yarmoth & Martha Bearse 27 Sep
Simon Pognit & Hannah Pease Sep. 27 1730
Thomas Crocker & Rebekah Hamlin Octo^r 4 1730
Solomon Davis & Mehitable Stewart of Sandwich Oct: 4 1730
Paul Abraham & Alma Moses Octo^r 11 1730
Stephen Weepkuck & Lois Popmunnuck Oct 18 1730
Phillip Symons Rochester* & Priscilla Parker. N 15 1730
Mr Lot Grey of Harwich & Mrs Jean Oris N. 20 1730
John Lumbart & Thankful Revis Jan 8th 1730/1
Experience Moses & Martha Paul Jan 22 1730/1
Jacob Hamlin Content Hamlin Feb 14 1730/1
Thomas Phinney & Meriah Lumbard March 6 1730/1
Jacob Hary & Sarah Popmunnucke July 4th 1731
Mr William Green & Mrs Mary Fuller July 18 1731
Josiah Morton of Plymouth & Melatiah Phinney August 15 1731
Gershom Cobb & Mrs Sarah Baxter of Yarmoth Aug 22: 1731
Gershom Davis & Mary Hinkley both of this Town 29† 1731
George Howland & Abigail Crocker Sep 19 1731

* Of Rochester, Mass.
† The month was not entered.

[p. 361] Persons Published by Nath¹ Otis Town Clerk . In the year 1724
James Cob . jur Hannah Rich the . 29th Day. of March
June 14th Solomon Barnabas . and Bethiah Wampom
Theophilus Wetherel & Ann Davis the 21st June
Seth Lewis And Sarah Revis the 21st June
July . 8th Hosea Richards And Mercy Pocknut
August. 23rd Moody Russell And Dinah Sturges
Augs't 27 . Thomas Adames And Sarah Phinney
Sep'br 26 . Samuel Hunt and Experience Paine
Oc'br 11th James Smith and Thankfull Hinckly
Oc'br 4th Shobal Wheten And Patience Will
Oc'br 11th Israel Buttler And Elizabeth Blosom
Oc'br 18th Eleazer Cob . And Relience Paine
Oc'br 24th David Crocker and Abigail Loringg
Oc'br 31 . Joshua Edward And Peace Parker
No'br 21 . Ebenezer Hamlin jur and Alice Phinney
Dec'r 3 . Samuel Bacon jur And Hannah Russell — widow
Dec'r 4 . Joseph Dexter And Rebekah Lovel
Dec'r 5 Job Davis And Mary Phinney
January 1st Ebenezer Fuller And Martha Jones
January 2d Moses Peage And Isabel Paul
January 9th John Williams and Hannah Dexter
January 20th Elisha Cob And Mary Hardin

Published by Nath¹ Otis Cl . In the year 1725.
Fe'ry. 6th Benj'a Lumbert jur and Sarah Crocker
Fe'ry. 20th Joseph Studly and Mary Jankens
March 4th Benj'a Sennit and Jemimiah Manasses
April 2d Ebenezer Scuder And Lydia Cobb
June 23rd M'r Joseph Hinckly jur And M'rs Mary Otis Situate*
July 27th Jacob Chipman And Bethiah Thomas
Aug't 12th Joseph Buttler. vineyard,† Thankfull Isum
Aug't 21st M'r Joseph Green And M'rs Hannah Russell
Aug't 28th 1725 Jonathan Linnel jur Eastham‡ & Abigail Phinney
[p. 362] Ebenezer Landers . Rochister§ . & Content Dexter . Barnstable
Sep'ber 13th 17[25]
Sep'tr 14th 1725 James Lothrop . & Sarah Cobb . both of Barnstable
Sep'b 24th 1725 Samuel Fuller and Melatiah Bodfish
Oc'br 14th 1725 Samuel Linnel Hannah Scuder
oc'br 15th 1725 Thomas Foster Lois Fuller
Oc'ber 16th 1725 Joseph Lothrop and Rebekah Parker
Oc'br 30th 1725 Gershom Lumbert and Thankfull Lewis
No'vr the 27th 1725 Samuel Cob & Hannah Cole

* Of Scituate, Mass.
† Of Martha's Vineyard.
‡ Of Eastham, Mass.
§ Rochester, Mass.

Fe'ry 4th 1725/6 Gersham Davis & Elizabeth Sturges
Fe'ry 19th 1725/6 Moses Goodspeed Hannah Allen
A D 1726. By N. Otis Clr*
March the 10th Job Bacon . and . Elizabeth Miles 1725.
March the 18th Thomas Phiney jur & Reliance Goodspeed
March 26th 1726 Jn'o Bacon jur & Elizabeth Freeman
May 2d 1726 Daniel Stuwart & Prudence Parker
June 11th 1726 Nath'll Bacon and Sarah Cob.
June 14th 1726 George Robin And Abigail Durfe In'd
June 24th 1726 Eben'r Wood Midleboro‡ & Lydia Lovel jur
July 2d 1726 . Eben'r Case And Elizabeth Lewis published
July 16th 1726 Solomon . Bacon . And Ann Capron
Aug't 13th 1726 . Daniel Smith & . Abigail Jones
Aug't 13th 1726 Zebulon Brown & Tabitha Lewis
Aug't 26th 1726 John Lewis jur & Mercy Hopkins
Aug't 27th 1726 Isaac Crocker of East-Haddam‡ & Elizabeth Fuller of Barnsble
Sep'br 9th 1726 John Bacon Esq'r & Mad'a Sarah Warrin
Sep'br 17th 1726 John Hinckly & Bethiah Robinson
Sep'br 21st: Thomas White & Hope Jankens
Sep'ber 27th 1726 Thomas Davis Susanah Sturges
[p. 363] 1726 Pharoah Negro And Hannah Samson
Samuel Anible . Bethiah Daniel Oc'br 22d 1726
No'vr 1st 1726 John Blossom And Thankfull Burg.
No'br 12 James Barse . And Thankfull Linnel
Dec'b 3d Samuel Fuller . And Lydia Lovel . widow
Dec'br 10th 1726 Peleg Larrance, Mary Passifull
Ja'ry 13. Ins§ Jn'o Anible jur & Elizabeth Snow of Truroe
Ja'ry 27th 1726/7 Joseph Smith jur & Sarah Bodfish
Ja'ry 28th 1726/7 Joseph Hamlin third & Elizabeth Matthew
Same Day James Lewis the third & Abigail Taylor
Ja'ry 28th 1726/7 Joseph Blosom ju & Temperance Fuller
March 18th 1726/7 Jacob Paul Martha Pees
Isaac Tomshit Elizabeth Quoy . Barnstable
May 6th 1727 Thomas Crocker & Mehitable Dimuck
June 3d 1727 . Shubal Davis & Patience Crocker
June 3d Daniel Atiquin Ind. & Hannah Nead
July 15th 1727 Peter Negro Serv't to M'r Anible, & Experience Pocknut
July 15th 1727 . James Oaker And Mercy Caine.
July 22d 1727 . George Lewis jur & Sarah Thacher of Yarmouth
Aug't 12th 1727 . Isaac Tomshit . Mehitable Semanna
Ag't 12th 1727 Simon Pocknut & Patience Late Serv't to M'r Silvanus Bourne

* This line is on the inner margin of the page.
† Middleborough, Mass.
‡ Connecticut.
§ Ensign.

Barnstable, Mass., Vital Records

Augt 22^d 1727 . Edward Morse And Margert White
August 27th 1727 Mathew Lumbert & Remember Mercy Davis
Sep^br 2^d 1727 Wm Paine & Sarah Bacon
Sep^br 16th 1727 Cuffee & Hagar Sev^ts to D Perker
[p. 364] Jno Bacon jur his Daug^tr Mary died the 17th day of July 1727
[*The following entries, on original page 364, are intentions of marriage.—Editor.*]
Sep^br 22^d 1727 Eben^r Gorham & Temperance Hawes
 James Davis & Thankfull Hinckly
Ob^r 7th 1727 . Joseph Gates, & Prudence Hamlin of Preson*
Oc^br 13th 1727 . Cornelius Crocker & Lydia Jankens
Oc^br 13th 1727 . Jerimiah Atiquin & Hester Francis Alias Robin
Nov^br 17th 1727 Jabez Howland & Elizabeth Pasifull
Dec^br 2^d 1727 . Benj^a Lothrop jur & Experence Howland
Ja^ry 3^d 1727/8 Barnabas Chipman & Elizabeth Hamlin
Jan^ry 5th 1727/8 James Coleman and Patience Phiney
Ja^ry 5th 1727/8 Jon^th Lumbert And Martha Phiney
Fe^ry 15th 1727/8 Jno Lothrop And Hannah Hadeway
April 30th 1728. Lamuel Nye & Sarah Jankens
June 3^d 1728 . Augustin Barse And Bethiah Linnil
June 29th 1728 Jno Sturges Mer^t And Abigail Allen
July 12th 1728 . James Stuwart . And Sarah Taylor
Aug^st 2^d : Jno Fuller jur, & Meriah Nye
Aug^st 3^d John Howland jur & Alice Hamlin
Elisha Lumbert . Rebecca Taylor†
Joseph Jankens the third & Martha Hinckly†
Silvanus Cob & Mercy Baker aug^t 31st 1728
[p. 365] Oc^t 16th 1728 . Then Wm Blackford, & Elizabeth Lewis published
Oc^br 26th 1728 . Mr Joseph Russell & Mrs Anna Vessele
Oc^br 28th 1728 Jacob Hary And Bette Caine—Jos Cains Daug^t oc^r 20th 1729 . Publish again
Jan^ry 25th 1728/9 Sam^ll Phiney & Hannah Ray
Ja^ry 25th 1728/9 Joshua Menasses & Sarah Caine
Fe^ry 8th 1728/9 John Hatch jur vid Mercy Crocker
Fe^ry 20th 1728/9 Benj^a Fuller jur And Mercy Fuller

In the year 1728/9

March 11th 1728/9 . Solomon Robin And Sarah Job
Sackfield West, Ruth Jankens†
Benj^a Lothrop Publish 2^d May 1729‡
May 10th 1729 Joseph Woies Jur And Mary Atiquin
May 24th Nehemiah Parker & Bethiah Basset

June 20th Cornelus Anible & Experience Goodspeed
July 12th 1729 . John Bumpas of Rochister*; and vid Jane Cleghorn
Oc^br 8th 1729 . Edmond Hawes, And Mary Freeman
Oc^br 28 . 1729 . Robert Bodfish & Jemima Nye
Thankful blish the Daughter of Reuben Blish born May 30 1727

[*The Second Volume of Original Records Ends Here.—Editor*]

THE MAYFLOWER DESCENDANT ceased publication at the end of Vol. 34. These vital records were not continued.

---

* Preston, Conn.?
† The date was not entered.
‡ The name of the bride was not entered.

PART II
Sandwich

THE MAYFLOWER DESCENDANT

An Illustrated Quarterly Magazine

OF

Pilgrim Genealogy, History and Biography

1912

VOLUME XIV

BOSTON
PUBLISHED BY THE
MASSACHUSETTS SOCIETY OF MAYFLOWER DESCENDANTS
1912

SANDWICH, MASS., VITAL RECORDS

Transcribed from the Original Records

BY GEORGE ERNEST BOWMAN

The earliest original entries of births, marriages and deaths on the records of Sandwich, Mass., are found in a volume now labelled: General Records 1651-1691 Births, Marriages and Deaths, but this label is misleading, as the book contains a number of birth records prior to 1651, and one as early as 1636. The vital records are scattered through the latter part of the book, among records of town proceedings, cattle marks, etc. The book was repaired by the Emery process, and rebound, in 1901.

In the June and September, 1900, and the March and December, 1901, issues of the "Genealogical Advertiser," a small portion of the Sandwich records were printed, with the following introduction:

[496] The following records of Marriages Births &c were taken from the oldest known Records of the Town & are true Copies of said Record as follows Attest H G O Ellis Town Clerk Sandwich Sept 15. 1869

Unfortunately, Mr. Ellis was not expert in reading old records, and evidently did not know that, in the old style calendar, the "tenth mounth" was December, not October, and that the second month was April, not February, consequently he made serious errors, some of which should be especially noted here. "Sarah" Adkins, born 1692, should be "Hanah". "Catherine" Bourne, born 1686, should be "bethshua". "Elehanan" Willis, born 1639, should be "Elchanan". James Percival was born "1671" not "1778" as copied. Ebenezer Lawrence, born 1676, was son of "Robert", not of "Ebenezer". Peleg Nie was son of "John & easther", not of "John & Dasther". Johanna daughter of George "Feilds" not "Fish" was born 1691. John Dillingham married Elizabeth "Feake", not "Peake", and the original record adds that she was daughter of Henry. "Marienne" Skiff, born 1652, should be "Pacience". Four times on one page "Mercy" was copied as "Mary". Robert "Harpper" not "Tupper", married Deborah Perry in 1654. Thomas "Hamblin", born 1671, should be "Hambleton", and "born at Rohd Iland" *was* omitted from the copy. "Henry" Tupper, born 1638, should be "Thomas". "Jefferson" Gifford, born 1676, should be "yellverton". "Drsula" Dillingham, died 1656, should be "Ursula". And at least one original entry was omitted in the Ellis copy.

The pages of the original book are not numbered, therefore I have arranged the copy here presented with a dash at the end of each original page, to facilitate comparison with the original entries. It should be borne in mind that such a dash in the following printed copy sometimes represents several pages of town proceedings.

William Adkins the son of James Adkins was borne the 2 July 1691
Hanah Adkins the daughter of James Adkins was borne the 17th december 1692

Bethiah Willis the daughter of Nathanael Willis was borne the 14th of September Anno Dom: 1643:
bethiah Nie the Daughter of Ebenezer Nie was borne the 5 of october anno domini 1675
Bethiah Gibb the Daughter of Thomas Gibbs Junior was borne the 10 of December anno dom 1675
Jobe Bourne and Ruhamah Hallett were marred the 14th of December anno : Domini 1664
Timothy Bourne sonn of Jobe Bourne and Ruhamah his wyfe : was Borne the 18 of april ano : dom: 1666
hannah Bourne the Daugter of Jobe Bourne and Ruhamah his wife : was borne the 18 of november 1667
Eleazer Bourne the Sonn of Jobe Bourne and Ruhamah his wife : was borne the 20th of July 1670:

108 Sandwich, Mass., Vital Records

John Bourne the Sonn of Jobe Bourne and Ruhamah his wife was borne the 2 of november 1672

hezechiah Bourne the sonn of Jobe Bourne and Ruhamah his wife was borne the 25 of September anno domini 1675

Benjamin Nie the Son of Ebenezer nie was borne the 27 of november anno dom 1677

Mary Basett the daughter of william baset was borne the 20 of october 1676

Rahell * Baset the daughter of william baset was borne the 25 of october 1679

Jonathan Bassett deceased the 13th of december 1683 and was buried the 14th

Ezra bourne the sone of Sherejashub bourne was borne the 6 of august 1676

Mary bourne the daughter of Sherejashub bourne was bourne the 21rst of october 1678

Sary bourne the daughter of sherejashub Bourne was borne the 6 febuary 1680

Mary bourne the daughter of Elisha Bourne was borne the 4th ofe february anno domini 1681

Joshua Blackwell sone sone of Joshua Blackwell borne the 12 Jenuary ann: domi 1682

mercy Blackwell the Daughter of Joshua Blackwell was borne the 5 day of october anno domi : 1684

bethshua bourne the daughter of Elisha bourn was borne the 20th of december anno domini 1686

Thomas Burge deceased the 23 february annodom 1685

dorithy burge deceased the 27 feberary 1687/8

Remembranc Bourne the daughter of Mr Sherejashub and bethshua his wife was borne the 6 of february anno domini 1683

Patience Bourney e daughter of Mr Sherejashub Bourne and Bethshua his wife was borne the 20 day of aprill anno domini 1686

benjamin Tobie the son of ephraim tobie was borne the 24 day of march 1691

Darity Butler the daughter of Thomas Butler was borne the 23th of January Anno Dom: 1650.

Dorty butler was died the 9th of august and bured the 10 day anno dom 1675

Theophilus Dotey the son of Joseph Doty was borne the 22 of Febuary 1674

Elles Dotey the son of Joseph Dotey was borne the 16 day of aprill 1677

Desire Blackwell the Daughter of John and Sary Blackwell was borne the 20th of December anna domini 1678

* Sic.

Sandwich, Mass., Vital Records 109

Allis Blackwell the daughter of John blackwell and Sarah his wife was borne the eight day of may anno dom 1681

Jane Blackwell the daughter of John Blackwell was borne the 3d of march anno dom 1683/4

[*Joshua Blackwell the Son of Joshua Blackwell was Borne the 12th of January anno domini 1682* *]

Nathanall Blackwell the son of John Blackwell was borne the 27 December anno do 1686

Samuell blackwell the son of Joshua blackwell was borne the 13 april ano dom 1689

Elizabeth Dextor the daughter of John Dextor was borne the second † of november anno dom 1683

abigail Dextor the daughter of Mr Thomas Dextor was borne the twelfe day of June 1663

John Dextor and Mehetable Hallett were married the tenth of november 1682

Mr Thomas Dextor Sen deceased the 29 december 1686

Elizabeth Dextor the daughter of John Dextor was born the first † of november 1683

Thomas Dextor the son of John Dextor was borne the 26 of august 1686

abagail Dextor the daughter of John dextor was borne the 26 of may 1689

Elchanan Willis the sone of Nathanail Willis was borne May the 20th Anno Domini. 1639.

Edmond ffreman junior and Margeret Perry wer maried the 18th of July Anno. Dom. 1651.

Elizabeth Dexter the daughter of Thomas Dexter junior was borne the 21th of September An: Dom: 1651

Experience Allin the daughter of Ralphe Allin mason was borne the 14th of March Anno Domini. 1651.

Ezra Perry and Elizabeth Burge Wer maried the 12th of february Anno Dom. 1651.

Epherim Allin the sonn of Ralfe Allin was borne 20th of march 1656

Edmon Freeman the sonn of Edmon Freeman iuner was borne the 5th of october : 1655:

Eales Freeman the Daughter of Edmon Freeman iuner was borne the 29th of march : 1658

Elezebeth Nuland the Daughter of William Nuland was buried the 4th of September : 1658 :

EPherim Allin the sonn of of Gorg Allin was borne the 14th of January 1652

Elezebeth Allin the Daughtter of Gorg Allin was borne the 10th of January 1654

* This entry has been crossed out. See second original page preceding.

† Sic.

Epherim Swift the sonn of william Swift was borne the 7th of June 1656

Rachell ffreemand The Daftar of Emond Freemond was Boarne the fourth of Septembar : In 165[*]

Sarath Freeman the Daftar of Edmond Freemond was Boarne the sixt of Feburary In 1662

Deboroath Freemond the Daftar. of Edmond Freemond was boarne The 9th of August In 1665

Edmond Freeman the son of Edmond Freeman Ju was borne †

Elisabeth Percevell the daugher of Jams Persevell was borne the tenth of September annodomini 1675

James percevell the Sonn of James persevell was bourné the 18 day of January 1671 ‡

Elisha Bourne and Patience Skiffe were married the 26 of october anno : dom: 1675

Ebenezer Nie and Sarah Gibbs was marred the 17 of december anno dom 1675

Mrs Elizabeth ffreman deceased the 14 of February ann domini 1675

Ebenezer Perry the Sonn of Ezra Perry Ju: was borne the 18 of november 1673

Mary Perry the Daughter of Ezra Perry Ju was borne the 21 of december 1675

Hannah Briggs Daughter of Samuell Briggs bourne the 14th of Febuary anno dominy 1675

John Nie Sonn of John Nie borne the 22 november anno domini 1675

Benjamin Nye Sonn of John Nie Junior borne the 25 of november anno domini 1673

Abigail Nie the daughter of John Nie was borne ye 18 april ano do 1678

Experience Nie the daughter of John Nie was borne the 16 december annod 1682

Hannah Nie the daughter of John Nie was borne the 19 June annod 1685

Ebenezer Nie the Son of John Nie was borne the 23 of September annod 1687

michall Blackwell . Jun. Died the twenti Eight Dam* of may . In . 1673 . And . was Buried the Last Day of the Same mounth

Ebenezer Lawrance Son of Robert Lawrance borne the 16 day of Janary 1676

Ellener Redding the Daughter of John Redding was bourne the 22th of February anno domini 1677

Elizabeth Bourne the Daughter of Elisha bourn was borne the 28 Jun anno domini 1679

Peleg Nie The Son of John and easther Nie was borne the 12th day of november 1689

Ephraim ffish the sonn of Ambros and Hannah fish was borne the 16 day of December anno domino 1676

Ephraim Fish the sone of Ambros and hannah ffish deceased the 17th of october anno : dom: 1677

Abia ffish The Daughter of Ambros ffish was Borne the 2d of September anno dom 1678

Mehittabell ffish The Daughter of Ambross ffish and Hannah his wife was borne the 19th of may in the year of our lord 1680

Johanna Fish daughter of Ambrose Fish was borne the 20th of may anno domini 1689

Joannah ffeilds The daughter of Georg Feilds was borne the 30th day november 1691

John ffish the Son of John ffish was borne The 19th day of september ann: dom: 1679

Josiah ffish the son of John ffish was borne the 13th day of Febuary anno : dom: 1681

George Benett died the 11 of november anno domini 1675

Thomas Lander Died the 11 of november anno domini 1675

Thomas Gibbs Ju: and Elles warran weare married the 23 of December anno domini 1674

John Ross died the 8th of December ano dom: 1675

Samuell Gibbs and Patience Butler were married the 5 day of march anno : Domini 1676

Thomas Gibbs The Sone of Thomas Gibbs was borne The 28 of January anno : dom: 1679

Barnabas Gibbs the son of John Gibbs was borne the 24 of June anno domini 1684

Elezebeth gifart the Daftar of John gifart was boarne : the 25 . of . 12 . 1665

* Sic.

---

* The last figure has been marked over and is now practically illegible. Savage's Genealogical Dictionary, in 1860, and Freeman's History of Cape Cod, in 1862, both give the year as 1659, and it seems unlikely that Rachel was born only eleven months after her sister Margaret, as the date in the Ellis copy, "1653," would have it.

† This entry is not in the same hand as the three preceding entries, and was left unfinished, probably because the clerk noted the birth of Edmund had already been recorded in the middle of the page. "Oct 5 . 1658" has been added in a modern hand, apparently by Mr. Ellis, in 1869. A comparison of his "copy" with the original records makes it evident that he intended to complete the original entry from the one above, but made an error in the year.

‡ The last "1" was made over a "5". This year was copied as "1778" in 1869.

Samuel gifart the Sonn of John gifart was boarn the 12 . of march .
1666
John gifart the Sonn of John gifart was boarn the 12 of June 1668
mary gifart the Daftar of John gifart was boarne the : 9 : of Octobr
1669
grase gifart the Daftar of John gifart was Boarne the 17 . of August
In . 1671
william gifard the Sonn of John gifart was Boarne the 7 . 3 . 1673
yellverton Gifford the Son of John Gifford was borne the 22 aprill
anod 1676
Josiah Gifford the Son of John Gifford was Borne ye 27 Feber anno :
1681

(*To be continued*)

SANDWICH, MASS., VITAL RECORDS

(Continued from page 112)

[As the pages of the original are not numbered, a dash has been inserted in the copy at the end of each page.]

Hannah Swift the daughter of William Swift was borne the 11th of March Anno. Dom: 1651.
Henery Dilingham the sone of mr Edward Dillingham and Hanna perry was marryed the 24th of June Anno Dom 1652
Henry Vinsent and Mary Matthewes were married the 15th day of desember 1657
Hasadiah Lander the daugter of Thomas lander was borne the 31 of January 1674
Elisha Hunter The son of william Hunter was borne The 10 day of august 1679
William Hunter The son of william Hunter was borne the 21 of march anno dom: 1681
allis hunter The daughter of william Hunter was borne the 25 of febuary 1682

———

John blackwell The Sonn of John Blackwell was Bourne The twenteth six Day of the tenth mounth one thousand Six houndreid Seventi befor

———

Judeth Willis the daughter of Nathanael Willis was borne June the 14th Anno Domini 1641.
Judah Allen the sone of George Allin was borne the 30th of January Anno Dom: 1650.
Joseph Bodfish the sone of Robert Bodfish was borne the 3d of April Anno 1651.
John ffish the sone of Nathanael ffish was borne the 13th of April Anno 1651.
John Dillingham the sone of mr Edward Dillingham and Elizabeth ffeake the daughter of mr Henery ffeake wer maried the 24th of March Anno Dom 1650
Jediah Allen The soone of Ralphe Allen was Borne the 3d of January 1646:
Job Cooke Jukin the sonn of John Jukin was borne the 14 day of aprill Anno 1655
Joell Ellis the sonn of John Ellis was borne 20th of march Anno 1654
Job Gibbs the sonn of Tho: Gibbs was borne The 15 of April Ano 1655

Allso Beththia Gibbs The daughter of Tho: Gibbs was borne 15th of April 1655
James skeff the sonn of James skeff was borne 12th of September Anno. 1638.
Steven Skeff the sonn of James Skeff was borne the 14th of April An 1641
Nathanniell Skeff the sonn of James Skeff was borne the 20th of march Anno. 1645.
Sare Skeff the Daughtter of James Skeff was borne the 19th of October 1646
Bathshua Skeff the Daughtter of James Skeff was borne the 26th of april 1648
Mary Skeff the Daughter of James Skeff was borne the 25th of march Anno. 1650.
Pacience Skeff the Daughter of James Skeff wa[s] borne the 25th of march Anno 1652/3
Beniamine Skeff the sonne of James skeff was borne the 15 of November 1655
John Borg and Mary Wordden were married the 8th Day of Desember: 1657
Nathan Skeff the sonn of James Skeff was Borne the 27th of may: 1658
John Dillingham the sonn of Henry Dillingham was borne the 24th of february 1658
James and John Allin sonns of Gorg Allin was born the 5th of Agust 1658
Judah Allin the sonn of Gorg Allin was borne the 14th of Jenuary 1650
John Gibbs the sonn of Thomas Gibbs was borne the 12th of September 1634
James Skeff and Elezebeth Nabor were maried the 18th of November 1659
John Greene was buried the 4th of April 1660
Jacob Borg and Mary Nie was married the first of June 1660

———

Sary Holly the dafter of Joseph Holley was born the 25 day of Aprell 1664
mary Holley the dafter of Joseph Holley was borne the 16 day of febereway 1665
Amey Allen the daufter of Jeames Allen was borne : the 14 day of Agust 1663
mary Allen the daufter of Jeames Allen was borne the 22 of desembar 1665
Abigale* Allen the Daftar of James Allen was Boarne the twenty Eight of Desembar 1667 Abigill naimeid

* "James" has been crossed out and "Abigale" interlined.

Sandwich, Mass., Vital Records

Caleb Allin the sonn of Gorg Allin was borne the 24th of June 1648
Elezibeth nuland The wife of John nuland was Buried the 2[*] of May : 1671

Samuel ffish the Son of nathanell ffish was borne the 10th day of august 1668

Hanna wing the dather of Daniell wing borne the 28 July 1642
Leidia wing dafter of Daniell wing of sandwige borne the 23 of may 1647
Samuell wing borne the 28 of august 1652
John Lander the sonn of Tho: Lander was Borne the seond of Jenuary Ano 1653
Hepthzibath the dather of daniell wing borne the 7 of of november 1654
Merty Lander the dafter of Thomas Lander Died the 7 of march Ano 1654
John wing the sonn of Daniell wing borne the 14 of november 1656
Bwela wing the dafter of daniell wing borne the 16 of november in the yeear 1658

Mary Willis the daughter of Nathanaell Willis was borne the 14th of April Anno . 1648.
Mary Skiff the daughter of James Skiff was borne the 24th of March Anno Dom: 1650.
Mercy Wing the daughter of Steven Wing was borne the 13th of November Anno . 1650.
Mordicai Ellis the sone of John Ellis was borne the 24th of March. Anno Dom. 1650.
Mercy Wright the daughter of Nicolas Wright borne the 4th of June An: 1651.
Mercy Lander the daughter of Thomas Lander was borne the 23th of January Anno Dom: 1651
Mercy Nie the daughter of Beniamen Nie was borne the 8th of April Anno Dom: 1652.
Mary Dillingham Daughtter of Henry Dillingham was borne 26th ‡ of Desember Ano Dom: [1654 †]
Mary Dillingham ye Daughtter of Henry Dillingham was borne the 25 ‡ of Desember Ano 1653:
Mary Basset the daughtter of will: Basset was borne the 21 of november ano 1654
Mary Harper the Daughtter of Robbert Harper was borne the 25 of Desember Anno . 1655.

** "4" has been made almost illegible, by what may have been an accidental blot.

† This year has been crossed out. Compare the next entry.

‡ Sic.

Matthyas Ellis the sonn of John Ellis was borne the 2tb of June Anno Dom: 1657 :*
Margret freeman the Dafter of Edmon freeman was borne the 2th of october . 1652 :
Mary Gibbs the Daughter of Thomas Gibbs was borne the 12th of Agust 1657
Mara Swift the Daughter of william Swift was borne the 7th of aprill 1659

Matthew Allin the son of Gorg Allin Sener and Sara Kerby were maried the 6th of June 1657
Dorryty Allin the Daughter of matthew Allin was Borne the 9th of April 1659
Meary presbury Daftar of John presbury was Boarne the 10 . Day . 3 . mo. 1644
Thomas Tupper Junior and Martha Mayhew the 27 of December anno dom 1661 (were married) †

meary Allen the Daftar of Ralph Allen Senour was buried the . 18 . 2 . 1675
Martha Tupper the Daugter of Thomas Tupper was bourne 13 of October ano domini 1662
Thomas Tupper the son of Thomas Tupper was bourne the 11 of august anno domini 1664
Israell Tupper the son of Thomas Tupper was bourne the 22 of september anno domini 1666
Elisha Tupper the son of Thomas Tupper was bourne the 17 of march anno domini 1668
Jane Tupper was bured the 28 of apriell 1672
Ichabod Tupper the Son of Thomas Tupper was bourne the 11 of apriell 1673
Eldad Tupper the sonn of Thomas and martha Tupper was borne the last day of may anno dom: 1675
Samuell burge the sonn of Jacob burge was borne the 8 of march anno domini 1671
Ebenezer burge the sonn of Jacob burge was borne the 2 of october anno domini 1673
malletiah bourne the Son : of SheareJashub bourne was borne 12 of January anno domini 1673
michaell Blackwell the sonn of John Blackwell borne the 16th of december 1676
Jakob Burge The son of Jakob Burge was Borne the 18th off October andom 1676
Medad Tupper the sonn of Thomas and martha Tupper was borne the 22 of September anndom 1677

* This record has been copied, in a modern hand, on the opposite page.

† Sic.

Ann Tupper The daughter of Thomas Tupper and martha his wife was borne the 14th of december anno dom 1679
Thomas Burge The sonn off Jacob Burge was Borne the 29th off march anno dom 1679 or 1680
Eliakim Tupper the son of Thomas Tupper and martha his wife was borne the 29th of december anno domini 1681
Bethiah Tupper was borne the 25 of april 1685

Bethiah Tupper the Daughter of Thomas Tupper and Martha his wife was born 25 april 1685
elisha Tupper the Son of Israell and Elisabeth Tupper was borne th 4 may 1692 This boys name is changed from Elisha to Samuel
Jane Tupper the daughter of Thomas and mary Tupper was borne 18 febury 1688
Thomas Tupper the son of Thomas Tupper and mary his wife was Born 25th of July 1693

Thomas Tupper the sonn of Thomas Tupper wa[s] the 16 day of January anno dom 1638
Thomas Tobie and Martha Knott wer maried the 18th of November Anno . 1650.
Thomas Lander and Jane Kerbie wer maried the 2^d of July . Anno . 1651.
Thomas Tobie the sone of Thomas Tobie was borne the 8th of December Anno 1651.
Thomas Johnsonn and Prissilla Goznee was maryed The 5th of Jannuary Ann 1656
Thomas Gibbs the sonn of Thomas Gibbs was borne the 23th of march 1636
Thomas Tupper Senior desceased the 28th of march and buried the 30th anno domini 1676
Thomas Tupper now disceassed was borne in the yeare of our lord 1578 his age at his disceas was about 98 yeares and two moneth
An Tupper the wife of Thomas Tupper deceased The 4th of June anno dominy 1676
An Tupper deceased in or about the 90th yeare of her age
Thomas Hambleton the son of Thomas Hamblton and lidia his wife was bourne the 17 of Febuary 1671 borne at Rohd Iland
Martha Tupper the Daughter of Thomas Tupper deceased the first day of november an dom 1680

Oseth Wing the wife of Steven wing Died 29th of april Ano : 1654
hanati: Dillinham the wife of henery Dillenham Died the : 9 . of 6 . 1673
mary Skffe the wife of James Skffe Sen Died the 21 . of Septembar . 1673.

Samuell perry of sandwich and Easher Tabor of dartmouth were married the 23 day of october anno dom 1689
Elizabeth perry ye daughter of Samuell Perry of monent was borne ye fifteenth day of July anno domini 1690

Peter Wright the sone of Peter Wright died the 28th of februrary Anno . Dom. 1651.
Patience Skeff the Daughtter James Skeff was borne 25th of march Anno Dom: 1653:
Ezra Perry the sonn of Ezra Perry was the 11 of febriary Ano Domy 1652
Debbora Perry the dafter of Ezra perry was borne the 28th of November 1654
John Perry the sonn of Ezra Perry was borne the first of Jeneway 1656
Prissilla Johnson the Daughter of Thomas Johnson was Borne the 20th of november 1657
Beniamine Perry t^he Sonn of Ezra Perry was Borne the 15th of January 1670
Remembrance Pery the daughter of Ezra perry sen was borne the first of January 1676
Samuell Perry son of Ezra Perry was borne about the midle of march 1667

Robert Bodfish died 19th of November An: 165[*worn off*]
Robert Harpper and Debbora Perry was marryed may 9th 1654
Rebekca burge the Daughter of Joseph burge was borne the 17 day of January an dom 1667
Dorite burge the Daughter of Joseph Burge was borne the 12 day of november ano domini 1670
Joseph burge the son of Joseph burge was borne the 18 day of november 1673
benjam burge the son of Jo Joseph Burge was borne the fift day of may 1681
Robert Harper and Prudence Butler were married the 22 of June 1666
Deborah Harper deceased the 14th day of october 1665
Mercy harper the daughter of Robert Harper and prudence * harper was bourn the 12 day of the the 4 mounth 1675
hannah harper the daughter of Robert and Prudence harper was bourn in the [*16 day of 8* †] 3 month 1670
Elizabeth harper the daughter of Robert and prudence harper was bourne the 16 day 8 mounth 1672
Mary harper the Daughter of Robert and Deborah harper was bourne the 5 day of the tenth mounth 1665

* "deborah" was first written, but was crossed out and "prudence" interlined, in the same hand.

† The words in italics have been crossed out. See next entry.

Sandwich, Mass., Vital Records

Experience harper the Daughter of Robert harper was bou£n in the 9 mounth 1657

Steven Harper the son of Robert and Deborah Harper was borne in the 4 moneth 1662

Remembranc Perry the daughter of Ezra Perry Sen: was borne the first of January 1676

Rose hamond the Daughter of Benjamine and Mary hamond Deceased the 20th of november ano dominy 1676

M**r** Richard Bourne and M**rs** Ruth winslow were married the Second of July anno dom: 1677

Richard handy the son of Richard handy was borne the 21th of may 1672

Jonathan haandy the son of Richard handy was Borne the 3rd Day of november 1675

Richard Chadwell deceased the 27 day of november and was buried the 28 ano : dom: 1681

Joseph Buck and Rose Newland was married the 2d of February 1682

Rose Buck the wife of Joseph Buk deceased the 25 day of november 1683

Joseph Buck and Remembrance Jening was married togeather the twenteth of september 168[*]

Remembrance Nie the daufhter of Nathan Nie was borne the last day of Feburary anno : dom: 168$\frac{6}{7}$

Sarah Gibbs the daughter of Thomas Gibbs was borne the 11th of Aprill Anno Dom: 1652.

Sammuell Gibbs the sonn of Thomas Gibbs was borne the 23th of June 1639

Sammuell Swift the Son of william Swift was borne the the 10 day of Ouggust 1662

Elesabeth Swift the daughter of Ephraim Swift was borne the 30 day of december anno : dom: 1674

William Swift The sonn of william Swift Ju: was borne The 24th day off January anno dom 1679

Samuell Sanerson the son of henry Sanderson was borne the tenth day of Febuary 1670

henry Sanderson the son of henry Sanderson was borne the 18 day of Jully anno dominy 1676

Shubael Smith and Mara Swift were married the sixt day of February anno : dom: 1677

Marcy Smith the daughter of Shubael Smith was borne the third day of January anno dom : 1678

Susanna Smith the daught of Shubael Smith was borne the sixteenth day of January anno dom 1680

Abigail Smith the daughter of Shubael Smith and mary his wife was born the second of Febuary 16[*worn off*]

* The last figure is doubtful, but probably was "6."

Mara Smith wif of Shubael Smith deceased The first day of march anno : dom: 168[*]

Elisabath Swift the daughter of Ephraim Swift was borne 29 december anno domini 1680

Johanah Swift Swift The daughter of Ephraim Swift was borne the 7 July anno : dom: 1684

Samell Swift Swift the son of Ephram Swift was borne the 9 april anno : dom: 1686

Ephraim Swift the son of Ephraim Swift was borne the 16 december anno : dom 1688

1690 † Seth Stuard the son of James Stuard was borne the 2d april anno domini 1691 †

Seth Tobie son of Nathan Tobie was Borne the 24 march monday 1686 1686

Deborah Tobie the daughter of Nathan Tobie was borne the 26 January 168$\frac{8}{9}$

Ursula Dillingham the wife of mr Edward Dillingha[m] was buried the 9th of febreary Anno Domyni 1656

William Johnson the sonn of Thomas Johnso[n] the 9th of June 1659 William Swift the sonn of william Swift was bor[ne] the 28th of agust ‡ 1654

Remembrance Jeninge The Daftar of John Jeninge was boarne the 17th of Septembar 1668

Ann Jenens the Dafter of John Jenens was Boarne the 17th of the Eight mounth . 1670

John Jenens the sonn of John Jenens & Ruhamah his wife was Boarne the 12 day of the 3 : 167[*worn off*]

William Bassett of Sandwich and Rachell willasson of taunton were married the 9 of october 1675

John Redding and mary Bassett were married the 22 of 8 moneth 1676

Isaak Jening the sonn of John and Ruhamah Jening was Bourne the third of July anno : 1677

Elizebeth Jening The daughter of John Jening was borne the 14th day of aprill anno dom 1680

Elizabeth Jening the daughter of John Jening deceased the 13th day of September anno : domini 1682

* "Febuary" was crossed out and "march" interlined; and "1682" was crossed out and "168", with a fourth figure, now worn off, was added. These changes apparently were made by the clerk who made the original entry.

† Sic.

‡ "last of September" was crossed out and "the 28th of agust" interlined, in the same hand.

Samuell Jening the Sonn of John Jening and Ruhamah his wife was borne The eighteenth day of February anno dom 1684

[St]ephen Wing And Sarath Bridggs was mareid the 7 of 11 . 1654
Stephen winge the sonn of Stephen wing was boarne the 2 . Day of Septembar In the yeare 1656
Sarath wing the Daftar of Stephen wing was boarne the 5 Day Feburay In the yeare 1658
John wing the sonn of Stephen winge was boarne the 25 of Septem In the yeare 1661
Abigirl Wing the Daftar of Stephen wing was boarne The first Day of may* In the yeare 1664
Ebenezar wing The Sonn of Stephen wing was Boarne the . 11 . 5 . 1671
matthew wing the Sonn of Stephen wing was Boarne the 1 . Day . 1 mo. 1673
Bethshoa Hakse The Daftar of Lodawick Hakse was boarne The 15 . Day of octobar . in the . yeare . 1665.
Josepth Hackse the Sonn of Lodawick Hackse was Boarne The 15 Daye of march in the yeare 1667
giddion Hackse the Sonn of Lodawick Hackse was . 25 . of feburary . 1670
Elezebeth Briggs the Daftar of Samuell Bridgs was Boarne the . 3 of 2 : 1665.
Benet Briggs was Boarne the . 14 . of october . 1667.
And Ebenesar Brigg The Sonn of Samuell Brigg was Boarne In the yeare of or Loard . 1671 . the 9 . of June.
Samuell bridgs the Sonn of Samuell Bridgs was Boarne the 12 . 12 . 1673
Anne the Daftar of Susana Tourner was boarne the . 13 . 11 . In 1671
John Landar the Sonn of Thomas Landar was boarne : 2 . 11 . mo. 1653

[worn off] gibbs The sonn of John gibbs was Boarne [t]wenti Eight Day of July : 1670
[worn off] gibbes The Sonn of John gibbs was Boarne [worn off] of Desember In . 1673.
[worn off] gibbs the sonn of John Gibbs was borne the 27th [worn off] Jy anno domini 1676
[worn off] hua Gibbs the sonn John Gibbs was borne [worn off] of aprill anno dom: 1679
[worn off] b Gibbs the Son of John Gibbs was borne the [worn off] of august anno dom 1681
[The vital records in the oldest volume end here. — *Editor.*]

(*To be continued*)

* "Febuary" was crossed out and "may" interlined in the same ink.

THE MAYFLOWER DESCENDANT

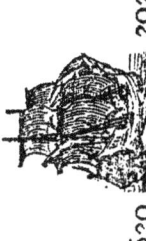

1620 2020

A QUARTERLY MAGAZINE OF
PILGRIM GENEALOGY AND HISTORY

VOLUME XXIX

1931

PUBLISHED BY THE
MASSACHUSETTS SOCIETY OF
MAYFLOWER DESCENDANTS
BOSTON

SANDWICH, MASS., VITAL RECORDS
Transcribed from the Original Records
By George Ernest Bowman
(Continued from Vol. XIV, p. 174)

Literal copies of all the original entries of births, marriages and deaths found in the oldest volume of records of the Town of Sandwich, Mass., were printed in the fourteenth volume of this magazine.

In the introduction to those articles especial attention was called to some of the many serious errors found in the copy of the town records which had been made in 1869.

The 1869 copy contains also a number of early records copied from original record pages which have not been found. Probate and gravestone records prove that some of these copies are very inaccurate, as shown by my notes in the following pages. Those for which no evidence, either confirming or correcting, has been found are here printed without comment.

In a number of cases the copyist overlooked or ignored the second figure in cases of double dating, and these incomplete dates were printed in the Genealogical Advertiser, 4: 101, 102.

All persons interested in the records of Sandwich are indebted to Mrs. C. Griffin Martin, of Chattanooga, Tenn., a member of the Massachusetts Society of Mayflower Descendants, who has contributed the amount necessary to pay the expense of preparing this article, and two to follow, on the Sandwich records.

Mrs. Martin is a descendant of Richard Warren, the Mayflower Passenger, through Abigail Gibbs[4] (*Alice*[3] *Warren, Nathaniel*[2], *Richard*[1]), whose marriage, in 1697, to Jirah Swift, recorded on the eleventh page of the second volume of the original records, is included in the present article.

In the following pages we print, first, the unverified entries found in the modern "copy". We then begin printing literal copies of the entries found in the second volume of the original records, which is labelled "Births Marriages and Deaths Ear Marks Town of Sandwich".

[From the Modern Copy—Original not found]

[p. 507] Deborah, daughter of Stephen Skiff, born 14 July, 1668
Marcy, daughter of Stephen Skiff, born 13 November, 1671

Steven, son of Stephen Skiff, born 4 February, 1685

[p. 509]
Died

Jennings Wife of Isaac Jennings Dec 21st 1720
Fish son of Seth Fish & Mary his wife died Feb 2 1720
Hannah Jennings died the last day of March 1721.
Wing—Wife of Jashub Wing died Dec 16. 1721
Mary Wing daughter of Jashub Wing died
Rev Rowland Cotten died March 18—1700*
John Gibbs Died April 30 1725
James Stuart died Oct 3d 1720†
Elizabeth Perry wife of John Perry died Apl 23d 1727
Died Elizabeth Barlow Wife of John Barlow May 16 1726
Ezra Perry died Jany 31. 1729
Thos Gibbs Sen died Jan 7. 1732
Samuel Wing died Feb 12 1732
Samuel Swift Sen died May 25 1730‡
Mordecai Ellis died Feb 5 in 1600 perhaps 80 or 90§
John Chipman died Apl 7th 1600 perhaps 80 or 90¶
[p. 510] The omitted dates & names were torn from the margin.
Probably the years omitted were from 1680 to 1700‖
died

William Allen Oct 1
Michael Blackwell Jan 6th 1710**
Stephen Skiff Esqr June 8th††
Seth Fish son of Seth died Aug 30

* This is an error. He died in 1722.—*Editor.*

† A James Stuart of Sandwich made his will, 26 December, 1723. and it was probated, 3 November, 1726.—*Editor.*

‡ Samuel Swift, Sr., of Sandwich, made his will 5 October, 1730: witnesses were sworn, 6 June, 1733.—*Editor.*

§ A settlement of the estate of Lieut. Mordecai Ellis, of Sandwich, was dated 20 February, 1709/10.—*Editor.*

¶ He died 7 April, 1708. His will, dated 12 November, 1702, and probated, 17 May, 1708; and the will of his second wife, Ruth, dated 6 December, 1710, and probated 8 October, 1713, will be found in our third volume. The records on their gravestones, in our twenty-fourth volume, show that Elder John Chipman died 7 April, 1708; and his widow Ruth died 4 October, 1713.—*Editor.*

‖ This note is on the outside margin of the page, in the same hand as the death records.

** "1710" is a later addition, in pencil.

†† His will was made 7 May, 1701; a codicil added, 20 August, 1708: probated, 28 June, 1710. The inventory notes that he "died the 8th day of June 1710."—*Editor.*

Elisha Bourne Son of Elisha Dec 10th*
John Abbit May 16
Widow Faith Fish Augt 7
Mr John Smith Oct 22d
Edward Perry Feb 16, 1690
Deborah Baxter Wife of Saml Oct 24
Mrs Ruth Chipman Oct 4th 1710†
Thomas Tobey Jan 9, 1710
Mrs. Lydia Skiff, Widow, Mch 17 1711‡
Mrs. Elizabeth Dexter, Mch. 19. 1712
Hannah Johnson Nov 4th 1712
Sarah Allen Widow March 22. 1711.
Elizabeth Pope Apl 15, 1715
Abigail Smith Apl 20 1715
Patience Bourne Widow Oct 25 1715§
Elizabeth Perry Widow died
Sarah Ellis Widow died Oct 25 1716
Mordecai Ellis Nov 1 1717¶
Martha Tupper Nov 15 1717
John Allen Dec 3, 1717
John Ellis Dec 12 1717
Remembrance Jennings wife of Saml June 21. 1718‖

[FROM ORIGINAL VOLUME, MARKED "BIRTHS MARRIAGES AND DEATHS EAR MARKS TOWN OF SANDWICH"]

[p. 5] [*worn*]n of Samuel prince [Born] may 1 [*worn*]
[*worn*]aughter of Saml prince Born January 8th: [*worn*]
[*worn*] the Son of Samuel prince Born Septemr 19th: [*worn*]
[*worn*] prince the Son of Samuel Prince Born Novemr 26th: [*worn*]
[*worn*]h prince the son of Samuel prince & Mercy prince his wife Born aprill: 1 : 1 [*worn*]

* 10 December, 1710, in 19th year, according to gravestone record.

† This should be 1713. See preceding note on John Chipman.—*Editor.*

‡ 1713, according to her gravestone.

§ 1716, according to her gravestone.

¶ On 29 March, 1718, Rebecca Ellis, widow of Mordicai Ellis of Sandwich, and John Ellis, his brother, appointed administrators.—*Editor.*

‖ A gravestone of Remember Jennings states that she died 23 January, 1717/18, aged about 28 years. It is near that of Samuel Jennings, Esqr. who died 13 May, 1764, in his 80th year.

[worn]rince son of Sam[ll] Prince and Mercy prince his wife Born 22 february 16[worn]

[worn]n Prince Son of the above named Samuel Prince & mercy prince born the last of November Anno Dom [worn]

[worn]y Prince the Daughter of the above named Samuel Prince & mercy [Pr]ince was born the 21th day of December Anno Dom 170[worn]

[worn] Prince the Daughter of the sd Sam[ll] and mercy Born the 13th day o[f Au]gust Anno Domini 170[worn]

[Be]niamin Prince son of the sd Sam[ll] and Mercy Prince was born the 23th day of [Fe]bruary Anno Domini ζ70[*] [worn]l† Ellis the son of Matthias Ellis and Mercy Ellis his wife [was Bor]n the 17th day of January 167⁹⁄₈₀

[Mat]thias Ellis the son of Matthias Ellis and Mercy Ellis his wife [was] Born the 5th of November 1681

[worn‡] Ellis the Son of Matthias Ellis and Mercy Ellis his wife [was] Born the 17th day of august 1683

[Mer]cy§ Ellis the Daughter of Matthias Ellis and of Mercy Ellis [his] wife was Born the 17th day of august 1685

[Ex]perience Ellis the Daughter of Matthias Ellis and of Me[rcy] his wife was born the 26th day of July 1687

[worn]chi‖ Ellis the son of Matthias Ellis and of Mercy Ellis [his wife] was Born the 8th day of october 1689

[Rem]ember Ellis the Daughter of Matthias Ellis and of Mercy [Ellis hi]s wife was Born the first day of December 1691

[worn]abel‖ Ellis the Daughter of Matthias Ellis and of Mercy [Ellis his] wife was Born the last day of Decem[r] 1693

[worn]uel** Ellis son of Matthias Ellis and Mercy Ellis his wife was bo[rn th]e 12[th] day of novem[r] Anno Dom 1699

[p. 6] [worn] 18 day of January [worn]

[worn] Smith the son of Thomas Smith an[worn]e was Born the 7[th] day of february ann[worn]

---

* The last figure is uncertain. It is either 9 or 5.

† "Joel" in the modern copy. The names Joel, Mehitable, Mary and Samuel, in that copy, are in a different hand and ink, and were inserted above lines which had been drawn by the copyist, to indicate that the baptismal names, on the original record, were either missing or illegible.

‡ "Mehitable" was added, in the modern copy, as in the preceding footnote; but the original record calls the child a "Son".

§ "Mary" was added in the modern copy, but the final "cy" indicates "Marcy" or "Mercy".

¶ Probably "Malachi"—so given in the modern copy.

‖ "Isabel" in modern copy.

** "Samuel" was added, in the modern copy, as in the earlier footnote.

[T]homas Smith the son of Thomas Smith and [worn] wife was Born the 25th of December anno 1691

Isaac Smith the son of Thomas Smith and Abigail his wife was Born the 11th day of february anno 169¾

[A]bigail Smith the Daughter of Thomas Smith and Abigale [his] wife was Born the 17th day of january in y[e] evening anno: 169⅝

[Re]beckah Smith the Daughter of Thomas Smith and Abigail Sm[ith] his wife was Born the 7th day of novem[r] Anno: 1697

Shubal Smith Son of Thomas Smith and Abigale Smith his wife was born the 20th of novem[r] 12 aClock at night: 1699

The above named Thomas Smith Died the 9th of December 1700 [a]nd buryed the next day

Nathan Bourne the son of Elisha Bourne and Patience Bou[rne] his wife was Born the last of august anno domini 1676

Abigail Bourne the Daughter of Elisha Bourne and patience Bou[rne] his wife was Born the 22th of July anno domini 1684

Elisha Bourne the son of Elisha Bourne and patience B[ourne his] wife was Born the 27th of July anno domini 1692

Elizabeth Bourne the Daughter of Elisha Bourne and p[atience] Bourne his wife was Borne the 26th of june 1679

Mary Bourne the Daughter of Elisha Bourne and pat[ience] Bourne his wife was Born the 4th of february 168½

Bershebe Bourne the Daughter of Elisha Bourne and p[atience] Bourne his wife was Born the 12th of December 1686

Hannah Bourne the Daughter of Elisha Bourne and p[atience] Bourne his wife was Born the 4th day of may 1689

[p. 8*] [worn]ere maryed the tenth of November anno domini 168[worn]

[E]lizabeth Dexter the Daughter of John Dexter and Mehitabel [his w]ife was Born the second of November anno domini 1683

Thomas Dexter the son of John Dexter and Mehitabel his wife was Born the 26th of august anno domini 1686

Abigail Dexter the Daughter of John Dexter and Mehitabe[l] his wife was Born the 26th of May anno domini 1689

John Dexter the son of s[d] John Dexter and of mehetabel his wife was born the 11th day of Septem[r] Anno 1692

Joshua Blackwell Son of Joshua Blackwell and mercy Blackwel his w[ife] was Born the 12th of january anno domini 1682

Mercy Blackwell the Daughter of Joshua Blackwel and Mercy Blackwel was Born the 5th day of october anno domini 1684

---

* In rebinding the original, the loose leaf containing pages 7 and 8 was reversed. This is shown by the references in the old index of this volume.

Michael Blackwell the son of Joshua Blackwell and Mercy Blackwell his wife was Born the: 23ᵈ: day of July anno domini 1687

Samuel Blackwell the son of Joshua Blackwell and mercy Blackwell his wife Born the 13ᵗʰ day of april anno domini 1689

Sarah Blackwell the daughter of Joshua Blackwell and Mercy [his] wife was Born the 11ᵗʰ of january Anno Domini 169⁰/₉₁

Jeane Blackwell the Daughter of Joshua Blackwell and mercy [his] wife was Born the 30ᵗʰ day of July anno Domini 1693

Abia Blackwell the Daughter of Joshua Blackwell and mercy Blackwel h[is] Wife was Born the 21ᵗʰ day of march anno domini 169⁵/₆

Hannah Blackwell Daughter of Joshua Blackwell and Mercy blackwell his wi[fe] was born the 21ᵗʰ day of June Anno Dom 1698

Deborah Blackwell Daughter of sᵈ Joshua Blackwell and Mercy Blackwell born the 8ᵗʰ day of July Anno Domini 1701

John Perry the Son of John Perry and Elizabeth Perry his wife w[as] Born the latter end of aprill anno Domini 1684

Johanah Perry the Daughter of John Perry and Elizabeth his wife was Born about the last of august anno Domini 1686

Timothy Perry the Son of John Perry and Elizabeth his wife was Born about the latter end of September anno domᵈ 1689

Experience Perry the daughter of John Perry and Eliza[beth] his wife was Born the first day of march anno domini 169½

Ezra Perry the son of John Perry and Elizabeth his wife w[as] Born the last of May anno Domini 1693

Arther Perry the son of the above named John Perry and Elizabeth Perry was Born the 27ᵗʰ day of november Anno Domini 1698

[worn]lijah Perry the son of the sᵈ John Perry and Elizabeth Perry was Born the second day of April Anno Domini 1701

[worn] Perry the son of the sᵈ John Perry and Elizabeth Perry was [worn] first day of December Anno Domini 1696

[worn] and Elizabeth Perry born last week in decemʳ Anno 1698

[worn] and Elizabeth Perry born April 2ᵈ Anno Domini 1701

[worn] Elizabeth* Pe[rry] [worn]

[p. 7†] [worn] of S[worn]

[worn] Cotton the Son of Rowland Coton & Elizabeth his wi[fe] was Born the 15ᵗʰ of july a little past one in yᵉ morning anno dom [worn]

Johanah Cotton the Daughter of Rowland Cotton and Eliz[abeth] Cotton his wife was Born the 16ᵗʰ: of august in yᵉ morning anno: 169[worn]

Elizabeth Cotton the Daughter of Rowland Cotton and Elizabeth Cot[ton] his wife was Born the 3ᵈ day of Novemʳ in the morning anno: 169[worn]

Sarah Cotton the Daughter of Rowland Cotton and Elizabeth Coto[n] his wife was Born the 26ᵗʰ day of Decemʳ in the evening Anno 169[worn]

Nathaniel Cotton the son of Rowland Cotton and Elizabeth Cotton [his] wife was Born the 13ᵗʰ day of June Anno dom 169[worn]

Abigail Cotton the Daughter of Rowland Cotton and Elizabeth Cott[on] his wife was Born the 9ᵗʰ day of July Anno Domⁿ: 169[worn]

Meriel Cotton the Daughter of Rowland Cotton and Elizabeth Cotton his wife was Born the 19ᵗʰ day of July Anno Dom 170[worn]

Rowland Cotton the Son of sᵈ Rowland and Elizabeth Cotton was born the 13ᵗʰ day of november Anno Dom 1701

Josiah Cotton the son of sᵈ Rowland and Elizabeth Cotton was born the [worn]ᵗʰ day of June Anno Domini 1703

Ruth Cotton the Daughter of the above named Rowland Cotton & Elizabeth Cotton Born the 22ᵈ of July Anno dom 1710

Ward Cotton the Son of the above named Rowland Cotton and Elizabeth Cotton Born the 8ᵗʰ day of Septemʳ Anno Dom 1711

Samuel Gibs Sen Died the 19ᵗʰ Day of November Anno 1732

Mercy Blackwel wife of Joshua Blackwell died March 29ᵗʰ 1734

Sarah Swift wife of Ephraim Swift died August 13ᵗʰ 1734

James Gifford Died October the 20ᵗʰ Anno Domini 1734

Jonathan Gifford Died February the 10ᵗʰ Anno Domini 1734/5

Silvanus Jones Son of Ralph Jones Died January the 14ᵗʰ Anno Domini 1734/5

Joanna Bodfish Daughter of John Bodfish Died January 20ᵗʰ Anno 1735/6

[B]ethiah Jones daughter of Ralph Jones died February 28ᵗʰ Anno 1735/6

Sarah Hoxie wife of Solomon Died March 18ᵗʰ Anno Domini 1735/6

Keziah Swift wife of William Swift Died March 23ᵈ Anno 1736

Mʳ William Newcomb Died April the 8ᵗʰ Anno Domini 1736

Abigail Toby wife of Jonathan Toby Juⁿ Died November the 30ᵗʰ 1736

---

* This is evidently the mother's name.

† In rebinding the original, the loose leaf containing pages 7 and 8 was reversed. This is shown by the references in the old index of this volume.

Deborah Toby wife of Cornelius Toby Died December the 2d 1736
John Landers sen Died April the 15th Anno Domini 1737
Sarah Stephens Died June the 9th Anno Domini 1737
John Bourn Son of Jonathan Bourn Died August 3d 1737
[Ge]rshom Pope Son of Seth Pope Ju Died August 8th 1737
[worn]ward Pope Son of Thomas Pope Died August 12th 1737
[worn]m[worn]s* Freeman Son of John Freeman Died August 24th 1737
[worn]hen Toby Son of Nathan Toby died September 7th 1737
[p. 9] [Ebe]nezer Wing the son of Batchelder Wing and Joanah Wing his wife [was] Borne the 20th day of November anno domini 1694
[worn]s† Wing the son of Batcheler Wing and Joana Wing his wife [was] Born the 13th day of October Anno Domini 1697
Joseph Holway the son of Joseph Holway and Ann Holway his wife was Born the sixth day of November anno domini 1694
Relyance Holway Daughter of the sd Joseph and Ann Holway was Borne the 16th day of February Anno Domini 169⁴/₅
Mary Holway the Daughter of the sd Joseph and Anne Holway was born the 18th day of June Anno Domini 1699
Anne Holway the Daughter of the sd Joseph and Anne Holway was borne the the first day of June Anno Domini 1702
Gidion Holway the son of the sd Joseph Holway and Ann Holway was born the 5th day of October Anno Dom 1704
Elkenah Smith the son of Benjamin Smith and Elizabeth Smith his wife was Born the 7th day of march anno : domini: 168⁵/₆
Ruth Smith the Daughter of Benjamin Smith and Elisabeth Smith his wife was Born the 17th day of December anno domini 1687
Hannah Smith the daughter of Benjamin Smith and Elisabeth Smith his wife was born the 10th day of march anno domini 168⁹/₉₀
Elisha Smith the son of Benjamin Smith and Elisabeth Smith his wife was Born the 26th of February anno domini 169½
Bathsheba Smith the daughter of Benjamin Smith and Elisabeth Smith his wife was born the 13th day of june anno: 1694
Elizabeth Smith Daughter of Benjamin Smith and Elizabeth Smith his wife was Born the the 4th day of august Ann Domini 1696
Pinninah Smith the Daughter of Benjamin Smith and Elizabeth Smith his wife was Born the 29th day of April Anno dom 1699

* Probably this name was either James or Thomas. One letter is illegible between m and s.
† "Thomas" in the modern copy.

Ichabod Smith the son of the above named Benjamin and Elizabeth Smith born the 27th day of June Anno domini 1702
Ebenezer Smith son of the above named Benjamin and Elizabeth Smith was born the 4th of September Anno Dom 1704
[p. 10] Mary Smith the Daughter of John Smith and Mehetab[el] Smith his wife was Born the 17th of January anno domini 1694
Martha Smith the Daughter of John Smith and Mehetabel Smith his wife was Born the 25th day of February anno: 169⁵/₆
John Smith the son of John Smith and Mehetabel Smith his wife was Born the 18th day of septem' Anno dom 1697
Susanna Smith the Daughter of sd John Smith and Mehetabel his wife was born the Eleventh day of march Anno Dom 169⁸/₉
Sarah Smith the Daughter of sd John Smith and Mehetabel Smith was Born the 23th day of February Anno Dom: 1700/701
Desire Smith Daughter of sd John and Mehetable Smith born the 5th day of July Anno Domini 1703
Thomas Smith son of the sd John and Mehetable Smith was born the 11th day of August Anno Domini 1705
Ichabod Smith Son of the above named John and Mehetable Smith was Borne the 16th day of February Anno Dom 1707/8
Jane Smith Daughter of the sd John and Mehetabel Smith was Born the 29th day of September Anno Domini 1710
Samuel Tupper the son of Israel Tupper and Elizabeth Tupper his wife was Born the 4th day of may anno 1692
Thankful Tupper the Daughter of Israel Tupper and Elisabeth Tupper his wife was Born the 9th day of october Anno dom 1696
Meribah Tupper Daughter of the sd Israel Tupper and Elizabeth Tupper was born the 28th day of august Anno Domini 1699
Elizabeth Tupper the Daughter of sd Israel Tupper and Elizabeth Tupper was born the 19th day of october Anno Domini 1701
Elizabeth Tupper the Wife of sd Israel Tupper died the 19th day of october Anno Domini 1701
Israel Tupper the son of Israel Tupper & of Elizabeth Tupper his wife was born the 18th day of June Anno Dom 1705
Meribah* Perry the Daughter of Benjamin Perry and Dinah Perry his wife was Born the 11th day of june anno: 1695
Remember Perry the Daughter of Benjamin Perry and Dinah Perry his wife was Born the 13th day of March Anno domini 169⁶/₇

* "Temperance" was first written; but it was crossed out, and "Meribah" interlined above, in the same hand and ink.

Seth Perry and Benjamin Perry sons of Benjamin Perry and Dinah Perry his wife was born the 19th day of march Anno Domini 1699/1700

Susannah* Perry daughter* of sd Benjamin and Dinah Perry was born the 27th* day of December Anno Domini 1701

Abner Perry son of sd Benjamin and Dinah Perry was born the 10th day of March Anno domini 1703/4

Josiah Perry Son of Benjamin Perry and Dinah his wife was Born the eighteenth Day of October Anno Domini 1709

Nathaniel Perry Son of Benjamin Perry & Dinah his wife was born the second Day of July Anno Domini 1713

Eliakim Perry Son of sd Benjamin Perry & Dinah his wife was born the eighth Day of May Anno Domini 1716

[p. 11] [J]oseph Benson and Charity Clap both of Rochester were maryed at Sandwich the 20th day of august 1695

Edward Dillingham and Abigail Nye Both of Sandwich were maryed ₱ Justice Skeffe the 26th day of Septemr anno: 1695

Richard Launders and Sarah Freeman were maryed ₱ justice Skeffe the 6th day of january Anno 1695/6

Joseph Foster now of Sandwich and Rachel Bassett of the Same Town was maryed ₱ mr Rowland Cotton Septemr 8th 1696

John Goodspeed of Barnestable and Remember Buck of Sandwich were maryed ₱ mr Stephen Skeffe the 16 day of February Anno domd 1696/7

Judith Bates and Job Gibs both of agawam were maryed ₱ Mr Rowland Cotton the 28th day of aprill Anno Domd 1697

Jirah Swift and Abigail Gibbs both of Sandwich were mary pr mr Stephen Skeffe in Sandwich novemr the 26th Anno: 1697

Garshom Tobye and Mehetabel Fish Both of Sandwich were maryed ₱ mr Rowland Cotton the 29th day of aprill Anno domd: 1697

John Mulford of Rhoad Island and peace Perry Late of Sandwich who were maryed ₱ mr Stephen Skeffe in Sandwich October the 20th Anno: 1697

Nathan Bourne and Mary Bassett Both of Sandwich were Maryed by Mr Rowland Cotton in Sandwich the 3d day of February Anno 1697:8

Ezra Bourne and Martha Prince both of Sandwich were maryed by mr Rowland Cotton in Sandwich the 27th day of December† at night anno domd 1698

Benjamin Gibbs and Ann Tupper both of Sandwich were maryed by mr Rowland Cotton in Sandwich the 4th* Anno Domini 1698/9

Benjamin Nye of Falmouth and Hannah Backhouse of Barnstable were maryed by Mr Justice Skeffe in Sandwich the 23th day of February Annd 1698/9

Ebenezer Wing and Elizabeth Backhouse both of Sandwich were maryed By Mr Justice Skeffe in Sandwich the 23 day of February Annod 1698/9

Isaac Benson and Mary Bumpas both of Rochester were maryed by Justice Skeff in Sandwich the 17th day of march Anno domd 1698/9

Joseph Dimick and Lydia Fuller both of Barnestable were Maryed by Justice Skeffe in Sandwich the 17th day of may 1699

The Maryage between Samuel Joy and Lydia Hanmor was solemniz[ed] Before Stephen Skeffe Esqr Justice of Peace in Sandwich the 31th of October 1699

The maryage between Samuel Gifford and Jane Loring both of Sandwich was solemn[ized] before Stephen Skeffe Esqr Justice of Peace in Sandwich the second day of november 1699

The maryage between Nathan Skeffe of Chilmark and Mercy Chipman of Barnstable was solemnized before Stephen Skeffe Esqr Justice of Peace In Sandwich the 13th day of December 1699

John Pope of Dartmouth and Elizabeth Bourne of Sandwich Joyned in covenant of maryage which was solemnized before mr Rowland Cotton January 2nd 1699 al 1700

Peter Newcomb late of Edgertown† and Mercy Smith of Sandwich Joyned in a covenant of maryage solemnised before Stephen Skeffe Esqr Justice of Peace in Sandwich the eleventh day of march Anno domini 1699 als 1700

Eldad‡ Tupper and Martha Wheaten Joyned in a maryage Covenant solemn[ised] before mr Rowland Cotton the 30th day of Decemr 1701

William Gifford and Elizabeth Wheaten entered into a maryage covenant solemnized before Stephen Skeffe Just Peace march 13th Anno 1701/2

[p. 12] Peleg Hauksie son of Joseph Hauksie and Sarah Hauksie his wife was Born the 23d day of aprill Anno domini 1695

Alce Launders the Daughter of John Launders and Rachel Launders his wife was Born aprill the 15th anno dom 1687

---

* "Samuel" and "son" and "Last" were first written; but they were crossed out and "Susannah", "daughter", and "27th" were interlined above, probably by the town clerk who recorded the sons Josiah, Nathaniel and Eliakim.

† "January" was crossed out and "December" written above, in the same hand and ink.

* The month was omitted.
† Edgartown, Mass.
‡ Incorrectly printed "Elead" in Genealogical Advertiser, 4: 102.

Richard Launders the Son of John Launders and Rachel Launders his Wife was Born the 6ᵗʰ day of march anno dom: 1688%

Deborah Launders the Daughter of John Launders and Rachel Launders his Wife was Born the 19ᵗʰ day of october anno dom 1691

John Launders the son of John Launders and Rachel Launders his wife was Born the 9ᵗʰ day of aprill anno dom 1694

Margerett Launders the Daughter of John Launders, and Rachel Launders his wife was born the 30ᵗʰ day of august Anno Domᵈ 1697

Ebenezer Launders the son of sᵈ John Launders and Rachel Launders was born the 13ᵗʰ day of march Anno Domᵈ 1699/700

Elizabeth Swift the Daughter of Ephraim Swift and Sarah Swift his wife was Born the 29ᵗʰ day of Decemʳ anno domᵈ 1679

Joanna Swift the Daughter of Ephraim Swift and Sarah Swift his wife was Born the the 7ᵗʰ day of July anno 1683

Samuel Swift Son of Ephraim Swift and Sarah Swift his wife was Born the 9ᵗʰ day of aprill anno domini 1686

Ephraim Swift the son of Ephraim Swift and Sarah Swift his wife was Born the 16ᵗʰ day of Decemʳ anno dom 1688

Sarah Swift the Daughter of Ephraim Swift and Sarah Swift his wife was Born the 12ᵗʰ day of aprill 1692

Hannah Swift the Daughter of Ephraim Swift and Sarah Swift his wife was Born the 19ᵗʰ day of may anno 1695

Moses Swift the son of the above named Ephraim and Sarah Swift was born the 15ᵗʰ day of Septemʳ Anno Dom 1699

[p. 13] Edmond Freeman the Son of Edmond Freeman and Sarah Freeman his wife was Born the 30ᵗʰ day of august anno domini 1683

Benjamin Freeman the Son of Edmond Freeman and Sarah Freeman his wife was Born the 6ᵗʰ day of january anno domini 1685:6:

Mary Freeman the Daughter of Edmond Freeman and Sarah Freeman his wife was Born the 13 day of march anno domᵈ 1687

John Freeman the Son of Edmond Freeman and Sarah Freeman his wife was Born the 12ᵗʰ day of June anno domᵈ 1693

Thomas Freeman the son of Edmond Freeman and Sarah Freeman his wife was Born the 26ᵗʰ day of march Anno Domini 1696

Joseph Freeman the son of Edmond Freeman and Sarah Freeman his wife was Born the 18ᵗʰ day of July Anno Domᵈ 1698

William Freeman the son of the above named Edmond Freeman & Sarah Freeman was born the 4ᵗʰ day of December Anno Dom 1700

Sarah Freeman son* of sᵈ Edmund and Sarah Freeman was born the 6ᵗʰ day of December Anno domini 1703

Isaac Freeman son of sᵈ Edmond and Sarah Freeman was born the 20ᵗʰ day of October Anno Domini 1706†

Christopher Gifford Son of Wᵐ Gifford Born in July anno: 1658

Deborah Gifford his wife was Born aprill the 2ᵈ anno 1665

Meribah Gifford Daughter of sᵈ Christopher and Deborah Gifford was Born the last day of october anno domd 1687

Addree Gifford their daughter Born Septem 17ᵗʰ anno 1689

Christopher Gifford their son Born may: 5ᵗʰ: 1687: and died march 29ᵗʰ 1689

Enos Gifford their Son was Born February yᵉ first anno 1693:4

Mary Gifford their Daughter was Born october yᵉ 6ᵗʰ anno: 1695

Christopher Gifford their son was born the 15 day of aprill Anno 1698

Deborah Gifford their Daughter was born the 2ᵈ day of February Anno: 1700

Mary Hoxe the Daughter of Gidion Hoxe and Grace Hoxe his wife was Born the: 1: day of February anno domd 1695/6

Content Hoxie the Daughter of Gidion Hoxie and Grace Hoxie his wife was Born the 13 day of July Anno 1697

Bathsheba Hoxie the Daughter of Gidion Hoxie and Grace Hoxie his wife was Born the 14 day of august Anno 1698

Elizabeth Hoxie Daughter of sᵈ Gidion and Grace Hoxie was born the 10ᵗʰ day of march Anno dom 1699/700

Joseph Hoxie Son of Sᵈ Gidion and Grace Hoxie was born the first of march Anno domini 1701/2

Simeon Hoxie Son of sᵈ Gidion Hoxie and Grace hoxie his wife was born the 13ᵗʰ of march Anno 1703/4

Anne Hoxie the Daughter of sᵈ Gidion & Grace Hoxie was born the Last day of march Anno Dom 1706

Giddion Hoxie the son of the sᵈ Gidion and Grace Hoxie born the fifth day of July Anno Domini 1707

Kezia Hoxie Daughter of sᵈ Gideon and Grace Hoxie Born yᵉ 13ᵗʰ of may 1710

Lodowick Hoxie son of sᵈ Gideon and Grace Hoxie Born yᵉ 29ᵗʰ of march 1712

Grace Hoxie Daughter of sᵈ Gideon & Grace Hoxie Born yᵉ 28ᵗʰ of April 1714

[*Desier Hoxie Daughter of sᵈ Gidion & Grace Hoxie born 5 november anno‡]

(To be continued)

* So recorded.

† This is the last record printed in the Genealogical Advertiser.

‡ This entry printed in italics was crossed out.

SANDWICH, MASS., VITAL RECORDS

(Continued from p. 34)

[p. 14] Hannah the Daughter of Mehetabel Jones and Reputed Daughter of Gidion Gifford was Born the 12th day of aprill anno domini: 1696

Benjamin Norris the son of Olliver Norris and Margery Norris his wife was Born the 11 day of march Anno 1695/6

Samuel Norris the son of olliver Norris and Margery Norris his wife was Born the 20th day of march Anno dom 1698/9

John Norris son of the s^d Olliver Norris and Margery his wife was born the second of July Anno Don 1710

Samuel Jennings the Son of John Jennings & Ruhamah his wife was Born the 19th Day of February Anno Dom: 1684/5

Caleb Allen son of Richard Allen and Hannah Allen his wife was Born the 29th day of aprill Anno Dom 1696

Daniel Allen the son of Richard Allen and Hannah Allen his wife was born the 12th day of septem^r Anno Domini 1699

Elizabeth Allen Daughter of the s^d Richard Allen and Hannah Allen was born the 21th day of septem^r Anno Domini 1702

Dorothy Allen Daughter of the s^d Richard and Hanah Allen was born the 4th day of July Anno Domini 1706

James Allen Son of the above named Richard and Hannah Allen was born the 9th day of august Anno Domini 1712

Paul Jones Son of Timothy Jones & Elizabeth his wife was Born the 15th Day of April Anno Domini 1721

Timothy Jones the Son of Timothy Jones & Elizabeth his wife was Born the 16th Day of May Anno Domini 1726

[p. 15] Jemimah Tobye Daughter of Nathan Tobye and Sarah Tobye his wife was Born the last day of March Anno Domini 1697

Susannah Toby Daughter of Nathan Toby and Sarah Toby his wife was Born the 11th day of March Anno dom: 1698/9

Nathan Toby son of the s^d Nathan Toby and Sarah Toby was Born the 28th day of September Anno dom 1701

Wm Toby son of the s^d Nathan and Sarah Toby was born the third day of may Anno Domini 1706

Sarah Toby Daughter of the s^d Nathan and Sarah Toby was Born the 30th day of August Anno Domini 1708

Hannah Dillingham Daughter of Edward Dillingham and Abigail Dillingham his wife was Born the 12th day of July Anno Dom: 1696

Abigail Dillingham Daughter of the s^d Edward Dillingham and Abigail Dillingham was Born the 26th day of February Anno Dom 1697/8

Simion Dillingham son of s^d Edward and Abigail Dillingham was born the 24th day of September Anno Dom 1700

Edward Dillingham son of the s^d Edward and Abigail Dillingham was Born the 12th day of march Anno Dom 1703/4

Mary Dillingham Daughter of the s^d Edward and Abigail Dillingham was Born the 22th day of October Anno Dom 1705

Experience Dillingham Daughter of the s^d Edward and Abigail Dillingham was born the 9th day of march Anno Dom 1707/8

Mary Dillingham Daughter of s^d Edward & Abigail Dillingham Born 22th October Anno: 1705*

Experience Dillingham Daughter of s^d Edward & Abigail Dillingham Born march 9th 1707/8*

John Dillingham son of s^d Edward & Abigail Dillingham was Born 14 novem^r 1710

Debora Dillingham daughter of s^d Edward & Abigail Dillingham born June 7th 1716

Joana Tobye Daughter of Samuel Tobye and Abia Tobye his wife was Born the 22th day of may Anno Dom: 1697

Cornelious Toby the son of Samuel Toby and Abia Toby his wife was born the 12th day of September Anno Dom 1699

Tabitha Toby Daughter of the s^d Samuel Toby and Abia Toby was born the 9th day of November Anno domini 1701

Zacheus Toby son of the above named Samuel Toby and abia Toby was Born the 14th day of January Anno 1703/4

Ruth Toby Daughter of the s^d Samuel and Abia Toby was born the 8th Day of September Anno Domini 1706

Jonathan Toby the Son of the s^d Samuel & Abia Toby was born the 13th day of may Anno Dom 1709

Eliakim Toby Son of the s^d Sam^ll and Abia Toby born the 19th day of october Anno dom 1711

Thomas Toby son of s^d Samuel and Abia Toby born 14th of August Anno 1720

Samuel Toby the Son of Samuel Toby & Abia his wife was Born the 8th Day of May Anno Domini 1715

[p. 16] Stephen Skeffe the son of James Skeffe and Mary Skeffe his wife was Born the 14th day of Aprill Anno Dom 1641

*These two duplicate entries are in the same hand and ink as the rest of the family.

Abigail Skeffe the Daughter of Stephen Skeffe and Ledia Skeffe his wife was Born the second day of may Anno Dom 1666

Melatiah Bourne and Desier Chipman both of Sandwich wer maryed by Stephen Skeffe Esq' Just peace the 23ᵈ day of February Anno 1692/3

Silvenus Bourne the son of Melatiah Bourne and Desier Bourne his wife was Born the 10ᵗʰ day of aprill Anno Dom 1694

Richard Bourne the son of Melatiah Bourne and Desier Bourne his wife was Born the 13ᵗʰ day of august Anno Dom 1695

Samuel Bourne and Sarah Bourne Son and Daughter of Melatiah Bourne and Desier Bourne his wife was Born the 7ᵗʰ day of February and died the 17ᵗʰ day of the same month Anno Domini 1696/7

John Bourne the son of Melatiah Bourne and Desire bourne his wife was borne the 10ᵗʰ day of march Anno Dom 1697/8

Shearjashub Bourne the son of Melatiah Bourne and Desire Bourne his wife was Borne the 21ᵗʰ day of December Anno dom 1699

Sylas Bourne the son of sᵈ Melatiah and Desire Bourne was born the tenth day of December Anno Domini 1701

Bethsheba Bourne the Daughter of the sᵈ Meletiah and Desire Bourne Borne the 11ᵗʰ day of november Anno Dom 1703

The above named Desire bourne died march 28ᵗʰ Anno 1705

Remember Laurance the daughter of Experience Laurance was Born the 26ᵗʰ Day of November Anno Domini 1714

Sarah Barber daughter of John Barber & Meribah his wife was Born the 4ᵗʰ Day of June Anno Domini 1732

Patience Barber daughter of John Barber & Meribah his wife was Born the 16ᵗʰ Day of April Anno Domini 1736

Elizabeth Barber daughter of John Barber & Meribah his wife was Born the 19ᵗʰ Day of April Anno Domini 1738

John Barber Son of John Barber & Meribah his wife was Born the 9ᵗʰ Day of March Anno Domini 1739/40

[p. 17] James Chipman the son of John Chipman and Mary Chipman his wife was Born the 18ᵗʰ day of Decemʳ Anno Dom: 1694

John Chipman the son of John Chipman and Mary Chipman his Wife was Born the 18ᵗʰ day of Septemʳ Anno Dom 1697

Mary Chipman and Bethyah Chipman Daughters of John Chipman and Mary Chipman his wife was born the 11ᵗʰ day of Decemʳ Anno 1699

Perez Chipman the son of sᵈ John and Mary Chipman was Born the 28ᵗʰ day of September Anno Domini 1702

Deborah Chipman the Daughter of the sᵈ John and mary Chipman was Born the 6ᵗʰ day of December Anno Domini 1704

Stephen Chipman and Lydia Chipman the Son & Daughter of the above named John and Mary Chipman Born yᵉ 9ᵗʰ of June Anno dom 1708

Ebenezer Chipman son of the sᵈ John and Mary Chipman Born the 13ᵗʰ day of November Anno Domini 1709

Handley Chipman son of the sᵈ John Chipman and Elizabeth Chipman his now wife was Born the Last Day of August Early in yᵉ morning Anno Dom 1717

Rebecca Chipman Daughter of the sᵈ John and Elizabeth Chipman was Born the 10ᵗʰ day of Novemʳ Anno Domini 1719

Mary Presbury the Daughter of Stephen Presbury and Deborah Presbury his wife was Born the 28ᵗʰ day of August Anno Dom 1694

Keturah Presbury the Daughter of Stephen Presbury & Deborah Presbury his wife was Born the 28ᵗʰ day of aprill Anno Dom 1696

Abigail Pope The Daughter of Seth Pope & Hannah Pope his Wife was Born yᵉ 2ⁿᵈ Day of Augst Ano Domini 1710

Bathsheba Pope The Daughter of Seth Pope & Hannah Pope his Wife was Born The 2ⁿᵈ Day of December Anno Domini 1713

John Pope yᵉ son of Seth Pope & Hannah Pope his Wife was Born The 25ᵗʰ Day of November Anno Domini 1716*

Hannah Pope yᵉ Daughter of Seth & Hannah Pope his Wife was born The 25ᵗʰ Day of April Anno Domini 1720

Patience Pope the Daughter of Seth Pope & Hannah his wife was Born the 29ᵗʰ Day of November Anno Domini 1725

[p. 18] Deborah Tobye the Daughter of Jonathan Toby and Remember Tobye his wife was Born the 30ᵗʰ day of Decemʳ Anno Dom 1694

Elisabeth Tobye Daughter of Jonathan Tobye and Remember Tobye his wife was Born the 15ᵗʰ day of Septemʳ Anno dom 1697

Maria Toby the Daughter of the abovenamed Jonathan toby and Remember Toby Was born the 12ᵗʰ day of Jenuary Anno Domini 1700/1

Remember Toby the Daughter of the sᵈ Jonathan and Remember toby was born the 16ᵗʰ day of August Annodom 1703

Samuel Toby the son of the sᵈ Jonathan and Remember† Toby was born the eleventh day of September Anno Domini 1707

---

* "1717" appears to have been altered to "1716".
† "Deborah" was first written, but was crossed out and "Remember" was interlined in the same hand and ink.— *Editor.*

Mercy Toby the Daughter of the s^d Jonathan and Remember Toby was Born the sixth day of October Anno Domini 1710

Abigail Toby Daughter of the above named Jonathan and Remember Toby Born the 28th day of may Anno Dom 1713

Mary Toby Daughter of the S^d Jonathan & Remember Toby born the Second day of February Anno Domini 1715

Jonathan Toby the Son of S^d Jonathan & Remember Toby was born the sixth day of August Anno Domini 1718

Nathaniel Toby ye Son of Jonathan Toby & Remember Toby was born the Last Day of June Anno Domini 1721

Mary Foster the Daughter of Joseph Foster and Rachell Foster his wife was Born the first day of September Anno 1697

Joseph Foster the son of Joseph Foster and Rachel Foster his wife was Born the 19th day of September Anno Dom 1698

Benjamin Foster the son of s^d Joseph & Rachel Foster was Born the 16th day of november Anno Dom 1699

William Foster the son of the abovenamed Joseph Foster and Rachel Foster was Born the last day of march Anno Dom 1702

Thankfull Foster the Daughter of the s^d Joseph and Rachell Foster was born the third day of november at night Anno Dom 1703

John Foster the son of the s^d Joseph and Rachel Foster was Born the 12th day of Aprill Anno domini 1705

Nathan Foster the son of Joseph and Rachell Foster was born the third day of January Anno Domini 1707/8

Abigail Foster the Daughter of s^d Joseph and Rachel Foster born the 27th day of February Anno Dom 1708/9

Deborah Foster the Daughter of s^d Joseph and Rachel Foster was born the 18th day of January Anno Domini 1710/11

Ebenezer Foster Son of s^d Joseph & Rachel Foster Born the 10th may 1713

Solomon Foster Son of s^d Joseph & Rachel Foster born 4th day of Septem^r 1714

Rachel Foster Daughter of s^d Joseph & Rachel Foster born ye 30th day of October Anno: 1716

Hannah Foster Daughter of s^d Joseph & Rachel Foster born ye 17th day of June Anno dom 1718

Sarah Foster Daughter of s^d Joseph & Rachel Born the 23^d Day of September 1721

[p. 19] Huldah Barlow the daughter of Zebulun Barlow & Elizabeth his wife was Born April 3^d Anno Domini 1730

Hannah Barlow daughter of Zebulun Barlow & Elizabeth his wife was Born the 3^d Day of August Anno Dom: 1733

Mary Barlow Daughter of Zebulun Barlow & Elizabeth his wife was Born the 24th day of March Anno Domini 1735/6

Peter Barlow Son of Zebulun Barlow & Elizabeth his wife was Born the 25th Day of July Anno Domini 1738

Elizabeth Nye and Hannah Nye the Daughter of Caleb Nye and Elizabeth Nye his wife were born the 2^d day of october anno: 1697

Sarah Cleavs the Daughter of William Cleavs and Hannah Cleavs his wife was borne the 18th day of november Anno Dom 1704

Mercy Smith the daughter of Daniel Smith & Abigail his wife was Born the 21st Day of June Anno Domini 1731

Elizabeth Smith the Daughter of Elkenah Smith and of Elizabeth Smith his wife was Born the 15th day of October Anno Dom 1708

Lydia Smith daughter of Elkanah Smith & Mary his wife was Born the 22^d day of February Anno Domini 1718/9

Elisha Smith Son of Elkanah Smith & Mary his wife was Born the first day of February Anno Domini 1720/1

Hannah Smith Daughter of Elkanah Smith & Mary his wife was Born the 23^d Day of May Anno Domini 1723

[p. 20] Nathan Launders the son of Thomas Launders and Deborah Launde[rs] his wife was Born the 20th day of August Anno Dom 1687

Joseph Launders the son of s^d Thomas and Deborah Launders was Born the 14th day of February Anno Dom 1688: or [89]

Benjamin Launders their son Born the 13th of october Anno dom: 1692

Anna Launders their Daughter Born the first day of may Anno 1695

Ebenezer Launders the son of s^d Thomas Launders and Deborah Launders was born the 17th day of September Anno dom 1699

Abigail Handy Daughter of Ebenezer Handy & Rebecca his wife was born the 18th Day of Sepr Anno Domini 1757

Benjamin Handy Son of Eben^r Handy & Rebecca his wife was born the 10th of May A Domini 1759

Elizabeth Handy Daughter of Ebenezer Handy & Rebecca his wife was born ye 18th Day of Sepr A Domini 1764

David Handy Son of Ebenezer Handy & Rebecca his wife was born the 18th of July A Domini 1766

Israel Handy Son of Ebenezer Handy & Rebecca his wife was born the last Day of August A Domini 1768

Nathan Handy Son of Eben^r Handy & Rebecca his wife was born the 5th Day of August A Domini 1770

Ebenezer Handy Son of Ebenezer & Rebecca his wife was born the 13th of June A Domini 1772

Mary Toby the Daughter of John Toby and Jane Toby his Wife was born In the moneth of march Anodom 1684-5

John Toby son of s^d John and Jane Toby born February Anno dom: 1686:7

Martha Toby Daughter of s^d John Toby and Jane Toby born jan^r 1688

Thomas Toby son of s^d John Toby and Jane Toby born in august 1690

Ebenezer Toby son of s^d John Toby and Jane Toby born in September 1692

Reliance Toby Daughter of s^d John Toby and Jane Toby born in march 1695

Eliezer Toby son of s^d John Toby and Jane Toby born in 2^d janu^y 1699/700

Deborah Fish Daughter of Ebenezer Fish & abigail his wife was born the 29th Day of July Anno Domini 1726

Patience Fish Daughter of Ebenezer Fish & Abigail his wife was Born the 28 day of September Anno 1727

Mary Hicks the daughter of Thomas Hicks & Abigail his wife was Born the 4th Day of May Anno Domini 1732

Remember Hicks daughter of Thomas Hicks & Abigail his wife was Born the 11th Day of September Anno Domini 1733

Rebekah Hicks the daughter of Thomas Hicks & Abigail his wife was Born the 27th Day of February Anno Domini 1736/7

Mehetable Fish the Daughter of Ebenezar Fish & Abigail his wife was Born June ye 2^d Day Anno Domini 1729

[p. 21] Maria Bourne the Daughter of Nathan Bourne and mary Bourne his Wife was Born the 24th day of May Anno: 1699

Jonathan Bourne the son of the above named Nathan and Mary Bourne born the 21th day of January Anno Domini 1702/3

Elizabeth Bourne the Daughter of the above named Nathan Bourne was born the Last day of June Anno domini 1704

John Bourne son of the above named Nathan Bourne and Mary Bourne was Born the Last day of July Anno Domini 1706

Nathan Bourne son of Nathan and Mary Bourne was born the 16th of January Anno domini 1709/10

Elisha Bourne the son of the above named Nathan Bourne and Mary Bourne was Born the 27th day of July Anno dom 1711

Mary Bourne Daughter of s^d Nathan and Mary Bourne was Born the twelfth day of august Anno domini 1714

Thomas Bourne Son of s^d Nathan and Mary Bourne born the 16th day of May Anno Domini 1716

Martha Gibbs the Daughter of Benjamin Gibbs and Ann Gibbs his wife was Born the Last day of october Anno Domini 1699

Silvanus Gibbs Son of s^d Benjamin and Ann Gibbs born the 20th of April Anno Domini 1702

Abigail Gibbs Daughter of the above named Benjamin & Anne Gibbs was Born the 8th day of September Anno Domini 1705

Jedidah Gibbs Daughter of the above named Benjamin & Anne Gibbs was Born the 30th of October Anno Domini 1707

Anne Gibbs Daughter of the above named Benjamin & Anne Gibbs was Born the 21th day of April Anno Domini 1710

Elizabeth Gibbs Daughter of s^d Benjamin and Anne Gibbs born the tenth day of April Anno Dom 1712

Jane Gibbs Daughter of s^d Benjamin & Anne Gibbs born the 7th day of Decem^r 1714

Benjamin Gibbs Son of s^d Benjamin And Anne Gibbs Born the 1st of march 1716/17

Reliance Gibbs Daughter of s^d Benjamin & Anne Gibbs Born y^e 11th day of July 1719

Job Gibbs Son of s^d Benjamin & Anne Gibs Born March 22^d 1723/4

(To be continued)

THE MAYFLOWER DESCENDANT

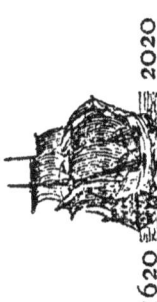

1620 2020

A QUARTERLY MAGAZINE OF
PILGRIM GENEALOGY AND HISTORY

VOLUME XXX

1932

PUBLISHED BY THE
MASSACHUSETTS SOCIETY OF
MAYFLOWER DESCENDANTS
BOSTON

SANDWICH, MASS., VITAL RECORDS

Transcribed by George Ernest Bowman

(*Continued from Vol. XXIX, p. 75*)

[p. 22] Sarah Bourne the Daugter of Ezra Bourne and Martha Bourne his wife was born the 7th day of January Anno Domini 1699/1700

The above named Sarah Bourne died the 11th & buried ye 12 of July 1700

Joseph Bourne the son of the above named Ezra Bourne and Martha Bourne was Borne the 10th day of may Anno Dom 1701

Lemuel Fish the Son of Bartholomey Fish & Hannah Fish was born the 10th of August Anno Domini 1727.

Ebenezer Handy the Son of Benjamin Handy & Elizabeth his wife was born ye 25th of October 1732 entred Apr 4th 1768 by Desire of Said Ebenr

Hanibal Handy the son of Richard Handy and Hanah Handy his wife was born the last week in October Anno Don 1685

Isaac Handy the son of Richard Handy and Hanah Handy his wife was born the 20th day of may Anno Domini 1688

[p. 23] Marriages from 1695

The Marriage Between Thomas Blossom and Feere Robinson solemnised before Shearjashub Bourne Esqr Decenr ye 3d Anno: 1695

The marriage between Saml Parker and Hannah Bumpas solemnized before Shearjashub Bourne Esqr the 14th day of Decemr Anno 1695

The Marriage between James Parsivel and Abigale Robinson solemnized before Shearjashub Bourne Esqr the the 18th of february Anno 1695-6

The Marriage between John Gifford and Desire Sprague solemnised before Shearjashub Bourne Esqr the 24th of novemr Anno 1696

The Marriage Betweene William Cleaves and Hannah Lovel solemnised before Shearjashub Bourne Esqr the 28th day of January Anno 1699/700

The Marriage between Richard Handy and Patience Randal solemnized Before Shearjashub Bourne Esqr the 21th day of february 1699/700

the Marriage between John Lovel and Mary Worthylake solemnized Before Shearjashub Bourne Esqr the the 6th day of March Anno 1699/700

The Marriage between Isaac Jenning and Rose Goodspeed solemnized before Shearjashub Bourne Esqr the 10th day of July Anno 1700

The Marriage between Joseph Laurance of Sandwich and Hannah Chaddack of falmouth solemnized before Shearjashub Bourne Esqr Justice of Peace the 25th day of January 1699/700

The Marriage betweene Benjamin Curtiss of Plimouth and Mary Bessie ye Daughter of Nehemiah Bessie of Sandwich solemnized before Stephen Skeefe Esqr Decemr 23: 1700

The marriage between Jashub Wing and Ann hoxie Both of Sandwich solemnized before Stephen Skeffe Esqr. Just of peace the 11th of february Anno dom: 1700/1

The narriage Between John Allen and Alce Worthilake Solemnized Before Stephen Skeffe Esqr Just peace the [*] day of april Anodom 1701

The Marriage Between Eldad Tupper and Martha Wheaten both of Sandwich Solemnized before Mr Rowland Cotton Minester the 30th day of Decemr Anno dom 1701

The marriage between Hezekiah Hoxie and Dinah Butler both of Sandwich Solemnized before Stephen Skeffe Esqr Just peace april 23: Anno Dom: 1702

The Marriage between Joshua Laurance and Elizabeth Swift both then of Sandwich Solemnized before Stephen Skeffe Esqr just of peace the 16 day of Decembr Anno dom 1702

*The day of the month was omitted.

The marriage between Seth Fish and Mary Turner both of Sandwich Solemnized Before M[r] Rowland Cotton minester the 30th of December Anno Domini 1702

The marriage between Anthony Savory and Margerett Price both of Rochester Solemnized before Stephen Skeffe Esq[r] Justice of Peace in Sandwich the second day of february Anno Domini 1702/3

The Marriage between James Bunpass and Mary Savory both of Rochester solemnized Before Stephen Skeffe Esq[r] Jus[t] of peace in Sandwich february 17th anno Dom 1702/3

Abial Fuller and Anness Parker one of Plimouth the other late Resident att Sandwich Married before Stephen Skeffe Esq[r] Jus[t] of peace in Sandwich february 19th Anno dom 1702/3

The marriage Between John Parsival of Barnestable and Mary Bourne of Sandwich Solemnized Before M[r] Rowland Cotton Minester June the 3[d] Anno 1703

The marriage between Abraham ashley and Susanna White both of Rochester Solemnized before Stephen Skeffe Esq[r] Just peace Septem[r] 9 1703

The marriage between Samuel Moxie* and Hannah Perry both of Sandwich solemnized before m[r] Rowland Cotton minester att Sandwich the 13th day of January Anno dom 1703/4

Jabez Hiller of Rochester and Elizabeth Butler of Sandwich were married before Stephen Skeffe Esq[r] att Sandwich february 21 Anno dom 1703/4

The marriage between Solomon Hoxie and Elizabeth Wing and the mariage between Benjamin Swift and Hannah Wing all of Sandwich solennized before Stephen Skeffe Esq[r] just of peace att Sandwich february 24th Anno Dom 1703/4

[p. 24] Stephen Wing the Son of Ebenezer Wing and Elizabeth Wing his wife was born the second day of august Anno Dom 1700

Rebecca Wing the Daughter of the s[d] Ebenezer and Elizabeth wing Born the 29th day of May Anno Domini 1702

Samuel Wing Son of the above named Ebenezer and Elizabeth Wing was born the 24th day of march Anno dom 1703/4

Joshua Wing son of the s[d] Ebenezer Wing & Elizabeth Wing born the 9th Day of September Anno Domini 1706

Sarah Wing the Dauhter of s[d] Ebenezer and Elizabeth Wing was born the fourth day of March Anno Dom 1708/9

Benjamin Laurance the son of Joseph Laurance and Hannah Laurance his wife was born the 12th day of august Anno Domini 1700

* So recorded.

Samuel Laurance son of s[d] Joseph Laurance and Hannah Laurance his wife was born the 8th day of october Anno domini 1703

Joseph Laurance son of s[d] Joseph and Hannah Laurance was born the 29th day of march Anno Domini 1705

Thomas Laurance son of s[d] Joseph and Hannah Laurance born the 20th day of february Anno Dom 1706/7

Jemimah Laurance the Daughter of s[d] Joseph and Hannah Laurance was born the 9th day of february Anno Dom 1708/9*

Robert Laurance the Son of Joseph Laurance & Hannah his wife was Born the 22[d] Day of January Anno Domini 1710/11

Benjamin Laurance the Son of Joseph Laurance & Hannah his wife was Born the 3[d] Day of June Anno Domini 1714

[p. 25] Robert Jones the Son of Adam Jones and of Mary Jones his wife was Born the 28th day of august Anno Domini 1700

Benjamin Smith the Son of Benjamin Smith of Dartmouth & Hannah his wife was Born at Sandwich the 6th Day of August Anno 1729

Samuel Hilliard the Son of Samuel Hilliard & Bathsheba his wife was Born the 20th Day of February Anno Dom 1729/30.

Gideon Hilliard Son of Samuel Hilliard & Bathsheba his wife was Born the 29th Day of August Anno Domini 1735

Elizabeth Perry the Daughter of Samuel Perry and Easter Perry his wife was Born the 17th day of July Anno Domini 1690

Deborah Perry the Daughter of the s[d] Samuel and Easter Perry was Born the 16th day of June Anno Domini 1692

Thomas Perry the son of the S[d] Samuel and Easter Perry was Born februar[y] y[e] 24th Anno Domini 1693/4

Sarah Perry the Daughter of the S[d] Samuel and Easter Perry was born the 8th day of June Anno Domini 1696

Nathan Perry the son of the s[d] Samuel and Easter Perry was born the 12th day of January Anno Domini 1700/1

Mary Perry Daughter of the s[d] Samuel and Esther Perry was born the 10th of December Anno Dom 1702

Ebenezer Perry the son of s[d] Samuel and Esther Perry born the fifth day of March Anno Domini 1705/6

Seth Perry the Son of S[d] Samuel and Esther Perry was born the 24th day of february Anno Dom 1707/8

Mercy Perry Daughter of the above named Sam[ll] and Esther Perry was Born the Eighth day of December Anno Dom 1710

[p. 26] Joseph Bourne the Son of Ezra Bourne and Martha Bourn his wife was born the 10th day of May Anno Domini 1701

Benjamin Howland Son of Justus Howland & Abigail his wife was Born the 18th Day of November Anno Domini 1737

* So recorded.

Elizabeth Howland Daughter of Justus Howland & Abigail his wife was Born the 13th Day of December Anno Domini 1739
Lemuel Howland Son of Justus Howland & Abigail his wife was Born the 28th Day of October Anno Domini 1742
Nathaniel Howland Son of Justus Howland & Abigail his wife was Born the 6th Day of January Anno Domini 1744/5
Ellis Howland the Son of Justus Howland & Abigail his wife was Born the 25th Day of May Anno Domini 1747
Benjamin Howland Son of Lemuel Howland & Abigail his wife was born on January ye 3d 1767
Nathaniel Howland Son of Lemuel Howland & Abigail his wife was born on June ye 17th 1769
Elisabeth Howland Daughter of Lemuel Howland & Abigail his wife was born on October ye 4th 1772
Micah Gibbs the son of Job Gibbs and Judeth his wife was born the 27th day of Novemr Anno dom 1701
Lydia Gibbs the Daughter of sd Job Gibbs & judith his wife was born the 15th day of may Anno Domini 1704
Solomon Perry the Son of Elisha Perry & Anna his wife was Born the 4th Day of April Anno Domini 1726.
Ruth Perry the daughter of Elisha Perry & Anna his wife was Born the 29th Day of August Anno Domini 1728
Elisha Perry the Son of Elisha Perry & Anna his wife was Born the 25th Day of June Anno Domini 1731
John Perry the Son of Elisha Perry & Anna his wife was Born the 22d Day of November Anno Domini 1733
James Perry the Son of Elisha Perry & Anna his wife was Born the 24th Day of December Anno Domini 1735
Maria Perry the Daughter of Elisha Perry & Anna his wife was Born the 6th Day of April Anno Domini 1738
[p. 27] Josiah Gifford the son of Samuel Gifford and Jean Gifford his wife was born the 12th day of february Anno Dom 1700/1
[Hannah Wing daughter of Zachery Wing & Content his wife was Born the 20th Day of January Anno Domini 1732/3*]
Mary Swift the Daughter of Samuel Swift and of Mary Swift his wife was born the 18th day of march Anno Domini 1690/91
Seth Swift the son of the sd Samuel and Mary Swift born the 17th day of march Anno Domini 1692/3
Jemimah Swift the Daughter of the sd Samuel and Mary Swift born the 12th day of October Anno Domini 1695
Ebenezer Swift the Son of the sd Samuel and Mary Swift born the 7th day of June Anno Domini 1698

* This entry has been crossed out. It was repeated on original page 45, with four more children of "Zacheus & Content".

Ketura Swift the Daughter of the sd Samuel and Mary Swift born the 30th day of april Anno Domini 1700
Zakeas Swift the son of sd Samuel and Mary Swift born the first day of february Anno Domini 1701/2
Temperance Swift Daughter of sd Samuel and Mary Swift was born the 7th day of may Anno Domini 1704
Ephraim swift son of the sd Samuel and Mary Swift was born the 17th day of June 1706
Elizabeth Swift the Daughter of the sd Samuel and Mary Swift was born the 7th day of Aprill anno Domini 1708
[p. 28] Abigail Wing the Daughter of Jashub Wing and of Anne Wing his wife, was Born the 7th day of november Anno Domini 1702
Daniel Wing son of the sd Jashub an Anne Wing was born the 30th day of march Anno Dom 1704
Joseph Wing son of the sd Jashub and Anne Wing was born the third day of may Anno dom 1706
Experience Wing the Daughter of the above named Jashub and Anne Wing was Born the 8th day of march Anno Donmini 1707/8
Barnabas Wing the Son of the sd Jashub and Anne Wing was Born the 27th of June Anno Domini 1710
Mary Wing Daughter of sd Jashub and Anne Wing born the 16th day of June Anno Domini 1716
Samll Wing Son of Sd Jashub & Anne Wing was Born the third day of June Anno Domini 1719
Mary Bessie the Daughter of Nehemiah Bessie and of Mary Bessie his wife was born in the moneth of november Anno Domini 1680
Nehemiah Bessie the son of sd nehemiah and Mary Bessie born in the moneth of July Anno Domini 168[*]
Hannah Bessie the Daughter of sd Nehemiah and Mary Bessie born in the moneth of January Anno Domini 1684/5
Robert Bessie the son of sd Nehemiah and Mary Bessie born the last day of april Anno Domini 1690
Joshua Bessie son of sd Nehemiah and Mary Bessie born the 14th day of february Anno Domini 1692/3
David Bessie the son of sd nehemiah and Mary Bessie born the 23d day of December Anno Domini 1693
Benjamin Bessie the son of sd Nehemiah and Mary Bessie was born the the 20th day of Septenber Anno domini 1695
Ebenezer Bessie son of sd Nehemiah Bessie and of sd Mary Bessie was Borne the 30th day of april Anno Domini 1692

* "1684/5" was first entered, but was altered to "1682/3"

[p. 29] Ezra Perry the son of Ezra Perry and of Rebecca Perry his wife was born the second day of february Anno Domini 1679

Hannah Perry the Daughter of s^d Ezra and Rebecca Perry Born the 10th day of September Anno Domini 1681

Edmond Perry the son of s^d Ezra and Rebecca Perry born the 20th day of october Anno Domini 1683

Freelove Perry the Daughter of s^d Ezra and Rebecca Perry was born the 28th day of november Anno Domini 1685

Samuel Perry the son of s^d Ezra and Rebecca Perry born the 20th day of march Anno Domini 1688

Rebecca Perry the Daughter of s^d Ezra and Rebecca Perry was bor the 2^d day of october Anno Domini 1689

Patience Perry the Daughter of s^d Ezra and Rebecca Perry was born the 2^d day of february Anno Domini 1691/2

Seth Burge the Son of Benjamin Burge & Mercy his wife was Born the 22d Day of May Anno Domini 1736

Thankfull Hiller the Daughter of Samuel Hiller and of Mary Hiller his wife was born the 10th day of December Anno Domini 1692

Samuel Hiller the son of the s^d Samuel and Mary Hiller born the 20th day of December Anno Domini 1694

Joseph Swift son of William Swift and of Elizabeth Swift his wife was born In november in the year 1687

Samuel Swift son of s^d William and Elisabeth Swift born in december Anno 1690

Joanna Swift Daughter of s^d William & Elisabeth Swift born march 9th Anno 169[*]

Thomas Swift son of s^d William and Elisabeth Swift born Decem^r Anno 169[*]

Elizabeth and thankfull Swift Son† and daughter of s^d William and Elizabeth Swift was born January 11th Anno domini 169[*]

Josiah Swift son of s^d William and Elizabeth Swift was born the ‡

Ebenezer Swift son of s^d William and Elizabeth Swift was born the ‡

[p. 30] Mehetabel Tupper the Daughter of Eldad Tupper and and of Martha Tupper his wife was born the 9th day of November Anno Domini 1702

*The year was not completed.
†So recorded.
‡The date was not entered.

Jemima Tupper the Daughter of the s^d Eldad Tupper and Martha Tupper his wife was born the 22th day of October Anno: 1704

Elisha Tupper the son of the above named Eldad and Martha Tupper was born the 17th day of July Anno Dom 1707

Isaiah Tupper the son of the s^d Eldad and Martha Tupper was Born the 11th day of December Anno Dom 1709

Eldad Tupper son of s^d Eldad and Martha Tupper Born 4th of march 1713/14

Prince Tupper son of s^d Eldad & Martha Tupper Born 24th of July 1716

Mayhew Tupper son of s^d Eldad and Martha Tupper Born 13th of July 1719

Benjamin Tupper. Son of Eldad Tupper & Martha his wife was Born the 4th Day of October Anno Domini 1722.

Martha Tupper the daughter of Eldad Tupper & Martha his wife was Born the 13th Day of February Anno Domini 1724/5.

Seth Pope the Son of John Pope and of Elizabeth Pope his wife born the 30th day of January Anno Domini: 1700/1

Deborah Pope the daughter of s^d John and Elizabeth Pope born the 6th day of January Anno domini 1702/3

Sarah Pope the Daughter of s^d John Pope and of Elizabeth Pope his wife was born the 25th day of march Anno domini 1705

Elizabeth Pope the Daughter of s^d John and Elizabeth Pope was Born the third day of January Anno Dom 1706/7

Thomas Pope Son of s^d John Pope and Elizabeth Pope his wife was Born the *

Mary Pope Daughter of s^d John and Elizabeth Pope his wife was Born the [†] Day of December Anno 1713.

Ezra Pope Son of s^d John Pope and of Experience Pope his now wife was Born the third day of April Anno Domini 1719

Joannah Pope the Daughter of John Pope & Experience his wife was Born the third day of March Anno Domini 1721/2

Charles Pope Son of John Pope & Experience his wife was Born the 28th Day of February Anno Domini 1724/5

[p. 31] Remember Nye the Daughter of Nathan Nye and of Mercy Nye his wife was born the Last day of february Anno domini 1686/7

Temperance Nye the Daughter of them the s^d Nathan and Mercy Nye born the 7th day of april Anno dom 1689

Thankfull Nye the Daughter of them the s^d Nathan and mercy Nye born the Eleventh day of august Anno dom 1691

*The record was not completed.
†The day of the month was not entered.

Content Nye the Daughter of them the s^d Nathan and Mercy Nye born the 25th day of September Anno dom 1693

Jemima Nye the Daughter of them the s^d Nathan and Mercy Nye born the 20th day of february Anno dom 1695/6

Lemuel Nye the son of the s^d Nathan and Mercy Nye was born the 21th day of March Anno Domini 1698/9

Deborah Nye the Daughter of them the s^d Nathan and mercy Nye born the 8th day of april Anno Domini 1700

Maria Nye the daughter of them the s^d Nathan and Mercy Nye born the 2^d day of april Anno Dom 1702

Caleb Nye the son of the s^d Nathan and Mercy Nye was born the 28th day of June Anno Domini 1704

Nathan Nye Son of the s^d Nathan and Mercy Nye was Born the 28th day of September Anno Domini 1708

Solomon Hoxie the son of Hezekiah hoxie and of Dinah Hoxie his wife was born the last day of february Anno^d 1702/3

James Hoxie Son of the s^d Hezekiah and Dinah Hoxie was born the 13th day of June Anno Domini 1704

Desier Hoxie Daughter of the s^d Hezekiah and Dinah Hoxie was born the fifth day of november Anno Domini 1705

Hannah Hoxie Daughter of the above named Hezekiah and Dinah Hoxie was born the second day of October Anno dom 1708

[p. 32] Margerett Fish the Daughter of John Fish and of Mehetable Fish his wife was born the 24th day of December Anno dom 1702

Mary Fish Daughter of the s^d John and Mehetable Fish was Born the 20th day of December Anno Dom 1704

John Fish son of the s^d John and Mehetabel Fish born the fifth day of January Anno Domini 1708/9

Hannah Fish the Daughter of the s^d John & Mehetable Fish was Born the 8th day of July Anno Domini 1711

Rachel Fish Dauhter of the s^d John and Mehetabel Fish born the fourth day of July Anno Domini 1714

Josiah Fish Son of the S^d John Fish & of Mehetable Fish his wife was Born the fourth day of January Anno Domini 1716/17

Edmond Fish Son of the s^d John and Mehitabel Fish was Born the first day of April Anno Domini 1721

Seth Stewart the son of James Stewart and Desire Stewart his wife was born the 2^d day of april Anno Dom 1690

Abigail Stewart the Daughter of s^d James and Desire Stewart born the 4th day of June Anno Dom 1692

Gemaliel Stewart the Son of the s^d James and Desire Stewart was born the 15th day of march Anno Dom 1694/5

Mary Stewart the Daughter of s^d James and desire Stewart was born the 22th day of July Anno Dom 1698

James Stewart the son of s^d James and Desire Stewart was born the 24th day of february Anno dom 1700/1

Mehetabel Stewart the daughter of James Stewart & Desire his wife was Born the 10th Day of April 1704

Silvanus Stewart the Son of James Stewart & Desire his wife was Born the 19th Day of March 1705/6

[Deborah Fish the Daughter of Ebenezer Fish & Abigail his wife was Born the 21st Day of July Anno Domini 1726*]

[Patience Fish the daughter of Ebenezer Fish & Abigail his wife was Born the 28 Day of September Anno Domini 1727*]

[p. 33] Joanna Nye the Daughter of Jonathan Nye and of Hannah his wife was born the 16th day of January 1686/7

Ichabod Nye the son of s^d Jonathan and Hannah Nye was born in the moneth of May Anno Domini 1689

Jonathan Nye the son of s^d Jonathan Nye and of Patience Nye his now wife was born in the moneth of november Anno 1691

Joseph Nye the son of the s^d Jonathan and Patience nye his wife was born in the moneth of november Anno Dom 1695

Benjamin Nye the son of s^d Jonathan and Patience Nye was born in october Anno Domini 1697

Thomas Nye the son of s^d Jonathan and Patience Nye was born in the moneth of august Anno Domini 1699

And Abigale Nye and Isaac Nye the son and Daughter of them the s^d Jonathan and Patience Nye was born the second day of September Anno Domini 1702

Patience Nye the Daughter of them the s^d Jonathan and Patience Nye was born in the moneth of november Anno dom 1693

David Nye and Zerviah Nye the Son and Daughter of the above-named Jonathan and Patience nye was Born the first day of July Anno dom 1706

Hannah Laurance daughter of Joseph Laurance Ju & Bette his wife was Born the 4th Day of September Anno Domini 1735

Justus Laurance Son of Joseph Laurance Ju & Bette his wife was Born the 20th Day of January Anno Domini 1736/7

Peninah Laurance daughter of Joseph Laurance Ju & Bette his wife was Born the 7th Day of June Anno Domini 1738

Martha Laurance daughter of Joseph Laurance Ju & Bette his wife was Born the first Day of September Anno Domini 1741

Seth Laurance Son of Joseph Laurance Ju & Bette his wife was Born the 11th Day of August Anno Domini 1743

James Laurance Son of Joseph Laurance Ju & Bette his wife was Born the 16th Day of November Anno Domini 1745

*These two entries have been crossed out.

SANDWICH, MASS., VITAL RECORDS

(Continued from page 68)

[p. 34] Elizabeth Jennings the Daughter of Isaac Jennings and of Rose Jennings his wife was Borne the 12th day of april Anno 1701

Experience Jennings the Daughter of the s^d Isaac and Rose Jennings was Born the 10th day of march Anno dom 1702/3

John Jennings the son of the s^d Isaac and Rose Jenning was born the Last day of July Anno Domini 1706

Rose Jenings the Daughter of the s^d Isaac and Rose Jenings was born the 27th day of August Anno Dom 1710

Isaac Jenings Son of the s^d Isaac and Rose Jenings Borne the 24th day of April Anno Domini 1714

Mary Jenings Daughter of the s^d Isaac & Rose Jenings Born the first day of Septem^r 1717

Benjamin Jenings Son of s^d Isaac and Rose Jenings born the 12th day of December Anno Domini 1720

Hannah Jennings the daughter of Isaac Jennings & Hannah his wife was Born the 12 Day of April Anno Domini 1725

Lois Jennings daughter of Isaac Jennings & Hannah his wife was Born the 7th Day of February Anno Domini 1726/7

Eunice Jennings the daughter of Isaac Jennings & Hannah his wife was Born the 25th Day of May Anno Domini 1729

Ales Swift Daughter of Jirah Swift and of Abigail Swift his wife was born the 23^d day of July Anno Domini 1698

Susanna Swift Daughter of the s^d Jirah and Abigail Swift was born the 6th day of October Anno Domini 1699

Jabez Swift the son of the s^d Jirah Swift & Abigail Swift was born the 16th day of march Anno Domini 1700

Zepheniah Swift son of the s^d Jirah Swift & abigail his wife was born the 6th day of march Anno dom 1702/3

William Swift Son of s^d Jirah & Abigail swift was born the fifth day of July Anno Domini 1705

Nathaniel Swift Son of s^d Jirah and Abigail Swift was born the fourteenth day of march Anno dom 1707/8

Jirah Swift Son of s^d Jirah and Abigail Swift was born the 23th day of november Anno Domini 1709

Job Swift Son of the S^d Jirah and Abigail Swift was born the third day of October Anno domini 1711

Jonathan Gifford the son of William Gifford and of Mary Gifford his wife was Born the 4th day of May Anno 1684

James Gifford the son of the s^d William and Mary Gifford was Born the 10th day of march Anno dom 1685/6

Eunice Fish daughter of John Fish Ju & Mercy his wife was Born August 10th Anno Domini 1736

(To be continued)

Silas Swift son of the s^d Jirah And Abigail Swift was born the second day of August Anno Domini 1713
Abigail Swift Daughter of s^d Jirah and Abigail Swift was born the 26th day of July Anno Domini 1715
Isaac Swift Son of the s^d Jirah and Abigail Swift Born the third day of may Anno Domini 1720
Rowland Swift the Son of Jirah Swift & Abigail his wife was Born the 24th Day of March Anno Domini 1721/2
[p. 35] Gidion Allen son of Daniel Allen and Bethshua Allen his wife was Borne the 17th day of may Anno Domini 1686
Hannah Allen Daughter of s^d Daniel and Bethsheua Allen was born the second day of June Anno Domini 1688
Lydia Allen Daughter of s^d Daniel and Bethua Allen was Born the Last day of April Anno Domini 1692
Cornelius Allen son of the s^d Daniel and Bethsua Allen was born the 22th day of May Anno Domini 1694
Daniel Allen the son of s^d Daniel and Bethshua Allen was born the Last day of June Anno Domini 1701
Benjamin Gifford the Son of William Gifford and of Elizabeth Gifford his wife, was Born August the 20th Anno dom^d 1703
Nathon Gifford son of s^d William and Elizabeth Gifford was Born the 16th day of february Anno Dom 1704/5
Elizabeth Gifford the Daughter of the above named William and Elizabeth Gifford was born the Last day of May Anno dom 1710
William Chipman the Son of Ebenezer Chipman & Mary his wife was Born the 6th Day of May anno Domini 1731
Martha Lawrence Daughter of Justus Lawrence & Deborah his wife was born the 20th of Novr 1763
Paddock Lawrence Daughter of Justus Lawrence & Deborah his wife born the first Day of July 1767
Lydia Lawrence Daughter of Justus Lawrence & Deborah his Wife was born the 25th of June* 1769
Asa Lawrence Son of James Lawrence and Abigail his wife was born on Octr 26th 1771
Temperance Lawrance Daughter of James Lawrence and Abigail his wife was born on Novr 1st 1775
[p. 36] Mercy Bourne the Daughter of Eliezer Bourne & of Abigale Bourne his Wife was born the Last day of May Anno Domini 1704
Isaac Bourne the son of s^d Eliazer and Abigail Bourn was born the first day of March Anno Dom 1706/7

* "July" was first written, but was altered to "June".

Job Bourne the son of s^d Eleazer and Abigal Bourne was Born the Last Day of March Anno Domini 1717
Elisha Ellis Son of Gideon Ellis & Anna his wife was Born the 19th Day of January Anno Domini 1736/7
Annah Ellis daughter of Gideon Ellis & Annah his wife was Born the 5th Day of June Anno Domini 1738
Elnathan Ellis Son of Gideon Ellis & Jemimah his wife was Born the 5th Day of January Anno Domini 1739/40
Seth Ellis the Son of Gideon Ellis & Jemimah his wife was Born the 23d Day of May Anno Domini 1741
Abiel Ellis Son of Gideon Ellis & Jemimah his wife was born the 6th Day of October Anno Domini 1744
John Ellis Son of Gideon Ellis & Jemimah his wife was Born the 2d Day of March Anno Domini 1745/6
Samuel Ellis Son of Gideon Ellis & Jemima his wife was born the 22th Day of September Anno Domini 1753
Reuben Ellis Son of Gideon Ellis & Jemima his wife was born the 25th Day of August Anno Domini 1755
Memorandum that Mr Gideon Ellis was with me on Apr. 26. 1758 & Saith that his Son. Seth ought to have been recorded to have been born on May 23. 1742 Benj. Fessenden. Clerk
Zacheus Moxum the son of Samuel Moxum and of Hanah Moxum his wife was born the 5th day of October Anno Domini. 1704
Mehetabel Stewart daughter of James Stewart & Mehetabel his wife was Born the 17th Day of July Anno Domini 1735
Joseph Wing the son of Nathaniel Wing and Sarah Wing his wife was Born the 30th day of march Anno Domini 1709
Thomas Snell Son of Thomas Snell and of Faith Snell his wife was Born the 24th day of September Anno Domini 1715
Gamaliel Fuller Son of Abiel Fuller and Sarah his wife was born on Sepr 27th A Domini 1765
[p. 37] The Marriage between John Bodfish and Sarah Nye both of Sandwich Solemnized Before Mr Rowland Cotton in Sandwich May 24th Anno: 1704
The marriage Between Joshua Blackwell and Sarah Ellis both of Sandwich Solemnized before Stephen Skeffe Esqr Justice of Peace in Sandwich the 8th day of June Anno Domini 1704
The maryage between Jonathan Weeks and Mercy Robinson both of Falmouth Solemnized before Stephen Skeffe Esqr Justice of Peace att Sandwich the 26th day of october Anno 1704
The Marriage beween John Handy and Keziah Wing both of Sandwich Solemnized before Stephen Skeffe Esqr Justice of Peace in Sandwich the 14th day of November Anno: 1704

The marriage between Ezra Perry and mary Swift both of Sandwich was Solemnized before m^r Rowland Cotton minester January 11th Anno dom 1704

The marriage between Thomas Doty of Plimouth and Mercy Ellis of Sandwich was Solemnized before m^r Rowland Cotton minestr at Sandwich Apil: 18th 1705

The marriage between Jacob Mott of Portsmouth and Rest Perry of Sandwich was solemnized before Stephen Skeffe Esqr Sandwich novem^r the 20th 1705

The marriage between Isaac Holms of Plimouth and mary nye of Sandwich was Solemnized before m^r Rowland Cotton minester in Sandwich novem^r 21: 1705

The Marriage between Thomas Savory of Rochester and Esther Saunderson of Sandwich was Solemnized before m^r Rowland Cotton minester in Sandwich Decem^r 14: 1705

The Marriage between Josiah Swift of Sandwich and Mary Bodfish of Barnestable was Solemnized before m^r Rowland Cotton minester in Sandwich April: 19th 1706

The marriage between Stephen Wanton of Scituate and Hanah Allen of Sandwich was Solemnized before Stephen Skeff Esqr Justice of Peace in Sandwich on the 10th day of Septem^r Anno Domini 1706

The marriage between Daniel Butler of Falmouth and Joanna Mendal of Rochester Solemnized before Stephen Skeffe Esqr Justice of Peace att Sandwich the 17th day of July Anno Domini 1707

Joseph Bennett of Middleborough and Joanna Perry of Sandwich was Marryed before Mr Rowland Cotton Minester in Sandwich on the 18th day of December Anno Dom 1707

Roger Haskall of Rochester and Joanna Swift of Sandwich were married before m^r Rowland Cotton minester In Sandwich the 25th day of February Anno Dom 1707/8

Gidion Allen and Anne Buck both of Sandwich Entred into a Covenant of Marriage Before Stephen Skeffe Esqr Justice of Peace att Sandwich the 23th day of march Anno Dom 1707/8

The Marriage Between Jonathan Bassett and Mary Gale both of Sandwich was Solemnized before m^r Rowland Cotton minester att Sandwich the 14th day of May Anno Domini 1708

The marriage between Thomas Jones and Hannah Bessie both of Sandwich was Solemnized Before Stephen Skeffe Esqr Justice of Peace att Sandwich the first day of October Anno Domini 1708

The marriage between Stephen Churchel of Plimouth & Experience Ellis of Sandwich Solemnized before Stephen Skeffe Esqr Justice of Peace att Sandwich the second day of Decem^r Anno Dom 1708

[p. 38] Sarah Barlow the Daughter of John Barlow and Elizabeth Barlow his wife was born the 15th day of october Anno dom 1693

Keturah Barlow daughter of the s^d John and Elizabeth Barlow as born the 29th day of may Anno Domini 1698

Samuel Barlow the son of the s^d John and Elizabeth Barlow was Born the 14th day of February Anno Dom 1700/701

John Barlow son of s^d John & Elizabeth Barlow Born the last of October 1706

Nathan Barlow son of s^d John & Elisabeth Barlow Born the last of October 1710

William Barlow son of s^d John & Elisabeth Barlow Born the 14th of April 1713

Zacheus Burge the son of Jacob Burg and of Mary Burg his wife was Born the 9th day of march Anno Domini 1704/5

Jedidah Burge Daughter of the s^d Jacob and Mary Burg his wife was born the 29th day of July Anno Dom 1706

Abia Burge the Daughter of the s^d Jacob and Mary Burg his wife was Born the 14th day of Aprill Anno Dom 1708

Abigail Burge Daughter of s^d Jacob and mary Burge was born the 29th day of June Anno Dom 1709

Samuel Burge the son of s^d Jacob and Mary Burge born the second day of november Anno Domini 1711

Jacob Burge son of s^d Jacob and Mary Burge was Born the 9th day of November Ann Domini 1715

John Hamett Son of Micah Hamett & Hannah his wife was Born the 19th Day of October Anno Domini 1740

Barnabas Hamett Son of Micah Hamett & Hannah his wife was Born the 5th Day of February Anno Domini 1741/2.

[p. 39] Nathaniell Ellis son of John Ellis and Sarah Ellis his wife was Born the 23th day of December Anno dom 1702

John Ellis son of s^d John and Sarah Ellis was born the 4th of February Anno domini 1704/5

Sarah Ellis Daughter of s^d John and Sarah Ellis Born 3^d day of February 1706

Rebecca Ellis Daughter of s^d John & Sarah Ellis Born 28th day of March 1709

Mercy Ellis Daughter of s^d John and Sarah Ellis Born 31th day of May 1711

Sandwich, Mass., Vital Records

Mordicai Ellis son of s^d John and Sarah Ellis Born 29th of October 1713

Jonathan Ellis son of s^d John and Sarah Ellis Born 1st day of may 1717

Jerusha Toby Daughter of Garshom Toby and of Mehetabel his wife was Born the 23th day of march Anno Domini 1697/8

Temperance Toby Daughter of the s^d Garshom and Mehetabel toby was born the 21th day of Aprill Anno Dom 1701

Silas Toby son of the s^d Garshom Toby and Mehetabel Toby was born the the 4th day of november Anno dóm 1704

Barnabas Toby son of s^d Garshom and Mehetabel Toby born the 22th day of July Anno domini 1708

Ephraim Toby son of s^d Garshom and mehetabel Toby was Born the 23th day of July Anno domini 1711

Mehetabel Toby the daughter of Gershom Toby & Mehetabel his wife was Born the 23d Day of December Anno Domini 1714

Gershom Toby Son of Gershom Toby & Mehetabel his wife was Born the 24th Day of September Anno Domini 1720

[p. 40] Job Bourne the sonn of Timothy Bourne and Temperance his wife was Born the Last day of October Anno Domini 1689

Benjamin Bourne Son of the s^d Timothy Bourne and Temperance Bourne was born the 27th day of October Anno Domini 1692

Joanna Bourne the Daughter of s^d Timothy and Temperance Bourne was born the 20th day of January Anno Dom 1695/6

Mehetabel Bourne the Daughter of s^d Timothy Bourne and Temperance bourne was born the second day of January Anno 1699/700

Timothy Bourne the son of s^d Timothy Bourne and Temperance Bourne was born the 5th day of December Anno dom 1703

Samuel Swift son of Benjamin Swift and of Hannah Swift his wife was born the 11th day of Septem^r Anno dom 1704

Mary Swift Daughter of the aboves^d Benjamin Swift and Hannah Swift was born the 11th day of October Anno Domini 1706

Content Swift the Daughter of the s^d Benjamin Swift & of Hannah Swift his wife was born the 12th day of Decenber Anno Dom 1708

Zebulun Swift Son of s^d Benjamin & Hannah Swift born the 15th day of April Anno Domini 1712

(To be continued)

THE MAYFLOWER DESCENDANT ceased publication at the end of Vol. 34. These vital records were not continued.

INDEX

INDEX - BARNSTABLE

This is NOT an all-name index. References in the text to religious and civil officials, as such, have been omitted. Names may appear more than once on the same page.

— A —

AAMES, Enos	52
ABRAHAM, Paul	110
ABRAHAM, Paul	116
ABRAHAM, Paul	120
ADAMES, Thomas	121
ADAMS, Edward	64
ADAMS, Edward	66
ADAMS, Edward	91
ADAMS, Elizabeth	81
ADAMS, Elizabeth	91
ADAMS, Hannah	91
ADAMS, Martha	54
ADAMS, Martha	91
ADAMS, Mercy	52
ADAMS, Nathanael	61
ADAMS, Nathanael	62
ADAMS, Nathll.	91
ADAMS, Sarah	72
ADAMS, Sarah	77
ADAMS, Sarah	91
ADAMS, Thomas	91
ADAMS, Walley	91
AERY, Sarah	39
AGRY, Hannah	76
AGRY, John	76
AGRY, Thomas	76
ALLEN, Abia	72
ALLEN, Abiah	103
ALLEN, Abigail	122
ALLEN, Andrew	48
ALLEN, Andrew	103
ALLEN, Anna	110
ALLEN, Anna	117
ALLEN, Benjamin	50
ALLEN, Bethiah	82
ALLEN, Bethiah	103
ALLEN, Bethiah	109
ALLEN, Beulah Lovel	103
ALLEN, Ebenezer	48
ALLEN, Elisha	103
ALLEN, Elizabeth	118
ALLEN, Hannah	78
ALLEN, Hannah	80
ALLEN, Hannah	97
ALLEN, Hannah	104
ALLEN, Hannah	113
ALLEN, Hannah	114
ALLEN, Hannah	121
ALLEN, James	77
ALLEN, James	97
ALLEN, John	118
ALLEN, John	119
ALLEN, Mary	75
ALLEN, Mary	114
ALLEN, Mary	116
ALLEN, Mehitable	103
ALLEN, Nathanael	66
ALLEN, Nathaniel	48
ALLEN, Nathaniel	56
ALLEN, Nathaniel	57
ALLEN, Nathll.	60
ALLEN, Nathll.	103
ALLEN, Olive	71
ALLEN, Olive	72
ALLEN, Rebekah	114
ALLEN, Sally	51
ALLEN, Sarah	53
ALLEN, Susannah	26
ALLEN, Susannah	117
ALLEN, Susannah	119
ALLEN, Thomas	65
ALLEN, Thomas	66
ALLEN, William	77
ALLEN, William	83
ALLEN, William	103
ALLEN, Zacheus	56
ALLEN, Zacheus	58
ALLIN, Abigail	99
ALLIN, Abigail	106
ALLIN, Anna	99
ALLIN, Elizabeth	99
ALLIN, Hannah	99
ALLIN, James	99
ALLIN, Martha	99
ALLIN, Mary	99
ALLIN, Olive	99
ALLIN, Rebakah	99
ALLIN, Sarah	99
ALLIN, Susanah	99
ALLIN, Thomas	99
ALMONY, Hannah	111
ALMONY, Hannah	114
ALLYN, Andrew	56
ALLYN, Benjn.	79
ALLYN, Elizabeth	10
ALLYN, Elizabeth	39
ALLYN, Elizabeth	110
ALLYN, Hannah	10
ALLYN, Isaac	10
ALLYN, James	10
ALLYN, James	79
ALLYN, John	10
ALLYN, John	79
ALLYN, Joseph	10
ALLYN, Lydia	79
ALLYN, Marston	79
ALLYN, Mary	10
ALLYN, Mary	77
ALLYN, Mary	99
ALLYN, Matthew	10
ALLYN, Mehitable	10
ALLYN, Nymphas	79
ALLYN, Olive	73
ALLYN, Rebecca	52
ALLYN, Rebekah	113
ALLYN, Saml.	10
ALLYN, Samuel	10
ALLYN, Sarah	72
ALLYN, Thomas	10
ALLYN, Thomas	56
ALLYN, Thomas	75
ALLYN, Thomas	76
ALLYN, Thomas	79
Amariah	116
Amaritta	80
Amaritta	113

Name	Page	Name	Page	Name	Page
AMES, Chloe	52	ANNABLE, Benjamin	108	ANNIS, Thomas	72
AMES, Elizabeth	76	ANNABLE, Bethiah	93	ANNIS, Thos.	72
AMES, Elizabeth	82	ANNABLE, Cornelius	10	ANSEL, Mary	34
AMES, Elizabeth	113	ANNABLE, Cornelius	106	ARNOLD, Hester	109
AMES, Enos	76	ANNABLE, David	108	ARNOLD, Hester	113
AMES, Isaac	76	ANNABLE, Desire	10	ATIQUIN, Daniel	121
AMES, Jerusha	76	ANNABLE, Desire	13	ATIQUIN, Jerimiah	122
AMES, John	52	ANNABLE, Elijah	106	ATIQUIN, Mary	122
AMES, Josiah	51	ANNABLE, Elizabeth	105	ATKINS, Bethiah	72
AMES, Josiah	54	ANNABLE, Experience	106	ATKINS, Hannah	119
AMES, Lydia	114	ANNABLE, Ezekel	10	ATKINS, Tabitha	73
AMES, Margaret	96	ANNABLE, Hannah	10	ATTAQUIN, Desire	110
AMES, Mehetable	76	ANNABLE, Hannah	12	ATTAQUIN, Desire	119
AMES, Mehitable	53	ANNABLE, Isaac	105	ATTAQUIN, Sarah	110
AMES, Sally	51	ANNABLE, Jane	10	ATTCHEHOO, John	97
AMES, Thomas	76	ANNABLE, John	10	ATWOOD, Rhoda	52
AMES, Thomas	109	ANNABLE, John	105		
AMES, Zephorn	76	ANNABLE, John	106	— B —	
Amos	73	ANNABLE, John	113		
AMOS, Elizabeth	61	ANNABLE, John	114	BACHOUSE, Dorcas	118
AMOS, Elizabeth	66	ANNABLE, Joseph	75	BACHOUSE, Remember	118
AMOS, Thomas	114	ANNABLE, Joseph	108	BACKHOUSE, Joshua	119
ANABLE, Anna	49	ANNABLE, Joseph	113	BACKHOUSE, Nathaniel	63
ANABLE, Annah	15	ANNABLE, Joseph	114	BACKHOUSE, Sarah	56
ANIBLE, Anna	98	ANNABLE, Martha	108	BACKOUS, Hannah	116
ANIBLE, Cornelus	122	ANNABLE, Mary	10	BACKOUSE, Joshua	118
ANIBLE, Jean	98	ANNABLE, Mary	96	BACKOUSE, Remember	73
ANIBLE, Jno.	121	ANNABLE, Mary	108	BACKOUSE, Remember	86
ANIBLE, Mary	96	ANNABLE, Mehitable	10	BACKUS, Crocker	52
ANIBLE, Mary	98	ANNABLE, Mehitable	11	BACKUS, Heman	51
ANIBLE, Mehitable	97	ANNABLE, Mehitable	93	BACKUS, Lydia	51
ANIBLE, Patience	96	ANNABLE, Mehitable	106	BACKUS, Rebecca	51
ANIBLE, Samuel	121	ANNABLE, Patience	10	BACKUS, Remember	67
ANNABLE, -----	10	ANNABLE, Remember	72	BACKUS, Reuben	51
ANNABLE, Abigail	10	ANNABLE, Saml.	78	BACKUS, Thomas	52
ANNABLE, Abigail	105	ANNABLE, Saml.	80	BACON, -----	88
ANNABLE, Abigail	119	ANNABLE, Saml.	93	BACON, Abigail	99
ANNABLE, Abigail	120	ANNABLE, Samuel	10	BACON, Abigail	106
ANNABLE, Abigil	75	ANNABLE, Samuel	50	BACON, Abigail	118
ANNABLE, Abishai	105	ANNABLE, Samuel	108	BACON, Abigail	119
ANNABLE, Ann	75	ANNABLE, Susanah	106	BACON, Alice	113
ANNABLE, Anna	10	ANNABLE, Temporance	108	BACON, Anna	11
ANNABLE, Anna	15	ANNABLE, Thankfull	75	BACON, Anna	97
ANNABLE, Anna	108	ANNABLE, Thomas	10	BACON, Annah	96
ANNABLE, Anne	106	ANNABLE, Thomas	75	BACON, Asa Doctor	84
ANNABLE, Ansel	106	ANNABLE, Thomas	82	BACON, Barnabas	88
ANNABLE, Ansel D.	52	ANNABLE, Thomas	93	BACON, Barnabas	102
ANNABLE, Anthony	10	ANNABLE, Thomas	115	BACON, Barnabas	105
ANNABLE, Anthony	108	ANNABLE, Thomas	118	BACON, Benjamin	15
ANNABLE, Bachelder	75	ANNABLE, William	105	BACON, Benjamin	52
ANNABLE, Barnabas	93	ANNABLLE, Abigil	75	BACON, Benjamin	76

INDEX - BARNSTABLE

BACON, Daniel	15	BACON, Jeremiah	69	BACON, Mercy	66
BACON, David	11	BACON, Jeremiah	77	BACON, Mercy	78
BACON, David	106	BACON, Jeremiah	80	BACON, Mercy	96
BACON, Deborah	91	BACON, Jeremiah	84	BACON, Mercy	102
BACON, Deborah	97	BACON, Jeremiah	91	BACON, Mercy	113
BACON, Deborah	111	BACON, Jerimiah	99	BACON, Mercy	114
BACON, Deborah	115	BACON, Jno.	121	BACON, Nathan	58
BACON, Desere	91	BACON, Jno.	122	BACON, Nathaniel	11
BACON, Desier	96	BACON, Job	11	BACON, Nathaniel	15
BACON, Desire	11	BACON, Job	121	BACON, Nathaniel	91
BACON, Desire	50	BACON, John	11	BACON, Nathaniel	120
BACON, Desire	88	BACON, John	15	BACON, Nathll.	91
BACON, Ebenezer	11	BACON, John	75	BACON, Nathll.	98
BACON, Ebenezer	48	BACON, John	88	BACON, Nathll.	121
BACON, Ebenezer	52	BACON, John	105	BACON, Nymphas	85
BACON, Ebenezer	85	BACON, John	113	BACON, Olive	69
BACON, Ebenezer	102	BACON, John	121	BACON, Oris	91
BACON, Ebenezer	110	BACON, Jonathan	11	BACON, Oris	110
BACON, Ebenezer	118	BACON, Jonathan	67	BACON, Orren	116
BACON, Edward	11	BACON, Jonathan	70	BACON, Orrice	97
BACON, Edward	56	BACON, Jonathan	72	BACON, Patience	11
BACON, Edward	58	BACON, Jonathan	106	BACON, Patience	64
BACON, Edward	85	BACON, Jonathan	114	BACON, Patience	65
BACON, Edward	115	BACON, Joseph	11	BACON, Patience	85
BACON, Elisabath	73	BACON, Joseph	75	BACON, Patience	96
BACON, Elizabeth	11	BACON, Joseph	81	BACON, Polly	106
BACON, Elizabeth	48	BACON, Joseph	96	BACON, Prince	99
BACON, Elizabeth	72	BACON, Josiah	113	BACON, Rebekah	91
BACON, Elizabeth	88	BACON, Judah	54	BACON, Rebekah	106
BACON, Elizabeth	91	BACON, Jude	11	BACON, Ruth	106
BACON, Elizabeth	105	BACON, Lamuill	73	BACON, Samll.	11
BACON, Ezekiel	106	BACON, Lemuel	71	BACON, Samll.	48
BACON, Hannah	11	BACON, Lemuel	76	BACON, Samll.	77
BACON, Hannah	22	BACON, Lemuel	91	BACON, Samuel	11
BACON, Hannah	50	BACON, Lydia	85	BACON, Samuel	75
BACON, Hannah	69	BACON, Lydia	102	BACON, Samuel	85
BACON, Hannah	110	BACON, Mark	88	BACON, Samuel	96
BACON, Hannah	118	BACON, Martha	11	BACON, Samuel	97
BACON, Isaac	11	BACON, Martha	102	BACON, Samuel	121
BACON, Isaac	61	BACON, Mary	11	BACON, Sarah	11
BACON, Isaac	63	BACON, Mary	17	BACON, Sarah	64
BACON, Isaac	88	BACON, Mary	88	BACON, Sarah	73
BACON, Isaac	113	BACON, Mary	102	BACON, Sarah	85
BACON, Isaac	114	BACON, Mary	105	BACON, Sarah	91
BACON, Jabez	15	BACON, Mary	122	BACON, Sarah	97
BACON, Jabez	91	BACON, Mercy	11	BACON, Sarah	106
BACON, James	85	BACON, Mercy	15	BACON, Sarah	110
BACON, Jean	96	BACON, Mercy	42	BACON, Sarah	118
BACON, Jean	113	BACON, Mercy	43	BACON, Sarah	122
BACON, Jean	114	BACON, Mercy	50	BACON, Simeon	88
BACON, Jeremiah	11	BACON, Mercy	60	BACON, Solomon	11

INDEX - BARNSTABLE

BACON, Solomon	121	BAKER, Hannah	114	BAKER, Saml.	118
BACON, Stephen	106	BAKER, Isaac	67	BAKER, Samll.	15
BACON, Susanah	97	BAKER, Isaac	71	BAKER, Samuel	60
BACON, Susannah	85	BAKER, Isaac	73	BAKER, Samuel	62
BACON, Susannah	110	BAKER, Isaac	74	BAKER, Samuel	89
BACON, Susannah	113	BAKER, James	73	BAKER, Samuel	109
BACON, Susannah	116	BAKER, John	15	BAKER, Samuel	119
BACON, Thankful	113	BAKER, John	49	BAKER, Sarah	15
BACON, Thankful	114	BAKER, John	74	BAKER, Sarah	110
BACON, Thomas	11	BAKER, John	84	BAKER, Sarah	118
BACON, Thomas	91	BAKER, John	89	BAKER, Stephen	69
BACON, Thomas	97	BAKER, Lewis	73	BAKER, Thankful	15
BACON, Thomas	109	BAKER, Lydia	69	BAKER, Thankful	84
BACON, William	102	BAKER, Martha	109	BAKER, Thankful	110
BACOR, Ebenezer	66	BAKER, Mary	15	BAKER, Thankful	118
BAKER, Abigail	15	BAKER, Mary	49	BAKER, William	64
BAKER, Abigail	89	BAKER, Mary	89	BAKER, William	66
BAKER, Abigail	118	BAKER, Mary	115	BALEY, Stephen	53
BAKER, Abigail	119	BAKER, Mary	116	BANGS, Joseph	110
BAKER, Anna	67	BAKER, Mary	118	BANGS, Joseph	117
BAKER, Anna	97	BAKER, Mehitable	15	BANGS, Mehitable	78
BAKER, Anna	109	BAKER, Mehitable	89	BANGS, Mehitable	81
BAKER, Annah	15	BAKER, Mehitable	118	BANGS, Mehitable	85
BAKER, Annah	89	BAKER, Mehitable	119	BANGS, Nathan	85
BAKER, Benney	15	BAKER, Mercy	15	BANGS, Nathan	111
BAKER, Benney	111	BAKER, Mercy	64	BANGS, Nathan	115
BAKER, Benny	84	BAKER, Mercy	66	BANGS, Samll.	48
BAKER, Benny	94	BAKER, Mercy	67	BANGS, Susannah	85
BAKER, Bethiah	109	BAKER, Mercy	89	BARBER, Solomon	111
BAKER, Binney	67	BAKER, Mercy	96	BARBER, Solomon	114
BAKER, Cynthia	53	BAKER, Mercy	105	BARDEN, Abraham	12
BAKER, Darcas	88	BAKER, Mercy	109	BARDEN, Anna	12
BAKER, David	60	BAKER, Mercy	122	BARDEN, Deborah	12
BAKER, David	62	BAKER, Nathaniel	15	BARDEN, John	12
BAKER, David	69	BAKER, Nathaniel	48	BARDEN, Joseph	12
BAKER, David	88	BAKER, Nathaniel	67	BARDEN, Mercy	12
BAKER, Dorcas	69	BAKER, Nathaniel	69	BARDEN, Stephen	12
BAKER, Dorcas	113	BAKER, Nathaniel	74	BARDEN, William	12
BAKER, Dorcas	114	BAKER, Nathaniel	88	BARKER, Anne	13
BAKER, Ebenezer	67	BAKER, Nathaniel	94	BARKER, Deborah	12
BAKER, Ebenezer	69	BAKER, Nathaniel	118	BARKER, Desire	13
BAKER, Ebenezer	88	BAKER, Nicholas	15	BARKER, Hannah	13
BAKER, Elizabeth	15	BAKER, Nicholas	88	BARKER, John	13
BAKER, Elizabeth	69	BAKER, Nicholas	94	BARKER, Samll.	110
BAKER, Elizabeth	115	BAKER, Nicolas	118	BARKER, Samuel	116
BAKER, Elizabeth	116	BAKER, Patience	84	BARLOW, Hannah	73
BAKER, Ezekiel	73	BAKER, Patience	94	BARLOW, John	110
BAKER, Grace	15	BAKER, Prudence	109	BARLOW, John	120
BAKER, Grace	48	BAKER, Rebacker	73	BARNABAS, Joseph	56
BAKER, Hannah	15	BAKER, Rebeckah	15	BARNABAS, Joseph	58
BAKER, Hannah	89	BAKER, Rebekah	89	BARNABAS, Moses	119

INDEX - BARNSTABLE

BARNABAS, Solomon	121	BASSETT, Nathll	75	BEARSE, Mahala	54
BARREY, Marey	73	BASSETT, Nathan	75	BEARSE, Martha	108
BARROW, Sylvanus	115	BASSETT, Nathanael	76	BEARSE, Martha	120
BARROW, Sylvanus	116	BASSETT, Olive	54	BEARSE, Melinda	52
BARROWS, Sally	54	BASSETT, Sophia	54	BEARSE, Mercy	75
BARSE, Anna	99	BASSETT, Thankfull	75	BEARSE, Mercy	77
BARSE, Augustin	122	BASSIT, Mary	31	BEARSE, Prince	75
BARSE, James	121	BATES, Abigail	90	BEARSE, Priscilla	109
BARSE, Jonathan	99	BATES, Hannah	52	BEARSE, Priscilla	117
BARSE, Joseph	94	BATES, Job	90	BEARSE, Ruth	64
BARSE, Josiah	99	BATES, John	58	BEARSE, Ruth	65
BARSE, Lois	99	BATES, John	90	BEARSE, Sally	53
BARSE, Martha	94	BATES, Joseph	114	BEARSE, Samuel	56
BARSE, Thomas	99	BATES, Margaret	118	BEARSE, Samuel	58
BARSE, Unis	99	BATES, Mehitable	90	BEARSE, Sarah	56
BARSE, Zerviah	99	BATES, Polly	52	BEARSE, Sarah	58
BARSLEY, Joanna	50	BATES, Samuel	90	BEARSE, Thankful	76
BARSLEY, Joanna	101	BATES, Seth	90	BEARSE, Thankful	109
BASSET, Bethiah	122	BATES, Susannah	65	BEARSE, Thankfull	76
BASSET, Ebenezer	82	BATES, Susannah	67	BEARSE, Thomas	54
BASSET, Elizabeth	72	BATES, Susannah	90	BEARSS, Lydia	85
BASSET, Experience	112	BATES, Thomas	90	BEARSS, Mercy	85
BASSET, Fear	115	Bathsheba	67	BEARSS, Prince	85
BASSET, Fear	116	BAXTER, Catharine B.	54	BEELS, Elizabeth	118
BASSET, Margaret	59	BAXTER, Elizebath	56	BEELS, Stephen	115
BASSET, Margaret	82	BAXTER, Joseph	82	BEELS, Stephen	117
BASSET, Martha	61	BAXTER, Joseph	113	BEETLE, Mary	48
BASSET, Martha	82	BAXTER, Sarah	120	BEETLE, Mary	50
BASSET, Mary	56	BAXTER, Shobal	82	BEETLE, Sarah	45
BASSET, Mary	58	BAXTER, Shobal	113	BEETLE, Sarah	114
BASSET, Mary	112	BAXTER, Silvester	53	BEETTLE, Sarah	43
BASSET, Nathan	114	BAXTER, Thankful	66	BEIRSE, Abigail	11
BASSET, Nathan	115	BAYLEY, Benjamin	65	BEIRSE, Austin	10
BASSET, Nathaniel	112	BAYLY, Elizabeth	42	BEIRSE, Hannah	11
BASSET, Nehemiah	82	BEARS, Lemuel	60	BEIRSE, Hester	11
BASSET, Saml.	82	BEARSE, Almond	54	BEIRSE, James	11
BASSET, Samuel	112	BEARSE, Bethiah	110	BEIRSE, Joseph	11
BASSET, Sarah	112	BEARSE, Bethiah	118	BEIRSE, Lydia	11
BASSET, Sussanah	82	BEARSE, Ebenezer	73	BEIRSE, Martha	11
BASSET, Thanckfull	56	BEARSE, Elisabeth	75	BEIRSE, Mary	10
BASSET, Thankful	82	BEARSE, Elisabeth	76	BEIRSE, Priscilla	11
BASSET, Thankfull	59	BEARSE, Hannah	60	BEIRSE, Rebekah	11
BASSET, William	82	BEARSE, Hannah	62	BEIRSE, Sarah	11
BASSET, William	96	BEARSE, Ira	54	BENIAH, Francis	110
BASSET, William	112	BEARSE, Jabez	60	BENIAH, Francis	116
BASSET, William	115	BEARSE, Jabez	62	BENJAMIN, Joseph	11
BASSETT, Cornelius	75	BEARSE, Joseph	118	BENJAMIN, Mary	20
BASSETT, Daniel	54	BEARSE, Lemuel	62	BENJAMIN, Mary	49
BASSETT, Elisabeth	77	BEARSE, Lucy	53	BENNET, Cornelius	107
BASSETT, Margarett	62	BEARSE, Lydia	110	BENNET, Cornelius	108
BASSETT, Martha	66	BEARSE, Lydia	119	BENNET, Cornelius	118

BENNET, Ruth	107	BERSE, Josiah	11	BLATCHFORD, Mercy	92
BERRY, Benjamin	53	BERSE, Lemuel	88	BLATCHFORD, Peter	91
BERRY, Ephraim	64	BERSE, Lydia	15	BLATCHFORD, Remember	66
BERRY, Ephraim	66	BERSE, Lydia	72	BLATCHFORD, Remember	92
BERRY, Marey	73	BERSE, Lydia	78	BLATCHFORD, William	91
BERRY, Rachel	53	BERSE, Martha	14	BLATCHFORD, William	92
BERSE, -----	15	BERSE, Martha	78	BLISH, Abigail	79
BERSE, Abigail	15	BERSE, Martha	82	BLISH, Abigail	110
BERSE, Abigail	42	BERSE, Mary	11	BLISH, Abigail	114
BERSE, Abigail	113	BERSE, Olive	78	BLISH, Abraham	13
BERSE, Abigail	114	BERSE, Peter	14	BLISH, Abraham	92
BERSE, Augustin	85	BERSE, Peter	83	BLISH, Abraham	110
BERSE, Augustin	113	BERSE, Peter	111	BLISH, Abraham	115
BERSE, Augustin	114	BERSE, Peter	115	BLISH, Abraham	118
BERSE, Augustine	14	BERSE, Priscilla	11	BLISH, Anna	13
BERSE, Benjamin	11	BERSE, Priscilla	14	BLISH, Anne	13
BERSE, Benjamin	14	BERSE, Rebecca	15	BLISH, Benjamin	13
BERSE, Benjamin	82	BERSE, Saml.	83	BLISH, Benjamin	92
BERSE, Bethiah	14	BERSE, Samuel	14	BLISH, David	84
BERSE, Bethiah	85	BERSE, Sarah	14	BLISH, Ebenezer	109
BERSE, Daniel	15	BERSE, Sarah	113	BLISH, Elijah	61
BERSE, David	14	BERSE, Sarah	114	BLISH, Elijah	66
BERSE, David	83	BERSE, Simeon	85	BLISH, Elijah	92
BERSE, Deborah	83	BERSE, Stephen	15	BLISH, Elisha	79
BERSE, Ebenezer	11	BERSE, Stephen	82	BLISH, Elisha	92
BERSE, Ebenezer	14	BERSE, Temperance	78	BLISH, Elizabeth	13
BERSE, Ebenezer	15	BERSE, Temperance	81	BLISH, Elizabeth	84
BERSE, Ebenezer	50	BERSE, Temperance	85	BLISH, George	53
BERSE, Edward	83	BERSE, Thankful	14	BLISH, Hannah	13
BERSE, Eleanor	72	BERSE, Thankful	88	BLISH, Hannah	109
BERSE, Elizabeth	14	BERSE, Thankful	113	BLISH, Hannah	110
BERSE, Elizabeth	15	Besse	113	BLISH, Hannah	113
BERSE, Enoch	78	Besse	114	BLISH, Hannah	114
BERSE, Gershom	78	BESSE, Elizabeth	12	BLISH, John	13
BERSE, Jabez	82	BESSE, Rebeca	31	BLISH, John	85
BERSE, Jabez	88	BIERSE, Sarah	31	BLISH, John	115
BERSE, Jabez	113	BILLE, Thos.	11	BLISH, John	116
BERSE, James	11	BLACHFORD, Benjamin	63	BLISH, Joseph	13
BERSE, James	50	BLACHFORD, David	58	BLISH, Joseph	49
BERSE, James	88	BLACHFORD, Remember	56	BLISH, Joseph	65
BERSE, Jesse	15	BLACK, Deborah	52	BLISH, Joseph	67
BERSE, Jesse	83	BLACK, Mehitable	115	BLISH, Joseph	109
BERSE, John	11	BLACKFORD, David	92	BLISH, Joseph	110
BERSE, John	15	BLACKFORD, William	106	BLISH, Joseph	118
BERSE, John	78	BLACKFORD, Wm.	122	BLISH, Joseph	119
BERSE, John	113	BLACKWEL, Mary	77	BLISH, Joseph	120
BERSE, John	114	BLACKWELL, Samuel	52	BLISH, Marcy	79
BERSE, Joseph	11	BLATCHFORD, Benjamin	92	BLISH, Martha	92
BERSE, Joseph	14	BLATCHFORD, David	92	BLISH, Mary	13
BERSE, Joseph	78	BLATCHFORD, Elizabeth	91	BLISH, Mary	50
BERSE, Joseph	80	BLATCHFORD, Lydia	92	BLISH, Mary	85

INDEX - BARNSTABLE

BLISH, Mary	114	BLOSSOM, Asenath	63	BLOSSOM, Sarah	113
BLISH, Mehitable	119	BLOSSOM, Benja.	77	BLOSSOM, Sarah	115
BLISH, Mehitable	120	BLOSSOM, Benjamin	75	OLOSSOM, Sarah	117
BLISH, Mehittable	110	BLOSSOM, Benjamin	77	BLOSSOM, Seth	69
BLISH, Mercy	79	BLOSSOM, Bithiah	63	BLOSSOM, Seth	75
BLISH, Mercy	109	BLOSSOM, Churchel	69	BLOSSOM, Seth	77
BLISH, Rebecakah	85	BLOSSOM, David	69	BLOSSOM, Seth	82
BLISH, Rebekah	79	BLOSSOM, Elizabeth	13	BLOSSOM, Sylvanus	14
BLISH, Rebekah	92	BLOSSOM, Elizabeth	93	BLOSSOM, Temperance	63
BLISH, Reuben	13	BLOSSOM, Hannah	59	BLOSSOM, Thankful	13
BLISH, Reuben	82	BLOSSOM, Hannah	63	BLOSSOM, Thankful	14
BLISH, Reuben	113	BLOSSOM, Hannah	69	BLOSSOM, Thankful	84
BLISH, Reuben	118	BLOSSOM, Hannah	84	BLOSSOM, Thankful	88
BLISH, Reuben	119	BLOSSOM, Hannah	85	BLOSSOM, Thankful	115
BLISH, Reuben	122	BLOSSOM, Jabez	13	BLOSSOM, Thomas	13
BLISH, Ruth	82	BLOSSOM, Jabez	14	BLOSSON, Thankful	118
BLISH, Sarah	13	BLOSSOM, James	63	BLUSH, Ann	102
BLISH, Sarah	85	BLOSSOM, James	65	BLUSH, Anna	102
BLISH, Sarah	92	BLOSSOM, James	67	BLUSH, Benja.	102
BLISH, Sarah	110	BLOSSOM, James	113	BLUSH, Mary	113
BLISH, Sarah	119	BLOSSOM, Jemima	56	BLUSH, Ruben	98
BLISH, Silas	13	BLOSSOM, Jemima	61	BLUSH, Silanus	102
BLISH, Silas	79	BLOSSOM, John	13	BLUSH, Trustrum	102
BLISH, Silas	82	BLOSSOM, John	121	BODFISH, Abigail	83
BLISH, Stacy	85	BLOSSOM, Joseph	13	BODFISH, Benjamin	12
BLISH, Temperance	92	BLOSSOM, Joseph	14	BODFISH, Benjamin	14
BLISH, Thankful	13	BLOSSOM, Joseph	65	BODFISH, Benjamin	63
BLISH, Thankful	15	BLOSSOM, Joseph	85	BODFISH, Benjamin	87
BLISH, Thankful	48	BLOSSOM, Joseph	113	BODFISH, Betsy	51
BLISH, Thankful	66	BLOSSOM, Levi	69	BODFISH, Bridget	29
BLISH, Thankful	67	BLOSSOM, Lucretia	63	BODFISH, David	51
BLISH, Thankful	122	BLOSSOM, Lydia	58	BODFISH, Deborah	63
BLISH, Thomas	82	BLOSSOM, Lydia	113	BODFISH, Desire	63
BLISH, Timothy	92	BLOSSOM, Mary	14	BODFISH, Ebenezer	12
BLISH, Timothy	109	BLOSSOM, Mary	113	BODFISH, Ebenezer	113
BLISH, Tristram	13	BLOSSOM, Mary	114	BODFISH, Elisebeth	82
BLISH, William	109	BLOSSOM, Mathias	63	BODFISH, Elizabeth	12
BLLOSSOM, Jabez	116	BLOSSOM, Mehetable	85	BODFISH, Elizabeth	13
BLOSOM, Abigail	81	BLOSSOM, Mercy	13	BODFISH, Elizabeth	14
BLOSOM, Beniman	81	BLOSSOM, Mercy	26	BODFISH, Elizabeth	113
BLOSOM, Elisabeth	81	BLOSSOM, Mercy	117	BODFISH, Elizabeth	115
BLOSOM, Elizabeth	101	BLOSSOM, Peter	13	BODFISH, Elizabeth	117
BLOSOM, Elizabeth	121	BLOSSOM, Peter	69	BODFISH, Elizabeth	118
BLOSOM, Joseph	104	BLOSSOM, Ruth	115	BODFISH, Hannah	12
BLOSOM, Joseph	121	BLOSSOM, Ruth	116	BODFISH, Hannah	14
BLOSOM, Peter	98	BLOSSOM, Samll.	84	BODFISH, Hannah	52
BLOSOMS, Peter	103	BLOSSOM, Samll.	113	BODFISH, Hannah	58
BLOSOMS, Seth	103	BLOSSOM, Samll.	114	BODFISH, Hannah	82
BLOSSOM, -----	13	BLOSSOM, Samule	85	BODFISH, Hannah	87
BLOSSOM, -----	14	BLOSSOM, Sarah	13	BODFISH, Hannah	113
BLOSSOM, Abigail	69	BLOSSOM, Sarah	69	BODFISH, Hannah	114

Name	Page	Name	Page	Name	Page
BODFISH, Hannah	118	BODFISH, Solomon	87	BOURNE, Silvanus	102
BODFISH, Hannah	119	BODFISH, Solomon	115	BOURNE, Sylvanus	50
BODFISH, Isaac	51	BODFISH, Solomon	116	BOURNE, William	102
BODFISH, Isaac	63	BODFISH, Sylvanus	14	BRADFORD, Jesse	52
BODFISH, John	12	BODFISH, Sylvanus	116	BRADFORD, Noah	53
BODFISH, John	63	BODFISH, Thankful	14	BRADLEY, Temperance	52
BODFISH, Jonathan	14	BODFISH, Thankful	82	BRIDGHAM, Catherine	58
BODFISH, Jonathan	63	BODFISH, Thankful	115	BRIDGHAM, Elisabeth	73
BODFISH, Jonathan	76	BODFISH, Thankful	118	BRIGEN, Elizabeth	44
BODFISH, Jonathan	77	BODFISH, Thankfull	82	BRIGGS, Cornelius	11
BODFISH, Joseph	12	BONHAM, Hannah	11	BRIMHORNE, George	97
BODFISH, Joseph	14	BONHAM, Mary	11	BROWN, Ann	49
BODFISH, Joseph	48	BONHAM, Nicholas	11	BROWN, Zebulon	121
BODFISH, Joseph	53	BONHAM, Sarah	11	BRYANT, Mary	114
BODFISH, Joseph	81	BOURMAN, Desire	13	BUCK, Rembranc	26
BODFISH, Joseph	82	BOURMAN, Hannah	12	BUCK, Thomas	75
BODFISH, Josiah	51	BOURMAN, Mary	13	BUCK, Thomas	77
BODFISH, Josiah	63	BOURMAN, Mehitable	13	BULLOCK, Hopestil	40
BODFISH, Lydia	82	BOURMAN, Samuel	13	BUMP, Benjamin	50
BODFISH, Lydia	87	BOURMAN, Thomas	12	BUMP, Bethia	80
BODFISH, Marey	82	BOURMAN, Thomas	13	BUMP, Bethiah	94
BODFISH, Martha	52	BOURMAN, Tristram	13	BUMP, Bethiah	113
BODFISH, Mary	12	BOURN, Abigail	71	BUMP, Jabez	93
BODFISH, Mary	14	BOURN, Abigail	75	BUMP, Joanna	93
BODFISH, Mary	17	BOURN, Desire	80	BUMP, John	93
BODFISH, Mary	115	BOURN, Desire	115	BUMP, Levi	108
BODFISH, Mehitable	82	BOURN, Desire	116	BUMP, Mary	94
BODFISH, Melatiah	12	BOURN, Eunice	72	BUMP, Phebe	94
BODFISH, Melatiah	121	BOURN, Hannah	78	BUMP, Samll.	93
BODFISH, Nathan	12	BOURN, Hannah	80	BUMP, Samuel	108
BODFISH, Nathan	83	BOURN, Hannah	86	BUMP, Sarah	93
BODFISH, Nathan	87	BOURN, John	48	BUMP, Sarah	108
BODFISH, Nathan	115	BOURN, Jonathan	78	BUMP, Thomas	82
BODFISH, Patience	83	BOURN, Jonathan	80	BUMP, Thomas	93
BODFISH, Prince	54	BOURN, Joseph	109	BUMP, Warren	94
BODFISH, Rachel	87	BOURN, Joseph	114	BUMPAS, Abigail	15
BODFISH, Rebecca	12	BOURN, Mary	114	BUMPAS, Benjamin	15
BODFISH, Rebekah	50	BOURN, Mercy	75	BUMPAS, Elizabeth	15
BODFISH, Robert	12	BOURN, Mercy	77	BUMPAS, Hannah	15
BODFISH, Robert	113	BOURN, Richard	102	BUMPAS, Jean	15
BODFISH, Robert	115	BOURN, Sylvanus	72	BUMPAS, Joanna	76
BODFISH, Robert	122	BOURN, Sylvanus	73	BUMPAS, Joanna	81
BODFISH, Ruth	82	BOURN, Timothy	117	BUMPAS, Joanna	83
BODFISH, Sarah	12	BOURNE, Abigail	102	BUMPAS, John	122
BODFISH, Sarah	13	BOURNE, Barachiah	53	BUMPAS, Mary	15
BODFISH, Sarah	14	BOURNE, Desier	102	BUMPAS, Samll.	15
BODFISH, Sarah	104	BOURNE, Eunice	102	BUMPAS, Samll.	50
BODFISH, Sarah	121	BOURNE, Hannah	102	BUMPAS, Samuel	118
BODFISH, Silvanus	63	BOURNE, Mary	102	BUMPAS, Sarah	15
BODFISH, Simeon	63	BOURNE, Melatiah	102	BUMPAS, Sarah	115
BODFISH, Solomon	14	BOURNE, Mercy	102	BUMPAS, Sarah	116

INDEX - BARNSTABLE

Name	Page	Name	Page	Name	Page
BUMPAS, Thankful	113	BURSLEY, John	84	BUTLER, Sarah	72
BUMPAS, Thankful	114	BURSLEY, John	114	BUTLER, Sarah	93
BUMPAS, Thomas	15	BURSLEY, Joseph	13	BUTTLER, Hannah	93
BUMPAS, Thomas	82	BURSLEY, Joseph	84	BUTTLER, Israel	101
BUMPS, Hannah	42	BURSLEY, Joseph	97	BUTTLER, Israel	121
BUMPUS, Jerimiah	96	BURSLEY, Joseph	104	BUTTLER, Joseph	121
BUMPUS, Phebe	98	BURSLEY, Joseph	115	BUTTLER, Mary	93
BURBANK, Mary	81	BURSLEY, Joseph	116		
BURBANK, Samuel	53	BURSLEY, Lamuel	104	— C —	
BURG, Thankfull	121	BURSLEY, Lemuel	83		
BURGE, Ebenezer	48	BURSLEY, Lemuel	84	CAHOON, Eliza	54
BURGES, Ephraim	64	BURSLEY, Lurana	53	CAHOON, James	22
BURGIS, Ephraim	73	BURSLEY, Martha	61	CAIN, Alice	72
BURLEY, Benjamin	117	BURSLEY, Martha	63	CAIN, Jos.	122
BURN, Rebecca	120	BURSLEY, Mary	13	CAIN, Samll.	118
BURSLEY, -----	13	BURSLEY, Mary	17	CAIN, Zaccheus	114
BURSLEY, Abigail	13	BURSLEY, Mercy	13	CAIN, Zaccheus	115
BURSLEY, Abigail	51	BURSLEY, Mercy	51	CAIN, Zechariah	118
BURSLEY, Abigail	97	BURSLEY, Mercy	67	CAINE, Bette	122
BURSLEY, Abigail	117	BURSLEY, Mercy	75	CAINE, Marcey	104
BURSLEY, Abigail	119	BURSLEY, Mercy	104	CAINE, Mercy	121
BURSLEY, Ausmon	52	BURSLEY, Sarah	104	CAINE, Sarah	122
BURSLEY, Barnabas	13	BURSLEY, Temperance	13	CAMET, David	85
BURSLEY, Barnabas	75	BURSLEY, Temperance	18	CAMET, Hannah	85
BURSLEY, Barnabas	89	BURSLEY, Thankful	89	CAMET, Peter	85
BURSLEY, Benjamin	13	BURSLY, Abigail	84	CAMET, Peter	115
BURSLEY, Benjamin	114	BURSLY, Barnabas	77	CAMET, Thankful	85
BURSLEY, Benjamin	115	BURSLY, Benjamin	83	CAMMET, Hannah	58
BURSLEY, Benjn.	113	BURSLY, Benjn.	83	CAMMET, Peter	51
BURSLEY, Bethiah	84	BURSLY, Elizabeth	83	CAMMET, Peter	115
BURSLEY, Charles H.	54	BURSLY, Jabez	83	CAMMET, Robert H.	53
BURSLEY, Elizabeth	13	BURSLY, Joanna	83	CANNON, Ebener	63
BURSLEY, Elizabeth	25	BURSLY, Martha	83	CANNON, Ebenezer	76
BURSLEY, Elizabeth	48	BURSLY, Mary	77	CANNON, Ebenezer	77
BURSLEY, Eunice	52	BURSLY, Mary	83	CANNON, Ebenezer	88
BURSLEY, Experience	13	BURSLY, Sarah	83	CANNON, Ebenezer	117
BURSLEY, Experience	119	BURSLY, Sarah	84	CANNON, Joanna	56
BURSLEY, Hannah	13	BUTLER, Benjamin	93	CANNON, Joanna	58
BURSLEY, Hannah	89	BUTLER, Daniel	93	CANNON, Joanna	88
BURSLEY, Hannah	115	BUTLER, Elizabeth	93	CANNON, Joanna	115
BURSLEY, Hannah	116	BUTLER, Hannah	65	CANNON, Joanna	117
BURSLEY, Jabez	13	BUTLER, Hannah	67	CANNON, Joseph	88
BURSLEY, Jabez	59	BUTLER, Israel	93	CANNON, Mercy	88
BURSLEY, Jabez	63	BUTLER, Israel	109	CANNON, Nathan	56
BURSLEY, Jabez	65	BUTLER, Israel	117	CANNON, Nathan	59
BURSLEY, Jabez	67	BUTLER, Israel	119	CANNON, Nathan	88
BURSLEY, Joann	20	BUTLER, James	93	CANNON, Ruth	88
BURSLEY, Joanna	13	BUTLER, Luke	56	CANNON, Timothy	97
BURSLEY, Joanna	114	BUTLER, Luke	66	CAPEE, Hannah	114
BURSLEY, John	13	BUTLER, Mary	93	CAPPEE, Hannah	116
BURSLEY, John	58	BUTLER, Nathll.	93	CAPRON, Ann	121

INDEX - BARNSTABLE

CARDER, Hannah	50	CASLY, Samuel	87	CHILDS, Dorcas S.	54
CARPENTER, Abigail	67	Cesar	78	CHILDS, Ebenezer	19
CARPENTER, Abigail	73	Cesar	81	CHILDS, Ebenezer	72
CARPENTER, Daniel	66	Cesar	82	CHILDS, Ebenezer	81
CARPENTER, Daniel	67	Cesar	113	CHILDS, Ebenezer	97
CARPENTER, Eliphalet	118	CHACE, Levi	63	CHILDS, Ebenezr.	81
CARPENTER, Eliphalet	119	CHADDOCK, Mary	115	CHILDS, Ebenr.	81
CARSLEY, Ambrose	61	CHADWICK, Thankful	61	CHILDS, Ebenr.	82
CARSLEY, John	61	CHADWICK, Thankful	62	CHILDS, Ebenr.	113
CARSLEY, John	63	CHAMBERLIN, Chloe	53	CHILDS, Edward	78
CARSLEY, Mary	51	CHAPMAN, Abigail	19	CHILDS, Edward	87
CARSLEY, Seth	52	CHAPMAN, Hannah	19	CHILDS, Elizabeth	19
CARSLY, Ambrose	63	CHAPMAN, Isaac	19	CHILDS, Elizabeth	67
CARVER, Hope	58	CHAPMAN, James	19	CHILDS, Elizabeth	78
CASE, Barnabas	90	CHAPMAN, James	49	CHILDS, Elizabeth	79
CASE, Betty	90	CHAPMAN, John	19	CHILDS, Elizabeth	82
CASE, Ebenezer	90	CHAPMAN, Lydia	19	CHILDS, Elizabeth	92
CASE, Ebenr.	121	CHAPMAN, Mary	47	CHILDS, Elizabeth	97
CASE, Elizabeth	90	CHAPMAN, Mary	81	CHILDS, Hannah	19
CASE, Isaac	72	CHAPMAN, Ralph	19	CHILDS, Hannah	73
CASE, Isaac	90	CHAPMAN, Rebecca	19	CHILDS, Hannah	78
CASE, James	115	CHARD, Samuel	98	CHILDS, Hannah	81
CASE, James	117	CHASE, Betsy	54	CHILDS, Hannah	82
CASE, Lot	54	CHASE, Jonathan	47	CHILDS, Hannah	87
CASE, Lot	90	CHASE, Levi	59	CHILDS, Hannah	89
CASE, Mary	90	CHASE, Levi	116	CHILDS, Hope	81
CASE, Sarah	90	CHEHU, Hannah	75	CHILDS, Isaac	61
CASE, Sophia	54	CHEHU, Hannah	77	CHILDS, James	19
CASE, William	50	CHILD, Abigail	49	CHILDS, James	52
CASELEY, Benjamin	87	CHILD, Hannah	13	CHILDS, James	53
CASELEY, David	87	CHILD, Hannah	49	CHILDS, James	67
CASELEY, Mehetible	87	CHILD, Hannah	109	CHILDS, James	69
CASELY, Ambrose	87	CHILDS, Abigail	81	CHILDS, James	73
CASELY, Dorcas	87	CHILDS, Anna	78	CHILDS, James	77
CASELY, Ebenezer	87	CHILDS, Anna	87	CHILDS, James	92
CASELY, Eunice	87	CHILDS, Asenah	87	CHILDS, James	96
CASELY, Isaac	87	CHILDS, Assenath	78	CHILDS, Job	87
CASELY, John	87	CHILDS, Benjamin	61	CHILDS, Jonathan	65
CASELY, Mary	87	CHILDS, Benjamin	73	CHILDS, Jonathan	67
CASELY, Seth	87	CHILDS, Benjamin	87	CHILDS, Jonathan	78
CASELY, Thomas	87	CHILDS, Benjamin	89	CHILDS, Jonathan	81
CASLEY, John	87	CHILDS, David	64	CHILDS, Jonathan	89
CASLY, -----	47	CHILDS, David	65	CHILDS, Joseph	19
CASLY, Benjamin	82	CHILDS, David	78	CHILDS, Joseph	65
CASLY, Benjamin	87	CHILDS, David	81	CHILDS, Joseph	96
CASLY, Benjamin	111	CHILDS, David	87	CHILDS, Josiah	78
CASLY, Benjamin	115	CHILDS, David	89	CHILDS, Josiah	81
CASLY, Hannah	87	CHILDS, David	118	CHILDS, Josiah	87
CASLY, John	110	CHILDS, David	119	CHILDS, Lewes	73
CASLY, John	116	CHILDS, Deliverance	65	CHILDS, Mary	67
CASLY, Lemuel	87	CHILDS, Deliverance	67	CHILDS, Mary	69

CHILDS, Mary	89	CHIPMAN, Bethiah	19	CHIPMAN, Saml.	72
CHILDS, Mehetable	58	CHIPMAN, Bethiah	78	CHIPMAN, Saml.	76
CHILDS, Mehitable	73	CHIPMAN, Betsey	51	CHIPMAN, Saml.	98
CHILDS, Mercy	19	CHIPMAN, Deborah	76	CHIPMAN, Samuel	19
CHILDS, Rebecca	61	CHIPMAN, Desire	19	CHIPMAN, Samuel	98
CHILDS, Richard	19	CHIPMAN, Ebenezer	98	CHIPMAN, Samuel	114
CHILDS, Richard	92	CHIPMAN, Ebenezer	107	CHIPMAN, Sarah	19
CHILDS, Ruth	82	CHIPMAN, Elisabeth	66	CHIPMAN, Sarah	96
CHILDS, Ruth	113	CHIPMAN, Elisabeth	67	CHIPMAN, Seth	19
CHILDS, Ruth D.	53	CHIPMAN, Elizabeth	69	CHIPMAN, Thomas	19
CHILDS, Saml.	69	CHIPMAN, Elizabeth	72	CHIPMAN, Thomas	66
CHILDS, Samuel	19	CHIPMAN, Elizabeth	96	CHIPMAN, Thomas	78
CHILDS, Samuel	53	CHIPMAN, Elizabeth	107	CHIPMAN, Thomas	107
CHILDS, Samuel	69	CHIPMAN, Hannah	19	CHIPMAN, Timothy	72
CHILDS, Samuel	92	CHIPMAN, Hannah	32	CHIPMAN, Timothy	77
CHILDS, Sarah	71	CHIPMAN, Hannah	53	CHIPMAN, Timothy	98
CHILDS, Sarah	75	CHIPMAN, Hannah	69	CHIPMAN, Timothy Fuller	78
CHILDS, Sarah	92	CHIPMAN, Hannah	97	CHIPMAN, William	72
CHILDS, Shubael Davis	87	CHIPMAN, Hannah	98	CHURCHEL, James	75
CHILDS, Silas	89	CHIPMAN, Hannah	107	CHURCHEL, James	77
CHILDS, Susannah	87	CHIPMAN, Hope	19	CHURCHEL, Lyda	73
CHILDS, Thankful	19	CHIPMAN, Hope	32	CHURCHELL, Thomas	66
CHILDS, Thankful	32	CHIPMAN, Isaac	78	CHURCHELL, Thomas	67
CHILDS, Thankful	64	CHIPMAN, Jacob	19	CHURCHIL, James	72
CHILDS, Thankful	66	CHIPMAN, Jacob	96	CHURCHIL, James	73
CHILDS, Thankfull	92	CHIPMAN, Jacob	98	CHURCHIL, James	78
CHILDS, Thomas	19	CHIPMAN, Jacob	121	CHURCHIL, Martha	78
CHILDS, Thomas	61	CHIPMAN, Joanna	54	CHURCHIL, Sarah	78
CHILDS, Thomas	89	CHIPMAN, John	19	CHURCHIL, Sarah	82
CHILDS, Timothy	19	CHIPMAN, John	72	CLAGHORN, Abia	19
CHILES, Benjamin	75	CHIPMAN, John	98	CLAGHORN, Benjamin	20
CHILES, Benjamin	77	CHIPMAN, Joseph	19	CLAGHORN, Benjamin	103
CHILES, Samuel	75	CHIPMAN, Joseph	69	CLAGHORN, Ebenezer	20
CHILES, Samuel	77	CHIPMAN, Joseph	77	CLAGHORN, Ebenezer	56
CHIN, Amos	77	CHIPMAN, Joseph	98	CLAGHORN, Ebenezer	85
CHIPMAN, -----	98	CHIPMAN, Joseph	107	CLAGHORN, Ebenezer	117
CHIPMAN, Abiah	76	CHIPMAN, Josiah	76	CLAGHORN, Ebenezer	119
CHIPMAN, Abiah	98	CHIPMAN, Lydia	19	CLAGHORN, Eleanor	87
CHIPMAN, Abigail	19	CHIPMAN, Martha	69	CLAGHORN, Elinor	103
CHIPMAN, Abigail	54	CHIPMAN, Mary	69	CLAGHORN, Elizabeth	19
CHIPMAN, Abigail	72	CHIPMAN, Mary	72	CLAGHORN, Elizebeth	85
CHIPMAN, Abigail	96	CHIPMAN, Mary	76	CLAGHORN, Eunice	75
CHIPMAN, Abigail	97	CHIPMAN, Mary	77	CLAGHORN, Eunice	77
CHIPMAN, Abigail	114	CHIPMAN, Mary	98	CLAGHORN, Eunice	103
CHIPMAN, Abigail	119	CHIPMAN, Mary	107	CLAGHORN, Jabez	59
CHIPMAN, Barnabas	19	CHIPMAN, Mercy	19	CLAGHORN, Jabez	66
CHIPMAN, Barnabas	69	CHIPMAN, Nathaniel	98	CLAGHORN, Jabez	103
CHIPMAN, Barnabas	75	CHIPMAN, Rebecca	78	CLAGHORN, James	19
CHIPMAN, Barnabas	77	CHIPMAN, Ruth	19	CLAGHORN, James	20
CHIPMAN, Barnabas	107	CHIPMAN, Ruth	19	CLAGHORN, James	82
CHIPMAN, Barnabas	122	CHIPMAN, Saml.	50	CLAGHORN, James	103

CLAGHORN, James	117	CLARCK, Anne	10	COB, Hannah	37
CLAGHORN, Jane	20	CLARK, Ebenezer	120	COB, Hannah	118
CLAGHORN, Jane	85	CLARK, Elisabeth	66	COB, Hannah	119
CLAGHORN, Jean	70	CLARK, Elizabeth	48	COB, Henry	15
CLAGHORN, Jean	72	CLARK, John	20	COB, Henry	71
CLAGHORN, Jean	87	CLARK, John	49	COB, James	15
CLAGHORN, Jean	103	CLARK, Josiah	53	COB, James	16
CLAGHORN, Joanna	87	CLARK, Nathll.	114	COB, James	85
CLAGHORN, Joseph	20	CLARK, Obed	54	COB, James	121
CLAGHORN, Joseph	85	CLARK, Priscilla	53	COB, Jesse	16
CLAGHORN, Lois	87	CLEGHORN, Jane	122	COB, Jesse	92
CLAGHORN, Mary	19	CLERK, Susannah	35	COB, Jesse	110
CLAGHORN, Mary	20	COB, Abigail	71	COB, Jesse	118
CLAGHORN, Mary	22	COB, Abigail	82	COB, John	15
CLAGHORN, Mary	120	COB, Abigail	85	COB, John	16
CLAGHORN, Nathaniel	20	COB, Abigail	119	COB, John	49
CLAGHORN, Nathaniel	103	COB, Abigail	119	COB, John	96
CLAGHORN, Nathll.	112	COB, Anne	16	COB, Jonathan	15
CLAGHORN, Nehemiah	103	COB, Benjamin	78	COB, Jonathan	16
CLAGHORN, Reuben	87	COB, Benjamin	80	COB, Jonathan	17
CLAGHORN, Reuben	103	COB, Benniy	105	COB, Joseph	17
CLAGHORN, Reuben	120	COB, Benniy	110	COB, Joseph	72
CLAGHORN, Robert	19	COB, David	114	COB, Joseph	73
CLAGHORN, Robert	20	COB, David	116	COB, Joseph	92
CLAGHORN, Robert	48	COB, Ebenezer	16	COB, Joseph	104
CLAGHORN, Robert	49	COB, Ebenezer	17	COB, Josiah	16
CLAGHORN, Robert	103	COB, Ebenezer	77	COB, Judah	85
CLAGHORN, Samll.	113	COB, Ebenezer	105	COB, Jude	16
CLAGHORN, Samll.	114	COB, Ebenezer	110	COB, Lois	15
CLAGHORN, Samuel	20	COB, Ebenr.	81	COB, Lydia	15
CLAGHORN, Samuel	112	COB, Edward	16	COB, Lydia	17
CLAGHORN, Sarah	19	COB, Eleazer	15	COB, Martha	15
CLAGHORN, Sarah	85	COB, Eleazer	121	COB, Mary	15
CLAGHORN, Seth	87	COB, Elisha	16	COB, Mary	16
CLAGHORN, Shobal	19	COB, Elisha	121	COB, Mary	50
CLAGHORN, Shobal	20	COB, Elizabeth	14	COB, Mary	79
CLAGHORN, Thankful	20	COB, Elizabeth	15	COB, Mary	113
CLAGHORN, Thankful	103	COB, Elizabeth	16	COB, Mary	114
CLAGHORN, Thomas	20	COB, Elizabeth	110	COB, Matthew	77
CLAP, Charity	19	COB, Elizabeth	118	COB, Matthew	83
CLAP, George	72	COB, Ephraim	96	COB, Mehitable	15
CLAP, Increase	19	COB, Eunice	15	COB, Mehitable	47
CLAP, John	19	COB, Experience	15	COB, Mercy	77
CLAP, Mary	72	COB, Experience	48	COB, Mercy	15
CLAP, Mary	77	COB, Experience	113	COB, Mercy	105
CLAP, Nathaniel	115	COB, Gershom	15	COB, Mercy	110
CLAP, Nathll.	116	COB, Gershom	16	COB, Nathan	16
CLAP, Stephen	48	COB, Gideon	15	COB, Nathan	119
CLAP, Stephen	110	COB, Hannah	15	COB, Nathaniel	110
CLAP, Thomas	19	COB, Hannah	16	COB, Nathaniel	112
CLAPP, Stephen	118	COB, Hannah	21	COB, Nathaniel	116

INDEX - BARNSTABLE

COB, Oris	112	COBB, Eleazer	104	COBB, Rowland	56
COB, Patience	15	COBB, Elisebeth	91	COBB, Samuel	64
COB, Patience	41	COBB, Elizabeth	92	COBB, Samuel	94
COB, Rebecca	105	COBB, Elizabeth	94	COBB, Sarah	121
COB, Rebecca	110	COBB, Enoch T.	53	COBB, Susanna	58
COB, Reliance	82	COBB, Eunice	61	COBB, Sussanna	56
COB, Reliance	110	COBB, Eunice	63	COBB, Thankful	66
COB, Reliance	117	COBB, Eunice	73	COBB, Thankfull	58
COB, Saml.	113	COBB, Ezekel	92	COBB, Thankfull	91
COB, Samuel	15	COBB, Gershom	75	COBB, Thomas	94
COB, Samuel	17	COBB, Gershom	77	COFFEN, Abner	57
COB, Samuel	121	COBB, Gershom	120	COGGIN, Abigail	42
COB, Sarah	14	COBB, Hannah	73	COGGIN, Thomas	42
COB, Sarah	15	COBB, Hannah	92	COGNIHU, Moses	80
COB, Sarah	16	COBB, Henery	75	COHANNET, Joseph	109
COB, Sarah	19	COBB, Henery	94	COLBY, Philip	52
COB, Sarah	29	COBB, Henry	53	COLE, Hannah	121
COB, Sarah	47	COBB, Huldy	73	COLE, Mary	35
COB, Sarah	114	COBB, Isaac	92	COLEMAN, -----	20
COB, Sarah	121	COBB, James	66	COLEMAN, Alvan	52
COB, Seth	16	COBB, James	92	COLEMAN, Ebenezer	20
COB, Silvanus	105	COBB, Jonathan	91	COLEMAN, Edward	20
COB, Silvanus	122	COBB, Joseph	64	COLEMAN, Edward	47
COB, Stephen	16	COBB, Joseph	66	COLEMAN, Hannah	82
COB, Stephen	79	COBB, Joseph	104	COLEMAN, James	20
COB, Stephen	114	COBB, Lois	92	COLEMAN, James	59
COB, Stephen	119	COBB, Lucy	64	COLEMAN, James	61
COB, Susannah	112	COBB, Lydia	66	COLEMAN, James	62
COB, Sylvanus	16	COBB, Lydia	73	COLEMAN, James	91
COB, Sylvanus	105	COBB, Lydia	121	COLEMAN, James	105
COB, Sylvanus	110	COBB, Mary	56	COLEMAN, James	122
COB, Thankful	15	COBB, Mary	57	COLEMAN, John	20
COB, Thankful	16	COBB, Mary	64	COLEMAN, John	56
COB, Thankful	92	COBB, Mary	66	COLEMAN, John	91
COB, Thankful	113	COBB, Mary	73	COLEMAN, John	110
COB, Thankful	114	COBB, Mathew	94	COLEMAN, John	114
COB, Thomas	15	COBB, Mercy	15	COLEMAN, John	117
COB, Thomas	112	COBB, Mercy	75	COLEMAN, Martha	20
COBB, Abigail	94	COBB, Nathaniel	94	COLEMAN, Martha	71
COBB, Abigaill	75	COBB, Nathaniel	113	COLEMAN, Martha	75
COBB, Abigaill	82	COBB, Nicholas	58	COLEMAN, Martha	77
COBB, Anna	64	COBB, Oris	56	COLEMAN, Martha	91
COBB, Banjamin	64	COBB, Oris	58	COLEMAN, Martha	97
COBB, Benjamin	104	COBB, Partience	56	COLEMAN, Martha	105
COBB, David	91	COBB, Patience	57	COLEMAN, Mary	56
COBB, David	94	COBB, Rachel	73	COLEMAN, Mary	91
COBB, Desire	66	COBB, Rachel	94	COLEMAN, Meriam	75
COBB, Ebenezer	73	COBB, Reliance	64	COLEMAN, Miriam	81
COBB, Ebenezer	66	COBB, Reliance	104	COLEMAN, Patence	20
COBB, Eber	94	COBB, Relience	104	COLEMAN, Patience	50
COBB, Eleazer	64	COBB, Remember Mercy	66	COLEMAN, Patience	110

INDEX - BARNSTABLE

Name	Page	Name	Page	Name	Page
COLEMAN, Sarah	78	COOMER, Mary	48	CROCKER, Anna	79
COLEMAN, Sarah	81	CORY, Elizabeth	117	CROCKER, Anna	93
COLEMAN, Thankful	20	CORY, Mary	91	CROCKER, Ansel	88
COLEMAN, Thankful	48	COTTELLE, Hannah	52	CROCKER, Arthur B.	53
COLLIER, Abigail	117	COUET, Jesse	58	CROCKER, Asa	58
COLLIER, Abigail	120	COVEL, Drusilla	81	CROCKER, Asa	79
COLMAN, James	56	COVET, Jesse	61	CROCKER, Azubah	79
COLMAN, John	54	COWET, Mary	110	CROCKER, Barnabas	51
COLMAN, John	119	COWET, Mary	118	CROCKER, Barnabas	58
COLMAN, Patience	118	COWET, Richard	52	CROCKER, Barnabas	61
COLMON, Martha	73	CROCKER, -----	17	CROCKER, Barnabas	104
CONANT, Asa	51	CROCKER, -----	18	CROCKER, Barsheba	101
CONANT, Crocker	67	CROCKER, -----	95	CROCKER, Bathsheba	18
CONANT, Elisabeth	67	CROCKER, -----	104	CROCKER, Bathsheba	78
CONANT, George	62	CROCKER, Abel	19	CROCKER, Bathsheba	79
CONANT, George	65	CROCKER, Abel	50	CROCKER, Bathsheba	79
CONANT, George	67	CROCKER, Abiah	53	CROCKER, Bathsheba	115
CONANT, George	74	CROCKER, Abigail	17	CROCKER, Bathsheba	116
CONANT, George	76	CROCKER, Abigail	18	CROCKER, Bathshua	17
CONANT, Gorge	67	CROCKER, Abigail	68	CROCKER, Benjamin	17
CONANT, Gorge	73	CROCKER, Abigail	69	CROCKER, Benjamin	18
CONANT, Lot	50	CROCKER, Abigail	75	CROCKER, Benjamin	48
CONANT, Lydia	74	CROCKER, Abigail	77	CROCKER, Benjamin	66
CONANT, Mary	113	CROCKER, Abigail	78	CROCKER, Benjamin	78
CONANT, Mary	114	CROCKER, Abigail	79	CROCKER, Benjamin	82
CONANT, Sarah	74	CROCKER, Abigail	88	CROCKER, Benjamin	97
CONANT, Susannah	67	CROCKER, Abigail	95	CROCKER, Benjamin	116
CONANT, Thacher	74	CROCKER, Abigail	99	CROCKER, Benoni	19
CONNEAT, Asa	83	CROCKER, Abigail	104	CROCKER, Benoni	20
CONNEAT, Barnabas	83	CROCKER, Abigail	108	CROCKER, Benoni	95
CONNEAT, Benjamin	83	CROCKER, Abigail	115	CROCKER, Benoni	101
CONNEAT, Charles	83	CROCKER, Abigail	119	CROCKER, Benoni	117
CONNEAT, Charles	114	CROCKER, Abigail	120	CROCKER, Benoni	119
CONNEAT, Elisabeth	83	CROCKER, Abner	95	CROCKER, Bethiah	19
CONNEAT, George	67	CROCKER, Achsah	74	CROCKER, Bethiah	48
CONNEAT, George	77	CROCKER, Alice	17	CROCKER, Bethiah	92
CONNEAT, Hannah	83	CROCKER, Alice	18	CROCKER, Betsey	51
CONNEAT, Joanna	83	CROCKER, Alice	37	CROCKER, Betsey	52
CONNEAT, John	83	CROCKER, Alice	99	CROCKER, Betsy B.	53
CONNEAT, Lemuel	83	CROCKER, Alice	104	CROCKER, Clarisa	53
CONNEAT, Martha	83	CROCKER, Alice	115	CROCKER, Clarissa	52
CONNEAT, Mary	83	CROCKER, Alice	117	CROCKER, Cornelius	17
CONNEAT, Olive	83	CROCKER, Allyn	79	CROCKER, Cornelius	104
CONNEAT, Sarah	83	CROCKER, Alvan	74	CROCKER, Cornelius	107
CONNEAT, Susannah	67	CROCKER, Ann	92	CROCKER, Cornelius	122
CONNEAT, Thomas	83	CROCKER, Anna	56	CROCKER, Daniel	73
COOK, Bethiah	75	CROCKER, Anna	59	CROCKER, Daniel	17
COOK, Bethiah	77	CROCKER, Anna	65	CROCKER, Daniel	19
COOMBS, Polly	52	CROCKER, Anna	67	CROCKER, Daniel	78
COOMBS, Simeon	54	CROCKER, Anna	68	CROCKER, Daniel	79
COOMBS, Stephen	53	CROCKER, Anna	81	CROCKER, Daniel	82

CROCKER, David	17	CROCKER, Elizabeth	79	CROCKER, Jabez	101
CROCKER, David	67	CROCKER, Elizabeth	88	CROCKER, Jabez	115
CROCKER, David	69	CROCKER, Elizabeth	95	CROCKER, Jabez	116
CROCKER, David	72	CROCKER, Elizabeth	96	CROCKER, Jabez	118
CROCKER, David	79	CROCKER, Elizabeth	102	CROCKER, Jabez	119
CROCKER, David	81	CROCKER, Elizabeth	104	CROCKER, James	17
CROCKER, David	79	CROCKER, Elizebeth	107	CROCKER, James	66
CROCKER, David	98	CROCKER, Enoch	87	CROCKER, James	67
CROCKER, David	104	CROCKER, Enock	85	CROCKER, James	78
CROCKER, David	115	CROCKER, Ephraim	17	CROCKER, James	99
CROCKER, David	121	CROCKER, Ephriam	102	CROCKER, James P.	52
CROCKER, Deborah	17	CROCKER, Esther	104	CROCKER, Jerusha	18
CROCKER, Deborah	58	CROCKER, Experience	17	CROCKER, Jerusha	115
CROCKER, Deborah	61	CROCKER, Ezekiel	52	CROCKER, Joanna	18
CROCKER, Deborah	79	CROCKER, Ezekiel	68	CROCKER, Joanna	50
CROCKER, Deborah	97	CROCKER, Ezekiel	92	CROCKER, Joanna	51
CROCKER, Deliverance	79	CROCKER, Ezra	52	CROCKER, Joanna	92
CROCKER, Desire	82	CROCKER, George	52	CROCKER, Joanna	93
CROCKER, Desire	97	CROCKER, George	74	CROCKER, Joanna	101
CROCKER, Desire	113	CROCKER, Gershom	17	CROCKER, Job	17
CROCKER, Dorcas	81	CROCKER, Gershom	92	CROCKER, Job	79
CROCKER, Ebenezer	17	CROCKER, Hannah	17	CROCKER, Job	94
CROCKER, Ebenezer	18	CROCKER, Hannah	18	CROCKER, John	17
CROCKER, Ebenezer	48	CROCKER, Hannah	34	CROCKER, John	53
CROCKER, Ebenezer	74	CROCKER, Hannah	50	CROCKER, John	60
CROCKER, Ebenezer	78	CROCKER, Hannah	65	CROCKER, John	66
CROCKER, Ebenezer	82	CROCKER, Hannah	67	CROCKER, John	77
CROCKER, Ebenezer	92	CROCKER, Hannah	82	CROCKER, John	78
CROCKER, Ebenezer	114	CROCKER, Hannah	85	CROCKER, John	79
CROCKER, Ebenezer	116	CROCKER, Hannah	88	CROCKER, John	88
CROCKER, Ebenezer	118	CROCKER, Hannah	92	CROCKER, John	95
CROCKER, Ebenr.	74	CROCKER, Hannah	93	CROCKER, John	96
CROCKER, Edmond	95	CROCKER, Hannah	94	CROCKER, John	101
CROCKER, Eleazer	17	CROCKER, Hannah	95	CROCKER, Jonathan	17
CROCKER, Eleazer	19	CROCKER, Hannah	104	CROCKER, Jonathan	48
CROCKER, Eleazer	50	CROCKER, Hannah	113	CROCKER, Jonathan	22
CROCKER, Elijach	79	CROCKER, Hannah	118	CROCKER, Jonathan	71
CROCKER, Elijah	68	CROCKER, Hannah	119	CROCKER, Jonathan	75
CROCKER, Elijah	107	CROCKER, Hope	104	CROCKER, Jonathan	79
CROCKER, Elisabeth	65	CROCKER, Huckins	104	CROCKER, Jonathan	102
CROCKER, Elisabeth	66	CROCKER, Isaac	17	CROCKER, Joseph	17
CROCKER, Elisabeth	67	CROCKER, Isaac	88	CROCKER, Joseph	18
CROCKER, Elisabeth	79	CROCKER, Isaac	101	CROCKER, Joseph	64
CROCKER, Elisha	68	CROCKER, Isaac	103	CROCKER, Joseph	65
CROCKER, Elisha	107	CROCKER, Isaac	116	CROCKER, Joseph	66
CROCKER, Elizabeth	17	CROCKER, Isaac	121	CROCKER, Joseph	78
CROCKER, Elizabeth	19	CROCKER, Jabes	75	CROCKER, Joseph	79
CROCKER, Elizabeth	50	CROCKER, Jabez	17	CROCKER, Joseph	107
CROCKER, Elizabeth	53	CROCKER, Jabez	20	CROCKER, Joshua	74
CROCKER, Elizabeth	68	CROCKER, Jabez	77	CROCKER, Joshua	95
CROCKER, Elizabeth	78	CROCKER, Jabez	79	CROCKER, Josiah	17

CROCKER, Josiah	18	CROCKER, Mehitable	115	CROCKER, Reliance	99
CROCKER, Josiah	56	CROCKER, Mehitable	116	CROCKER, Relience	97
CROCKER, Josiah	58	CROCKER, Melatia	48	CROCKER, Remember	18
CROCKER, Josiah	78	CROCKER, Melatiah	18	CROCKER, Remember	50
CROCKER, Josiah	79	CROCKER, Melatiah	107	CROCKER, Remember	108
CROCKER, Josiah	88	CROCKER, Melatiah	118	CROCKER, Rouland	92
CROCKER, Josiah	107	CROCKER, Melatiah	119	CROCKER, Rowland	17
CROCKER, Josiah	113	CROCKER, Mercy	18	CROCKER, Ruth	19
CROCKER, Josiah	114	CROCKER, Mercy	119	CROCKER, Ruth	79
CROCKER, Knelm	74	CROCKER, Mercy	120	CROCKER, Ruth	93
CROCKER, Lemuel	56	CROCKER, Mercy	122	CROCKER, Saml.	93
CROCKER, Lemuel	95	CROCKER, Moodey	95	CROCKER, Samuel	17
CROCKER, Lidia	66	CROCKER, Moses	17	CROCKER, Samuel	52
CROCKER, Loisa	53	CROCKER, Moses	95	CROCKER, Samuel	64
CROCKER, Lot	51	CROCKER, Moses	119	CROCKER, Samuel	66
CROCKER, Louisa	52	CROCKER, Nathan	19	CROCKER, Samuel	68
CROCKER, Lucretia	52	CROCKER, Nathan	20	CROCKER, Samuel	76
CROCKER, Lucy	54	CROCKER, Nathan	50	CROCKER, Samuel	79
CROCKER, Lydia	14	CROCKER, Nathan	79	CROCKER, Samuel	81
CROCKER, Lydia	17	CROCKER, Nathan	97	CROCKER, Samuel	96
CROCKER, Lydia	64	CROCKER, Nathan	101	CROCKER, Samuel	107
CROCKER, Lydia	69	CROCKER, Nathan	115	CROCKER, Sarah	17
CROCKER, Lydia	79	CROCKER, Nathan	116	CROCKER, Sarah	19
CROCKER, Lydia	104	CROCKER, Nathaniel	17	CROCKER, Sarah	61
CROCKER, Lydia	107	CROCKER, Nathaniel	58	CROCKER, Sarah	62
CROCKER, Mahitable	51	CROCKER, Nathaniel	95	CROCKER, Sarah	63
CROCKER, Martha	18	CROCKER, Noah	18	CROCKER, Sarah	65
CROCKER, Martha	97	CROCKER, Noah	93	CROCKER, Sarah	67
CROCKER, Martha	53	CROCKER, Patience	17	CROCKER, Sarah	93
CROCKER, Martha	85	CROCKER, Patience	121	CROCKER, Sarah	95
CROCKER, Martha	97	CROCKER, Patty	52	CROCKER, Sarah	97
CROCKER, Martha	113	CROCKER, Peter	78	CROCKER, Sarah	101
CROCKER, Martha	114	CROCKER, Phebe	79	CROCKER, Sarah	104
CROCKER, Mary	13	CROCKER, Prince	79	CROCKER, Sarah	118
CROCKER, Mary	17	CROCKER, Prudence	17	CROCKER, Sarah	119
CROCKER, Mary	18	CROCKER, Prudence	97	CROCKER, Sarah	121
CROCKER, Mary	26	CROCKER, Prudence	102	CROCKER, Seth	18
CROCKER, Mary	52	CROCKER, Rachel	17	CROCKER, Seth	92
CROCKER, Mary	59	CROCKER, Rachel	81	CROCKER, Seth	114
CROCKER, Mary	63	CROCKER, Rachel	116	CROCKER, Seth	118
CROCKER, Mary	69	CROCKER, Rebecca	17	CROCKER, Seth	119
CROCKER, Mary	78	CROCKER, Rebecca	64	CROCKER, Seth	120
CROCKER, Mary	79	CROCKER, Rebecca	65	CROCKER, Simeon	99
CROCKER, Mary	85	CROCKER, Rebecca	66	CROCKER, Stephen	79
CROCKER, Mary	79	CROCKER, Rebecca	67	CROCKER, Susanea	67
CROCKER, Mary	98	CROCKER, Rebekah	19	CROCKER, Susanea	73
CROCKER, Mary	104	CROCKER, Rebekah	88	CROCKER, Susanna	59
CROCKER, Mary	107	CROCKER, Rebekah	104	CROCKER, Susanna	63
CROCKER, Mathias	69	CROCKER, Rebekah	116	CROCKER, Susanna	69
CROCKER, Mehitable	79	CROCKER, Reliance	17	CROCKER, Susanna	77
CROCKER, Mehitable	104	CROCKER, Reliance	45	CROCKER, Susannah	79

INDEX - BARNSTABLE

CROCKER, Sylvanus	95	CROCKER, Zacheus	118	CUMMINS, Sarah	66		
CROCKER, Tabitha	17	CROCKER, Zenas	74	CUSHING, Abel	65		
CROCKER, Tabitha	18	CROCKER, Zerviaah	74	CUSHING, Abel	67		
CROCKER, Tabitha	64	CROCKER, Zerviah	74	CUSHMAN, Seth	72		
CROCKER, Tabitha	66	CROEL, Thomas	73	CYPRUS, Peggy	57		
CROCKER, Tabitha	92	CROOK, Elizabeth	50				
CROCKER, Temperance	66	CROOK, Isaac	50	— D —			
CROCKER, Temperance	67	CROOK, Mary	119				
CROCKER, Temperance	69	CROSBEE, Thomas	96	DANIEL, Bethiah	121		
CROCKER, Temperance	85	CROSBEY. Jesse	62	DANIEL, Dinah	97		
CROCKER, Temperance	102	CROSBY, Andrew	53	DANIEL, John	114		
CROCKER, Temperance	108	CROSBY, Asenath H.	54	DANIEL, John	115		
CROCKER, Temperance	113	CROSBY, Caroline	54	DANIEL, Mercy	82		
CROCKER, Temperance	114	CROSBY, Ebenezer	118	DANIEL, Mercy	113		
CROCKER, Temperence	18	CROSBY, Ebenezer	119	DARBY, Elizabeth	39		
CROCKER, Temperence	79	CROSBY, Edward	78	DAVIS, -----	90		
CROCKER, Thankful	17	CROSBY, Edward	80	DAVIS, Abegail	107		
CROCKER, Thankful	18	CROSBY, Eunice	52	DAVIS, Abigail	22		
CROCKER, Theophilus	19	CROSBY, Freeman	53	DAVIS, Abigail	76		
CROCKER, Thomas	17	CROSBY, Harriet	54	DAVIS, Abigail	79		
CROCKER, Thomas	22	CROSBY, Jesse	59	DAVIS, Abigail	97		
CROCKER, Thomas	72	CROSBY, Mercy	87	DAVIS, Andrew	21		
CROCKER, Thomas	88	CROSBY, Mercy	115	DAVIS, Ann	78		
CROCKER, Thomas	92	CROSBY, Mercy	117	DAVIS, Ann	80		
CROCKER, Thomas	104	CROSBY, Nathaniel A.	52	DAVIS, Ann	103		
CROCKER, Thomas	119	CROSBY, Oliver	54	DAVIS, Ann	121		
CROCKER, Thomas	120	CROSBY, Ruth	52	DAVIS, Anna	21		
CROCKER, Thomas	121	CROSBY, Samuel	52	DAVIS, Anna	109		
CROCKER, Timothy	17	CROSBY, Sophia	52	DAVIS, Anna	113		
CROCKER, Timothy	18	CROSBY, Watson	54	DAVIS, Annah	69		
CROCKER, Timothy	48	CROSBY, William	52	DAVIS, Ansel	78		
CROCKER, Timothy	78	CROSBY, Wilson	54	DAVIS, Bathsheba	22		
CROCKER, Walley	17	CROSMAN, Nathaniel	82	DAVIS, Benjamin	21		
CROCKER, Walley	104	CROSMAN, Nathll.	82	DAVIS, Benjamin	22		
CROCKER, Walley	108	CROWEL, -----	19	DAVIS, Benjamin	64		
CROCKER, Walley	119	CROWEL, Bathshua	19	DAVIS, Benjamin	65		
CROCKER, Walley	120	CROWEL, Benjamin	19	DAVIS, Benjamin	104		
CROCKER, William	17	CROWEL, Edward	19	DAVIS, Catharine	76		
CROCKER, William	18	CROWEL, Joseph	19	DAVIS, Content	81		
CROCKER, William	54	CROWEL, Lydia	26	DAVIS, Cornelius	69		
CROCKER, William	56	CROWEL, Mary	19	DAVIS, Cornelius	78		
CROCKER, William	57	CROWEL, Melintha	54	DAVIS, Cornelius	80		
CROCKER, William	69	CROWEL, Paul	82	DAVIS, Daniel	21		
CROCKER, William	76	CROWEL, Paul	113	DAVIS, Daniel	22		
CROCKER, William	85	CROWEL, Thomas	71	DAVIS, Daniel	61		
CROCKER, William	104	CROWEL, Yelverton	19	DAVIS, Daniel	62		
CROCKER, William	114	Cuffee	77	DAVIS, Daniel	77		
CROCKER, Winslow	79	Cuffee	122	DAVIS, Daniel	90		
CROCKER, Zaccheus	17	CULLIO, John	110	DAVIS, Daniel	107		
CROCKER, Zaccheus	95	CULLIO, John	119	DAVIS, Daniel	111		
CROCKER, Zacheus	95	CUMMINS, Sarah	64	DAVIS, Daniel	114		

INDEX - BARNSTABLE

DAVIS, David	104	DAVIS, Isaac	105	DAVIS, Lucy	64
DAVIS, Deborah	21	DAVIS, Isaac	107	DAVIS, Lucy	66
DAVIS, Deborah	56	DAVIS, Isaac	109	DAVIS, Lucy	105
DAVIS, Deborah	58	DAVIS, Jabez	21	DAVIS, Lydia	21
DAVIS, Deborah	78	DAVIS, Jabez	22	DAVIS, Marcy	107
DAVIS, Desire	78	DAVIS, Jacob	22	DAVIS, Marey	107
DAVIS, Desire	83	DAVIS, James	21	DAVIS, Martha	56
DAVIS, Desire	94	DAVIS, James	22	DAVIS, Martha	57
DAVIS, Doler	21	DAVIS, James	83	DAVIS, Martha	76
DAVIS, Doller	21	DAVIS, James	99	DAVIS, Martha	94
DAVIS, Dorcas	115	DAVIS, James	104	OAVIS, Mary	21
DAVIS, Ebenezer	22	DAVIS, James	107	DAVIS, Mary	22
DAVIS, Ebenezer	107	DAVIS, James	113	DAVIS, Mary	26
DAVIS, Edward	22	DAVIS, James	114	DAVIS, Mary	38
DAVIS, Elisabeth	64	DAVIS, James	122	DAVIS, Mary	60
DAVIS, Elisabeth	65	DAVIS, Jean	83	DAVIS, Mary	66
DAVIS, Elisabeth	107	DAVIS, Jesse	105	DAVIS, Mary	72
DAVIS, Elizabeth	21	DAVIS, Jesse	107	DAVIS, Mary	75
DAVIS, Elizabeth	83	DAVIS, Job	22	DAVIS, Mary	77
DAVIS, Elizebath	61	DAVIS, Job	96	DAVIS, Mary	81
DAVIS, Elizebath	63	DAVIS, Job	107	DAVIS, Mary	94
DAVIS, Elizebath	76	DAVIS, Job	121	DAVIS, Mary	107
DAVIS, Eunice	59	DAVIS, John	21	DAVIS, Mary	110
DAVIS, Eunice	66	DAVIS, John	22	DAVIS, Mary	118
DAVIS, Eunice	104	DAVIS, John	47	DAVIS, Mehetable	75
DAVIS, Experience	50	DAVIS, John	78	DAVIS, Mehetable	77
DAVIS, Experience	78	DAVIS, John	106	DAVIS, Mehetable	78
DAVIS, Gershom	21	DAVIS, John	108	DAVIS, Mehitable	22
DAVIS, Gershom	66	DAVIS, John	110	DAVIS, Mehitable	61
DAVIS, Gershom	107	DAVIS, John	117	DAVIS, Mehitable	76
DAVIS, Gershom	119	DAVIS, John	120	DAVIS, Mehitable	77
DAVIS, Gershom	120	DAVIS, Jonathan	21	DAVIS, Mehitable	90
DAVIS, Gershom	121	DAVIS, Jonathan	91	DAVIS, Mehitable	106
DAVIS, Hannah	16	DAVIS, Jonathan	108	DAVIS, Mehitable	107
DAVIS, Hannah	21	DAVIS, Jonathan	117	DAVIS, Mehitable	111
DAVIS, Hannah	22	DAVIS, Jonathan	119	DAVIS, Mehitable	115
DAVIS, Hannah	33	DAVIS, Joseph	21	DAVIS, Mercy	22
DAVIS, Hannah	64	DAVIS, Joseph	22	DAVIS, Mercy	69
DAVIS, Hannah	65	DAVIS, Joseph	56	DAVIS, Mercy	91
DAVIS, Hannah	75	DAVIS, Joseph	83	DAVIS, Nathan	21
DAVIS, Hannah	77	DAVIS, Joseph	104	DAVIS, Nathan	22
DAVIS, Hannah	83	DAVIS, Joseph	107	DAVIS, Nathaniel	22
DAVIS, Hannah	99	DAVIS, Josiah	21	DAVIS, Nicholas	22
DAVIS, Hannah	107	DAVIS, Josiah	22	DAVIS, Noah	22
DAVIS, Hannah	109	DAVIS, Josiah	64	DAVIS, Noah	96
DAVIS, Hopestill	77	DAVIS, Josiah	66	DAVIS, Patience	83
DAVIS, Isaac	21	DAVIS, Josiah	97	DAVIS, Phebe	52
DAVIS, Isaac	22	DAVIS, Josiah	107	DAVIS, Prince	78
DAVIS, Isaac	75	DAVIS, Josiah	114	DAVIS, Prince	81
DAVIS, Isaac	77	DAVIS, Lothrop	78	DAVIS, Prince	103
DAVIS, Isaac	103	DAVIS, Louis	96	DAVIS, Priscilla	81

INDEX - BARNSTABLE

DAVIS, Rebeca	75	DAVIS, Stephen	94	DELAP, Hannah	90
DAVIS, Rebeca	77	DAVIS, Stephen	103	DELAP, James	90
DAVIS, Rebecca	103	DAVIS, Stephen	108	DELAP, James	110
DAVIS, Rebekah	103	DAVIS, Stephen	120	DELAP, James	116
DAVIS, Remember	22	DAVIS, Susanah	105	DELAP, Jean	90
DAVIS, Remember Mercy	122	DAVIS, Susannah	91	DELAP, Mary	90
DAVIS, Robert	21	DAVIS, Susannah	103	DELAP, Rose	64
DAVIS, Robert	21	DAVIS, Susannah	111	DELAP, Rose	66
DAVIS, Robert	22	DAVIS, Susannah	114	DELAP, Rose	90
DAVIS, Robert	77	DAVIS, Susannah	114	DELAP, Sarah	90
DAVIS, Robert	83	DAVIS, Thankful	22	DELAP, Thomas	90
DAVIS, Robert	98	DAVIS, Thankful	80	DERBY, Sarah	39
DAVIS, Robert	107	DAVIS, Thankful	99	DERRICK, Richard	52
DAVIS, Ruth	21	DAVIS, Thankful	104	DEWY, Augusta M.	54
DAVIS, Ruth	39	DAVIS, Thankfull	56	DEXTER, -----	22
DAVIS, Ruth	47	DAVIS, Thankfull	58	DEXTER, Abigail	22
DAVIS, Ruth	76	DAVIS, Thankfull	96	DEXTER, Anna	22
DAVIS, Saml.	64	DAVIS, Thomas	21	DEXTER, Benjamin	21
DAVIS, Samuel	21	DAVIS, Thomas	78	DEXTER, Content	22
DAVIS, Samuel	22	DAVIS, Thomas	104	DEXTER, Content	121
DAVIS, Samuel	65	DAVIS, Thomas	105	DEXTER, Cornelius	22
DAVIS, Samuel	107	DAVIS, Thomas	106	DEXTER, Drusilla	59
DAVIS, Sarah	21	DAVIS, Thomas	107	DEXTER, Drusilla	62
DAVIS, Sarah	21	DAVIS, Thomas	121	DEXTER, Hannah	121
DAVIS, Sarah	48	DAVIS, Timothy	64	DEXTER, James	21
DAVIS, Sarah	67	DAVIS, Timothy	66	DEXTER, John	21
DAVIS, Sarah	70	DAVIS, Unis	96	DEXTER, Joseph	121
DAVIS, Sarah	72	DAVIS, William	76	DEXTER, Mary	21
DAVIS, Sarah	103	DAVIS, William	106	DEXTER, Mary	22
DAVIS, Seth	21	DAVIS, William	107	DEXTER, Mary	98
DAVIS, Seth	72	DAVIS, William	113	DEXTER, Mercy	22
DAVIS, Seth	72	DAVIS, William	114	DEXTER, Meribah	65
DAVIS, Seth	107	DEAN, Abigail	74	DEXTER, Miriam	22
DAVIS, Shobal	21	DEAN, Archelaus	74	DEXTER, Philippi	56
DAVIS, Shobal	22	DEAN, Elijah	115	DEXTER, Phillip	21
DAVIS, Shobal	107	DEAN, Elijah	115	DEXTER, Stephen	21
DAVIS, Shoble	75	DEAN, Ephraim	108	DEXTER, Stephen	22
DAVIS, Shoble	76	DEAN, Eunice	108	DEXTER, Stephen	117
DAVIS, Shubal	98	DEAN, Hannah	74	DEXTER, Thomas	21
DAVIS, Shubal	121	DEAN, Jonas	108	DEXTER, William	21
DAVIS, Simeon	94	DEAN, Lydia	78	DIC, Rachel	62
DAVIS, Simon	21	DEAN, Lydia	80	DIER, Ebenezer	22
DAVIS, Simon	22	DEAN, Lydia	108	DIER, Henry	22
DAVIS, Simon	81	DEAN, Thomas	74	DIER, Isabel	22
DAVIS, Simon	99	DEAN, Thomas	77	DIER, Jonathan	22
DAVIS, Simon	111	DEAN, Thomas	108	DIER, Judah	22
DAVIS, Simon	115	DEAN, William	108	DIER, Lydia	22
DAVIS, Solomon	106	DELAP, Abigail	56	DIER, Saml.	22
DAVIS, Solomon	120	DELAP, Abigail	56	DIER, William	22
DAVIS, Stephen	21	DELAP, Abigail	90	DIER, William	22
DAVIS, Stephen	22	DELAP, Catharine	90	DILLINGHAM, Edward	96

DILLINGHAM, John	115	DIMOCK, Samuel	21	DRAPER, Mary	98
DILLINGHAM, John	115	DIMOCK, Sarah	21	DRODY, Allen G.	53
DIMMOCK, Elizabeth	112	DIMOCK, Shobal	20	Dublin	66
DIMMOCK, Ensign	21	DIMOCK, Shobal	21	DUN, Dorothy	21
DIMMOCK, Hannah	112	DIMOCK, Shobal	22	DUN, Dorothy	114
DIMMOCK, Mehitable	106	DIMOCK, Temperance	47	DUN, Elizabeth	82
DIMMOCK, Thomas	112	DIMOCK, Temporance	20	DUN, Experience	21
DIMOCK, Abigail	21	DIMOCK, Thankful	20	DUN, John	21
DIMOCK, Abigail	82	DIMOCK, Thankful	21	DUN, John	81
DIMOCK, Abigail	108	DIMOCK, Theophilus	21	DUNHAM, Benjamin	21
DIMOCK, Anna	21	DIMOCK, Theophilus	48	DUNHAM, David	113
DIMOCK, Anna	78	DIMOCK, Thomas	20	DUNHAM, David	114
DIMOCK, Anna	81	DIMOCK, Thomas	21	DUNHAM, Desire	21
DIMOCK, Anna	108	DIMOCK, Thomas	61	DUNHAM, Ebenezer	21
DIMOCK, Benjamin	20	DIMOCK, Thomas	72	DUNHAM, Elisha	21
DIMOCK, Bethiah	21	DIMOCK, Thomas	73	DUNHAM, John	21
DIMOCK, Charles	61	DIMOCK, Thomas	108	DUNHAM, Mary	31
DIMOCK, Charles	112	DIMOCK, Thomas	108	DUNHAM, Mercy	21
DIMOCK, David	21	DIMOCK, Timothy	20	DUNHAM, Susannah	32
DIMOCK, David	113	DIMOCK, Timothy	21	DUNHAM, Thomas	21
DIMOCK, David	114	DIMUCK, Daniel	99	DUNN, Elizabeth	115
DIMOCK, Desire	20	DIMUCK, Hannah	99	DURFE, Abigail	121
DIMOCK, Desire	47	DIMUCK, Joseph	99		
DIMOCK, Desire	78	DIMUCK, Mehitable	99	— E —	
DIMOCK, Desire	80	DIMUCK, Mehitable	121		
DIMOCK, Desire	108	DIMUCK, Samuel	99	EASTERBROOK, Abigail	64
DIMOCK, Ebenezer	21	DIMUCK, Shobal	99	EASTERBROOK, Elisabeth	64
DIMOCK, Edward	20	DOANE, Eliza	52	EASTERBROOK, Gorham	64
DIMOCK, Edward	108	DOANE, Rachel	58	EASTERBROOK, John	64
DIMOCK, Elizabeth	21	DOGGED, Patience	10	EASTERBROOK, John	78
DIMOCK, Elizabeth	61	DOGGET, Ruth	11	EASTERBROOK, John	80
DIMOCK, Elizabeth	81	DONE, Saml.	48	EASTERBROOK, Mercy C.	52
DIMOCK, Ensign	108	DOWENS, Barnabas	94	EASTERBROOK, Rachel	64
DIMOCK, Ensign	118	DOWNES, Abigail	94	EASTERBROOK, Samuel	64
DIMOCK, Hannah	61	DOWNES, Barnabas	64	Ebad	48
DIMOCK, Hannah	108	DOWNES, Barnabas	66	Ebad	118
DIMOCK, Ichabod	21	DOWNES, Barnabus	94	EDEY, Elizabeth	40
DIMOCK, Joanna	20	DOWNES, David	94	EDWARD, Joshua	121
DIMOCK, Joannah	21	DOWNES, Desire	75	EDWARDS, Joshua	96
DIMOCK, John	20	DOWNES, Edward	94	EGARD, Hester	45
DIMOCK, John	61	DOWNES, Elisabeth	94	EGERTON, Miriam	66
DIMOCK, Joseph	20	DOWNES, James	94	EGERTON, Miriam	67
DIMOCK, Joseph	21	DOWNES, Mary	94	EGRED, Thomas	78
DIMOCK, Joseph	108	DOWNES, Mercy	94	EGRED, Thomas	81
DIMOCK, Mary	21	DOWNES, Prince	94	ELDREDGE, Ann	118
DIMOCK, Mehitable	20	DOWNES, Rachel	94	ELDRIDGE, Benjamin	54
DIMOCK, Mehitable	21	DOWNES, Samuel	94	ELDRIDGE, David H.	51
DIMOCK, Mehitable	47	DOWNS, Barnabas	76	ELDRIDGE, Jonathan	52
DIMOCK, Mehitable	106	DOWNS, Barnabas	76	ELIS, Prissilla	58
DIMOCK, Mehitable	108	DOWNS, Mary	72	ELLIS, Elizabeth	58
DIMOCK, Pharoh	21	DOWNS, Thankfull	76	ELLIS, Jonathan	78

Name	Page	Name	Page	Name	Page
ELLIS, Jonathan	80	EWER, Sarah	97	FITTS RANDLE, Thos.	22
ELLIS, Mary	116	EWER, Seth	63	FITTSRANDLE, Hannah	47
ELLIS, Mercy	65	EWER, Seth	65	FITTSRANDLE, Isaac	22
ELLIS, Meriah	76	EWER, Seth	73	FITTSRANDLE, John	22
ELLIS, Priscilla	61	EWER, Seth	97	FITTSRANDLE, Nathll.	22
EVERET, Noble	53	EWER, Shobal	22	FOLLAND, Margaret	39
EWER, Abigail	81	EWER, Silas	81	FORD, Phebe	51
EWER, Ansel	73	EWER, Silas	98	FOSTER, Abigail	66
EWER, Benjamin	22	EWER, Silas	109	FOSTER, Abigail	83
EWER, Benjamin	82	EWER, Susannah	81	FOSTER, Benjamin	23
EWER, David	88	EWER, Sylvanus	97	FOSTER, Chillingsworth	112
EWER, Desire	98	EWER, Thankful	22	FOSTER, Ebenezer	56
EWER, Ebenezer	88	EWER, Thomas	22	FOSTER, Ebenezer	59
EWER, Eleazer	73	EWER, Thomas	49	FOSTER, Ebenezer	66
EWER, Elizabeth	81	EWER, Thomas	73	FOSTER, Ebenezer	67
EWER, Gamaliel	72	EWER, Thomas	80	FOSTER, Elizabeth	83
EWER, Gamaliel	98	EWER, Thomas	97	FOSTER, Gershom	108
EWER, Hezekiah	22			FOSTER, James	66
EWER, Isaac	53	— F —		FOSTER, Joanna	75
EWER, Jean	88			FOSTER, John	83
EWER, John	22	FARRAR, Sarah	34	FOSTER, John Bursley	66
EWER, John	23	FARRIS, Orange	72	FOSTER, Joseph	23
EWER, John	88	Fench Betty	118	FOSTER, Joseph	83
EWER, John	97	FESSENDEN, Lucy	66	FOSTER, Lois	108
EWER, John	115	FICH, Unice	97	FOSTER, Mary	66
EWER, Jonathan	22	FISH, Betsy	54	FOSTER, Mercy	66
EWER, Jonathan	88	FISH, Calvan	54	FOSTER, Mercy	83
EWER, Joseph	22	FISH, Clarisa	54	FOSTER, Mercy	112
EWER, Lydia	73	FISH, Dorcas	115	FOSTER, Nathan	58
EWER, Lydia	81	FISH, Ebenezer	66	FOSTER, Nathan	66
EWER, Mary	34	FISH, Huldah	52	FOSTER, Nathan	76
EWER, Mary	66	FISH, Isaac	52	FOSTER, Nathan	77
EWER, Mary	67	FISH, John	98	FOSTER, Nathan	83
EWER, Mary	98	FISH, Lemuel	75	FOSTER, Thomas	66
EWER, Mehitable	22	FISH, Lemuel	77	FOSTER, Thomas	95
EWER, Mehitable	81	FISH, Mary	51	FOSTER, Thomas	108
EWER, Mercy	64	FISH, Mary	95	FOSTER, Thomas	121
EWER, Mercy	66	FISH, Mary	119	FOXWEL, Martha	22
EWER, Mercy	88	FISH, Phebe	118	FOXWEL, Mary	22
EWER, Mercy	97	FISH, Rachel	63	FOXWEL, Richard	22
EWER, Nathaniel	81	FISH, Rebeckah P.	53	FOXWEL, Ruth	22
EWER, Nathaniel	98	FISH, Ruben	61	FOXWELL, Martha	11
EWER, Nathl.	98	FISH, Seth	114	FRANCIS, Hester	122
EWER, Nathll.	22	FISH, Zenas	52	FREEMAN, Abigail	72
EWER, Prince	81	FITTRANDLE, Mary	29	FREEMAN, Abigail	108
EWER, Rebekah	22	FITTS RANDLE, Edward	22	FREEMAN, Benjamin	47
EWER, Rebekah	115	FITTS RANDLE, Hannah	22	FREEMAN, Bethiah	102
EWER, Rebekah	118	FITTS RANDLE, Hope	22	FREEMAN, Bethiah	113
EWER, Reliance	88	FITTS RANDLE, John	22	FREEMAN, Bethiah	114
EWER, Sarah	64	FITTS RANDLE, Joseph	22	FREEMAN, Bethiah	117
EWER, Sarah	65	FITTS RANDLE, Mary	22	FREEMAN, David	76

INDEX - BARNSTABLE

Name	Page	Name	Page	Name	Page
FREEMAN, David	79	FULLER, Benjamin	91	FULLER, Hannah	96
FREEMAN, David	108	FULLER, Benjamin	95	FULLER, Hannah	109
FREEMAN, Desire	118	FULLER, Bethia	23	FULLER, Hannah	114
FREEMAN, Edmond	110	FULLER, Bethiah	22	FULLER, Hannah	119
FREEMAN, Edmond	118	FULLER, Bethiah	23	FULLER, Hannah	120
FREEMAN, Elizabeth	88	FULLER, Bethiah	22	FULLER, Hester	79
FREEMAN, Elizabeth	121	FULLER, Bethiah	66	FULLER, Isaac	23
FREEMAN, Hannah	92	FULLER, Bethiah	108	FULLER, Isaac	75
FREEMAN, James	102	FULLER, Bethiah	115	FULLER, Isaac	89
FREEMAN, Keziah	92	FULLER, Bethiah	116	FULLER, Isaac	98
FREEMAN, Lydia	62	FULLER, Bethiah	117	FULLER, Jabez	23
FREEMAN, Mary	122	FULLER, Celio	53	FULLER, Jacob	79
FREEMAN, Nathaniel	102	FULLER, Charity	61	FULLER, James	23
FREEMAN, Nathl.	102	FULLER, Charity	66	FULLER, James	51
FREEMAN, Stephen	92	FULLER, Charity	89	FULLER, James	63
FREEMAN, Stephen	115	FULLER, Content	23	FULLER, James	91
FREEMAN, Stephen	118	FULLER, Cornelius	23	FULLER, James	118
FREEMAN, Thomas Davis	108	FULLER, Daniel	76	FULLER, James	118
FREEMAN, Warren	54	FULLER, Daniel	77	FULLER, James	119
French Betty	118	FULLER, Daniel	88	FULLER, James H.	54
FULER, Abigail	95	FULLER, David	23	FULLER, Jean	23
FULER, Benjamin	94	FULLER, David	63	FULLER, Jean	88
FULER, Benjamin	95	FULLER, David	88	FULLER, Jedidah	63
FULER, Elizabeth	95	FULLER, Desire	85	FULLER, Jerusha	63
FULER, Lidia	95	FULLER, Ebenezer	23	FULLER, Jerusha	77
FULER, Mary	94	FULLER, Ebenezer	88	FULLER, Jerusha	89
FULER, Rebecca	94	FULLER, Ebenezer	121	FULLER, Jno.	122
FULER, Rebecca	95	FULLER, Edward	85	FULLER, Joanna	108
FULER, Thomas	95	FULLER, Eleazer	72	FULLER, Job	85
FULLER, -----	23	FULLER, Eli	63	FULLER, John	22
FULLER, -----	35	FULLER, Eli	82	FULLER, John	23
FULLER, -----	91	FULLER, Eli	89	FULLER, John	35
FULLER, Abigail	23	FULLER, Eliezer	102	FULLER, John	85
FULLER, Abigail	91	FULLER, Elisabeth	73	FULLER, John	88
FULLER, Abigail	96	FULLER, Elizabeth	23	FULLER, John	91
FULLER, Abigail	98	FULLER, Elizabeth	44	FULLER, John	111
FULLER, Abijah	79	FULLER, Elizabeth	79	FULLER, Jonathan	23
FULLER, Abijah	91	FULLER, Elizabeth	102	FULLER, Jonathan	88
FULLER, Abijah	109	FULLER, Elizabeth	103	FULLER, Joseph	23
FULLER, Abijah	113	FULLER, Elizabeth	111	FULLER, Joseph	49
FULLER, Abram	53	FULLER, Elizabeth	115	FULLER, Joseph	66
FULLER, Allen	51	FULLER, Elizabeth	116	FULLER, Joseph	91
FULLER, Ann	45	FULLER, Elizabeth	121	FULLER, Joseph	95
FULLER, Ann	98	FULLER, Francis	85	FULLER, Joseph	108
FULLER, Anne	23	FULLER, Hannah	11	FULLER, Joshua	102
FULLER, Barnabas	23	FULLER, Hannah	23	FULLER, Josiah	23
FULLER, Barnabas	102	FULLER, Hannah	49	FULLER, Josiah	115
FULLER, Bathsheba	108	FULLER, Hannah	61	FULLER, Lemuel	66
FULLER, Benja.	122	FULLER, Hannah	63	FULLER, Lemuel	108
FULLER, Benjamin	23	FULLER, Hannah	79	FULLER, Lidia	102
FULLER, Benjamin	66	FULLER, Hannah	89	FULLER, Lois	23

INDEX - BARNSTABLE

FULLER, Lois	95	FULLER, Saml.	23	GARRET, Andrew	75
FULLER, Lois	121	FULLER, Saml.	91	GARRET, Andrew	77
FULLER, Lot	102	FULLER, Samuel	23	GARRET, Lydia	109
FULLER, Lydia	21	FULLER, Samuel	66	GARRET, Mary	77
FULLER, Lydia	114	FULLER, Samuel	73	GARRET, Mary	83
FULLER, Lydia	116	FULLER, Samuel	102	GARRETT, Andrew	64
FULLER, Mariah	109	FULLER, Samuel	103	GARRETT, Andrew	66
FULLER, Mariah	114	FULLER, Samuel	121	GARRETT, Olive	52
FULLER, Mariah	116	FULLER, Sarah	23	GARRITT, Andrew	70
FULLER, Marrah	85	FULLER, Sarah	102	GARRITT, Isaac	70
FULLER, Martha	59	FULLER, Seth	23	GARRITT, Jesse	70
FULLER, Martha	63	FULLER, Seth	64	GARRITT, Lucy	70
FULLER, Martha	72	FULLER, Seth	66	GARRITT, Susannah	70
FULLER, Martha	91	FULLER, Seth	89	GARRITT, Temperance	70
FULLER, Mary	23	FULLER, Seth	95	GARRITT, Thankfull	56
FULLER, Mary	56	FULLER, Shobal	49	GATES, Joseph	122
FULLER, Mary	59	FULLER, Temperance	23	George	113
FULLER, Mary	88	FULLER, Temperance	85	George	114
FULLER, Mary	91	FULLER, Temperance	91	GIFFORD, Abigail	66
FULLER, Mary	115	FULLER, Temperance	104	GIFFORD, Alfred	52
FULLER, Mary	116	FULLER, Temperance	108	GIFFORD, Binjn.	51
FULLER, Mary	119	FULLER, Temperance	115	GIFORD, Hannah	98
FULLER, Mary	120	FULLER, Temperance	118	GILBERT, Abigail	64
FULLER, Matthew	23	FULLER, Temperance	121	GILBERT, Abigail	102
FULLER, Matthias	58	FULLER, Thakful	67	GILBERT, Benjamin	64
FULLER, Matthias	108	FULLER, Thankful	23	GILBERT, Saml.	67
FULLER, Mehitable	89	FULLER, Thankful	23	GILBERT, Samuel	64
FULLER, Mehitable	109	FULLER, Thankful	66	GILBERT, Samuel	66
FULLER, Melatiah	79	FULLER, Thankful	95	GILBERT, Samuel	102
FULLER, Melatiah	91	FULLER, Thankful	114	GILBERT, Seth	64
FULLER, Mercy	23	FULLER, Thankful	115	GILBERT, Thankful	64
FULLER, Mercy	23	FULLER, Thomas	23	GILBERT, Thankfull	102
FULLER, Mercy	63	FULLER, Thomas	79	GILLMAN, Abigail	56
FULLER, Mercy	122	FULLER, Thos.	23	GILLMAN, Abigail	58
FULLER, Nathaniel	23	FULLER, Timothy	108	GILMAN, Nathaniel	82
FULLER, Nathll.	115	FULLER, Timothy	115	GILMAN, Nathll.	113
FULLER, Nathll.	116	FULLER, Timothy	116	GLOVER, Mary	29
FULLER, Phebe	109	FULLER, William	63	GODFREY, Sarah	63
FULLER, Phebe	113	FULLER, William	88	GOODSPEED, -----	26
FULLER, Rebecca	53	FULLER, Young	23	GOODSPEED, Abigail	55
FULLER, Rebecca	63	FULLER, Zaccheus	89	GOODSPEED, Abigail	56
FULLER, Rebecca	95	FULLER, Zacheus	76	GOODSPEED, Abigail	81
FULLER, Rebekah	23	FULLER, Zacheus	77	GOODSPEED, Abigail	99
FULLER, Rebekah	102			GOODSPEED, Abner	99
FULLER, Rebekah	108	— G —		GOODSPEED, Alice	26
FULLER, Reliance	22			GOODSPEED, Alice	22
FULLER, Remember	23	GAGE, Aurela	52	GOODSPEED, Allen	55
FULLER, Remember	75	GAGE, Caroline	54	GOODSPEED, Almon	51
FULLER, Remember	77	GAGE, Lot	53	GOODSPEED, Ann	63
FULLER, Ruth	53	GALLISON, John	72	GOODSPEED, Anna	51
FULLER, Ruth	102	GALLOP, Desire	81	GOODSPEED, Anna	55

181

INDEX - BARNSTABLE

GOODSPEED, Anne	99	GOODSPEED, Isaac	73	GOODSPEED, Mary	25
GOODSPEED, Anthony	99	GOODSPEED, Isaac	96	GOODSPEED, Mary	26
GOODSPEED, Bathshua	26	GOODSPEED, Jabez	26	GOODSPEED, Mary	29
GOODSPEED, Benja.	102	GOODSPEED, Jabez	59	GOODSPEED, Mary	30
GOODSPEED, Benjamin	25	GOODSPEED, Jabez	62	GOODSPEED, Mary	47
GOODSPEED, Benjamin	26	GOODSPEED, Jabez	81	GOODSPEED, Mary	53
GOODSPEED, Benjamin	58	GOODSPEED, Jabez	102	GOODSPEED, Mary	58
GOODSPEED, Benjamin	81	GOODSPEED, Jabez	118	GOODSPEED, Mary	81
GOODSPEED, Benjn.	26	GOODSPEED, James	26	GOODSPEED, Mary	85
GOODSPEED, Betsy	52	GOODSPEED, James	85	GOODSPEED, Mary	97
GOODSPEED, Charles	54	GOODSPEED, James	111	GOODSPEED, Mary	113
GOODSPEED, Charles	63	GOODSPEED, James	115	GOODSPEED, Mary	114
GOODSPEED, Cornelius	26	GOODSPEED, Jane	26	GOODSPEED, Mary	115
GOODSPEED, Cornelius	81	GOODSPEED, Jane	51	GOODSPEED, Mary	116
GOODSPEED, Cornelius	114	GOODSPEED, Jane	102	GOODSPEED, Mehitable	26
GOODSPEED, Cornelius	116	GOODSPEED, John	25	GOODSPEED, Mehitable	48
GOODSPEED, Daniel	63	GOODSPEED, John	26	GOODSPEED, Mehitable	81
GOODSPEED, David	26	GOODSPEED, John	51	GOODSPEED, Mehitable	104
GOODSPEED, David	85	GOODSPEED, John	53	GOODSPEED, Mercy	26
GOODSPEED, Ebenezer	25	GOODSPEED, John	67	GOODSPEED, Mercy	33
GOODSPEED, Ebenezer	26	GOODSPEED, John	75	GOODSPEED, Mercy	77
GOODSPEED, Ebenezer	22	GOODSPEED, John	91	GOODSPEED, Moses	26
GOODSPEED, Ebenezer	97	GOODSPEED, John	99	GOODSPEED, Moses	104
GOODSPEED, Ebenezer	113	GOODSPEED, John	118	GOODSPEED, Moses	121
GOODSPEED, Ebenezer	115	GOODSPEED, John	119	GOODSPEED, Nancy	53
GOODSPEED, Ebenezer	118	GOODSPEED, Jonathan	26	GOODSPEED, Nathan	26
GOODSPEED, Edward	113	GOODSPEED, Joseph	26	GOODSPEED, Nathan	52
GOODSPEED, Elisabeth	77	GOODSPEED, Joseph	52	GOODSPEED, Nathan	104
GOODSPEED, Eliza	53	GOODSPEED, Joseph	58	GOODSPEED, Nathaniel	25
GOODSPEED, Elizabeth	19	GOODSPEED, Joseph	72	GOODSPEED, Nathl.	104
GOODSPEED, Elizabeth	25	GOODSPEED, Joseph	77	GOODSPEED, Nathll.	19
GOODSPEED, Elizabeth	26	GOODSPEED, Joseph	81	GOODSPEED, Nathll.	25
GOODSPEED, Elizabeth	77	GOODSPEED, Joseph	96	GOODSPEED, Nathll.	73
GOODSPEED, Elizabeth	85	GOODSPEED, Joseph	113	GOODSPEED, Olive	55
GOODSPEED, Elizabeth	96	GOODSPEED, Joseph	114	GOODSPEED, Patience	26
GOODSPEED, Elizabeth	113	GOODSPEED, Joseph	116	GOODSPEED, Patience	23
GOODSPEED, Eljiah	63	GOODSPEED, Josiah	56	GOODSPEED, Patience	55
GOODSPEED, Eunice	55	GOODSPEED, Josiah	61	GOODSPEED, Patience	76
GOODSPEED, Eunice	99	GOODSPEED, Josiah	81	GOODSPEED, Patience	77
GOODSPEED, Experience	26	GOODSPEED, Luther	63	GOODSPEED, Patty	51
GOODSPEED, Experience	122	GOODSPEED, Lyddia	26	GOODSPEED, Philemon	91
GOODSPEED, Ezra	52	GOODSPEED, Lyddy	104	GOODSPEED, Rachel	52
GOODSPEED, Hannah	55	GOODSPEED, Lydia	23	GOODSPEED, Rebacca	97
GOODSPEED, Hannah	63	GOODSPEED, Lydia	61	GOODSPEED, Rebecca	91
GOODSPEED, Hannah	85	GOODSPEED, Lydia	62	GOODSPEED, Rebecca	119
GOODSPEED, Hannah	104	GOODSPEED, Lydia	91	GOODSPEED, Rebecka	118
GOODSPEED, Hannah	113	GOODSPEED, Martha	64	GOODSPEED, Rebekah	99
GOODSPEED, Heman	63	GOODSPEED, Martha	66	GOODSPEED, Reliance	26
GOODSPEED, Heman	102	GOODSPEED, Martha	85	GOODSPEED, Reliance	102
GOODSPEED, Isaac	63	GOODSPEED, Martha	113	GOODSPEED, Reliance	104
GOODSPEED, Isaac	71	GOODSPEED, Mary	14	GOODSPEED, Reliance	121

GOODSPEED, Remember	99	GOREHAM, Job	97	GORHAM, Elizabeth	91
GOODSPEED, Roger	25	GOREHAM, John	97	GORHAM, Elizabeth	105
GOODSPEED, Roger	26	GOREHAM, Mary	96	GORHAM, Elizabeth	112
GOODSPEED, Roger	96	GOREHAM, Temperance	97	GORHAM, Eunice	105
GOODSPEED, Rose	26	GOREHAM, Thomas	97	GORHAM, Experience	25
GOODSPEED, Rufus	113	GORHAM, -----	25	GORHAM, Experience	34
GOODSPEED, Ruth	22	GORHAM, Abigail	25	GORHAM, Experience	102
GOODSPEED, Ruth	25	GORHAM, Abigail	49	GORHAM, Ezekiel	69
GOODSPEED, Ruth	26	GORHAM, Abigail	72	GORHAM, George	25
GOODSPEED, Ruth	59	GORHAM, Abigail	73	GORHAM, George Lewis	74
GOODSPEED, Ruth	62	GORHAM, Abigail	78	GORHAM, Gershom	25
GOODSPEED, Ruth	104	GORHAM, Abigail	80	GORHAM, Hannah	25
GOODSPEED, Samuel	26	GORHAM, Abigail	102	GORHAM, Hannah	56
GOODSPEED, Samuel	99	GORHAM, Abigail	103	GORHAM, Hannah	69
GOODSPEED, Sarah	53	GORHAM, Abigail	112	GORHAM, Hannah	71
GOODSPEED, Sarah	63	GORHAM, Abraham	25	GORHAM, Hannah	75
GOODSPEED, Sarah	76	GORHAM, Ann	102	GORHAM, Hannah	78
GOODSPEED, Sarah	96	GORHAM, Annah	91	GORHAM, Hannah	80
GOODSPEED, Seth	53	GORHAM, Annar	74	GORHAM, Hannah	92
GOODSPEED, Seth	55	GORHAM, Anne	115	GORHAM, Hannah	106
GOODSPEED, Seth	56	GORHAM, Barnabas	105	GORHAM, Hezekiah	109
GOODSPEED, Seth	75	GORHAM, Benja.	106	GORHAM, Hezekiah	113
GOODSPEED, Seth	76	GORHAM, Benjamin	25	GORHAM, Isaac	69
GOODSPEED, Seth	104	GORHAM, Benjamin	86	GORHAM, Isaac	86
GOODSPEED, Silas	52	GORHAM, Benjamin	102	GORHAM, Isaac	109
GOODSPEED, Silas	113	GORHAM, Benjamin	112	GORHAM, Isaac	113
GOODSPEED, Sophia	55	GORHAM, Benjamin	114	GORHAM, Isaac	113
GOODSPEED, Susanna	51	GORHAM, Benjamin	115	GORHAM, Isaac	114
GOODSPEED, Susannah	26	GORHAM, Christopher	91	GORHAM, Jabez	25
GOODSPEED, Susannah	23	GORHAM, Daniel	25	GORHAM, Jabez	81
GOODSPEED, Susannah	73	GORHAM, David	57	GORHAM, James	25
GOODSPEED, Susannah	91	GORHAM, David	106	GORHAM, James	116
GOODSPEED, Temperance	26	GORHAM, David	110	GORHAM, Job	25
GOODSPEED, Temperance	23	GORHAM, David	112	GORHAM, Job	69
GOODSPEED, Temperance	55	GORHAM, David	118	GORHAM, Job	117
GOODSPEED, Temperance	82	GORHAM, Deborah	86	GORHAM, John	25
GOODSPEED, Temperance	99	GORHAM, Deborah	102	GORHAM, John	22
GOODSPEED, Thankful	64	GORHAM, Deborah	110	GORHAM, John	69
GOODSPEED, Thankful	65	GORHAM, Deborah	116	GORHAM, John	91
GOODSPEED, Thankful	113	GORHAM, Desire	25	GORHAM, John	102
GOODSPEED, Thomas	51	GORHAM, Desire	69	GORHAM, John	106
GOODSPEED, Thomas	64	GORHAM, Ebenezer	25	GORHAM, John	110
GOODSPEED, Thomas	66	GORHAM, Ebenezer	58	GORHAM, John	118
GOODSPEED, Thomas	96	GORHAM, Ebenezer	75	GORHAM, Joseph	25
GOODSPEED, Timothy	81	GORHAM, Ebenezer	76	GORHAM, Joseph	102
GOODSPEED, Timothy	82	GORHAM, Ebenezer	92	GORHAM, Joseph	106
GOODSPEED, William	61	GORHAM, Ebenr.	122	GORHAM, Joseph	115
GOODSPEED, William	63	GORHAM, Edward	86	GORHAM, Joseph	116
GOODSPEED, William	81	GORHAM, Edward	112	GORHAM, Josiah	72
GOREHAM, Desire	97	GORHAM, Elisabeth	69	GORHAM, Josiah	75
GOREHAM, Edward	97	GORHAM, Elizabeth	25	GORHAM, Josiah	77

INDEX - BARNSTABLE

Name	Page	Name	Page	Name	Page
GORHAM, Josiah	105	GORHAM, Ruth	25	GRAY, Susanna	57
GORHAM, Leuis	74	GORHAM, Ruth	108	GRAY, Susannah	63
GORHAM, Lowis	105	GORHAM, Ruth	118	GRAY, Thomas	53
GORHAM, Lydia	25	GORHAM, Samuel	25	GREEN, David	52
GORHAM, Lydia	56	GORHAM, Samuel	86	GREEN, Desier	99
GORHAM, Lydia	106	GORHAM, Sarah	86	GREEN, Desire	109
GORHAM, Lydia	112	GORHAM, Shobal	25	GREEN, Desire	113
GORHAM, Lydia	116	GORHAM, Shobal	106	GREEN, Desire	115
GORHAM, Lydia	119	GORHAM, Shobal	112	GREEN, Hannah	26
GORHAM, Mary	25	GORHAM, Shubal	106	GREEN, Hannah	102
GORHAM, Mary	29	GORHAM, Steph.	105	GREEN, Isaiah Lewis	102
GORHAM, Mary	64	GORHAM, Stephen	25	GREEN, James	99
GORHAM, Mary	65	GORHAM, Stephen	105	GREEN, Jno.	99
GORHAM, Mary	69	GORHAM, Sturges	86	GREEN, John	56
GORHAM, Mary	72	GORHAM, Sturgis	56	GREEN, John	77
GORHAM, Mary	73	GORHAM, Sturgis	57	GREEN, Joseph	102
GORHAM, Mary	86	GORHAM, Susannah	91	GREEN, Joseph	121
GORHAM, Mary	91	GORHAM, Sylvanus	25	GREEN, Martha	102
GORHAM, Mary	92	GORHAM, Temperance	25	GREEN, Mary	114
GORHAM, Mary	102	GORHAM, Temperance	48	GREEN, Mary	120
GORHAM, Mary	106	GORHAM, Temperance	56	GREEN, Samuel	26
GORHAM, Mary	110	GORHAM, Temperance	58	GREEN, Sarah	47
GORHAM, Mary	112	GORHAM, Temperance	92	GREEN, Sarah	99
GORHAM, Mary	116	GORHAM, Temperance	111	GREEN, Warren	99
GORHAM, Mary	118	GORHAM, Temporance	25	GREEN, William	49
GORHAM, Mary S.	53	GORHAM, Thankful	22	GREEN, William	99
GORHAM, Matthias	110	GORHAM, Thankful	25	GREEN, William	113
GORHAM, Matthias	118	GORHAM, Thankful	64	GREEN, William	114
GORHAM, Mehitable	25	GORHAM, Thankful	66	GREEN, William	119
GORHAM, Mehitable	47	GORHAM, Thankful	108	GREEN, William	120
GORHAM, Mehitable	86	GORHAM, Thankful	113	GREENE, Abigail	49
GORHAM, Mercy	25	GORHAM, Thankful	114	GREY, Elisha	111
GORHAM, Mercy	50	GORHAM, Thankful	120	GREY, Elisha	114
GORHAM, Mercy	102	GORHAM, Thankfull	102	GREY, Lot	110
GORHAM, Naomi	102	GORHAM, Theodate	25	GREY, Lot	120
GORHAM, Nathanael	75	GORHAM, Thomas	25	GUNDY, Jerusha	76
GORHAM, Nathanael	77	GORHAM, Thomas	58		
GORHAM, Nathaniel	102	GORHAM, Thomas	69	— H —	
GORHAM, Nathll.	74	GORHAM, Thomas	75		
GORHAM, Olive	86	GORHAM, Thomas	86	HACD, Joseph	50
GORHAM, Paul	25	GORHAM, Thos.	71	HADAWAY, Hannah	54
GORHAM, Peter	25	GORHAM, William	106	HADDEWAY, Bethiah	89
GORHAM, Princ	73	GORHAM, William	112	HADDEWAY, Bethiah	111
GORHAM, Prince	72	GORHAM, Zacheus	105	HADDEWAY, Elizabeth	115
GORHAM, Prince	92	GOSNOLD, Remington	73	HADDEWAY, James	72
GORHAM, Priscilla	25	GRAY, Elisha	63	HADDEWAY, James	89
GORHAM, Prudence	102	GRAY, John	56	HADDEWAY, James	110
GORHAM, Rachel	60	GRAY, John	59	HADDEWAY, James	120
GORHAM, Rachel	62	GRAY, John	62	HADDEWAY, Lois	89
GORHAM, Rebeckah	69	GRAY, John	63	HADDEWAY, Lot	102
GORHAM, Reuben	25	GRAY, Susanna	56	HADDEWAY, Patience	102

INDEX - BARNSTABLE

HADDEWAY, Sarah	50	HALLET, Jonathan	78	HAMBLIN, Elizabeth	56
HADDEWAY, Sarah	102	HALLET, Jonathan	87	HAMBLIN, Joanna	77
HADDEWAY, Susannah	102	HALLET, Jonathan	96	HAMBLIN, Joseph	77
HADDEWAY, Temperance	102	HALLET, Jonathan	113	HAMBLIN, Joshua	69
HADDEWAY, Temperance	111	HALLET, Jonathan	114	HAMBLIN, Lewes	115
HADDEWAY, Temperance	114	HALLET, Joseph	66	HAMBLIN, Lewes	116
HADDEWAY, Thomas	102	HALLET, Joseph	90	HAMBLIN, Martha	48
HADEWAY, -----	27	HALLET, Jula Ann	54	HAMBLIN, Martha	69
HADEWAY, Edward	27	HALLET, Lois	15	HAMBLIN, Mercy	72
HADEWAY, Elizabeth	113	HALLET, Lothrop	78	HAMBLIN, Ruth	69
HADEWAY, Elizabeth	115	HALLET, Mary	61	HAMBLIN, Sarah	69
HADEWAY, Hannah	122	HALLET, Mary	62	HAMBLIN, Shobal	69
HADEWAY, John	27	HALLET, Mary	87	HAMBLIN, Southworth	59
Hagar	122	HALLET, Mary	90	HAMBLIN, Southworth	73
HALL, Bathsheba	82	HALLET, Mary	116	HAMBLIN, Susannah	69
HALL, Hannah	18	HALLET, Mehitable	82	HAMBLIN, Tabitha	59
HALL, Hannah	48	HALLET, Mehitable	87	HAMBLIN, Timothy	69
HALL, John	110	HALLET, Mehitable	113	HAMLEN, Abigail	53
HALL, John	116	HALLET, Melissa	54	HAMLEN, Abigail	63
HALL, Mary	114	HALLET, Nathaniel	78	HAMLEN, Ansel	54
HALL, Priscilla	48	HALLET, Remember	75	HAMLEN, Benjamin	59
HALLET, Abigail	87	HALLET, Remember	76	HAMLEN, Benjamin	62
HALLET, Abigail	90	HALLET, Remember	87	HAMLEN, Benjamin	66
HALLET, Abigail	110	HALLET, Samuel	78	HAMLEN, Daniel	63
HALLET, Abigail	116	HALLET, Sarah	75	HAMLEN, Daniel	65
HALLET, Abner	78	HALLET, Sarah	77	HAMLEN, Daniel	67
HALLET, Abner	87	HALLET, Sarah	87	HAMLEN, Deliverance	63
HALLET, Andrew	97	HALLET, Seth	54	HAMLEN, Eleazar	97
HALLET, Annah	64	HALLET, Seth	90	HAMLEN, Hope	76
HALLET, Annah	66	HALLET, Temperance	90	HAMLEN, Jerusha	66
HALLET, Annah	87	HALLET, Thankful	60	HAMLEN, Job	66
HALLET, Anner	78	HALLET, Thankful	66	HAMLEN, Joseph	77
HALLET, Benjamin	78	HALLET, Thankful	90	HAMLEN, Martha	76
HALLET, Clarissa	52	HALLET, Timothy	114	HAMLEN, Mehetable	77
HALLET, David	72	HALLET, Timothy	116	HAMLEN, Mercy	76
HALLET, David	76	HALT, Andrew	97	HAMLEN, Rebeca	76
HALLET, David	87	HAM, Isaac	61	HAMLEN, Ruth	76
HALLET, David	96	HAM, Isaac	66	HAMLEN, Samuel	75
HALLET, David	98	HAMBELTON, Daniel	47	HAMLEN, Samuel	76
HALLET, Deborah	90	HAMBLEN, Abigail	56	HAMLEN, Sarah	66
HALLET, Desire	109	HAMBLEN, Abigail	58	HAMLEN, Sarah	67
HALLET, Elizabeth	16	HAMBLEN, Benjamin	58	HAMLEN, Sarah	76
HALLET, Elizabeth	87	HAMBLEN, Benjamin	59	HAMLEN, Shobal	76
HALLET, Elizabeth	96	HAMBLEN, Jerusha	59	HAMLEN, Shoble	62
HALLET, Elizabeth	113	HAMBLEN, Shoble	61	HAMLEN, Shoble	75
HALLET, Elizebeth	82	HAMBLEN, Timothy	61	HAMLEN, Susannah	76
HALLET, Hannah	27	HAMBLEN, Timothy	62	HAMLES, Ansel	54
HALLET, Hannah	72	HAMBLIN, Abigail	56	HAMLIN, -----	31
HALLET, Hannah	90	HAMBLIN, Bethiah	59	HAMLIN, -----	32
HALLET, Harvey	54	HAMBLIN, Ebenezer	77	HAMLIN, Abigail	20
HALLET, John	78	HAMBLIN, Eleazer	59	HAMLIN, Abigail	31

HAMLIN, Abigail	86	HAMLIN, Enoch	91	HAMLIN, John	86
HAMLIN, Abigail	92	HAMLIN, Esther	31	HAMLIN, John	115
HAMLIN, Abigail	110	HAMLIN, Experience	31	HAMLIN, John	116
HAMLIN, Abigail	120	HAMLIN, Experience	32	HAMLIN, Jonathan	31
HAMLIN, Alice	31	HAMLIN, Experience	34	HAMLIN, Jonathan	86
HAMLIN, Alice	92	HAMLIN, Experience	38	HAMLIN, Jonathan	113
HAMLIN, Alice	122	HAMLIN, Experience	83	HAMLIN, Jonathan	114
HAMLIN, Ann	32	HAMLIN, Experience	89	HAMLIN, Joseph	31
HAMLIN, Bartholomew	31	HAMLIN, Experience	110	HAMLIN, Joseph	32
HAMLIN, Bartholomew	32	HAMLIN, Experience	118	HAMLIN, Joseph	85
HAMLIN, Benjamin	31	HAMLIN, George	91	HAMLIN, Joseph	97
HAMLIN, Benjamin	32	HAMLIN, Gershom	32	HAMLIN, Joseph	115
HAMLIN, Benjamin	86	HAMLIN, Gershom	91	HAMLIN, Joseph	116
HAMLIN, Benjamin	88	HAMLIN, Gershom	92	HAMLIN, Joseph	121
HAMLIN, Benjamin	92	HAMLIN, Gershom	111	HAMLIN, Joshua	32
HAMLIN, Benjamin	115	HAMLIN, Gershom	114	HAMLIN, Joshua	95
HAMLIN, Bethiah	32	HAMLIN, Hannah	31	HAMLIN, Josiah	109
HAMLIN, Caleb	92	HAMLIN, Hannah	47	HAMLIN, Josiah	113
HAMLIN, Content	31	HAMLIN, Hannah	84	HAMLIN, Lemuel	86
HAMLIN, Content	81	HAMLIN, Hannah	85	HAMLIN, Lewes	31
HAMLIN, Content	110	HAMLIN, Hannah	91	HAMLIN, Lewes	83
HAMLIN, Content	120	HAMLIN, Hannah	92	HAMLIN, Lewes	89
HAMLIN, Cornelius	31	HAMLIN, Hester	31	HAMLIN, Lewis	88
HAMLIN, Daniel	32	HAMLIN, Hope	31	HAMLIN, Lydia	86
HAMLIN, David	31	HAMLIN, Hope	50	HAMLIN, Lydia	95
HAMLIN, David	92	HAMLIN, Hope	86	HAMLIN, Martha	31
HAMLIN, Deborah	92	HAMLIN, Hope	114	HAMLIN, Martha	91
HAMLIN, Deliverance	96	HAMLIN, Hope	116	HAMLIN, Martha	92
HAMLIN, Dorcas	32	HAMLIN, Hopestil	31	HAMLIN, Mary	22
HAMLIN, Dorcas	110	HAMLIN, Ichabud	88	HAMLIN, Mary	32
HAMLIN, Dorcas	116	HAMLIN, Isaac	31	HAMLIN, Mary	86
HAMLIN, Ebenezer	31	HAMLIN, Israel	31	HAMLIN, Mary	88
HAMLIN, Ebenezer	32	HAMLIN, Israel	32	HAMLIN, Mary	114
HAMLIN, Ebenezer	72	HAMLIN, Jacob	32	HAMLIN, Mary	119
HAMLIN, Ebenezer	121	HAMLIN, Jacob	110	HAMLIN, Mehitable	31
HAMLIN, Eleanor	95	HAMLIN, Jacob	120	HAMLIN, Mehitable	73
HAMLIN, Eleazer	31	HAMLIN, James	31	HAMLIN, Mehitable	88
HAMLIN, Eleazer	48	HAMLIN, James	92	HAMLIN, Mehitable	95
HAMLIN, Elenor	32	HAMLIN, Jean	88	HAMLIN, Mehitable	97
HAMLIN, Elenor	95	HAMLIN, Jemima	32	HAMLIN, Melatiah	31
HAMLIN, Elisabeth	107	HAMLIN, Jerusha	32	HAMLIN, Mercy	31
HAMLIN, Elisha	31	HAMLIN, Jerusha	797	HAMLIN, Mercy	32
HAMLIN, Elizabeth	31	HAMLIN, Jerusha	95	HAMLIN, Mercy	47
HAMLIN, Elizabeth	32	HAMLIN, Jerusha	115	HAMLIN, Mercy	86
HAMLIN, Elizabeth	46	HAMLIN, Jerusha	116	HAMLIN, Mercy	92
HAMLIN, Elizabeth	97	HAMLIN, Joanna	72	HAMLIN, Micah	85
HAMLIN, Elizabeth	122	HAMLIN, Job	31	HAMLIN, Nathan	32
HAMLIN, Elkanah	20	HAMLIN, John	20	HAMLIN, Nathan	111
HAMLIN, Elkanah	31	HAMLIN, John	31	HAMLIN, Nathan	115
HAMLIN, Elkanah	86	HAMLIN, John	32	HAMLIN, Nathaniel	86
HAMLIN, Elkanah	118	HAMLIN, John	53	HAMLIN, Nathll.	88

HAMLIN, Patience	20	HAMLIN, Sylvanus	115	HATCH, Nathaniel	28
HAMLIN, Patience	32	HAMLIN, Tabitha	20	HATCH, Rebekah	118
HAMLIN, Patience	114	HAMLIN, Tabitha	81	HATCH, Saml.	28
HAMLIN, Perez	86	HAMLIN, Tabitha	82	HATCH, Sarah	28
HAMLIN, Philemon	86	HAMLIN, Tabitha	113	HATCH, Silvanus	53
HAMLIN, Priscilla	31	HAMLIN, Thankful	31	HATCH, Thomas	27
HAMLIN, Priscilla	111	HAMLIN, Thankful	32	HATCH, Tibitha	53
HAMLIN, Priscilla	115	HAMLIN, Thankful	81	HATHAWAY, James	89
HAMLIN, Prudence	32	HAMLIN, Thankful	110	HATHAWAY, Mary	89
HAMLIN, Prudence	122	HAMLIN, Thankful	117	HATHEWAY, James	72
HAMLIN, Rachel	20	HAMLIN, Thomas	31	HATHEWAY, Thomas	65
HAMLIN, Rebecca	32	HAMLIN, Thomas	86	HATHEWAY, Thomas	67
HAMLIN, Rebecca	84	HAMLIN, Timothy	32	HATHEWAY, Thomas	82
HAMLIN, Rebekah	119	HAMLIN, Zaccheus	31	HATHEWAY, Thomas	109
HAMLIN, Rebekah	120	HAMLIN, Zaccheus	110	HAUXAY, Grace	116
HAMLIN, Reliance	32	HAMLIN, Zaccheus	117	HAUXEY, Grace	114
HAMLIN, Reuben	20	HAMMET, Michael	115	HAWES, Bayes	113
HAMLIN, Reuben	86	HANDY, Anna	66	HAWES, Bayes	114
HAMLIN, Reuben	114	HANDY, Elisabeth	66	HAWES, David	110
HAMLIN, Reuben	116	HANDY, Micajah	51	HAWES, David	118
HAMLIN, Ruth	31	HANDY, Micajah	52	HAWES, Dorcas	56
HAMLIN, Ruth	96	HARDEN, Bethiah	119	HAWES, Edmond	58
HAMLIN, Saml.	32	HARDIN, Mary	121	HAWES, Edmond	102
HAMLIN, Saml.	77	HARLOW, Elisabeth	63	HAWES, Edmund	122
HAMLIN, Saml.	81	HARLOW, Lydia	73	HAWES, John	25
HAMLIN, Samuel	32	HARLOW, Lydia	80	HAWES, Mary	11
HAMLIN, Samuel	83	HARLOW, Temperance	54	HAWES, Mary	66
HAMLIN, Sarah	31	HARPER, Experience	27	HAWES, Mary	102
HAMLIN, Sarah	86	HARRIS, Sarah G.	54	HAWES, Mary	118
HAMLIN, Sarah	89	HARRY, Shobal	110	HAWES, Rebecca	53
HAMLIN, Sarah	92	HARY, Jacob	120	HAWES, Sarah	102
HAMLIN, Sarah	110	HARY, Jacob	122	HAWES, Sophrona	54
HAMLIN, Sarah	117	HARY, Shobal	118	HAWES, Temperance	122
HAMLIN, Sarah	119	HASKELL, William	65	HAWES, Thankful	118
HAMLIN, Seth	31	HASKELL, William	67	HAWES, Thomas	108
HAMLIN, Seth	92	HATCH, Amos	71	HAWES, Thomas	120
HAMLIN, Seth	119	HATCH, Amos	75	HAWLEY, Gideon	66
HAMLIN, Shobal	31	HATCH, Benjamin	27	HAYMAN, Grace	42
HAMLIN, Shobal	32	HATCH, Benjamin	50	HAYMAN, Grace	43
HAMLIN, Shobal	77	HATCH, Eliphalet	52	HEDGE, Abigail	32
HAMLIN, Shobal	82	HATCH, Elizabeth	72	HEDGE, Elisha	49
HAMLIN, Shobal	95	HATCH, Experience	94	HEDGE, Elizabeth	35
HAMLIN, Silas	92	HATCH, Experience	115	HEDGE, John	32
HAMLIN, Solomon	31	HATCH, Exsperience	111	HEDGE, John	49
HAMLIN, Solomon	84	HATCH, John	122	HEDGE, Lemuel	118
HAMLIN, Solomon	119	HATCH, Jonathan	27	HEDGE, Thomas	110
HAMLIN, Southward	31	HATCH, Joseph	27	HEDGE, Thomas	116
HAMLIN, Southward	114	HATCH, Joseph	119	HERSEY, Abner	78
HAMLIN, Southworth	113	HATCH, Lydia	47	HERSEY, Abner	113
HAMLIN, Susannah	32	HATCH, Mary	27	HERSEY, Abner	114
HAMLIN, Sylvanus	20	HATCH, Moses	28	HERSEY, Ezekiel	90

Name	Page	Name	Page	Name	Page
HERSEY, Hannah	78	HINCKLEY, Warren	53	HINKLEY, Admire	29
HERSEY, James	90	HINCKLEY, William	52	HINKLEY, Albert	53
HERSEY, James	111	HINCKLY, Abiah	105	HINKLEY, Bathsheba	93
HERSEY, James	115	HINCKLY, Abigail	86	HINKLEY, Bathshua	29
HERSEY, James	116	HINCKLY, Adino	105	HINKLEY, Benjamin	29
HERSEY, Lydia	90	HINCKLY, Bathsheba	75	HINKLEY, Benjamin	30
HERSEY, Mary	78	HINCKLY, Bethiah	75	HINKLEY, Benjamin	50
HERSEY, Mehitable	90	HINCKLY, Bethiah	105	HINKLEY, Benjamin	73
HERSEY, Mehitable	113	HINCKLY, Daniel	63	HINKLEY, Benjamin	78
HERSEY, Mehitable	114	HINCKLY, Elisabeth	86	HINKLEY, Benjamin	93
HERSEY, Thomas	119	HINCKLY, Hodiah	63	HINKLEY, Bethia	30
HEWETT, Eliza	52	HINCKLY, Hodiah	105	HINKLEY, Bethiah	30
HIGGINS, Saml.	50	HINCKLY, Isaac	86	HINKLEY, Bethiah	71
HILLIARD, Bartlet	51	HINCKLY, John	60	HINKLEY, Bethiah	83
HILLIARD, Chloe	52	HINCKLY, John	62	HINKLEY, Daniel	30
HILLIARD, Maria	52	HINCKLY, John	75	HINKLEY, David	30
HILLIER, Deborah	45	HINCKLY, John	77	HINKLEY, Ebenezer	29
HILMAN, Reuben	54	HINCKLY, John	105	HINKLEY, Ebenezer	30
HINCKLEY, Abraham	53	HINCKLY, John	121	HINKLEY, Ebenezer	31
HINCKLEY, Adino	61	HINCKLY, Joseph	86	HINKLEY, Ebenezer	49
HINCKLEY, Adino	63	HINCKLY, Joseph	121	HINKLEY, Ebenezer	84
HINCKLEY, Alpheus	51	HINCKLY, Martha	76	HINKLEY, Ebenezer	114
HINCKLEY, Alvin	52	HINCKLY, Martha	77	HINKLEY, Ebenr.	84
HINCKLEY, Benjamin	54	HINCKLY, Martha	105	HINKLEY, Edmond	93
HINCKLEY, Charles	86	HINCKLY, Martha	122	HINKLEY, Edmond	113
HINCKLEY, Chipman	53	HINCKLY, Mary	96	HINKLEY, Edmond	114
HINCKLEY, Chloe	52	HINCKLY, Nathanael	63	HINKLEY, Elijah	106
HINCKLEY, Edmond	51	HINCKLY, Nathanael	66	HINKLEY, Elizabeth	29
HINCKLEY, Eli	54	HINCKLY, Nathanael	67	HINKLEY, Elizabeth	41
HINCKLEY, Eunice	86	HINCKLY, Nathaniel	61	HINKLEY, Elizabeth	73
HINCKLEY, George	54	HINCKLY, Patience	63	HINKLEY, Elizabeth	83
HINCKLEY, Hannah	52	HINCKLY, Phebe	63	HINKLEY, Elnathan	29
HINCKLEY, Hannah	86	HINCKLY, Prince	73	HINKLEY, Experience	29
HINCKLEY, Harvey	53	HINCKLY, Samuel	65	HINKLEY, Freeman	83
HINCKLEY, Hodiah	61	HINCKLY, Silvanus	73	HINKLEY, Gershom	30
HINCKLEY, Huldah	87	HINCKLY, Silvanus	76	HINKLEY, Hannah	29
HINCKLEY, Ira	53	HINCKLY, Thankfull	97	HINKLEY, Hannah	30
HINCKLEY, Isaac	86	HINCKLY, Thankfull	104	HINKLEY, Hannah	32
HINCKLEY, Jabez	56	HINCKLY, Thankfull	105	HINKLEY, Hannah	49
HINCKLEY, Josiah	52	HINCKLY, Thankfull	121	HINKLEY, Hannah	113
HINCKLEY, Lorinza	52	HINCKLY, Thankfull	122	HINKLEY, Hannah	114
HINCKLEY, Luther	52	HINCKLY, Thomas	63	HINKLEY, Huldah	32
HINCKLEY, Mary	75	HINCKLY, Thomas	76	HINKLEY, Huldah	111
HINCKLEY, Mary	77	HINKLEY, -----	48	HINKLEY, Huldah	115
HINCKLEY, Mary Ann	54	HINKLEY, Abia	50	HINKLEY, Ichabod	30
HINCKLEY, Oliver	52	HINKLEY, Abiah	29	HINKLEY, Ichabod	31
HINCKLEY, Richard	86	HINKLEY, Abigail	29	HINKLEY, Ichabod	105
HINCKLEY, Sarah	54	HINKLEY, Abigail	48	HINKLEY, Isaac	29
HINCKLEY, Sarah	56	HINKLEY, Abigail	93	HINKLEY, Isaac	78
HINCKLEY, Sophia	51	HINKLEY, Abigail	115	HINKLEY, Isaac	106
HINCKLEY, Timothy	58	HINKLEY, Abigail	116	HINKLEY, Jabez	105

INDEX - BARNSTABLE

HINKLEY, James	29	HINKLEY, Saml.	109	HINKLY, Nathll.	81
HINKLEY, James	83	HINKLEY, Samuel	28	HINKLY, Nathll.	113
HINKLEY, Job	29	HINKLEY, Samuel	29	HINKLY, Saml.	113
HINKLEY, Job	32	HINKLEY, Samuel	30	HINKLY, Sarah	79
HINKLEY, Job	49	HINKLEY, Samuel	31	HINKLY, Sarah	81
HINKLEY, John	28	HINKLEY, Samuel	93	HODGDON, David	96
HINKLEY, John	29	HINKLEY, Sarah	11	HODGDON, Hannah	96
HINKLEY, John	30	HINKLEY, Sarah	15	HODGDON, Mehitabe	96
HINKLEY, John	31	HINKLEY, Sarah	28	HODGDON, William	96
HINKLEY, John	47	HINKLEY, Sarah	29	HODGES, Harcules	52
HINKLEY, John	83	HINKLEY, Sarah	30	HOLDEN, John	50
HINKLEY, John	113	HINKLEY, Sarah	32	HOLLEY, Experience	26
HINKLEY, John	114	HINKLEY, Sarah	48	HOLLEY, Mary	22
HINKLEY, Jonathan	30	HINKLEY, Sarah	73	HOLMES, Betsey	51
HINKLEY, Joseph	29	HINKLEY, Sarah	83	HOLMES, Elisha	64
HINKLEY, Joseph	77	HINKLEY, Sarah	84	HOLMES, Elisha	65
HINKLEY, Joseph	83	HINKLEY, Seth	29	HOLMES, Lydia	63
HINKLEY, Joseph	93	HINKLEY, Seth	106	HOLWAY, Joseph	65
HINKLEY, Joseph	112	HINKLEY, Shobal	29	HOLWAY, Lemuel	54
HINKLEY, Josiah	29	HINKLEY, Susannah	30	HOLWAY, Thankful	52
HINKLEY, Levi	73	HINKLEY, Sylvanus	73	HOLWAY, William	51
HINKLEY, Lydia	73	HINKLEY, Sylvanus	93	HOMES, Phebe	76
HINKLEY, Marcy	29	HINKLEY, Temperance	106	HOPE, Abigail	75
HINKLEY, Martha	31	HINKLEY, Temperance	115	HOPE, Sarah	75
HINKLEY, Martha	72	HINKLEY, Temprence	84	HOPE, Thankfull	75
HINKLEY, Martha	93	HINKLEY, Thankful	29	HOPE, Timothy	75
HINKLEY, Mary	29	HINKLEY, Thankful	31	HOPE, Timothy	76
HINKLEY, Mary	30	HINKLEY, Thankful	48	HOPKINS, Elisha	49
HINKLEY, Mary	31	HINKLEY, Thankful	49	HOPKINS, Mercy	121
HINKLEY, Mary	48	HINKLEY, Thankful	114	HOPKINS, Patty	51
HINKLEY, Mary	105	HINKLEY, Thankful	116	HORSFIELD, Timothy	52
HINKLEY, Mary	106	HINKLEY, Thomas	29	HORTEN, Abigail	77
HINKLEY, Mary	112	HINKLEY, Thomas	30	HOWES, Abigail	103
HINKLEY, Mary	119	HINKLEY, Thomas	106	HOWES, Barnabas	72
HINKLEY, Mary	120	HINKLEY, Thos.	29	HOWES, Barnabas	103
HINKLEY, Mehitable	29	HINKLEY, Timothy	93	HOWES, Deliverance	61
HINKLEY, Melatiah	17	HINKLEY, Zaccheus	73	HOWES, Deliverance	62
HINKLEY, Melatiah	29	HINKLEY, Zaccheus	93	HOWES, Elizabeth	11
HINKLEY, Mercy	29	HINKLY, Abner	79	HOWES, Jeremiah	103
HINKLEY, Mercy	48	HINKLY, Anna	79	HOWES, Peter	51
HINKLEY, Mercy	105	HINKLY, Bathsheba	77	HOWES, Prince	110
HINKLEY, Mercy	106	HINKLY, Benjamin	79	HOWES, Prince	116
HINKLEY, Nathaniel	29	HINKLY, Benjamin	81	HOWES, Saml.	48
HINKLEY, Nathaniel	109	HINKLY, Desire	81	HOWES, Sarah	103
HINKLEY, Nathll.	93	HINKLY, Edmond	79	HOWES, Susanna	53
HINKLEY, Nymphas	73	HINKLY, Enock	79	HOWES, Thankful	77
HINKLEY, Oliver	54	HINKLY, Heman	79	HOWLAND, -----	98
HINKLEY, Rachel	29	HINKLY, Isaac	80	HOWLAND, Abigail	69
HINKLEY, Reliance	29	HINKLY, Mary	79	HOWLAND, Abigail	93
HINKLEY, Reliance	48	HINKLY, Mary	83	HOWLAND, Alice	75
HINKLEY, Reliance	73	HINKLY, Nathaniel	81	HOWLAND, Alice	77

INDEX - BARNSTABLE

HOWLAND, Alice	109	HOWLAND, Jabez	104	HOWLAND, Mary	85
HOWLAND, Alice	110	HOWLAND, Jabez	107	HOWLAND, Mary	107
HOWLAND, Alice	113	HOWLAND, Jabez	122	HOWLAND, Mehitable	69
HOWLAND, Ann	26	HOWLAND, James	49	HOWLAND, Mercy	26
HOWLAND, Ann	85	HOWLAND, James	51	HOWLAND, Mercy	31
HOWLAND, Ann	98	HOWLAND, James	69	HOWLAND, Mercy	69
HOWLAND, Ann	113	HOWLAND, James	107	HOWLAND, Mercy	107
HOWLAND, Anne	17	HOWLAND, James N.	53	HOWLAND, Mercy	115
HOWLAND, Anne	26	HOWLAND, Jason	53	HOWLAND, Mercy	117
HOWLAND, Anne	114	HOWLAND, Joanna	69	HOWLAND, Nathaniel	63
HOWLAND, Ansel	107	HOWLAND, Joanna	77	HOWLAND, Nathaniel	107
HOWLAND, Benjamin	56	HOWLAND, Joannah	26	HOWLAND, Rachel	61
HOWLAND, Benjamin	69	HOWLAND, Joannah	81	HOWLAND, Rachel	63
HOWLAND, Benjamin	98	HOWLAND, Job	26	HOWLAND, Rachel	85
HOWLAND, Benjn.	59	HOWLAND, Job	52	HOWLAND, Rachel	98
HOWLAND, David	56	HOWLAND, Job	69	HOWLAND, Rebecca	69
HOWLAND, David	110	HOWLAND, Job	75	HOWLAND, Rebeckah	69
HOWLAND, Deborah	56	HOWLAND, Job	77	HOWLAND, Samuel	98
HOWLAND, Deborah	59	HOWLAND, Job	107	HOWLAND, Sarah	98
HOWLAND, Deborah	110	HOWLAND, John	26	HOWLAND, Sarah	113
HOWLAND, Desire	76	HOWLAND, John	69	HOWLAND, Sarah	114
HOWLAND, Desire	77	HOWLAND, John	93	HOWLAND, Sarah Nye	54
HOWLAND, Desire	110	HOWLAND, John	98	HOWLAND, Seth	93
HOWLAND, Ebenezer	26	HOWLAND, John	107	HOWLAND, Shobal	26
HOWLAND, Ebenr.	97	HOWLAND, John	110	HOWLAND, Shove	69
HOWLAND, Elisabeth	69	HOWLAND, John	122	HOWLAND, Shove	93
HOWLAND, Elizabeth	13	HOWLAND, Jonathan	110	HOWLAND, Southward	69
HOWLAND, Elizabeth	31	HOWLAND, Joseph	26	HOWLAND, Susannah	75
HOWLAND, Elizabeth	77	HOWLAND, Joseph	56	HOWLAND, Susannah	77
HOWLAND, Elizabeth	107	HOWLAND, Joseph	59	HOWLAND, Susannah	110
HOWLAND, Experience	26	HOWLAND, Joseph	69	HOWLAND, Thankful	65
HOWLAND, Experience	122	HOWLAND, Joseph	85	HOWLAND, Thankful	67
HOWLAND, George	26	HOWLAND, Joseph	98	HOWLAND, Timothy	69
HOWLAND, George	93	HOWLAND, Joseph	109	HOWLAND, Zaccheus	26
HOWLAND, George	119	HOWLAND, Joseph	114	HOWSE, Mary	76
HOWLAND, George	120	HOWLAND, Joseph	116	HOXIE, Alice	52
HOWLAND, Hanah	62	HOWLAND, Josiah	48	HUBBARD, Justin	72
HOWLAND, Hannah	17	HOWLAND, Lemuel	56	HUCKENS, -----	105
HOWLAND, Hannah	26	HOWLAND, Lemuel	58	HUCKENS, Elizabeth	32
HOWLAND, Hannah	59	HOWLAND, Lydia	26	HUCKENS, Elizabeth	37
HOWLAND, Hannah	69	HOWLAND, Lydia	34	HUCKENS, Experience	32
HOWLAND, Hannah	85	HOWLAND, Martha	113	HUCKENS, Experience	37
HOWLAND, Hannah	93	HOWLAND, Martha	114	HUCKENS, Experience	49
HOWLAND, Hannah	118	HOWLAND, Mary	10	HUCKENS, Hannah	25
HOWLAND, Hannah	118	HOWLAND, Mary	26	HUCKENS, Hannah	32
HOWLAND, Hannah	119	HOWLAND, Mary	58	HUCKENS, Hope	16
HOWLAND, Isaac	26	HOWLAND, Mary	59	HUCKENS, Hope	32
HOWLAND, Isaac	94	HOWLAND, Mary	63	HUCKENS, Jabez	32
HOWLAND, Isaac	98	HOWLAND, Mary	69	HUCKENS, Jabez	105
HOWLAND, Jabez	26	HOWLAND, Mary	75	HUCKENS, James	32
HOWLAND, Jabez	69	HOWLAND, Mary	77	HUCKENS, James	105

INDEX - BARNSTABLE

HUCKENS, John	32	ISHAM, Polly	52	JANKENS, Sarah	122
HUCKENS, John	105	ISHAM, Samuel	61	JANKENS, Simeon	61
HUCKENS, Joseph	32	ISHAM, Samuel	62	JANKINS, David	103
HUCKENS, Joseph	49	ISHAM, Thomas	51	JANKINS, Elizabeth	103
HUCKENS, Joseph	105	ISHAM, Thomas	54	JANKINS, Joseph	63
HUCKENS, Lydia	32	ISSUM, Abigail	77	JANKINS, Lot	59
HUCKENS, Mary	32	ISSUM, Hannah	33	JANKINS, Phillip	103
HUCKENS, Mary	45	ISSUM, Isaac	33	JENKINS, -----	61
HUCKENS, Mary	48	ISSUM, Jane	33	JENKINS, Abigail	34
HUCKENS, Rose	32	ISSUM, Jane	50	JENKINS, Abigail	50
HUCKENS, Samuel	32	ISSUM, John	33	JENKINS, Abigail	98
HUCKENS, Sarah	49	ISSUM, Joseph	33	JENKINS, Abigail	116
HUCKENS, Snow	105	ISSUM, Mary	33	JENKINS, Alvin	61
HUCKENS, Thomas	32	ISSUM, Patience	33	JENKINS, Ann	34
HUCKENS, Thos.	32	ISSUM, Sarah	33	JENKINS, Ann	98
HUCKINGS, Elizabeth	105	ISSUM, Sarah	50	JENKINS, Anne	71
HUCKINGS, Rachel	105	ISSUM, Thankful	33	JENKINS, Anne	73
HUCKINGS, Samuel	105	ISUM, Abigail	97	JENKINS, Bathsheba	98
HUCKINGS, Thomas	105	ISUM, Daniel	97	JENKINS, Bathshuah	34
HUCKINS, James	64	ISUM, Ebenezer	97	JENKINS, Benjamin	34
HUCKINS, James	65	ISUM, Hannah	98	JENKINS, Benjamin	98
HUCKINS, Joseph	53	ISUM, Isaac	97	JENKINS, Benjamin	119
HUCKINS, Rachel	53	ISUM, John	97	JENKINS, Benjamin	120
HULL, Hannah	13	ISUM, Joshua	97	JENKINS, Bethiah	98
HULL, Hannah	27	ISUM, Mary	50	JENKINS, Charlotte	52
HULL, John	27	ISUM, Samuel	97	JENKINS, Dorcas	98
HULL, Joseph	27	ISUM, Thankfull	121	JENKINS, Ebenezer	34
HULL, Mary	27	ISUM, Timothy	97	JENKINS, Ebenezer	48
HULL, Sarah	27			JENKINS, Ebenezer	66
HULL, Trustram	27	— J —		JENKINS, Ebenezer	92
HUMFREY, Micah	61			JENKINS, Ebenezer	118
HUMFREY, Micah	63	JACKSON, Hezekiah	58	JENKINS, Ebenezer	119
HUNT, Samuel	121	JACKSON, Nathaniel	97	JENKINS, Elis	61
HUNTER, William	31	James	80	JENKINS, Elizabeth	92
HUSSEY, Puelia	25	James	82	JENKINS, Ellis	51
HYLLIER, Deborah	32	JAMES, Sarah	40	JENKINS, Experience	34
HYLLIER, Hugh	32	JANKENS, Ann	98	JENKINS, Experience	92
HYLLIER, Rose	32	JANKENS, Darkis	98	JENKINS, Experience	98
HYLLIER, Samuel	32	JANKENS, Hope	104	JENKINS, Experience	115
		JANKENS, Hope	121	JENKINS, Experience	116
— I —		JANKENS, Joseph	61	JENKINS, Hannah	75
		JANKENS, Joseph	96	JENKINS, Hannah	77
Ichabod	75	JANKENS, Joseph	98	JENKINS, Hannah	98
Ichabod	77	JANKENS, Joseph	122	JENKINS, Hannah	115
Ichabod	82	JANKENS, Lydia	104	JENKINS, Hannah	118
Ichabod	113	JANKENS, Lydia	122	JENKINS, Hope	34
ISCHAM, Sarah	97	JANKENS, Mary	121	JENKINS, John	34
ISHAM, Abigail	83	JANKENS, Nathan	61	JENKINS, John	49
ISHAM, Betsy	54	JANKENS, Nathan	63	JENKINS, John	50
ISHAM, Isaac	50	JANKENS, Ruth	122	JENKINS, Joseph	34
ISHAM, Lucretia	53	JANKENS, Sarah	96	JENKINS, Joseph	98

JENKINS, Joseph	115	JENKINS, Thankful	34	JONES, Deliverance	64
JENKINS, Joseph	117	JENKINS, Thomas	34	JONES, Deliverance	66
JENKINS, Josiah	34	JENKINS, Thomas	77	JONES, Deliverance	79
JENKINS, Josiah	116	JENKINS, Thomas	92	JONES, Deliverance	118
JENKINS, Judith	92	JENKINS, Timothy	98	JONES, Deliverance	119
JENKINS, Keziah	98	JENKINS, Zaccheus	98	JONES, Eben	119
JENKINS, Lot	63	Jenny	120	JONES, Ebenezer	33
JENKINS, Lot	92	JO, Jeremiah	59	JONES, Ebenezer	116
JENKINS, Lydia	34	JO, Jeremy	62	JONES, Ebenezer	118
JENKINS, Lydia	72	JOB, Experience	119	JONES, Eliphalet	52
JENKINS, Lydia	91	JOB, Hannah	66	JONES, Elizabeth	33
JENKINS, Marcy	50	JOB, Mehitable	113	JONES, Elizabeth	97
JENKINS, Mariah	61	JOB, Mehtable	82	JONES, Ephraim	79
JENKINS, Martha	92	JOB, Sarah	77	JONES, Experience	33
JENKINS, Mary	92	JOB, Sarah	111	JONES, Goodspeed	72
JENKINS, Mary	98	JOB, Sarah	114	JONES, Grace	81
JENKINS, Mehitable	31	JOB, Sarah	122	JONES, Hannah	33
JENKINS, Mehitable	34	JOB, Thomas	76	JONES, Hannah	53
JENKINS, Mehitable	98	JOEL, Patience	110	JONES, Hannah	75
JENKINS, Mercy	34	JOEL, Patience	118	JONES, Hannah	115
JENKINS, Mercy	98	JOEL, Sarah	97	JONES, Hannah	118
JENKINS, Nathan	92	JOHNSON, Mary	76	JONES, Hannah	119
JENKINS, Nathanael	76	JONES, Abigail	33	JONES, Isaac	33
JENKINS, Nathaniel	61	JONES, Abigail	73	JONES, Isaac	72
JENKINS, Nathaniel	92	JONES, Abigail	103	JONES, Isaac	77
JENKINS, Olive	61	JONES, Abigail	121	JONES, Isaac	93
JENKINS, Patience	98	JONES, Abner	72	JONES, Jeddediah	33
JENKINS, Phillip	34	JONES, Adam	49	JONES, Jedediah	33
JENKINS, Phillip	48	JONES, Ann	67	JONES, Jedediah	52
JENKINS, Prudence	118	JONES, Ann	73	JONES, Jedediah	75
JENKINS, Prudence	119	JONES, Anna F.	53	JONES, Jedediah	85
JENKINS, Rebekah	98	JONES, Asa	75	JONES, Jedediah	93
JENKINS, Reliance	34	JONES, Benjamin	33	JONES, Jedediah	115
JENKINS, Ruth	34	JONES, Benjamin	52	JONES, Jedidiah	116
JENKINS, Ruth	110	JONES, Benjamin	81	JONES, John	33
JENKINS, Sally	53	JONES, Benjamin	98	JONES, John	118
JENKINS, Saml.	34	JONES, Benjamin	112	JONES, Joseph	33
JENKINS, Saml.	48	JONES, Benjamin	114	JONES, Joseph	75
JENKINS, Saml.	77	JONES, Benjamin	116	JONES, Joseph	81
JENKINS, Saml.	81	JONES, Bethiah	33	JONES, Joseph	112
JENKINS, Saml.	92	JONES, Betsey	51	JONES, Josiah	33
JENKINS, Samuel	34	JONES, Betsy	53	JONES, Lyddy	93
JENKINS, Samuel	76	JONES, Catharine	85	JONES, Lydia	72
JENKINS, Sarah.	34	JONES, Cornelius	33	JONES, Mariah	52
JENKINS, Sarah	52	JONES, Cornelius	51	JONES, Mariah	75
JENKINS, Sarah	98	JONES, Cornelius	52	JONES, Mariah	88
JENKINS, Simeon	63	JONES, Cornelius	115	JONES, Marsena	51
JENKINS, Simeon	92	JONES, Cornelus	117	JONES, Martha	53
JENKINS, Southworth	98	JONES, David	81	JONES, Martha	121
JENKINS, Tabitha	98	JONES, Deborah	33	JONES, Mary	33
JENKINS, Temperance	61	JONES, Deborah	52	JONES, Mary	81

INDEX - BARNSTABLE

JONES, Mary	85	OONES, Thankful	33	LAWRENCE, Robert	67
JONES, Mary	112	JONES, Thankful	114	LAYTON, Alice	25
JONES, Matthew	33	JONES, Thankful	116	LEONARD, Prudence	36
JONES, Mercy	33	JONES, Thankful	118	LEONARD, Rebecca	19
JONES, Mercy	72	JONES, Thomas	52	LEUIS, David	74
JONES, Meriah	85	JONES, Timothy	33	LEUIS, Deborah	74
JONES, Micah	63	JONES, Timothy	63	LEUIS, Ebenezer	74
JONES, Micah	93	JONES, Timothy	72	LEUIS, John	74
JONES, Nathan	52	JONES, Timothy	97	LEUIS, Peter	74
JONES, Nye	51	JONES, Zenas	53	LEUIS, Rebakah	73
JONES, Nye	58	JONES, Zilpha	52	LEUIS, Sarih	73
JONES, Nye	61	JORDAN, Samuel	75	LEVET, Joanna	119
JONES, Nye	85	JORDAN, Samuel	77	LEVET, Joanna	120
JONES, Patience	72	JOYCE, Mary	25	LEWES, -----	39
JONES, Patience	93	JOYCE, Thomas	50	LEWES, Abigail	37
JONES, Patience M.	53	JUSTICE, Elizabeth	97	LEWES, Abigail	82
JONES, Polly	52			LEWES, Abigail	112
JONES, Ralp	33	— K —		LEWES, Abigail	118
JONES, Ralph	32			LEWES, Abigail	119
JONES, Ralph	33	KEEN, Lemuel	65	LEWES, Alice	37
JONES, Ralph	96	KEEN, Rebekah	120	LEWES, Anna	37
JONES, Rebecca	58	KELLEY, Clement	54	LEWES, Anna	87
JONES, Rebecca	118	KENEWAY, Aaron	110	LEWES, Anna	118
JONES, Rebecca	119	KENEWAY, Aaron	118	LEWES, Annah	109
JONES, Reuben	53	KENEWAY, Jacob	116	LEWES, Annah	119
JONES, Reuben	79	KENEWAY, Patience	111	LEWES, Antipas	108
JONES, Reuben	114	KENEWAY, Patience	115	LEWES, Antipas	120
JONES, Reuben	116	KENT, Elisha	64	LEWES, Barnabas	36
JONES, Rosanna	51	KENT, Elisha	66	LEWES, Barnabas	112
JONES, Saml.	50	KENT, William	118	LEWES, Bathshua	35
JONES, Saml.	67	KENT, Wm.	119	LEWES, Benjamin	35
JONES, Saml.	73	KNOWLES, Lydia	76	LEWES, Benjamin	39
JONES, Samuel	33			LEWES, Benjn.	49
JONES, Samuel	112	— L —		LEWES, Bethiah	112
JONES, Sarah	76			LEWES, Daniel	39
JONES, Sarah	77	LANDERS, Ebenezer	121	LEWES, David	36
JONES, Sarah	93	LANDERS, Hannah	114	LEWES, David	37
JONES, Saul	81	LANDERS, Jemima	76	LEWES, David	91
JONES, Shobal	32	LANE, Sarah	36	LEWES, Desire	37
JONES, Shobal	33	LARRANCE, Peleg	103	LEWES, Desire	73
JONES, Shobal	85	LARRANCE, Peleg	121	LEWES, Desire	108
JONES, Shobal	114	LAUNDERS, Cyntha	52	LEWES, Desire	120
JONES, Shobal	116	LAWRENCE, Hannah	82	LEWES, Ebenezer	36
JONES, Silas F.	53	LAWRENCE, Hannah	103	LEWES, Ebenezer	37
JONES, Simon	33	LAWRENCE, Hester	109	LEWES, Ebenezer	91
JONES, Simon	75	LAWRENCE, John	103	LEWES, Ebenezer	112
JONES, Simon	80	LAWRENCE, Joseph	64	LEWES, Edward	37
JONES, Simon	82	LAWRENCE, Joseph	66	LEWES, Eleazer	37
JONES, Simon	93	LAWRENCE, Mary	103	LEWES, Elinor	15
JONES, Simon	119	LAWRENCE, Peleg	103	LEWES, Elizabeth	39
JONES, Susannah	72	LAWRENCE, Robert	65	LEWES, Elizabeth	94

INDEX - BARNSTABLE

Name	Page	Name	Page	Name	Page
LEWES, Elizabeth	112	LEWES, John	112	LEWES, Saml.	36
LEWES, Elnathan	109	LEWES, Jonathan	35	LEWES, Samuel	36
LEWES, Elnathan	117	LEWES, Jonathan	39	LEWES, Samuel	35
LEWES, Ephraim	36	LEWES, Jonathan	110	LEWES, Samuel	112
LEWES, Ephraim	37	LEWES, Jonathan	117	LEWES, Sara	71
LEWES, Ephraim	110	LEWES, Jonathan	118	LEWES, Sarah	15
LEWES, Ephraim	117	LEWES, Joseph	36	LEWES, Sarah	30
LEWES, Experience	37	LEWES, Josiah	37	LEWES, Sarah	31
LEWES, Fear	112	LEWES, Josiah	109	LEWES, Sarah	36
LEWES, George	36	LEWES, Lemuel	78	LEWES, Sarah	37
LEWES, George	37	LEWES, Lemuel	81	LEWES, Sarah	35
LEWES, George	35	LEWES, Leonard	112	LEWES, Sarah	39
LEWES, George	39	LEWES, Levi	39	LEWES, Sarah	49
LEWES, George	109	LEWES, Levi	82	LEWES, Sarah	94
LEWES, Gershom	37	LEWES, Lothrop	37	LEWES, Sarah	109
LEWES, Hannah	36	LEWES, Lot	39	LEWES, Seth	39
LEWES, Hannah	37	LEWES, Martha	91	LEWES, Shobal	37
LEWES, Hannah	35	LEWES, Mary	36	LEWES, Shobal	49
LEWES, Hannah	39	LEWES, Mary	37	LEWES, Shobal	94
LEWES, Hannah	50	LEWES, Mary	35	LEWES, Shobal	117
LEWES, Hannah	110	LEWES, Mary	39	LEWES, Solomon	36
LEWES, Hannah	112	LEWES, Mary	87	LEWES, Solomon	112
LEWES, Hannah	116	LEWES, Mary	91	LEWES, Susanah	37
LEWES, Isaac	78	LEWES, Mary	94	LEWES, Susanah	99
LEWES, Isaac	82	LEWES, Mary	110	LEWES, Susannah	71
LEWES, Isaac	110	LEWES, Mary	118	LEWES, Susannah	109
LEWES, Jabez	35	LEWES, Mehitable	112	LEWES, Susannah	112
LEWES, Jacob	86	LEWES, Melatiah	35	LEWES, Temperance	77
LEWES, James	36	LEWES, Melatiah	39	LEWES, Temperance	109
LEWES, James	37	LEWES, Melatiah	82	LEWES, Thankful	36
LEWES, James	35	LEWES, Melatiah	113	LEWES, Thankful	37
LEWES, James	48	LEWES, Melatiah	114	LEWES, Thankful	39
LEWES, James	77	LEWES, Mercy	39	LEWES, Thankful	49
LEWES, James	81	LEWES, Mercy	48	LEWES, Thankful	78
LEWES, James	111	LEWES, Miriam	82	LEWES, Thankful	80
LEWES, James	112	LEWES, Naomi	87	LEWES, Thankful	109
LEWES, James	113	LEWES, Naomi	118	LEWES, Thankful	110
LEWES, James	114	LEWES, Nathan	35	LEWES, Thankful	116
LEWES, James	118	LEWES, Nathan	39	LEWES, Theodate	82
LEWES, Jane	39	LEWES, Nathaniel	37	LEWES, Thomas	37
LEWES, Jean	113	LEWES, Nathaniel	112	LEWES, Thomas	35
LEWES, Jean	114	LEWES, Nathaniel	117	LEWES, Thomas	49
LEWES, Jesse	37	LEWES, Nathll.	112	LEWES, Timothy	112
LEWES, Jesse	87	LEWES, Nathll.	119	LEWIS, -----	102
LEWES, Jesse	117	LEWES, Nehemiah	112	LEWIS, Abigail	108
LEWES, Jesse	118	LEWES, Rachel	58	LEWIS, Annah	75
LEWES, John	36	LEWES, Rebekah	71	LEWIS, Annah	77
LEWES, John	37	LEWES, Rebekah	85	LEWIS, Annah	108
LEWES, John	35	LEWES, Rebekah	112	LEWIS, Ansel	108
LEWES, John	94	LEWES, Reliance	112	LEWIS, Barnabas	76
LEWES, John	109	LEWES, Ruth	31	LEWIS, Benjamin	54

INDEX - BARNSTABLE

LEWIS, Daniel Davis	108	LEWIS, Mehitable	98	LINNEL, Hannah	39
LEWIS, Deborah	107	LEWIS, Mehitable	108	LINNEL, Hannah	80
LEWIS, Edward	98	LEWIS, Melatiah	103	LINNEL, Hannah	82
LEWIS, Elijah	54	LEWIS, Meltiah	82	LINNEL, Hannah	110
LEWIS, Elijah Phiney	74	LEWIS, Mercy	61	LINNEL, Heman	70
LEWIS, Elisabeth	76	LEWIS, Mercy	63	LINNEL, Jabez	39
LEWIS, Elizabeth	96	LEWIS, Patience	102	LINNEL, Jabez	91
LEWIS, Elizabeth	106	LEWIS, Patience	103	LINNEL, Jabez	110
LEWIS, Elizabeth	121	LEWIS, Rebecca	85	LINNEL, Jabez	118
LEWIS, Elizabeth	122	LEWIS, Rebeckah E.	54	LINNEL, Jean	91
LEWIS, Ephraim	85	LEWIS, Richard	112	LINNEL, John	39
LEWIS, Experience	107	LEWIS, Robert	108	LINNEL, John	91
LEWIS, George	60	LEWIS, Sarah	76	LINNEL, John	94
LEWIS, George	66	LEWIS, Sarah	85	LINNEL, John	110
LEWIS, George	108	LEWIS, Sarah	108	LINNEL, John	118
LEWIS, George	112	LEWIS, Seth	97	LINNEL, Jonathan	121
LEWIS, George	121	LEWIS, Seth	121	LINNEL, Joseph	39
LEWIS, Isaac	85	LEWIS, Solomon	85	LINNEL, Joseph	56
LEWIS, Isaac	99	LEWIS, Solomon	98	LINNEL, Joseph	58
LEWIS, Isaac	118	LEWIS, Susanah	97	LINNEL, Joseph	70
LEWIS, Jabez	107	LEWIS, Susannah	75	LINNEL, Joseph	91
LEWIS, James	76	LEWIS, Tabitha	121	LINNEL, Joseph	113
LEWIS, James	108	LEWIS, Temperance	75	LINNEL, Levi	70
LEWIS, James	109	LEWIS, Temperance	107	LINNEL, Lydia	70
LEWIS, James	121	LEWIS, Temperance	112	LINNEL, Mary	91
LEWIS, Jane	102	LEWIS, Thankful	75	LINNEL, Saml.	71
LEWIS, Joanna	61	LEWIS, Thankful	76	LINNEL, Samuel	39
LEWIS, Joanna	63	LEWIS, Thankful	85	LINNEL, Samuel	110
LEWIS, John	52	LEWIS, Thankfull	102	LINNEL, Samuel	121
LEWIS, John	74	LEWIS, Thankfull	103	LINNEL, Sarah	54
LEWIS, John	75	LEWIS, Thankfull	107	LINNEL, Sarah	91
LEWIS, John	76	LEWIS, Thankfull	121	LINNEL, Susanah	43
LEWIS, John	107	LEWIS, Theodate	56	LINNEL, Thankful	39
LEWIS, John	121	LEWIS, Theodate	58	LINNEL, Thankful	70
LEWIS, Jonathan	76	Limus	120	LINNEL, Thankful	88
LEWIS, Jonathan	102	LINCOLN, Ebenr.	97	LINNEL, Thankfull	121
LEWIS, Joshua	76	LINKHORN, Luke	110	LINNELL, Abigail	55
LEWIS, Leml.	112	LINKHORN, Luke	117	LINNELL, Abigail	75
LEWIS, Lemuel	103	LINKHORN, Thomas	37	LINNELL, Abigail	76
LEWIS, Lemuel	112	LINNEL, Abigail	40	LINNELL, David	39
LEWIS, Lois	103	LINNEL, Abigail	96	LINNELL, Deborah	60
LEWIS, Lot	102	LINNEL, Abigail	110	LINNELL, Deborah	66
LEWIS, Lothrop	85	LINNEL, Bethiah	39	LINNELL, Elisabeth	75
LEWIS, Lothrop	108	LINNEL, Bethiah	110	LINNELL, Elizabeth	77
LEWIS, Lydia	85	LINNEL, Deborah	91	LINNELL, Hannah	110
LEWIS, Lydia	107	LINNEL, Dorcas	70	LINNELL, Jabez	75
LEWIS, Major	108	LINNEL, Elisha	39	LINNELL, Jabez	77
LEWIS, Martha	85	LINNEL, Elisha	91	LINNELL, Nancy	54
LEWIS, Mary	61	LINNEL, Elizabeth	110	LINNELL, Samuel	75
LEWIS, Mary	63	LINNEL, Experience	22	LINNELL, Thomas	54
LEWIS, Mary	108	LINNEL, Hannah	21	LINNET, Joseph	82

Name	Page	Name	Page	Name	Page
LINNIL, Bethiah	122	LOTHROP, Abigail	35	LOTHROP, Hannah	92
LOGGEE, John	72	LOTHROP, Abigail	70	LOTHROP, Hannah	93
LOMBART, Lemuel	76	LOTHROP, Ann	35	LOTHROP, Hannah	96
LOMBART, Thankful	120	LOTHROP, Anna	35	LOTHROP, Hannah	105
London	62	LOTHROP, Anna	37	LOTHROP, Hope	34
LOOK, Saml.	49	LOTHROP, Ansel	34	LOTHROP, Ichabod	34
LOOKE, Patience	39	LOTHROP, Barnabas	34	LOTHROP, Ichabod	118
LORD, Joseph	48	LOTHROP, Barnabas	35	LOTHROP, Ichabod	119
LORING, Abigail	17	LOTHROP, Barnabas	49	LOTHROP, Isaac	34
LORING, Abigail	39	LOTHROP, Barnabas	70	LOTHROP, Isaac	66
LORING, Abigail	94	LOTHROP, Barnabas	93	LOTHROP, James	34
LORING, Abigail	98	LOTHROP, Barnabas	97	LOTHROP, James	35
LORING, Abigail	121	LOTHROP, Barnabas	105	LOTHROP, James	58
LORING, Abner	94	LOTHROP, Barnabas	113	LOTHROP, James	91
LORING, David	39	LOTHROP, Barnabas	114	LOTHROP, James	110
LORING, David	56	LOTHROP, Bathshua	35	LOTHROP, James	118
LORING, David	66	LOTHROP, Benja.	122	LOTHROP, James	121
LORING, David	94	LOTHROP, Benjamin	34	LOTHROP, Jno.	98
LORING, Desire	94	LOTHROP, Benjamin	35	LOTHROP, Jno.	122
LORING, Elijah	52	LOTHROP, Benjamin	86	LOTHROP, John	34
LORING, Elijah	94	LOTHROP, Benjamin	96	LOTHROP, John	35
LORING, Eliphalet	94	LOTHROP, Benjamin	96	LOTHROP, John	49
LORING, Eliphelet	66	LOTHROP, Benjamin	119	LOTHROP, John	70
LORING, Elizabeth	39	LOTHROP, Bethiah	30	LOTHROP, John	78
LORING, Elizabeth	94	LOTHROP, Bethiah	34	LOTHROP, John	92
LORING, Elizabeth	109	LOTHROP, Bethiah	35	LOTHROP, John	93
LORING, Elizabeth	116	LOTHROP, Bethiah	49	LOTHROP, John	94
LORING, Elizabeth	117	LOTHROP, Bethiah	93	LOTHROP, John	105
LORING, Elpalet	56	LOTHROP, Bethiah	105	LOTHROP, John	114
LORING, Elpalet	58	LOTHROP, David	53	LOTHROP, Jonathan	35
LORING, Elpalet	94	LOTHROP, David	70	LOTHROP, Jonathan	61
LORING, George	66	LOTHROP, David	91	LOTHROP, Jonathan	63
LORING, Joshua	94	LOTHROP, Deborah	34	LOTHROP, Jonathan	70
LORING, Lydia	39	LOTHROP, Deborah	63	LOTHROP, Jonathan	75
LORING, Lydia	110	LOTHROP, Deborah	91	LOTHROP, Jonathan	77
LORING, Lydia	117	LOTHROP, Ebenezer	91	LOTHROP, Jonathan	105
LORING, Mary	39	LOTHROP, Elijah	96	LOTHROP, Joseph	34
LORING, Mary	113	LOTHROP, Elizabeth	17	LOTHROP, Joseph	49
LORING, Mary	114	LOTHROP, Elizabeth	23	LOTHROP, Joseph	72
LORING, Mehitable	66	LOTHROP, Elizabeth	34	LOTHROP, Joseph	63
LORING, Otis	56	LOTHROP, Elizabeth	35	LOTHROP, Joseph	70
LORING, Otis	66	LOTHROP, Elizabeth	36	LOTHROP, Joseph	78
LORING, Otis	71	LOTHROP, Elizabeth	49	LOTHROP, Joseph	93
LORING, Otis	73	LOTHROP, Elizabeth	110	LOTHROP, Joseph	98
LORING, Otis	94	LOTHROP, Elizabeth	116	LOTHROP, Joseph	121
LORING, Sarah	66	LOTHROP, Experience	35	LOTHROP, Kembal	35
LORING, Sarah	94	LOTHROP, Experience	86	LOTHROP, Lemuel	35
LORING, Solomon	39	LOTHROP, Hannah	34	LOTHROP, Lot	93
LOTHROP, -----	34	LOTHROP, Hannah	35	LOTHROP, Kembal	35
LOTHROP, -----	35	LOTHROP, Hannah	49	LOTHROP, Lydia	110
LOTHROP, Abigail	34	LOTHROP, Hannah	70	LOTHROP, Lydia	118

LOTHROP, Martha	35	LOTHROP, Seth	115	LOVEL, Elenor	40
LOTHROP, Martha	60	LOTHROP, Seth	116	LOVEL, Eli	40
LOTHROP, Martha	62	LOTHROP, Shobal	34	LOVEL, Elinor	120
LOTHROP, Martha	91	LOTHROP, Susannah	35	LOVEL, Elizabeth	40
LOTHROP, Mary	19	LOTHROP, Susannah	110	LOVEL, Elizabeth	94
LOTHROP, Mary	34	LOTHROP, Susannah	120	LOVEL, Elizabeth	103
LOTHROP, Mary	35	LOTHROP, Tabitha	21	LOVEL, Elizabeth	116
LOTHROP, Mary	49	LOTHROP, Tabitha	34	LOVEL, Gorham	79
LOTHROP, Mary	70	LOTHROP, Tabitha	49	LOVEL, Hannah	94
LOTHROP, Mary	76	LOTHROP, Thankful	35	LOVEL, Hannah	115
LOTHROP, Mary	77	LOTHROP, Thankful	49	LOVEL, Hannah	116
LOTHROP, Mary	78	LOTHROP, Thankful	70	LOVEL, Jacob	40
LOTHROP, Mary	81	LOTHROP, Thankful	78	LOVEL, Jacob	82
LOTHROP, Mary	86	LOTHROP, Thankful	93	LOVEL, Jacob	93
LOTHROP, Mary	91	LOTHROP, Thankful	105	LOVEL, Jacob	94
LOTHROP, Mary	92	LOTHROP, Thomas	34	LOVEL, Jacob	109
LOTHROP, Mary	105	LOTHROP, Thomas	35	LOVEL, Jacob	113
LOTHROP, Mary D.	53	LOTHROP, Thomas	70	LOVEL, James	40
LOTHROP, Mehitable	34	LOTHROP, Thomas	110	LOVEL, James	50
LOTHROP, Mehitable	48	LOTHROP, Thomas	118	LOVEL, James	103
LOTHROP, Mehitable	106	LOTHROP, Thos.	34	LOVEL, Jane	40
LOTHROP, Mehitable	111	LOTHROP, Unis	70	LOVEL, Jane	96
LOTHROP, Mehitable	114	LOVEL, Abia	40	LOVEL, Jean	94
LOTHROP, Melatiah	34	LOVEL, Abia	48	LOVEL, Jean	115
LOTHROP, Mercy	35	LOVEL, Abigail	40	LOVEL, Jean	116
LOTHROP, Mercy	70	LOVEL, Abigail	79	LOVEL, Jemima	60
LOTHROP, Nathaniel	35	LOVEL, Abigail	97	LOVEL, Jerusha	40
LOTHROP, Nathaniel	63	LOVEL, Abigail	103	LOVEL, John	40
LOTHROP, Nathaniel	78	LOVEL, Abigail	116	LOVEL, John	81
LOTHROP, Nathaniel	96	LOVEL, Abigail	116	LOVEL, John	97
LOTHROP, Nathll.	92	LOVEL, Andrew	40	LOVEL, John	103
LOTHROP, Patience	91	LOVEL, Andrew	60	LOVEL, John	110
LOTHROP, Phebe	35	LOVEL, Andrew	94	LOVEL, John	118
LOTHROP, Prince	61	LOVEL, Anna	40	LOVEL, Jonathan	40
LOTHROP, Prince	66	LOVEL, Anna	103	LOVEL, Jonathan	94
LOTHROP, Rebecca	63	LOVEL, Benjamin	93	LOVEL, Jossph	40
LOTHROP, Rebecca	98	LOVEL, Bethia	103	LOVEL, Jossph	93
LOTHROP, Rebeckah	119	LOVEL, Beulah	40	LOVEL, Joshua	40
LOTHROP, Rebekah	70	LOVEL, Beulah	115	LOVEL, Joshua	50
LOTHROP, Saml.	34	LOVEL, Beulah	116	LOVEL, Joshua	97
LOTHROP, Saml.	86	LOVEL, Christopher	79	LOVEL, Lazarus	40
LOTHROP, Saml.	116	LOVEL, Content	93	LOVEL, Lazarus	88
LOTHROP, Samuel	34	LOVEL, Cornelius	93	LOVEL, Lazarus	117
LOTHROP, Samuel	105	LOVEL, Daniel	79	LOVEL, Lazarus	119
LOTHROP, Samuel	116	LOVEL, Daniel	103	LOVEL, Lida	104
LOTHROP, Sarah	34	LOVEL, Daniel	114	LOVEL, Lusana	94
LOTHROP, Sarah	35	LOVEL, Deborah	40	LOVEL, Lydia	40
LOTHROP, Sarah	49	LOVEL, Deborah	50	LOVEL, Lydia	72
LOTHROP, Seth	34	LOVEL, Deborah	103	LOVEL, Lydia	103
LOTHROP, Seth	56	LOVEL, Desier	103	LOVEL, Lydia	121
LOTHROP, Seth	78	LOVEL, Desire	79	LOVEL, Martha	40

INDEX - BARNSTABLE

LOVEL, Martha	60	LOVELL, Benjamin	77	LOVELL, Susannah	76
LOVEL, Martha	94	LOVELL, Charity	73	LOVELL, Susannah	77
LOVEL, Martha	98	LOVELL, Charrity	73	LOVELL, Sylvia	51
LOVEL, Martha	103	LOVELL, Chloe	51	LOVELL, Thirsa	53
LOVEL, Mary	40	LOVELL, Cornelius	76	LOVELL, Thomas	73
LOVEL, Mary	48	LOVELL, Cornelius	77	LOVELL, Zenas	52
LOVEL, Mary	88	LOVELL, Daniel	52	LUCE, Israel	48
LOVEL, Mary	94	LOVELL, Daniel	79	LUMBARD, Abia	19
LOVEL, Mary	103	LOVELL, David	52	LUMBARD, Bethiah	120
LOVEL, Mary	114	LOVELL, Deborah	75	LUMBARD, Chalana	52
LOVEL, Mary	116	LOVELL, Deborah	77	LUMBARD, Freelove	54
LOVEL, Mercy	40	LOVELL, Eliza	52	LUMBARD, James	54
LOVEL, Mercy	94	LOVELL, Elizabeth	22	LUMBARD, Jemima	11
LOVEL, Mercy	97	LOVELL, Elizabeth	56	LUMBARD, Meriah	120
LOVEL, Nehemiah	79	LOVELL, Elizabeth	114	LUMBARD, Sarah	39
LOVEL, Ollive	53	LOVELL, Elizebath	59	LUMBARD, Thomas	39
LOVEL, Patience	103	LOVELL, Eunice	52	LUMBARD, William	52
LOVEL, Phebe	15	LOVELL, Eunice	73	LUMBART, -----	39
LOVEL, Puelia	103	LOVELL, Ezra	52	LUMBART, -----	105
LOVEL, Rebeckah	40	LOVELL, Henry	52	LUMBART, Abigail	39
LOVEL, Rebeckah	88	LOVELL, Holbrook	53	LUMBART, Abigail	40
LOVEL, Rebekah	121	LOVELL, James	59	LUMBART, Abigail	78
LOVEL, Releif	60	LOVELL, James	63	LUMBART, Abigail	80
LOVEL, Relief	94	LOVELL, Jerusha	98	LUMBART, Abigail	82
LOVEL, Remember	97	LOVELL, John	103	LUMBART, Abigail	93
LOVEL, Ruth	103	LOVELL, Joseph	63	LUMBART, Alice	40
LOVEL, Sarah	40	LOVELL, Joseph	73	LUMBART, Ann	118
LOVEL, Sarah	79	LOVELL, Joshua	52	LUMBART, Anna	66
LOVEL, Sarah	97	LOVELL, Lazarus	64	LUMBART, Anna	78
LOVEL, Sarah	103	LOVELL, Lazarus	66	LUMBART, Anna	93
LOVEL, Sebra	60	LOVELL, Lazerus	88	LUMBART, Bathshua	39
LOVEL, Shobal	79	LOVELL, Levi	65	LUMBART, Bathshua	40
LOVEL, Shobal	103	LOVELL, Levi	67	LUMBART, Benjamin	39
LOVEL, Silas	40	LOVELL, Lydia	73	LUMBART, Benjamin	40
LOVEL, Silas	115	LOVELL, Maria	52	LUMBART, Benjamin	77
LOVEL, Simeon	88	LOVELL, Martha	73	LUMBART, Benjamin	93
LOVEL, Susannah	40	LOVELL, Mary	73	LUMBART, Bernard	39
LOVEL, Susannah	50	LOVELL, Mary	88	LUMBART, Bernard	114
LOVEL, Susannah	103	LOVELL, Owen	73	LUMBART, Bernard	115
LOVEL, Thankful	40	LOVELL, Puelia	64	LUMBART, Bethiah	39
LOVEL, William	40	LOVELL, Puelia	66	LUMBART, Bethiah	47
LOVEL, Zelotes	60	LOVELL, Relief	64	LUMBART, Bethiah	110
LOVEL, Zerviah	97	LOVELL, Relief	66	LUMBART, Daniel	78
LOVELL, Abigail H.	54	LOVELL, Relief	73	LUMBART, David	77
LOVELL, Amelia	52	LOVELL, Sarah B.	79	LUMBART, David	83
LOVELL, Andrew	73	LOVELL, Serena	52	LUMBART, Deborah	71
LOVELL, Andrew	76	LOVELL, Shobael	56	LUMBART, Desire	72
LOVELL, Anna	52	LOVELL, Shobael	59	LUMBART, Desire	73
LOVELL, Anna	56	LOVELL, Silas	61	LUMBART, Desire	91
LOVELL, Anna	57	LOVELL, Silas	66	LUMBART, Ebenezer	40
LOVELL, Benjamin	76	LOVELL, Silas	73	LUMBART, Ebenezer	77

LUMBART, Ebenezer	80	LUMBART, Joshua	105	LUMBART, Sarah	40
LUMBART, Ebenezer	106	LUMBART, Lemuel	106	LUMBART, Sarah	42
LUMBART, Elihu	39	LUMBART, Lydia	113	LUMBART, Sarah	49
LUMBART, Elizabeth	22	LUMBART, Lydia	114	LUMBART, Sarah	59
LUMBART, Elizabeth	39	LUMBART, Mariah	39	LUMBART, Sarah	85
LUMBART, Elizabeth	50	LUMBART, Mariah	110	LUMBART, Sarah	93
LUMBART, Elizabeth	93	LUMBART, Martha	39	LUMBART, Sarah	105
LUMBART, Gershom	39	LUMBART, Martha	40	LUMBART, Sarah	110
LUMBART, Gershom	91	LUMBART, Martha	42	LUMBART, Sarah	113
LUMBART, Hannah	39	LUMBART, Martha	77	LUMBART, Sarah	114
LUMBART, Hannah	40	LUMBART, Martha	105	LUMBART, Sarah	116
LUMBART, Hannah	59	LUMBART, Mary	35	LUMBART, Sarah	117
LUMBART, Hannah	82	LUMBART, Mary	39	LUMBART, Sarah	119
LUMBART, Hannah	105	LUMBART, Mary	40	LUMBART, Simeon	105
LUMBART, Hannah	109	LUMBART, Mary	47	LUMBART, Solomon	39
LUMBART, Hannah	110	LUMBART, Mary	59	LUMBART, Solomon	78
LUMBART, Hannah	113	LUMBART, Mary	72	LUMBART, Solomon	110
LUMBART, Hannah	114	LUMBART, Mary	93	LUMBART, Solomon	116
LUMBART, Hannah	118	LUMBART, Mary	110	LUMBART, Susana	105
LUMBART, Hepthsibah	39	LUMBART, Mary	117	LUMBART, Susanna	105
LUMBART, Hezekiah	39	LUMBART, Mary	119	LUMBART, Susannah	40
LUMBART, Hezekiah	118	LUMBART, Mathew	91	LUMBART, Susannah	105
LUMBART, Hope	26	LUMBART, Matthew	39	LUMBART, Temperance	40
LUMBART, Hope	40	LUMBART, Mehitable	39	LUMBART, Thankful	39
LUMBART, Hopestil	106	LUMBART, Mehitable	40	LUMBART, Thankful	47
LUMBART, Hopestill	40	LUMBART, Mercy	39	LUMBART, Thankful	50
LUMBART, Hopestill	105	LUMBART, Mercy	40	LUMBART, Thomas	39
LUMBART, Jabesh	39	LUMBART, Mercy	48	LUMBART, Thomas	50
LUMBART, Jabez	39	LUMBART, Mercy	49	LUMBART, Thos.	39
LUMBART, Jane	40	LUMBART, Mercy	93	LUMBART, Timothy	59
LUMBART, Jane	59	LUMBART, Mercy	105	LUMBART, Zaccheus	39
LUMBART, Jedediah	39	LUMBART, Nathaniel	39	LUMBARRT, Hezekiah	110
LUMBART, Jedediah	50	LUMBART, Nathaniel	82	LUMBER, Anna	56
LUMBART, Jemima	110	LUMBART, Nathll.	80	LUMBER, Anna	61
LUMBART, Jemima	118	LUMBART, Parker	40	LUMBER, Elisabeth	67
LUMBART, Joana	50	LUMBART, Patience	39	LUMBER, Elisabeth	71
LUMBART, Joanna	39	LUMBART, Patience	47	LUMBER, Elisabeth	79
LUMBART, John	39	LUMBART, Patience	111	LUMBER, Elizabeth	20
LUMBART, John	93	LUMBART, Rebecca	39	LUMBER, Experience	40
LUMBART, John	120	LUMBART, Rebekah	47	LUMBER, Hannah	40
LUMBART, Jonathan	40	LUMBART, Remember	91	LUMBER, Jabez	72
LUMBART, Jonathan	105	LUMBART, Saml.	59	LUMBER, Jededia	40
LUMBART, Joseph	93	LUMBART, Saml.	48	LUMBER, Jedediah	40
LUMBART, Joseph	105	LUMBART, Saml.	82	LUMBER, John	40
LUMBART, Joseph	113	LUMBART, Saml.	93	LUMBER, Jonathan	71
LUMBART, Joseph	114	LUMBART, Saml.	105	LUMBER, Jonathan	75
LUMBART, Joshua	40	LUMBART, Saml.	116	LUMBER, Joshua	63
LUMBART, Joshua	59	LUMBART, Samuel	40	LUMBER, Mary	42
LUMBART, Joshua	70	LUMBART, Samuel	93	LUMBER, Thomas	40
LUMBART, Joshua	72	LUMBART, Samuel	115	LUMBERT, Abigail	80
LUMBART, Joshua	93	LUMBART, Sarah	39	LUMBERT, Anna	64

INDEX - BARNSTABLE

LUMBERT, Annah	80	MAGS, Matthew	87	MEFFRECH, Gorge	73		
LUMBERT, Benja.	121	MAN, Charles	53	MEIGGS, Lydia	53		
LUMBERT, Benjamin	60	MANASSES, Jemimiah	121	MEIGGS, Seth	53		
LUMBERT, Benjamin	66	MANNING, John	113	MEIGS, Mary	61		
LUMBERT, Benjamin	72	MANNING, John	114	MEIGS, Mercy	61		
LUMBERT, Benjamin	75	MANTON, Desire	42	MEIGS, Mercy	63		
LUMBERT, Benjamin	101	MANTON, George	42	Melle	114		
LUMBERT, Debarah	73	MANTON, John	42	MENASSEH, Joshua	75		
LUMBERT, Ebenezer	75	MARCH, Barnabas	115	MENASSES, Joshua	77		
LUMBERT, Elisabeth	65	MARCH, Henry	49	MENASSES, Joshua	122		
LUMBERT, Elisabeth	75	MARCH, Nathaniel	111	MENDAL, Moses	115		
LUMBERT, Elisha	122	MARCH, Nathaniel	115	MENDAL, Moses	116		
LUMBERT, Elizabeth	40	MARCHANT, Crocker	52	MENDAL, Susannah	78		
LUMBERT, Elizabeth	76	MARCHANT, Lydia	52	MENDALL, Susannah	78		
LUMBERT, Elizabeth	99	MARSTON, Arthur B.	53	MENDALL, Susannah	80		
LUMBERT, Gershom	103	MARSTON, Benjamin	50	MERCHANT, Jabez	75		
LUMBERT, Gershom	121	MARSTON, Benjamin	63	MERCHANT, Jabez	76		
LUMBERT, Hannah	103	MARSTON, Charles	53	MERLL, Mary	47		
LUMBERT, Hannah	106	MARSTON, Isaiah	63	MERRYFIELD, Margaret	115		
LUMBERT, Hopestill	98	MARSTON, John	59	Micah	66		
LUMBERT, Ichabod	78	MARSTON, John	63	Micah	67		
LUMBERT, John	108	MARSTON, John	107	MILES, Elizabeth	121		
LUMBERT, Jonth.	122	MARSTON, Lydia	52	MILLER, John	110		
LUMBERT, Joseph	72	MARSTON, Lydia	63	MILLER, John	116		
LUMBERT, Joshua	61	MARSTON, Lydia	77	MILLER, Thankful	114		
LUMBERT, Joshua	106	MARSTON, Nymphas	77	MILTON, Edward	47		
LUMBERT, Lemuel	76	MARSTON, Nymphus	63	MOLOSSES, Mercy	115		
LUMBERT, Lemuel	78	MARSTON, Patience	51	MORDECAI, Tupper	82		
LUMBERT, Martha	72	MARSTON, Patience	116	MORSE, Edward	104		
LUMBERT, Martha	75	MARSTON, Polly	52	MORSE, Edward	122		
LUMBERT, Mary	72	MARSTON, Prince	63	MORTON, Ebenezer	50		
LUMBERT, Mathew	122	MARSTON, Prince	73	MORTON, John	48		
LUMBERT, Mercy	76	MARSTON, Sarah	63	MORTON, Josiah	109		
LUMBERT, Samuel	97	MARSTON, Sophia	53	MORTON, Josiah	120		
LUMBERT, Sarah	78	MARSTON, Sophrona	54	MORTON, Mehitable	114		
LUMBERT, Susannah	71	MARSTON, Winslow	63	MOSES, Alma	120		
LUMBERT, Susannah	73	Martha	48	MOSES, Amy	110		
LUMBERT, Thankful	60	MARYFIELD, Margaret	116	MOSES, Experience	120		
LUMBERT, Thankful	62	MASTAIN, Benja.	107	MORTON, Thankful	80		
LYNNEL, Hannah	21	MASTAIN, Benjamin	107				
		MASTAIN, John	107				
— M —		MASTAIN, Lidia	107	— N —			
		MASTAIN, Lydia	107				
MAGGS, Hannah	87	MASTAIN, Nimphas	107	NEAD, Hannah	121		
MAGGS, Josiah	87	MASTAIN, Patience	107	NEAL, John	120		
MAGGS, Mary	87	MASTAIN, Prince	107	NED, Lidia	75		
MAGGS, Mercy	87	MASTIN, Nymphas	75	NED, Lydia	79		
MAGGS, Rebekah	87	MATTHEW, Elizabeth	121	NED, Mercy	98		
MAGGS, Reuben	87	MATTHEWS, Thankful	114	Nero	61		
MAGGS, Reuben	118	MAYHEW, Experience	48	Nero	63		
MAGGS, Reuben	119	MAYO, Hannah	11	NETOMPOM, Abraham	114		
				NEWCOM, Mary	40		

INDEX - BARNSTABLE

Name	Page	Name	Page	Name	Page
NEWCOMB, Thomas	98	NYE, Joseph	64	OTIS, Jean	103
NICHOLS, Mary	47	NYE, Joseph	65	OTIS, John	42
NICHOLLS, -----	42	NYE, Joseph	115	OTIS, John	43
NICHOLLS, Abigail	42	NYE, Joshua	72	OTIS, John	67
NICHOLLS, Allin	42	NYE, Lamuel	122	OTIS, John	78
NICHOLLS, Experience	42	NYE, Lemuel	65	OTIS, John	94
NICHOLLS, James	42	NYE, Lemuel	67	OTIS, John	103
NICHOLLS, Joseph	42	NYE, Lydia	52	OTIS, John	115
NICHOLLS, Josiah	42	NYE, Mercy	53	OTIS, Jonathan	43
NICHOLLS, Mary	42	NYE, Meriah	122	OTIS, Joseph	66
NICHOLLS, Nathaniel	42	NYE, Nathan	118	OTIS, Joseph	76
NICHOLLS, Priscilla	42	NYE, Nathan	119	OTIS, Joseph	99
NICKERSON, Aaron	53	NYE, Rachel	53	OTIS, Marcy	73
NICKERSON, Anna	82	NYE, Stephen C.	53	OTIS, Maria	52
NICKERSON, Eleazer	113	NYE, Susannah	120	OTIS, Mariah	67
NICKERSON, Eleazer	114	NYE, Thomas S.	53	OTIS, Martha	43
NICKERSON, Shobal	109			OTIS, Martha	99
NICKERSON, Shobal	113	— O —		OTIS, Martha	110
NICKOLS, Thankfull	97			OTIS, Martha	118
NORMAN, Samll.	47	OAKER, James	104	OTIS, Mary	25
NORRIS, Jemima	54	OAKER, James	121	OTIS, Mary	42
NORTH, Daniel	21	OKILLEY, Benjamin	47	OTIS, Mary	43
NORTH, Hannah	21	OKILLEY, Mary	110	OTIS, Mary	44
NORTH, Hannah	82	OKILLEY, Mary	116	OTIS, Mary	59
NORTH, Hannah	113	OLDHAM, John	47	OTIS, Mary	62
NORTH, James	21	ORIS, -----	46	OTIS, Mary	99
NORTH, John	21	ORIS, Deborah	46	OTIS, Mary	103
NORTH, Mary	21	ORIS, Jane	46	OTIS, Mary	121
NORTH, Mary	114	ORIS, Jane	110	OTIS, Mary A.	67
NORTH, Winifred	21	ORIS, Jean	120	OTIS, Mercy	42
NORTON, Content	83	ORIS, Mary	45	OTIS, Mercy	43
NORTON, Content	118	ORIS, Mary	46	OTIS, Mercy	61
NOYES, Nathan	78	OTIS, -----	66	OTIS, Mercy	63
NOYES, Nathan	81	OTIS, -----	67	OTIS, Mercy	77
NYE, Benjamin	65	OTIS, Abigail	43	OTIS, Mercy	99
NYE, Benjamin	67	OTIS, Abigail	99	OTIS, Mercy	103
NYE, Benjamin	115	OTIS, Abigail	108	OTIS, Nathaniel	42
NYE, Benjamin	116	OTIS, Abigail	120	OTIS, Nathaniel	43
NYE, Benjamin	117	OTIS, Amos	103	OTIS, Nathaniel	48
NYE, Betsey	51	OTIS, Arthur	67	OTIS, Nathaniel	99
NYE, Caleb	118	OTIS, Charles	67	OTIS, Nathaniel Walter	67
NYE, Caleb	119	OTIS, Elisabeth	66	OTIS, Nathll.	99
NYE, Ebenezer	66	OTIS, Elizabeth	10	OTIS, Rebekah	66
NYE, Ebenezer	67	OTIS, Elizabeth	99	OTIS, Samll. Allen	99
NYE, Ichabod	73	OTIS, Hannah	99	OTIS, Sarah	99
NYE, Ichabud	67	OTIS, Heyman	78	OTIS, Solomon	42
NYE, Jemima	122	OTIS, James	42	OTIS, Solomon	43
NYE, John	78	OTIS, James	43	OTIS, Solomon	103
NYE, John	80	OTIS, James	66	OTIS, Temperance	78
NYE, Jonathan	72	OTIS, James	99	OTIS, Thomas	67
NYE, Joseph	52	OTIS, Jean	82	OTIS, William	67

INDEX - BARNSTABLE

Name	Page	Name	Page	Name	Page
Owet, Joab	116	PARKER, Anselm	52	PARKER, Mary	110
		PARKER, Benjamin	41	PARKER, Mary	117
— P —		PARKER, Benjamin	47	PARKER, Mary	118
		PARKER, Caroline	53	PARKER, Mary	119
PAGE, John	50	PARKER, Daniel	41	PARKER, Mercy	53
PAGE, Rebecca	61	PARKER, Daniel	42	PARKER, Mercy	108
PAGE, Rebeccah	63	PARKER, Daniel	53	PARKER, Mercy B.	53
PAIN, Bethiah	42	PARKER, Daniel	93	PARKER, Nehemiah	42
PAIN, Bethiah	110	PARKER, Daniel	94	PARKER, Nehemiah	122
PAIN, Bethiah	117	PARKER, Daniel	108	PARKER, Patience	15
PAIN, Dorcas	98	PARKER, David	42	PARKER, Patience	42
PAIN, Experience	42	PARKER, David	52	PARKER, Patience	98
PAIN, Experience	110	PARKER, David	53	PARKER, Patience	108
PAIN, Experience	118	PARKER, David	93	PARKER, Peace	42
PAIN, James	42	PARKER, David	108	PARKER, Peace	96
PAIN, Jedidah	64	PARKER, David	115	PARKER, Peace	121
PAIN, Jedidah	65	PARKER, David	118	PARKER, Priscilla	42
PAIN, Mary	42	PARKER, Deborah	109	PARKER, Priscilla	119
PAIN, Patience	50	PARKER, Deborah	113	PARKER, Priscilla	120
PAIN, Rebecca	42	PARKER, Desire	98	PARKER, Prudence	42
PAIN, Saml.	115	PARKER, Ebenezer	108	PARKER, Prudence	103
PAIN, Sarah	72	PARKER, Elisha	41	PARKER, Prudence	121
PAIN, Sarah	114	PARKER, Elisha	96	PARKER, Rebecca	42
PAIN, Sarah	118	PARKER, Elisha	98	PARKER, Rebecca	51
PAIN, Theophilus	110	PARKER, Elisha	108	PARKER, Rebekah	98
PAIN, Theophilus	118	PARKER, Ester	52	PARKER, Rebekah	121
PAIN, Thomas	42	PARKER, Experience	42	PARKER, Robert	40
PAINE, Dorcas	96	PARKER, Freman	98	PARKER, Robert	41
PAINE, Experience	121	PARKER, Hannah	41	PARKER, Robert	42
PAINE, Mary	102	PARKER, Hannah	42	PARKER, Saml.	42
PAINE, Rebecca	58	PARKER, Hannah	98	PARKER, Samuel	40
PAINE, Reliance	121	PARKER, Hannah	110	PARKER, Samuel	98
PAINE, Wm.	122	PARKER, Jabez	75	PARKER, Samuel	118
PALMER, Joseph	58	PARKER, Jabez	77	PARKER, Sarah	17
PALMER, Thomas	56	PARKER, James	42	PARKER, Sarah	40
PALMER, Thomas	61	PARKER, James	108	PARKER, Sarah	41
PARCEFULL, John	58	PARKER, Jane	33	PARKER, Sarah	42
PARCIVALL, Anna	63	PARKER, Jane	40	PARKER, Sarah	52
PARCIVALL, Hannah	63	PARKER, Jonathan	42	PARKER, Temperance	75
PARCIVALL, James	63	PARKER, Jonathan	54	PARKER, Temperance	77
PARCIVALL, Jemima	63	PARKER, Joseph	41	PARKER, Temperance	98
PARCIVALL, John	63	PARKER, Joseph	48	PARKER, Thomas	41
PARCIVALL, Mary	63	PARKER, Joseph	56	PARKER, Timothy	60
PARCIVALL, Mary	65	PARKER, Joshua	52	PARKER, Timothy	62
PARCIVALL, Sarah	63	PARKER, Mahitable	51	PARSEVEL, Mary	103
PARCKER, Marey	73	PARKER, Mary	40	PASAVIL, Hannah	115
PARKER, Abigail	42	PARKER, Mary	42	PASIFULL, Elisabeth	122
PARKER, Abigail	98	PARKER, Mary	77	PASIFULL, Elizabeth	104
PARKER, Abigail H.	54	PARKER, Mary	93	PASSAVAL, Sarah	79
PARKER, Alice	40	PARKER, Mary	98	PASSAVIL, Elizabeth	45
PARKER, Alice	41	PARKER, Mary	108	PASSAVIL, Hannah	117

INDEX - BARNSTABLE

Name	Page	Name	Page	Name	Page	Name	Page
PASSAVIL, James	45	Pharoah	103	PHINNEY, Freeman	54
PASSAVIL, James	116	Pharoah	121	PHINNEY, Hannah	43
PASSAVIL, John	45	PHINEY, -----	75	PHINNEY, Isaac	53
PASSAVIL, John	114	PHINEY, Anna	63	PHINNEY, Isaac	56
PASSAVIL, John	116	PHINEY, Bethiah	75	PHINNEY, Jabez	43
PASSAVIL, Patience	118	PHINEY, Deborah	75	PHINNEY, Jabez	118
PASSAVIL, Patience	119	PHINEY, Deborah	76	PHINNEY, Jane	54
PASSAVIL, Sarah	114	PHINEY, Edmond	96	PHINNEY, Jane	69
PASSAVIL, Sarah	116	PHINEY, Eli	75	PHINNEY, John	42
PASSIFULL, Mary	121	PHINEY, Elizabeth	96	PHINNEY, John	97
PASSIVAL, Bathsheba	77	PHINEY, Hannah	96	PHINNEY, Jonathan	100
Patience	121	PHINEY, Isaac	67	PHINNEY, Lemuel	100
PAUL, Isabel	121	PHINEY, Jabez	101	PHINNEY, Maria	54
PAUL, Jacob	115	PHINEY, Jane	101	PHINNEY, Martha	43
PAUL, Jacob	121	PHINEY, John	96	PHINNEY, Martha	72
PAUL, Martha	120	PHINEY, Joseph	101	PHINNEY, Martha	100
PEAGE, Moses	121	PHINEY, Lydia	60	PHINNEY, Mary	42
PEASE, Alice	76	PHINEY, Lydia	62	PHINNEY, Mary	69
PEASE, Hannah	120	PHINEY, Martha	96	PHINNEY, Mary	71
PEES, Martha	98	PHINEY, Martha	105	PHINNEY, Mary	96
PEES, Martha	121	PHINEY, Martha	122	PHINNEY, Mary	121
Pegg	61	PHINEY, Mary	75	PHINNEY, Melatiah	120
Pegg	63	PHINEY, Mary	101	PHINNEY, Patience	43
PEIRCE, Benjamin	81	PHINEY, Melatiah	109	PHINNEY, Patience	105
PEIRCE, Joseph	81	PHINEY, Patience	60	PHINNEY, Paul	69
PEIRCE, Mary	81	PHINEY, Patience	62	PHINNEY, Rebekah	99
PEIRCE, Samauel	81	PHINEY, Patience	122	PHINNEY, Richard	69
PEPENO, John	114	PHINEY, Samll.	122	PHINNEY, Robert	69
PERCIVAL, James	115	PHINEY, Sarah	75	PHINNEY, Sarah	43
PERCIVAL, Thankful	52	PHINEY, Sarah	76	PHINNEY, Sarah	100
PERCIVELL, Freeman	52	PHINEY, Seth	75	PHINNEY, Sarah	121
PERCIVELL, James	52	PHINEY, Silpah	75	PHINNEY, Solomon	69
PERKINS, Deborah	72	PHINEY, Stephen	96	PHINNEY, Susanna	69
PERRY, Ann	58	PHINEY, Susannah	65	PHINNEY, Temperance	119
PERRY, Caleb	66	PHINEY, Susannah	67	PHINNEY, Thomas	42
PERRY, Caleb	67	PHINEY, Thomas	121	PHINNEY, Thomas	51
PERRY, Zachariah	113	PHINNEY, Abigail	121	PHINNEY, Thomas	104
PERRY, Zechariah	114	PHINNEY, Alice	97	PHINNEY, Thomas	110
Peter	76	PHINNEY, Alice	121	PHINNEY, Thomas	120
Peter	80	PHINNEY, Anna	61	PHINNEY, William	69
Peter	82	PHINNEY, Barnabas	114	PHINNEY, Zaccheus	114
Peter	111	PHINNEY, Charles	54	PHINNY, Abigail	42
Peter	114	PHINNEY, David	53	PHINNY, Abigail	45
Peter	121	PHINNEY, David	118	PHINNY, Abigail	93
PETER, Ephraim	67	PHINNEY, Deborah	69	PHINNY, Anne	101
PETER, Ephraim	70	PHINNEY, Ebenezer	99	PHINNY, Barnabas	43
PETER, Ephraim	72	PHINNEY, Edward	69	PHINNY, Barnabas	81
PETER, Expeirience	113	PHINNEY, Eli	69	PHINNY, Benja.	113
PETER, Experience	82	PHINNEY, Elijah	54	PHINNY, Benjamin	42
PETER, Mary	114	PHINNEY, Eliza	54	PHINNY, Benjamin	43
PETER, Patience	119	PHINNEY, Elizabeth	42	PHINNY, Benjamin	81

INDEX - BARNSTABLE

PHINNY, Benjamin	82	PHINNY, Mercy	42	PITCHER, Jonathan	64
PHINNY, David	43	PHINNY, Mercy	45	PITCHER, Jonathan	65
PHINNY, David	86	PHINNY, Mercy	50	PITCHER, Jonathan	96
PHINNY, Deborah	86	PHINNY, Mercy	110	PITCHER, Jonathan	109
PHINNY, Ebenezer	42	PHINNY, Mercy	118	PITCHER, Joseph	96
PHINNY, Ebenezer	43	PHINNY, Nathaniel	109	PITCHER, Joseph	109
PHINNY, Ebenezer	120	PHINNY, Patience	93	PITCHER, Lydia	96
PHINNY, Eli	71	PHINNY, Peter	109	PITCHER, Mary	96
PHINNY, Eli	93	PHINNY, Rebekah	100	PITCHER, Mary	109
PHINNY, Elijah	86	PHINNY, Reliance	42	PITCHER, Mercy	109
PHINNY, Elizabeth	21	PHINNY, Reiiance	48	PITCHER, Reuben	96
PHINNY, Elizabeth	42	PHINNY, Reliance	93	PITCHER, Reuben	109
PHINNY, Elizabeth	43	PHINNY, Robert	42	PITCHER, Ruth	109
PHINNY, Elizabeth	87	PHINNY, Samuel	42	PITCHER, Samuel	52
PHINNY, Elizabeth	93	PHINNY, Samuel	43	PITCHER, Samuel	96
PHINNY, Gershom	45	PHINNY, Samuel	109	PITCHER, Samuel	109
PHINNY, Hannah	42	PHINNY, Sarah	93	PITCHER, Stephen	109
PHINNY, Hannah	42	PHINNY, Seth	43	PITCHER, William	96
PHINNY, Hannah	101	PHINNY, Seth	80	POCHNAT, Abigail	73
PHINNY, Hannah	109	PHINNY, Seth	100	POCKNUT, Bethiah	114
PHINNY, Ichabod	81	PHINNY, Seth	113	POCKNUT, Desire	110
PHINNY, Isaac	72	PHINNY, Seth	114	POCKNUT, Desire	116
PHINNY, Isaac	93	PHINNY, Silas	43	POCKNUT, Experience	121
PHINNY, Jabez	119	PHINNY, Susannah	81	POCKNUT, Hannah	97
PHINNY, James	45	PHINNY, Susannah	109	POCKNUT, John	114
PHINNY, Jeremiah	42	PHINNY, Temperance	43	POCKNUT, Mercy	121
PHINNY, John	42	PHINNY, Temperance	118	POCKNUT, Simon	121
PHINNY, John	101	PHINNY, Thankful	43	POCKNUT, Susannah	120
PHINNY, Jonathan	42	PHINNY, Thomas	42	POGMOT, Margaret	70
PHINNY, Jonathan	42	PHINNY, Thomas	43	POGNIT, Simon	120
PHINNY, Jonathan	43	PHINNY, Thomas	45	POGNUT, Margaret	67
PHINNY, Joseph	42	PHINNY, Thomas	78	POGNUT, Margaret	72
PHINNY, Joseph	43	PHINNY, Thomas	80	POGNUT, Peter	73
PHINNY, Joseph	101	PHINNY, Thomas	93	Pompey	113
PHINNY, Joshua	42	PHINNY, Timothy	81	Pompey	114
PHINNY, Josiah	42	PHINNY, William	109	POPE, Mary	118
PHINNY, Lydia	78	PHINNY, Zaccheus	81	POPE, Sarah	29
PHINNY, Lydy	93	PHINNY, Zacheus	43	POPMUNNUCK, Lois	120
PHINNY, Martha	43	PHINY, Bethiah	42	POPMUNNUCKE, Sarah	120
PHINNY, Martha	53	PHINY, Lydia	81	PORRIDGE, Ananias	116
PHINNY, Martha	72	PHINY, Samuel	42	PORRIDGE, Saml.	75
PHINNY, Mary	42	PIKE, Mary	116	PORRIDGE, Samuel	79
PHINNY, Mary	43	PINCHON, Mary	13	PORRIDGE, Simon	119
PHINNY, Mary	48	PINKAM, Alexander	53	PORRIGE, Ananias	109
PHINNY, Mary	86	PINNEY, Mehitable	54	PORRIGE, Hannah	115
PHINNY, Mary	87	PITCHER, Abigail	75	PRATT, David	54
PHINNY, Mehitable	43	PITCHER, Abigail	76	PRICE, Kezia	63
PHINNY, Mehitable	50	PITCHER, Abigail	96	Primus	80
PHINNY, Mehitable	81	PITCHER, Abner	109	Primus	113
PHINNY, Melatiah	42	PITCHER, Ezra	109	PRINC, Rebekah	45
PHINNY, Melatiah	43	PITCHER, Hannah	109	PRINCE, Hannah	45

INDEX - BARNSTABLE

Name	Page	Name	Page	Name	Page
PRINCE, John	45	ROBBINS, Lydia	52	RUSELL, Jonathan	102
PRINCE, Joseph	45	ROBBINS, Timothy	76	RUSELL, Mercy	102
PRINCE, Saml.	45	ROBEN, Mehitable	73	RUSSEL, Abigail	44
		Robin	97	RUSSEL, Abigail	48
— Q —		ROBIN, George	121	RUSSEL, Abigail	82
		ROBIN, Hester	122	RUSSEL, Abigail	102
QUASON, Betty	80	ROBIN, James	114	RUSSEL, Abigail	113
QUASON, Betty	82	ROBIN, James	116	RUSSEL, Anna	106
QUASON, Elizabeth	80	ROBIN, James	119	RUSSEL, Benjamin	44
QUOY, Elizabeth	121	ROBIN, Jeremiah	118	RUSSEL, Eleazer	44
QUOY, Patience	75	ROBIN, Mehitable	70	RUSSEL, Elizebeth	102
QUOY, Patience	77	ROBIN, Mehtiable	70	RUSSEL, Hannah	44
		ROBIN, Solomon	122	RUSSEL, John	44
— R —		ROBINS, Eleanor	114	RUSSEL, John	48
		ROBINS, Eleanor	119	RUSSEL, John	73
RAFE, Elisabeth	73	ROBINS, Jeduthan	98	RUSSEL, John	81
RALPH, Elizabeth	77	ROBINS, Rebacca	98	RUSSEL, John	102
RALPH, Joshua	58	ROBINS, Sarah	110	RUSSEL, John	113
RALPH, Joshua	67	ROBINS, Sarah	116	RUSSEL, John	114
RALPH, Joshua	70	ROBINSON, Abigail	44	RUSSEL, Jonathan	44
RALPH, Joshua	72	ROBINSON, Bethiah	121	RUSSEL, Jonathan	80
RALPH, Rachel	58	ROBINSON, Fear	13	RUSSEL, Jonathan	102
RALPH, Ruth	56	ROBINSON, Fear	44	RUSSEL, Joseph	44
RALPH, Ruth	58	ROBINSON, Isaac	44	RUSSEL, Joseph	106
RAY, Hannah	122	ROBINSON, Jabez	118	RUSSEL, Joseph	118
REDNDER, Leah	52	ROBINSON, Jabez	119	RUSSEL, Lothrop	81
REVIS, Sarah	97	ROBINSON, John	44	RUSSEL, Martha	44
REVIS, Sarah	121	ROBINSON, John	111	RUSSEL, Martha	45
REVIS, Thankful	120	ROBINSON, John	115	RUSSEL, Mehitable	71
REVIS, Thankfull	108	ROBINSON, Joseph	47	RUSSEL, Mehitable	73
Rheta	78	ROBINSON, Timothy	44	RUSSEL, Mehitable	81
Rheta	81	ROGERS, John	49	RUSSEL, Moody	44
RICH, Elisabeth	65	ROGERS, Joseph	115	RUSSEL, Otis	102
RICH, Hannah	92	ROGERS, Joseph	116	RUSSEL, Rebecca	48
RICH, Hannah	121	ROGERS, Juda	47	RUSSEL, Rebeckah	44
RICHARDS, Elizabeth	114	ROGERS, Mary	42	RUSSEL, Saml.	110
RICHARDS, Hosea	121	ROGERS, Mercy	82	RUSSEL, Saml.	117
RICHARDS, John	75	ROGERS, Sarah	118	RUSSEL, Samuel	44
RICHARDS, John	77	ROGGERS, Polly	54	RUSSELL, -----	44
RICHARDS, Mary	29	ROWLEY, -----	44	RUSSELL, Abigail	97
RICHARDS, Mercy	114	ROWLEY, Aaron	44	RUSSELL, Abigail	106
RICHARDS, Mercy	115	ROWLEY, Anne	115	RUSSELL, Desire	65
RIDER, Abigail	115	ROWLEY, John	44	RUSSELL, Hannah	102
RIDER, Isaih	53	ROWLEY, Mary	44	RUSSELL, Hannah	121
RIDER, Nathanll.	77	ROWLEY, Mehitable	44	RUSSELL, John	90
RIGHT, Timothy	111	ROWLEY, Moses	44	RUSSELL, John	106
RIGHT, Timothy	115	ROWLEY, Sarah	27	RUSSELL, Jonathan	106
RING, John	47	ROWLEY, Sarah	44	RUSSELL, Joseph	106
ROBBINS, Clarissa	53	ROWLEY, Shobal	44	RUSSELL, Joseph	122
ROBBINS, Hannah	53	RUMSEY, David	56	RUSSELL, Leonard	106
ROBBINS, James	53	RUMSEY, David	57	RUSSELL, Lothrop	90

INDEX - BARNSTABLE

Name	Page	Name	Page	Name	Page
RUSSELL, Lothrop	106	SCUDDER, Experience	46	SERJEANT, William	45
RUSSELL, Lucy	53	SCUDDER, Experience	49	SEVERNS, Hannah	114
RUSSELL, Moody	97	SCUDDER, Hannah	46	SHAW, Mary	94
RUSSELL, Moody	121	SCUDDER, Hannah	74	SHAW, Moses	61
RUSSELL, Rebekah	106	SCUDDER, Hannah	112	SHAW, Moses	63
RYDER, Barnabas	52	SCUDDER, Isaiah	64	SHAW, Oakes	56
RYDER, Nathanael	75	SCUDDER, James	64	SHELLY, Benj.	44
RYNG, Elizabeth	117	SCUDDER, James	74	SHELLY, Benjamin	44
		SCUDDER, James	112	SHELLY, Benjamin	49
— S —		SCUDDER, James D.	64	SHELLY, Joseph	44
		SCUDDER, John	46	SHELLY, Joseph	115
SAMPSON, Cornelius	82	SCUDDER, John	47	SHELLY, Joseph	117
SAMPSON, Cornelius	113	SCUDDER, John	112	SHELLY, Joseph	118
SAMPSON, Jerusha	116	SCUDDER, Jonathan	112	SHELLY, Lydia	45
SAMSON, Hannah	103	SCUDDER, Josiah	54	SHELLY, Robert	44
SAMSON, Hannah	121	SCUDDER, Josiah	64	SHELLY, Shobal	44
SAMSON, Jedida	109	SCUDDER, Josiah	74	SHELLY, Thankful	45
SAMSON, Jemima	109	SCUDDER, Josiah	75	SHERLY, Hannah	39
SAMSON, Martha	109	SCUDDER, Josiah	76	SHERMON, Ebenr. C.	51
SAMSON, Mary	109	SCUDDER, Josiah	112	SHOVE, Mercy	48
SAMSON, Sally	109	SCUDDER, Lucy	54	SIMMONS, Silvanus	54
SAMSON, Southworth	64	SCUDDER, Lydia	52	SIMON, Almy	115
SAMSON, Southworth	65	SCUDDER, Lydia	64	SIMON, Isaac	72
SAMSON, Southworth	109	SCUDDER, Lydia	65	SIMON, Isaac	120
SAMSON, William	109	SCUDDER, Mehitable	112	SKIFF, Thankfull	66
SANDERS, Anna	22	SCUDDER, Nathaniel	112	SMALLEY, Daniel	107
SANDERS, Thankful	114	SCUDDER, Oliver	52	SMALLEY, Martha	107
SANDERSON, John	79	SCUDDER, Puella	54	SMALLEY, Ruth	107
SANDERSON, John	82	SCUDDER, Reliance	46	SMITH, -----	97
SANDERSON, John	97	SCUDDER, Roose	64	SMITH, Abia	97
SANDERSON, John	113	SCUDDER, Rose	64	SMITH, Abigail	45
SANDERSON, Rebekah	79	SCUDDER, Rose D.	64	SMITH, Abigail	99
SANDERSON, Samuel	97	SCUDDER, Ruth	112	SMITH, Abigail	103
SANDERSON, Tabitha	79	SCUDDER, Saml.	58	SMITH, Abigail	108
SAVORY, George	54	SCUDDER, Sarah	74	SMITH, Abigail	114
SCUDDER, Ann	112	SCUDDER, Thomas	64	SMITH, Abigail	116
SCUDDER, Anne	111	SCUDDER, Thomas D.	64	SMITH, Abner	69
SCUDDER, Anne	115	SCUDER, David	104	SMITH, Ann	45
SCUDDER, Asa	64	SCUDER, Ebenezer	104	SMITH, Ann	58
SCUDDER, Benjamin	112	SCUDER, Ebenezer	121	SMITH, Ann	61
SCUDDER, Betty	74	SCUDER, Eliezer	104	SMITH, Ann	99
SCUDDER, David	112	SCUDER, Elizabeth	104	SMITH, Anna	51
SCUDDER, Ebenezer	46	SCUDER, Hannah	121	SMITH, Anne	82
SCUDDER, Ebenezer	64	SCUDER, Lydia	104	SMITH, Anne	97
SCUDDER, Ebenezer	66	SCUDER, Rebekah	104	SMITH, Anne	108
SCUDDER, Ebenezer	104	SCUDER, Samuel	104	SMITH, Benjamin	45
SCUDDER, Ebenezer	112	SEMANNA, Mehitable	121	SMITH, Benjamin	61
SCUDDER, Eleazer	61	SENNIT, Benja.	121	SMITH, Benjamin	63
SCUDDER, Eleazer	63	SERJANT, John	45	SMITH, Benjamin	108
SCUDDER, Elisabeth	112	SERJANT, Joseph	45	SMITH, Benjamin	110
SCUDDER, Elizabeth	64	SERJEANT, Sarah	45	SMITH, Benjamin	112

INDEX - BARNSTABLE

SMITH, Bethiah	65	SMITH, John	97	SMITH, Sarah	110
SMITH, Bethiah	67	SMITH, Joseph	45	SMITH, Sarah	112
SMITH, Bethiah	75	SMITH, Joseph	45	SMITH, Sarah	113
SMITH, Bethiah	77	SMITH, Joseph	56	SMITH, Shobal	45
SMITH, Bethiah	108	SMITH, Joseph	58	SMITH, Susanna	58
SMITH, Betsy	51	SMITH, Joseph	61	SMITH, Susanna	103
SMITH, Caroline C.	53	SMITH, Joseph	94	SMITH, Susannah	45
SMITH, Daniel	45	SMITH, Joseph	97	SMITH, Susannah	61
SMITH, Daniel	103	SMITH, Joseph	99	SMITH, Susannah	69
SMITH, Daniel	121	SMITH, Joseph	104	SMITH, Susannah	103
SMITH, David	45	SMITH, Joseph	110	SMITH, Susannah	110
SMITH, David	110	SMITH, Joseph	112	SMITH, Thankful	75
SMITH, David	112	SMITH, Joseph	118	SMITH, Thankful	77
SMITH, David	117	SMITH, Joseph	121	SMITH, Thankful	97
SMITH, David	119	SMITH, Josiah	61	SMITH, Thomas	45
SMITH, Dorcas	45	SMITH, Josiah	62	SMITH, Thomas	53
SMITH, Dorcas	70	SMITH, Josiah	114	SMITH, Timothy	61
SMITH, Dorcas	82	SMITH, Lydia	45	SMITH, William	98
SMITH, Dorcas	113	SMITH, Lydia	99	SNOW, David	54
SMITH, Ebenezer	45	SMITH, Lydia	108	SNOW, Elizabeth	121
SMITH, Ebenezer	61	SMITH, Manasseth	99	SNOW, Hannah	58
SMITH, Ebenezer	103	SMITH, Martha	61	SNOW, Jabez	96
SMITH, Ebenezer	110	SMITH, Mary	21	SNOW, Martha	56
SMITH, Ebenezer	112	SMITH, Mary	45	SNOW, Martha	59
SMITH, Elisha	61	SMITH, Mary	45	SNOW, Mary	58
SMITH, Elizabeth	45	SMITH, Mary	53	SNOW, Mary	117
SMITH, Elizabeth	61	SMITH, Mary	77	SNOW, Polly	51
SMITH, Elizabeth	97	SMITH, Mary	81	SOUTHWICK, Stephen	51
SMITH, Enoch	69	SMITH, Mary	108	SPARROW, Jonathan	47
SMITH, Epharim	99	SMITH, Mary	116	SPARROW, Richard	56
SMITH, Hannah	61	SMITH, Mathias	61	SPARROW, Richard	59
SMITH, Hannah	108	SMITH, Matthias	45	SPEAR, Samuel	97
SMITH, Huldah	65	SMITH, Matthias	63	SPOONER, Jane	77
SMITH, Huldah	67	SMITH, Matthias	108	SPOONER, Jean	83
SMITH, Huldah	108	SMITH, Matthias	118	SPRINGER, Desire	47
SMITH, Ichabod	45	SMITH, Matthias	120	STACEY, Joseph	46
SMITH, Ignatius	69	SMITH, Mercy	58	STACY, Mary	49
SMITH, Ignatius	75	SMITH, Mercy	97	STEPHENS, Asa	54
SMITH, Ignatius	103	SMITH, Peter	61	STEPHENS, John	110
SMITH, James	45	SMITH, Polycarpus	103	STETSON, Thomas	56
SMITH, James	61	SMITH, Rebecah	61	STETSON, Thomas	57
SMITH, James	73	SMITH, Rebekah	82	STEWARD, Bruce	77
SMITH, James	97	SMITH, Relience	99	STEWARD, Desire	67
SMITH, James	121	SMITH, Richard	120	STEWARD, Seth	77
SMITH, Jemima	45	SMITH, Saml.	45	STEWART, Levi	104
SMITH, Jemima	97	SMITH, Samuel	45	STEWART, Mehitable	120
SMITH, Jemimah	61	SMITH, Samuel	108	STEWART, Remember	61
SMITH, Joanna	53	SMITH, Sarah	45	STEWART, Remember	63
SMITH, John	45	SMITH, Sarah	97	STEWART, Sarah	61
SMITH, John	56	SMITH, Sarah	99	STEWART, Sarah	66
SMITH, John	61	SMITH, Sarah	109	STEWART, Sarah F.	53

INDEX - BARNSTABLE

STIRGIS, William W.	53	STURGES, David	76	STURGES, Mercy	91
STONE, Keziah	65	STURGES, Dinah	97	STURGES, Mercy	112
STONE, Mary	29	STURGES, Dinah	121	STURGES, Moses	45
STONE, Nathaniel	48	STURGES, Ebenezer	76	STURGES, Moses	79
STONE, Nathaniel	114	STURGES, Ebenezer	106	STURGES, Moses	114
STORES, Cordiel	45	STURGES, Edward	45	STURGES, Moses	118
STORES, Elizabeth	45	STURGES, Eleanor	79	STURGES, Nathanael	76
STORES, Hannah	45	STURGES, Elisabeth	75	OTURGES, Nathanall	76
STORES, Hester	45	STURGES, Elisabeth	76	STURGES, Nathaniel	45
STORES, Lydia	45	STURGES, Elizabeth	45	STURGES, Nathaniel	46
STORES, Mary	45	STURGES, Elizabeth	107	STURGES, Nathaniel	119
STORES, Saml.	45	STURGES, Elizabeth	121	STURGES, Nathll.	46
STORES, Samuel	45	STURGES, Ezekiel	79	STURGES, Rebeca	76
STORES, Sarah	45	STURGES, Fear	79	STURGES, Rebecah	76
STORES, Thomas	45	STURGES, Hannah	45	STURGES, Rebecca	45
STUARD, Lydia	92	STURGES, Hannah	106	STURGES, Saml.	45
STUARD, Puella	92	STURGES, James	76	STURGES, Saml.	64
STUARD, Remember	92	STURGES, Jno:	122	STURGES, Saml.	91
STUARD, Silvanus	92	STURGES, John	45	STURGES, Saml.	112
STUARD, Solomon	92	STURGES, John	64	STURGES, Samuel	64
STUART, Desire	72	STURGES, John	79	STURGES, Samuel	66
STUART, Desire	104	STURGES, John	106	STURGES, Samul	73
STUART, James	104	STURGES, John	107	STURGES, Sarah	75
STUART, Mary	67	STURGES, John	110	STURGES, Sarah	77
STUART, Mary	72	STURGES, John	118	STURGES, Sarah	112
STUART, Mary	104	STURGES, John	119	STURGES, Solomon	45
STUART, Mehitable	104	STURGES, Jonathan	45	STURGES, Solomon	91
STUART, Mercy	82	STURGES, Jonathan	76	STURGES, Solomon	112
STUART, Remember	104	STURGES, Jonathan	110	STURGES, Solomon	118
STUART, Sarah	104	STURGES, Jonathan	112	STURGES, Solomon	119
STUART, Seth	72	STURGES, Jonathan	118	STURGES, Susanah	104
STUART, Seth	77	STURGES, Joseph	76	STURGES, Susanah	121
STUART, Silvanus	104	STURGES, Josiah	107	STURGES, Susannah	45
STUART, Solomon	104	STURGES, Lucretia	64	STURGES, Susannah	49
STUART, Sylvanus	72	STURGES, Lucretia	107	STURGES, Susannah	115
STUART, Sylvanus	72	STURGES, Martha	45	STURGES, Susannah	116
STUDDLEY, Joseph	118	STUREGES, Mary	45	STURGES, Thomas	45
STUDLEY, Joseph	110	STURGES, Mary	71	STURGES, Thomas	114
STUDLY, Joseph	121	STURGES, Mary	75	STURGES, Timothy Crocker	107
STURGES, Abigail	45	STURGES, Mary	76	STURGIS, -----	72
STURGES, Abigail	64	STURGES, Mary	79	STURGIS, Abigail	45
STURGES, Abigail	66	STURGES, Mary	112	STURGIS, Abigail	72
STURGES, Abigail	67	STURGES, Mary	115	STURGIS, Abigail	72
STURGES, Abigail	76	STURGES, Mehetable	61	STURGIS, Abigail	106
STURGES, Abigail	91	STURGES, Mehetable	62	STURGIS, Abigail	118
STURGES, Abigail	106	STURGES, Mehitable	114	STURGIS, Daniel H.	53
STURGES, Abigail	109	STURGES, Melatiah	66	STURGIS, Elizabeth	72
STURGES, Abigail	110	STURGES, Melatiah	67	STURGIS, Hannah	72
STURGES, Abigail	112	STURGES, Melatiah	107	STURGIS, Hannah	73
STURGES, Abigail	113	STURGES, Mercy	48	STURGIS, John	71
STURGES, Abigail	118	STURGES, Mercy	79	STURGIS, John	72

INDEX - BARNSTABLE

Name	Page	Name	Page	Name	Page
STURGIS, John	73	TAYLER, Ann	88	TAYLER, Lydia	47
STURGIS, John	90	TAYLER, Annah	81	TAYLER, Martha	11
STURGIS, John	106	TAYLER, Anne	47	TAYLER, Martha	64
STURGIS, John	120	TAYLER, Bithiah	82	TAYLER, Martha	66
STURGIS, Jonathan	56	TAYLER, Christopher	59	TAYLER, Mary	22
STURGIS, Jonathan	58	TAYLER, Christopher	62	TAYLER, Mary	47
STURGIS, Josiah	72	TAYLER, Christopher	72	TAYLER, Mary	77
STURGIS, Martha	72	TAYLER, Christopher	82	TAYLER, Mary	83
STURGIS, Mehetable	84	TAYLER, Christopher	94	TAYLER, Mary	88
STURGIS, Moses	52	TAYLER, Daniel	84	TAYLER, Mary	94
STURGIS, Olive	72	TAYLER, Deborah	77	TAYLER, Mehitable	47
STURGIS, Rebekah	106	TAYLER, Deborah	84	TAYLER, Mercy	47
STURGIS, Russel	72	TAYLER, Deborah	94	TAYLER, Nathan	47
STURGIS, Saml.	71	TAYLER, Ebenezer	47	TAYLER, Olive	84
STURGIS, Saml.	72	TAYLER, Ebenezer	81	TAYLER, Phebe	81
STURGIS, Saml.	73	TAYLER, Ebenezer	88	TAYLER, Prince	78
STURGIS, Samuel	67	TAYLER, Ebenezer	110	TAYLER, Prince	84
STURGIS, Samuel	72	TAYLER, Ebenever	113	TAYLER, Rebeckah	47
STURGIS, Samuel	106	TAYLER, Ebenezer	118	TAYLER, Sarah	10
STURGIS, Sarah	72	TAYLER, Ebenr.	109	TAYLER, Sarah	47
STURGIS, Thomas	72	TAYLER, Edward	47	TAYLER, Sarah	88
STURGIS, Thos.	72	TAYLER, Elenor	47	TAYLER, Sarah	94
STURGIS, William	72	TAYLER, Eliphalet	84	TAYLER, Seth	47
STUWARD, Mary	98	TAYLER, Elisha	48	TAYLER, Seth	49
STUWART, Daniel	103	TAYLER, Experience	10	TAYLER, Seth	88
STUWART, Daniel	121	TAYLER, Experience	47	TAYLER, Susannah	88
STUWART, James	122	TAYLER, Hannah	17	TAYLER, Thankful	47
Sussex	82	TAYLER, Hannah	47	TAYLER, William	113
Sussex	113	TAYLER, Hannah	77	TAYLER, William	114
SWENTON, Sally	53	TAYLER, Hannah	80	TAYLOR, Abigail	121
SWIFT, James	109	TAYLER, Hannah	84	TAYLOR, Alice	61
SWIFT, James	116	TAYLER, Hannah	94	TAYLOR, Alice	63
SYMONS, Phillip	118	TAYLER, Henry	47	TAYLOR, Alice	113
SYMONS, Phillip	120	TAYLER, Hope	47	TAYLOR, Deborah	77
		TAYLER, Isaac	47	TAYLOR, Enoch	77
— T —		TAYLER, Isaac	83	TAYLOR, Mary	58
		TAYLER, Isaac	113	TAYLOR, Mehitable	97
TABOR, Content	51	TAYLER, Isaac	114	TAYLOR, Phebe	56
Tamar	113	TAYLER, Jacob	47	TAYLOR, Phebe	57
Tamar	114	TAYLER, Jane	118	TAYLOR, Prince	82
TAYLER, -----	47	TAYLER, Jasper	47	TAYLOR, Rebecca	118
TAYLER, Abigail	84	TAYLER, Jasper	48	TAYLOR, Rebecca	122
TAYLER, Abraham	47	TAYLER, Jasper	88	TAYLOR, Sarah	122
TAYLER, Abraham	48	TAYLER, Jean	94	TAYLOR, Susanna	63
TAYLER, Abraham	50	TAYLER, Jeremiah	84	THACHER, Abigail	47
TAYLER, Abraham	82	TAYLER, John	47	THACHER, Abigail	56
TAYLER, Abraham	94	TAYLER, Jonathan	47	THACHER, Abigail	56
TAYLER, Alice	88	TAYLER, Josiah	47	THACHER, Abigail	83
TAYLER, Ann	21	TAYLER, Josiah	88	THACHER, Anthony	89
TAYLER, Ann	26	TAYLER, Judeth	47	THACHER, Benjamin	110
TAYLER, Ann	83	TAYLER, Lot	84	THACHER, Benjamin	118

THACHER, Bethiah	42	THATCHER, Lot	66	TOBIE, Peter	97
THACHER, Content	83	THATCHER, Lott	64	TOBY, Abigail	118
THACHER, Desire	83	THATCHER, Mary	75	TOBY, Guinney	110
THACHER, Desire	113	THATCHER, Mary	76	TOBY, Guinny	118
THACHER, Desire	114	THATCHER, Mary	77	TOBY, Jane	63
THACHER, Elisha,	72	THAYER, Mary T.	54	TOBY, Jean	115
THACHER, Elisha	89	THAYR, Frederick N.	54	TOBY, Mercy	82
THACHER, Elizabeth	47	Thom	72	TOBY, Reliance	118
THACHER, Elizabeth	58	Thomas	77	TOBY, Saml.	115
THACHER, Elizabeth	83	THOMAS, Ann	88	TOBY, Saml.	116
THACHER, Elizebath	61	THOMAS, Ann	105	TOMPSON, Elizabeth	47
THACHER, Elizebeth	56	THOMAS, Ann	116	TOMPSON, Hester	47
THACHER, Fear	47	THOMAS, Anna	56	TOMPSON, Jacob	47
THACHER, Fear	83	THOMAS, Anna	115	TOMPSON, John	47
THACHER, Fear	117	THOMAS, Bethiah	121	TOMPSON, Lydia	47
THACHER, Fear	118	THOMAS, Ebenezer	88	TOMPSON, Sarah	47
THACHER, James	83	THOMAS, Ebenezer	115	TOMPSON, Thomas	47
THACHER, Jethro	83	THOMAS, Ebenezer	118	TOMSHIT, Isaac	121
THACHER, John	47	THOMAS, Elijah	88	TOWARDY, Bathsheba	62
THACHER, John	52	THOMAS, Elijah	106	TOWARDY, Bathsheba	66
THACHER, John	83	THOMAS, Elisha	88	Tony	116
THACHER, John	118	THOMAS, Hannah	105	TRAP, John	49
THACHER, Lot	47	THOMAS, Joseph	77	TREDDEWAY, Hannah	40
THACHER, Lot	109	THOMAS, Joseph	81	TRICK, Elizabeth	111
THACHER, Lot	120	THOMAS, Joseph	105	TRICK, Elizabeth	115
THACHER, Lucretia	56	THOMAS, Lydia	106	TROOP, Mary	47
THACHER, Lucretia	89	THOMAS, Mary	118	TROOP, William	47
THACHER, Martha	63	THOMAS, Mary	119	TROT, Thankful	29
OHACHER, Mary	83	THOMAS, Nathan	51	TROWBRIDGE, John	50
THACHER, Mary	106	THOMAS, Nathan	73	TRUET, Esther	65
THACHER, Mary	109	THOMAS, Nathan	106	TUNCAGAIN, Hannah	73
THACHER, Peter	118	THOMAS, Rebecca	106	TUNEGIN, Hannah	59
THACHER, Peter	118	THOMAS, Remember	106	TUPPER, Abigail	82
THACHER, Phebe	89	THOMAS, Richard	105	TUPPER, Allen	54
THACHER, Rebekah	83	THOMAS, Susanna	106	TUPPER, Eliza	54
THACHER, Rebekah	109	THOMAS, Thankfull	106	TUPPER, Elizabeth	118
THACHER, Rebekah	118	THOMAS, Thomas	115	TUPPER, Elizabeth	119
THACHER, Rouland	47	THOMAS, William	88	TUPPER, Elizebath	82
THACHER, Rowland	115	THOMAS, Zeruiah	59	TUPPER, Experience	63
THACHER, Rowlabd	115	THOMAS, Zilphah	106	TUPPER, Israel	48
THACHER, Samuel	83	THOMAS, Zurviah	62	TUPPER, Lothrop	82
THACHER, Samuel Sturges	89	THORP, Joseph	115	TUPPER, Mordecai	71
THACHER, Sarah	121	TOBEY, Charles B.	53	TUPPER, Mordecai	75
THACHER, Temperance	92	TOBEY, James	75	TUPPER, Mordecai	82
THACHER, Temperance	118	TOBEY, James	77	TUPPER, Rebecca	82
OOACHER, Thankful	82	TOBEY, Joseph	66	TUPPER, Susanna	82
THACHER, Thankfull	56	TOBEY, Mehetable	65	TUPPER, William	52
THACHER, Thankfull	58	TOBEY, Rebeca	76	TWEKIT, Mary	80
THARP, Mehitable	49	TOBEY, Rebeccah	77	TWEKIT, Mary	82
THATCHER, John	76	TOBIE, Eleazer	98	TWINING. Anna	11

INDEX - BARNSTABLE

Name	Page	Name	Page	Name	Page
TYLER, Jane	118	WHIPPO, Elizabeth	50	WILLIAMSON, Mary	50
		WHIPPO, George	50	WILLIAMSON, Sarah	50
— V —		WHIPPO, James	50	WILLIAMSON, Timothy	50
		WHIPPO, Jane	50	WILSON, Michael	50
VASSALL, Anna	106	WHIPPO, Lawrence	50	WING, Deborah	56
VESSELE, Anna	122	WHIPPO, Margaret	50	WING, Hannah	40
VINSEN, Sarah	21	WHIPPO, Martha	50	WING, Lot	52
VINSON, Thomas	53	WHITE, Dorcas	115	WING, Mary Ann	54
		WHITE, Hannah	50	WING, Thankful	77
— W —		WHITE, Immanuel	50	WINSLOW, Jedediah	77
		WHITE, James	50	WINSLOW, Jedidiah	77
WALDRON, William	96	WHITE, John	50	WINSLOW, Kenelm	71
WALKER, Sarah	40	WHITE, Judith	48	WINSLOW, Knelm	75
WALLEY, Hannah	10	WHITE, Margerent	104	WINSLOW, Phebe	73
WALLEY, Mary	17	WHITE, Margert	122	WINSLOW, Sarah	73
WALTER, Mariah	66	WHITE, Martha	50	WINSLOW, Saml.	64
WAMPOM, Bethiah	121	WHITE, Mary	50	WINSLOW, Samuel	66
WAMPOM, Hannah	115	WHITE, Saml.	50	WINSLOW, Thomas	115
WARDSWORTH, Susanah	75	WHITE, Samuel	50	WINSLOW, Thomas	118
WARIN, Jams	73	WHITE, Sarah	114	WINSLOW, Zerviah	82
WARREN, James	77	WHITE, Sarah	115	WITHEREL, Thomas	110
WARREN, Jane	40	WHITE, Thomas	104	WITHEREL, Thomas	116
WARREN, Joanna	50	WHITE, Thomas	121	WITTON, John	48
WARREN, Sarah	50	WHITMAN, Betsy	53	WOES, Mary	109
WARREN, Sarah	50	WHITMAN, Sally	53	WOES, Mary	116
WARRIN, Sarah	121	WHITMARSH, John	71	WOIES, Joseph	122
WASTE, Bezaleel	56	WHITMARSH, John	73	WOIS, Mary	114
WASTE, Bezaleel	58	WHITNE, Samuell	73	WOOD, Ansel	63
WEBB, Abigail	72	WHITNEY, Saml.	70	WOOD, Betsey H.	52
WEEDEN, Thomas	76	WICKNOT, Sarah	118	WOOD, David	63
WEEKS, Barzilla	66	WIDDUP, Paul	47	WOOD, Ebenr.	104
WEEKS, Barzilla	67	WILDER, Jabez	61	WOOD, Ebenr.	121
WEEKS, Elizabeth	44	WILDER, Jabez	63	WOOD, Elisabeth	63
WEEKS, Rebecca	47	WILEY, Liticier	52	WOOD, Elizebeth	64
WEEPKUCK, Stephen	120	WILL, Desire	118	WOOD, Francis	63
WELD, Elisabeth	56	WILL, Martha	67	WOOD, Francis	64
WELLS, Mary	32	WILL, Martha	70	WOOD, Francis	77
WEQUASH, Saml.	98	WILL, Martha	72	WOOD, Hipziba	98
WEST, Sackfield	110	WILL, Mary	49	WOOD, Jabez	63
WEST, Sackfield	122	WILL, Patience	121	WOOD, Maria E.	52
WETHEREL, Thophilus	121	WILL, Robin	97	WOOD, Mathew	56
WHELDEN, Eliza	53	WILL, Sarah	118	WOOD, Mathew	57
WHELDEN, Jane	52	WILL, Stephen	49	WOOD, Tilson	63
WHELDREN, Bela	53	WILL, Thankful	66	WOOD, Zenas	64
WHELDREN, Lucy	53	WILL, Tom	98	WOODCOCK, Mary	109
WHETEN, Shobal	121	WILLIAMS, Bradford B.	54		
WHETSTONE, Abigail	49	WILLIAMS, Elizabeth	49	**— Y —**	
WHETSTONE, Barshaba	97	WILLIAMS, John	121		
WHETSTONE, Hannah	40	WILLIAMSON, Caleb	50	YOUNG, Bangs	85
WHETSTONE, Mercy	48	WILLIAMSON, Ebenezer	50	YOUNG, Eliza	53
WHIPPO, Benjamin	50	WILLIAMSON, Martha	50	YOUNG, Elizabeth	23

INDEX - BARNSTABLE

YOUNG, Elizabeth	85	YOUNG, Rebecca	85	YOUNG, Thomas	72
YOUNG, Mary	85	YOUNG, Thomas	72	YOUNG, Thomas	85
YOUNG, Patience	23				

INDEX - SANDWICH

This is NOT an all-name index. References in the text to religious and civil officials, as such, have been omitted. Names may appear more than once on the same page.

UNKNOWN

-----, -----	137
-----, -----	138

— A —

ABBIT, John	136
ADKINS, Hanah	126
ADKINS, James	126
ADKINS, Sarah	126
ADKINS, William	126
ALLEN, Abigale	130
ALLEN, Abigill	130
ALLEN, Amey,	130
ALLEN, Bethsheua	153
ALLEN, Bethshua	153
ALLEN, Bethsua	153
ALLEN, Bethua	153
ALLEN, Caleb	142
ALLEN, Cornelus	153
ALLEN, Daniel	142
ALLEN, Daniel	153
ALLEN, Dorothy	142
ALLEN, Elizabeth	142
ALLEN, Gidion	153
ALLEN, Gidion	154
ALLEN, Hanah	142
ALLEN, Hanah	154
ALLEN, Hannah	142
ALLEN, Hannah	153
ALLEN, James	130
ALLEN, James	142
ALLEN, Jeames	130
ALLEN, Jediah	130
ALLEN, John	136
ALLEN, John	147
ALLEN, Judah	130
ALLEN, Lydia	153
ALLEN, Mary	130
ALLEN, Meary	131
ALLEN, Ralph	131
ALLEN, Ralphe	127
ALLEN, Richard	142
ALLEN, Sarah	136
ALLEN, William	136
ALLIN, Caleb	131
ALLIN, Dorryty	131
ALLIN, Elezebeth	127
ALLIN, Epherim	127
ALLIN, Experience	127
ALLIN, George	130
ALLIN, Gorg	127
ALLIN, Gorg	130
ALLIN, Gorg	131
ALLIN, James	130
ALLIN, John	130
ALLIN, Judah	130
ALLIN, Matthew	131
ALLIN, Ralfe	127
ALLIN, Ralphe	127
ASHLEY, Abraham	148

— B —

BACKHOUSE, Elizabeth	140
BACKHOUSE, Hannah	140
BARBER, Elizabeth	143
BARBER, John	143
BARBER, Meribah	143
BARBER, Patience	143
BARBER, Sarah	143
BARLOW, Elisabeth	154
BARLOW, Elizabeth	136
BARLOW, Elizabeth	144
BARLOW, Elizabeth	144
BARLOW, Elizabeth	154
BARLOW, Hannah	144
BARLOW, Huldah	144
BARLOW, John	136
BARLOW, John	154
BARLOW, Keturah	154
BARLOW, Mary	144
BARLOW, Nathan	154
BARLOW, Peter	144
BARLOW, Samuel	154
BARLOW, Sarah	154
BARLOW, William	154
BARLOW, Zebulun	144
BASET, Rahell	127
BASET, William	127
BASETT, Mary	127
BASSET, Mary	131
BASSET, Will:	131
BASSETT, Jonathan	127
BASSETT, Jonathan	154
BASSETT, Mary	133
BASSETT, Mary	140
BASSETT, Rachel	140
BASSETT, William	133
BATES, Judith	140
BAXTER, Deborah	136
BAXTER, Saml.	136
BENETT, George	128
BENNETT, Joseph	154
BENSON, Isaac	140
BENSON, Joseph	140
BESSIE, Benjamin	149
BESSIE, David	149
BESSIE, Ebenezer	149
BESSIE, Hannah	149
BESSIE, Hannah	154
BESSIE, Joshua	149
BESSIE, Mary	147
BESSIE, Mary	149
BESSIE, Nehemiah	147
BESSIE, Nehemiah	149
BESSIE, Robert	149
BLACKWEL, Joshua	137
BLACKWEL, Joshua	138
BLACKWEL, Mercy	137
BLACKWEL, Mercy	138
BLACKWELL, Abia	138
BLACKWELL, Allis	127
BLACKWELL, Deborah	138
BLACKWELL, Desire	127
BLACKWELL, Hannah	138
BLACKWELL, Jane	127
BLACKWELL, Jeane	138
BLACKWELL, John	127
BLACKWELL, John	130

INDEX - SANDWICH

Name	Page	Name	Page	Name	Page
BLACKWELL, John	131	BOURNE, Elisha	136	BOURNE, ShearJashub	131
BLACKWELL, Joshua	127	BOURNE, Elisha	137	BOURNE, Shearjashub	143
BLACKWELL, Joshua	137	BOURNE, Elisha	145	BOURNE, Sherejashub	127
BLACKWELL, Joshua	138	BOURNE, Elizabeth	128	BOURNE, Silvenus	143
BLACKWELL, Joshua	153	BOURNE, Elizabeth	137	BOURNE, Sylas	143
BLACKWELL, Mercy	127	BOURNE, Elizabeth	140	BOURNE, Temperance	155
BLACKWELL, Mercy	137	BOURNE, Elizabeth	145	BOURNE, Thomas	145
BLACKWELL, Mercy	138	BOURNE, Ezra	127	BOURNE, Timothy	126
BLACKWELL, Michael	136	BOURNE, Ezra	140	BOURNE, Timothy	155
BLACKWELL, Michael	138	BOURNE, Ezra	147	BRIDGGS, Sarath	134
BLACKWELL, Michaell	131	BOURNE, Ezra	148	BRIDGS, Samuell	134
BLACKWELL, Michall	128	BOURNE, Hannah	126	BRIGG, Ebensar	134
BLACKWELL, Nathanall	127	BOURNE, Hannah	137	BRIGG, Samuell	134
BLACKWELL, Samuel	138	BOURNE, Hezechiah	127	BRIGGS, Benet	134
BLACKWELL, Samuell	127	BOURNE, Isaac	153	BRIGGS, Elezebeth	134
BLACKWELL, Sarah	127	BOURNE, Joanna	155	BRIGGS, Hannah	128
BLACKWELL, Sarah	138	BOURNE, Job	153	BRIGGS, Samuell	128
BLACKWELL, Sary	127	BOURNE, Job	155	BUCK, Anne	154
BLOSSOM, Thomas	147	BOURNE, Jobe	126	BUCK, Joseph	133
BODFISH, Joanna	138	BOURNE, Jobe	127	BUCK, Remember	140
BODFISH, John	138	BOURNE, John	127	BUCK, Rose	133
BODFISH, John	153	BOURNE, John	143	BUK, Joseph	133
BODFISH, Joseph	130	BOURNE, John	145	BUMPAS, Hannah	147
BODFISH, Mary	154	BOURNE, Jonathan	145	BUMPAS, Mary	140
BODFISH, Robert	130	BOURNE, Joseph	147	BUMPASS, James	148
BODFISH, Robert	132	BOURNE, Joseph	148	BURG, Jacob	154
BORG, Jacob	130	BOURNE, Malletiah	131	BURG, Mary	154
BORG, John	130	BOURNE, Maria	145	BURGE, Abia	154
BOURN, Abigail	153	BOURNE, Martha	147	BURGE, Abigail	154
BOURN, Eliazer	153	BOURNE, Mary	127	BURGE, Benjam	132
BOURN, Elisha	127	BOURNE, Mary	137	BURGE, Benjamin	150
BOURN, Elisha	128	BOURNE, Mary	145	BURGE, Dorite	132
BOURN, John	139	BOURNE, Mary	148	BURGE, Dorithy	127
BOURN, Jonathan	139	BOURNE, Mehetabel	155	BURGE, Ebenezer	131
BOURN, Martha	148	BOURNE, Melatiah	143	BURGE, Elizabeth	127
BOURNE, Abigal	137	BOURNE, Mercy	153	BURGE, Jacob	131
BOURNE, Abigal	153	BOURNE, Nathan	137	BURGE, Jacob	132
BOURNE, Abigale	153	BOURNE, Nathan	140	BURGE, Jacob	154
BOURNE, Benjamin	155	BOURNE, Nathan	145	BURGE, Jakob	131
BOURNE, Bershebe	137	BOURNE, Patience	127	BURGE, Jedidah	154
BOURNE, Bethsheba	143	BOURNE, Patience	136	BURGE, Jo Joseph	132
BOURNE, Bethshua	126	BOURNE, Patience	137	BURGE, Joseph	132
BOURNE, Bethshua	127	BOURNE, Remembranc	127	BURGE, Mary	154
BOURNE, Catherine	126	BOURNE, Richard	133	BURGE, Mercy	150
BOURNE, Desier	143	BOURNE, Richard	143	BURGE, Rebekca	132
BOURNE, Desire	143	BOURNE, Ruhamah	126	BURGE, Samuel	154
BOURNE, Eleazer	126	BOURNE, Ruhamah	127	BURGE, Samuell	131
BOURNE, Eleazer	153	BOURNE, Samuel	143	BURGE, Seth	150
BOURNE, Eliezer	153	BOURNE, Sarah	143	BURGE, Thomas	127
BOURNE, Elisha	127	BOURNE, Sarah	147	BURGE, Thomas	132
BOURNE, Elisha	128	BOURNE, Sary	127	BURGE, Zacheus	154

INDEX - SANDWICH

BUTLER, Daniel	154	CURTISS, Benjamin	147	ELLIS, ---uel	137		
BUTLER, Darity	127			ELLIS, Abiel	153		
BUTLER, Dinah	147	— D —		ELLIS, Anna	153		
BUTLER, Dorty	127			ELLIS, Annah	153		
BUTLER, Elizabeth	148	DEXTER, Abigail	137	ELLIS, Elisha	153		
BUTLER, Patience	128	DEXTER, Elizabeth	127	ELLIS, Elnathan	153		
BUTLER, Prudence	132	DEXTER, Elizabeth	136	ELLIS, Experience	137		
BUTLER, Thomas	127	DEXTER, Elizabeth	137	ELLIS, Experience	154		
		DEXTER, John	137	ELLIS, Gideon	153		
		DEXTER, Mehetabel	137	ELLIS, Isabel	137		
— C —		DEXTER, Mehitabel	137	ELLIS, Jemima	153		
CHADDACK, Hannah	147	DEXTER, Thomas	127	ELLIS, Jemimah	153		
CHADWELL, Richard	133	DEXTER, Thomas	137	ELLIS, Joel	137		
CHIPMAN, Bethyah	143	DEXTOR, Abigail	127	ELLIS, Joell	130		
CHIPMAN, Deborah	143	DEXTOR, Elizabeth	127	ELLIS, John	130		
CHIPMAN, Desier	143	DEXTOR, John	127	ELLIS, John	131		
CHIPMAN, Ebenezer	143	DEXTOR, Thomas	127	ELLIS, John	136		
CHIPMAN, Ebenezer	153	DILLINGHAM, Abigail	142	ELLIS, John	153		
CHIPMAN, Handley	143	DILLINGHAM, Debora	142	ELLIS, John	154		
CHIPMAN, James	143	DILLINGHAM, Drsula	126	ELLIS, John	155		
CHIPMAN, John	136	DILLINGHAM, Edward	130	ELLIS, Jonathan	155		
CHIPMAN, John	143	DILLINGHAM, Edward	133	ELLIS, Malachi	137		
CHIPMAN, Lydia	143	DILLINGHAM, Edward	140	ELLIS, Marcy	137		
CHIPMAN, Mary	143	DILLINGHAM, Edward	142	ELLIS, Mary	137		
CHIPMAN, Mary	153	DILLINGHAM, Experience	142	ELLIS, Matthias	137		
CHIPMAN, Mercy	140	DILLINGHAM, Hannah	142	ELLIS, Matthyas	131		
CHIPMAN, Perez	143	DILLINGHAM, Henery	130	ELLIS, Mehitable	137		
CHIPMAN, Rebecca	143	DILLINGHAM, Henry	130	ELLIS, Mercy	137		
CHIPMAN, Ruth	136	DILLINGHAM, Henry	131	ELLIS, Mercy	154		
CHIPMAN, Stephen	143	DILLINGHAM, John	126	ELLIS, Mordecai	136		
CHIPMAN, William	153	DILLINGHAM, John	130	ELLIS, Mordicai	131		
CHURCHEL, Stephen	154	DILLINGHAM, John	142	ELLIS, Mordicai	136		
CLAP, Charity	140	DILLINGHAM, Mary	131	ELLIS, Mordicai	155		
CLEAVES, William	147	DILLINGHAM, Mary	142	ELLIS, Nathaniell	154		
CLEAVS, Hannah	144	DILLINGHAM, Simion	142	ELLIS, Rebecca	136		
CLEAVS, Sarah	144	DILLINGHAM, Ursula	126	ELLIS, Rebecca	154		
CLEAVS, William	144	DILLINGHAM, Ursula	133	ELLIS, Remember	137		
COTON, Elizabeth	138	DILLINHAM, Hanath	132	ELLIS, Reuben	153		
COTON, Rowland	138	DILLINHAM, Henery	132	ELLIS, Samuel	137		
COTTEN, Rowland	136	DIMICK, Joseph	140	ELLIS, Samuel	153		
COTTON, ------	138	DOTEY, Elles	127	ELLIS, Sarah	136		
COTTON, Abigail	138	DOTEY, Joseph	127	ELLIS, Sarah	153		
COTTON, Elizabeth	138	DOTEY, Theophilus	127	ELLIS, Sarah	154		
COTTON, Johanah	138	DOTY, Joseph	127	ELLIS, Sarah	155		
COTTON, Josiah	138	DOTY, Thomas	154	ELLIS, Seth	153		
COTTON, Meriel	138						
COTTON, Nathaniel	138	— E —		— F —			
COTTON, Rowland	138						
COTTON, Ruth	138	ELLIS, ---abel	137	FEAKE, Elizabeth	126		
COTTON, Sarah	138	ELLIS, ---chi	137	FEAKE, Henry	126		
COTTON, Ward	138	ELLIS, ---l	137	FEILDS, Georg	128		

INDEX - SANDWICH

FEILDS, George	126	FISH, Mehetable	151	FULLER, Gamaliel	153
FEILDS, Joanna	126	FISH, Mehitabel	151	FULLER, Lydia	140
FFEAKE, Elizabeth	130	FISH, Mercy	152	FULLER, Sarah	153
FFEAKE, Henery	130	FISH, Patience	145		
FFEILDS, Joannah	128	FISH, Patience	151	— G —	
FFISH, Abia	128	FISH, Rachel	151		
FFISH, Ambros	128	FISH, Seth	136	GALE, Mary	154
FFISH, Ambross	128	FISH, Seth	148	GIBB, Bethiah	126
FFISH, Ephraim	128	FOSTER, Abigail	144	8IBBES, -----	134
FFISH, Hannah	128	FOSTER, Benjamin	144	GIBBS, -----	134
FFISH, John	128	FOSTER, Deborah	144	GIBBS, -----b	134
FFISH, John	130	FOSTER, Ebenezer	144	GIBBS, -----hua	134
FFISH, Josiah	128	FOSTER, Hannah	144	GIBBS, Abigail	140
FFISH, Mehittabell	128	FOSTER, John	144	GIBBS, Abigail	145
FFISH, Nathanael	130	FOSTER, Joseph	140	GIBBS, Ann	145
FFISH, Nathanell	131	FOSTER, Joseph	144	GIBBS, Anne	145
FFISH, Samuel	131	FOSTER, Mary	144	GIBBS, Barnabas	128
FFREEMAND, Margaret	128	FOSTER, Nathan	144	GIBBS, Benjamin	140
FFREEMAND, Rachel	128	FOSTER, Rachel	144	GIBBS, Benjamin	145
FFREEMAND, Rachell	128	FOSTER, Rachell	144	GIBBS, Beththia	130
FFREMAN, Edmond	127	FOSTER, Sarah	144	GIBBS, Elizabeth	145
FFREMAN, Elizabeth	128	FOSTER, Solomon	144	GIBBS, Jane	145
FISH, -----	136	FOSTER, Thankfull	144	GIBBS, Jedidah	145
FISH, Abigail	145	FOSTER, William	144	GIBBS, Job	130
FISH, Abigail	151	FREEMAN, ----m----s	139	GIBBS, Job	145
FISH, Ambrose	128	FREEMAN, Benjamin	141	GIBBS, Job	149
FISH, Bartholomey	147	FREEMAN, Eales	127	GIBBS, John	128
FISH, Deborah	145	FREEMAN, Edmon	127	GIBBS, John	130
FISH, Deborah	151	FREEMAN, Edmon	131	GIBBS, John	134
FISH, Ebenezar	145	FREEMAN, Edmond	128	GIBBS, John	136
FISH, Ebenezer	145	FREEMAN, Edmond	141	GIBBS, Judeth	149
FISH, Ebenezer	151	FREEMAN, Edmund	128	GIBBS, Judith	149
FISH, Edmond	151	FREEMAN, Edmund	141	GIBBS, Lydia	149
FISH, Ephraim	128	FREEMAN, Isaac	141	GIBBS, Martha	145
FISH, Eunice	152	FREEMAN, James	139	GIBBS, Mary	131
FISH, Faith	136	FREEMAN, John	139	GIBBS, Micah	149
FISH, George	126	FREEMAN, John	141	GIBBS, Reliance	145
FISH, Hannah	147	FREEMAN, Joseph	141	GIBBS, Sammuell	133
FISH, Hannah	151	FREEMAN, Margret	131	GIBBS, Samuell	128
FISH, Joanna	126	FREEMAN, Mary	141	GIBBS, Sarah	128
FISH, Johanna	128	FREEMAN, Sarah	140	GIBBS, Sarah	133
FISH, John	151	FREEMAN, Sarah	141	GIBBS, Silvanus	145
FISH, John	152	FREEMAN, Sarath	128	GIBBS, Tho:	130
FISH, Josiah	151	FREEMAN, Thomas	139	GIBBS, Tho:.	130
FISH, Lemuel	147	FREEMAN, William	141	GIBBS, Thos.	136
FISH, Margarett	151	FREENMAN, Thomas	141	GIBBS, Thomas	126
FISH, Mary	136	FREEMOND, Deboroath	128	GIBBS, Thomas	128
FISH, Mary	151	FREEMOND, Edmond	128	GIBBS, Thomas	130
FISH, Mehetabel	140	FREEMOND, Emond	128	GIBBS, Thomas	131
FISH, Mehetabel	151	FULLER, Abial	148	GIBBS, Thomas	132
FISH, Mehetable	145	FULLER, Abiel	153	GIBBS, Thomas	133

INDEX - SANDWICH

Name	Page	Name	Page	Name	Page
GIBS, Job	140	HAKSE, Lodawick	134	HASKLL, Roger	154
GIBS, Samuel	138	HALLETT, Mehetable	127	HAUKSIE, Joseph	140
GIFART, Elezebeth	128	HALLETT, Ruhamah	126	HAUKSIE, Peleg	140
GIFART, Grase	129	HAMBLETON, Thomas	126	HAUKSIE, Sarah	140
GIFART, John	128	HAMBLETON, Thomas	132	HICKS, Abigail	145
GIFART, John	129	HAMBLIN, Thomas	126	HICKS, Mary	145
GIFART, Mary	129	HAMBLTON, Lidia	132	HICKS, Rebekah	145
GIFART, Samuel	129	HAMBLTON, Thomas	132	HICKS, Remember	145
GIFART, William	129	HAMETT, Barnabas	154	HICKS, Thomas	145
GIFFORD, Addree	141	HAMETT, Hannah	154	HILLER, Jabez	148
GIFFORD, Benjamin	153	HAMETT, John	154	HILLER, Mary	150
GIFFORD, Christopher	141	HAMETT, Micah	154	HILLER, Samuel	150
GIFFORD, Deborah	141	HAMOND, Benjamine	133	HILLER, Thankfull	150
GIFFORD, Elizabeth	153	HAMOND, Mary	133	HILLIARD, Bathsheba	148
GIFFORD, Enos	141	HAMOND, Rose	133	HILLIARD, Gideon	148
GIFFORD, Gidion	142	HANDY, Abigail	144	HILLIARD, Samuel	148
GIFFORD, Hannah	142	HANDY, Benjamin	144	HOLLEY, Joseph	130
GIFFORD, James	138	HANDY, Benjamin	147	HOLLEY, Mary	130
GIFFORD, James	152	HANDY, David	144	HOLLY, Sary	130
GIFFORD, Jean	149	HANDY, Ebenezer	144	HOLMS, Isaac	154
GIFFORD, Jefferson	126	HANDY, Ebenezer	145	HOLWAY, Ann	139
GIFFORD, John	129	HANDY, Ebenezer	147	HOLWAY, Anne	139
GIFFORD, John	147	HANDY, Ebenr.	144	HOLWAY, Gidion	139
GIFFORD, Jonathan	138	HANDY, Elizabeth	144	HOLWAY, Joseph	139
GIFFORD, Jonathan	152	HANDY, Elizabeth	147	HOLWAY, Mary	139
GIFFORD, Josiah	129	HANDY, Hanah	147	HOLWAY, Relyance	139
GIFFORD, Josiah	149	HANDY, Hanibal	147	HOWLAND, Abigail	148
GIFFORD, Mary	141	HANDY, Isaac	147	HOWLAND, Abigail	149
GIFFORD, Mary	152	HANDY, Israel	144	HOWLAND, Benjamin	148
GIFFORD, Meribah	141	HANDY, John	153	HOWLAND, Benjamin	149
GIFFORD, Nathon	153	HANDY, Nathan	144	HOWLAND, Elisabeth	149
GIFFORD, Samuel	140	HANDY, Rebecca	144	HOWLAND, Elizabeth	149
GIFFORD, Samuel	149	HANDY, Rebecca	145	HOWLAND, Ellis	149
GIFFORD, William	140	HANDY, Richard	133	HOWLAND, Justus	148
GIFFORD, William	152	HANDY, Richard	147	HOWLAND, Justus	149
GIFFORD, William	153	HAMMOR, Lydia	140	HOWLAND, Lemuel	149
GIFFORD, Wm.	141	HARPER, Deborah	132	HOWLAND, Nathaniel	149
GIFFORD, Yelverton	126	HARPER, Deborah	133	HOXE, Gidion	141
GIFFORD, Yelverton	129	HARPER, Elizabeth	132	HOXE, Grace	141
GOODSPEED, John	140	HARPER, Experience	133	HOXE, Mary	141
GOODSPEED, Rose	147	HARPER, Hannah	132	HOXIE, Ann	147
GOZNEE, Prissilla	132	HARPER, Mary	131	HOXIE, Anne	141
GREENE, John	130	HARPER, Mary	132	HOXIE, Bathsheba	141
		HARPER, Mercy	132	HOXIE, Content	141
— H —		HARPER, Prudence	132	HOXIE, Desier	141
		HARPER, Robbert	131	HOXIE, Desier	151
HAANDY, Jonathan	133	HARPER, Robert	132	HOXIE, Dinah	151
HACKSE, Giddion	134	HARPER, Robert	133	HOXIE, Elizabeth	141
HACKSE, Josepth	134	HARPER, Steven	133	HOXIE, Giddion	141
HACKSE, Lodawick	134	HARPPER, Robert	126	HOXIE, Gideon	141
HAKSE, Bethshoa	134	HARPPER, Robert	132	HOXIE, Gidion	141

INDEX - SANDWICH

HOXIE, Grace	141	JENNINGS, Rembrance	136	LAUNDERS, Benjamin	144
HOXIE, Hannah	151	JENNINGS, Rose	152	LAUNDERS, Deborah	141
HOXIE, Hezekiah	147	JENNINGS, Ruhamah	142	LAUNDERS, Deborah	144
HOXIE, Hezekiah	151	JENNINGS, Saml.	136	LAUNDERS, Ebenezer	141
HOXIE, James	151	JENNINGS, Samuel	136	LAUNDERS, Ebenezer	144
HOXIE, Joseph	141	JENNINGS, Samuel	142	LAUNDERS, John	140
HOXIE, Kezia	141	JOHNSON, Hannah	136	LAUNDERS, John	141
HOXIE, Lodowick	141	JOHNSON, Prissilla	132	LAUNDERS, Joseph	144
HOXIE, Sarah	138	JOHNSON, Thomas	132	LAUNDERS, Margerett	141
HOXIE, Simeon	141	JOHNSON, Thomas	133	LAUNDERS, Nathan	144
HOXIE, Solomon	138	JOHNSON, William	133	LAUNDERS, Rachel	140
HOXIE, Solomon	148	JOHNSONN, Thomas	132	LAUNDERS, Rachel	141
HOXIE, Solomon	151	JONES, Adam	148	LAUNDERS, Richard	140
HUNTER, Allis	130	JONES, Bethiah	138	LAUNDERS, Richard	141
HUNTER, Elisha	130	JONES, Elizabeth	142	LAUNDERS, Thomas	144
HUNTER, William	130	JONES, Hannah	142	LAURANCE, Benjamin	148
		JONES, Mary	148	LAURANCE, Bette	151
— J —		JONES, Mehetabel	142	LAURANCE, Experience	143
		JONES, Paul	142	LAURANCE, Hannah	148
JENENS, Ann	133	JONES, Ralph	138	LAURANCE, Hannah	148
JENENS, John	133	JONES, Robert	148	LAURANCE, Hannah	151
JENENS, Ruhamah	133	JONES, Silvanus	138	LAURANCE, James	151
JENING, Elizabeth	133	JONES, Thomas	154	LAURANCE, Jemima	148
JENING, Elizebeth	133	JONES, Timothy	142	LAURANCE, Joseph	147
JENING, Isaak	133	JOY, Samuel	140	LAURANCE, Joseph	148
JENING, John	133	JUKIN, Job Cooke	130	LAURANCE, Joseph	151
JENING, John	134	JUKIN, John	130	LAURANCE, Joshua	147
JENING, Remembrance	133			LAURANCE, Justus	151
JENING, Ruhamah	133	— K —		LAURANCE, Martha	151
JENING, Ruhamah	134			LAURANCE, Peninah	151
JENING, Samuell	134	KERBIE, Jane	132	LAURANCE, Remember	143
JENINGE, John	133	KERBY, Sara	131	LAURANCE, Robert	148
JENINGE, Remembrance	133	KNOTT, Martha	132	LAURANCE, Samuel	148
JENINGS, Benjamin	152			LAURANCE, Seth	151
JENINGS, Isaac	152	— L —		LAURANCE, Thomas	148
JENINGS, Mary	152			LAWRANCE, Ebenezer	128
JENINGS, Rose	152	LANDAR, John	134	LAWRANCE, Robert	128
JENNING, Isaac	147	LANDAR, Thomas	134	LAWRANCE, Temperance	153
JENNINGS, -----	136	LANDER, Hasadiah	130	LAWRENCE, Abigail	153
JENNINGS, Elizabeth	152	LANDER, John	131	LAWRENCE, Asa	153
JENNINGS, Eunice	152	LANDER, Mercy	131	LAWRENCE, Deborah	153
JENNINGS, Experience	152	LANDER, Merty	131	LAWRENCE, Ebenezer	126
JENNINGS, Hannah	136	LANDER, Tho:	131	LAWRENCE, James	153
JENNINGS, Hannah	152	LANDER, Thomas	128	LAWRENCE, Justus	153
JENNINGS, Isaac	136	LANDER, Thomas	130	LAWRENCE, Lydia	153
JENNINGS, Isaac	152	LANDER, Thomas	131	LAWRENCE, Martha	153
JENNINGS, John	142	LANDER, Thomas	132	LAWRENCE, Paddock	153
JENNINGS, John	152	LANDERS, John	139	LAWRENCE, Robert	126
JENNINGS, Lois	152	LAUNDERS, Alce	140	LORING, Jane	140
JENNINGS, Remember	136	LAUNDERS, Anna	144	LOVEL, Hannah	147

INDEX - SANDWICH

LOVEL, John	147	NYE, Benjamin	128	PERRY, Deborah	148
		NYE, Benjamin	140	PERRY, Dinah	139
— M —		NYE, Benjamin	151	PERRY, Dinah	140
		NYE, Caleb	144	PERRY, Easter	148
MATTHEWES, Mary	130	NYE, Caleb	151	PERRY, Ebenezer	128
MAYHEW, Martha	131	NYE, Content	151	PERRY, Ebenezer	148
MENDAL, Joanna	154	NYE, David	151	PERRY, Edmond	150
MOTT, Jacob	154	NYE, Deborah	151	PERRY, Edward	136
MOXIE, Samuel	148	NYE, Elizabeth	144	PERRY, Eliakim	140
MOXUM, Hanah	153	NYE, Hannah	144	PERRY, Elisha	149
MOXUM, Samuel	153	NYE, Hannah	151	PERRY, Elizabeth	132
MOXUM, Zacheus	153	NYE, Ichabod	151	PERRY, Elizabeth	136
MULFORD, John	140	NYE, Isaac	151	PERRY, Elizabeth	138
		NYE, Jemima	151	PERRY, Elizabeth	148
— N —		NYE, Joanna	151	PERRY, Experience	138
		NYE, Jonathan	151	PERRY, Ezra	127
NABOR, Elezebeth	130	NYE, Joseph	151	PERRY, Ezra	128
NEWCOMB, Peter	140	NYE, Lemuel	151	PERRY, Ezra	132
NEWCOMB, William	138	NYE, Maria	151	PERRY, Ezra	133
NEWLAND, Rose	133	NYE, Mary	154	PERRY, Ezra	136
NIE, Abigail	128	NYE, Mercy	150	PERRY, Ezra	138
NIE, Beniamen	131	NYE, Mercy	151	PERRY, Ezra	150
NIE, Benjamin	127	NYE, Nathan	150	PERRY, Ezra	154
NIE, Bethiah	126	NYE, Nathan	151	PERRY, Ezrra	132
NIE, Dasther	126	NYE, Patience	151	PERRY, Freelove	150
NIE, Easther	126	NYE, Remember	150	PERRY, Hanna	130
NIE, Easther	128	NYE, Sarah	153	PERRY, Hannah	148
NIE, Ebenezer	126	NYE, Temperance	150	PERRY, Hannah	150
NIE, Ebenezer	127	NYE, Thankfull	150	PERRY, James	149
NIE, Ebenezer	128	NYE, Thomas	151	PERRY, Joanna	154
NIE, Experience	128	NYE, Zerviah	151	PERRY, Johanah	138
NIE, Hannah	128			PERRY, John	132
NIE, John	126	— P —		PERRY, John	136
NIE, John	128			PERRY, John	138
NIE, Mary	130	PARKER, Anness	148	PERRY, John	149
NIE, Mercy	131	PARKER, Samll.	147	PERRY, Josiah	140
NIE, Nathan	133	PARSIVAL, John	148	PERRY, Margaret	127
NIE, Peleg	126	PARSIVEL, James	147	PERRY, Maria	149
NIE, Peleg	128	PEAKE, Elizabeth	126	PERRY, Mary	128
NIE, Remembrance	133	PERCEVELL, Elisabeth	128	PERRY, Mary	148
NORRIS, Benjamin	142	PERCIVAL, James	126	PERRY, Mercy	148
NORRIS, John	142	PERRY, -----	138	PERRY, Meribah	139
NORRIS, Margery	142	PERRY, -----ijah	138	PERRY, Nathan	148
NORRIS, Olliver	142	PERRY, Abner	140	PERRY, Nathaniel	140
NORRIS, Samuel	142	PERRY, Anna	149	PERRY, Patience	150
NULAND, Elezebeth	127	PERRY, Arther	138	PERRY, Peace	140
NULAND, Elezibeth	131	PERRY, Beniamine	132	PERRY, Rebecca	150
NULAND, John	131	PERRY, Benjamin	139	PERRY, Remember	139
NULAND, William	127	PERRY, Benjamin	140	PERRY, Remembranc	133
NYE, Abigail	140	PERRY, Debbora	132	PERRY, Rest	154
NYE, Abigale	151	PERRY, Deborah	126	PERRY, Ruth	149

INDEX - SANDWICH

PERRY, Saml.	148	PRINCE, Benianin	137	SKIFF, Marcy	135
PERRY, Samuel	140	PRINCE, Martha	140	SKIFF, Marienne	126
PERRY, Samuel	148	PRINCE, Mercy	136	SKIFF, Mary	131
PERRY, Samuel	150	PRINCE, Mercy	137	SKIFF, Pacience	126
PERRY, Samuell	132	PRINCE, Saml.	136	SKIFF, Stephen	135
PERRY, Sarah	148	PRINCE, Saml.	137	SKIFF, Stephen	136
PERRY, Seth	140	PRINCE, Samuel	136	SKIFF, Steven	136
PERRY, Seth	148	PRINCE, Samuel	137	SKIFFE, Patience	128
PERRY, Solomon	149			SMITH, -----	137
PERRY, Susannah	140	— R —		SMITH, -----	137
PERRY, Temperance	139			SMITH, Abigail	133
PERRY, Thomas	148	RANDAL, Patience	147	SMITH, Abigail	136
PERRY, Timothy	138	REDDING, Ellener	128	SMITH, Abigail	137
PERSEVELL, Jams	128	REDDING, John	128	SMITH, Abigail	144
PERY, Remembrance	132	REDDING, John	133	SMITH, Abigail	152
POPE, ----ward	139	ROBINSON, Abigale	147	SMITH, Abigale	137
POPE, Abigail	143	ROBINSON, Peere	147	SMITH, Bathsheba	139
POPE, Bathsheba	143	ROBINSON, Mercy	153	SMITH, Benjamin	139
POPE, Charles	150	ROSS, John	128	SMITH, Benjamin	139
POPE, Deborah	150			SMITH, Benjamin	148
POPE, Elizabeth	136	— S —		SMITH, Daniel	144
POPE, Elizabeth	150			SMITH, Desire	139
POPE, Experience	150	SANDERSON, Henry	133	SMITH, Ebenezer	139
POPE, Ezra	150	SANERSON, Samuell	133	SMITH, Elisabeth	139
POPE, Gershom	139	SAUNDERSON, Esther	154	SMITH, Elisha	139
POPE, Hannah	143	SAVORY, Anthony	148	SMITH, Elisha	144
POPE, Joannah	150	SAVORY, Mary	148	SMITH, Elizabeth	139
POPE, John	140	SAVORY, Thomas	154	SMITH, Elizabeth	144
POPE, John	143	SKEFF, Bathshua	130	SMITH, Elkanah	144
POPE, John	150	SKEFF, Beniamine	130	SMITH, Elkenah	139
POPE, Mary	150	SKEFF, James	130	SMITH, Elkenah	144
POPE, Patience	143	SKEFF, James	132	SMITH, Hannah	139
POPE, Sarah	150	SKEFF, Mary	130	SMITH, Hannah	144
POPE, Seth	139	SKEFF, Nathan	130	SMITH, Hannah	148
POPE, Seth	143	SKEFF, Nathaniell	130	SMITH, Ichabod	139
POPE, Seth	150	SKEFF, Pacience	130	SMITH, Isaac	137
POPE, Thomas	139	SKEFF, Patience	132	SMITH, Jane	139
POPE, Thomas	150	SKEFF, Sare	130	SMITH, John	136
PRESBURY, Deborah	143	SKEFF, Steven	130	SMITH, John	139
PRESBURY, John	131	SKEFFE, Abigail	143	SMITH, Lydia	144
PRESBURY, Keturah	143	SKEFFE, James	142	SMITH, Mara	133
PRESBURY, Mary	143	SKEFFE, Ledia	143	SMITH, Marcy	133
PRESBURY, Meary	131	SKEFFE, Mary	142	SMITH, Martha	139
PRESBURY, Stephen	143	SKEFFE, Nathan	140	SMITH, Mary	133
PRICE, Margarett	148	SKEFFE, Stephen	142	SMITH, Mary	139
PRINCE, -----	136	SKEFFE, Stephen	143	SMITH, Mary	144
PRINCE, -----	137	SKFFE, James	132	SMITH, Mehetabel	139
PRINCE, -----n	136	SKFFE, Mary	132	SMITH, Mehetable	139
PRINCE, -----n	137	SKIFF, Deborah	135	SMITH, Mercy	140
PRINCE, ----rince	137	SKIFF, James	131	SMITH, Mercy	144
PRINCE, -----y	137	SKIFF, Lydia	136	SMITH, Pinninah	139

INDEX - SANDWICH

Name	Page	Name	Page	Name	Page
SMITH, Rebeckah	137	SWIFT, Hannah	130	SWIFT, Zepheniah	152
SMITH, Ruth	139	SWIFT, Hannah	141		
SMITH, Sarah	139	SWIFT, Hannah	155	— T —	
SMITH, Shubael	133	SWIFT, Isaac	153		
SMITH, Shubael	133	SWIFT, Jabez	152	TABOR, Easher	132
SMITH, Shubaell	133	SWIFT, Jemimah	149	TOBIE, Ephraim	127
SMITH, Shubal	137	SWIFT, Jirah	140	TOBIE, Benjamin	127
SMITH, Susanna	133	SWIFT, Jirah	152	TOBIE, Deborah	133
SMITH, Susanna	139	SWIFT, Jirah	153	TOBIE, Ephraim	127
SMITH, Thomas	137	SWIFT, Joanna	141	TOBIE, Nathan	133
SMITH, Thomas	139	SWIFT, Joanna	150	TOBIE, Seth	133
SNELL, Faith	153	SWIFT, Joanna	154	TOBIE, Thomas	132
SNELL, Thomas	153	SWIFT, Job	152	TOBY, ----hen	139
SPRAGUE, Desire	147	SWIFT, Johanah Swift	133	TOBY, Abia	142
STEPHENS, Sarah	139	SWIFT, Joseph	150	TOBY, Abigail	138
STEWART, Abigail	151	SWIFT, Josiah	150	TOBY, Abigail	144
STEWART, Desire	151	SWIFT, Josiah	154	TOBY, Barnabas	155
STEWART, Desire	151	SWIFT, Ketura	149	TOBY, Cornelious	142
STEWART, Gamaliel	151	SWIFT, Keziah	138	TOBY, Cornelius	139
STEWART, James	151	SWIFT, Mara	131	TOBY, Deborah	139
STEWART, James	151	SWIFT, Mara	133	TOBY, Deborah	143
STEWART, James	153	SWIFT, Mary	149	TOBY, Ebenezer	145
STEWART, Mary	151	SWIFT, Mary	154	TOBY, Eliakim	142
STEWART, Mehetabel	151	SWIFT, Mary	155	TOBY, Eliezer	145
STEWART, Mehetabel	153	SWIFT, Moses	141	TOBY, Ephraim	155
STEWART, Seth	151	SWIFT, Nathaniel	152	TOBY, Garshom	155
STEWART, Silvanus	151	SWIFT, Rowland	153	TOBY, Gershom	155
STUARD, James	133	SWIFT, Samell Swift	133	TOBY, Jane	145
STUARD, Seth	133	SWIFT, Sammuell	133	TOBY, Jerusha	155
STUART, James	136	SWIFT, Samuel	136	TOBY, John	145
SWIFFT, William	133	SWIFT, Samuel	141	TOBY, Jonathan	138
SWIFT, Abigail	153	SWIFT, Samuel	149	TOBY, Jonathan	142
SWIFT, Ales	152	SWIFT, Samuel	150	TOBY, Jonathan	143
SWIFT, Benjamin	148	swuft, Samuel	155	TOBY, Jonathan	144
SWIFT, Benjamin	155	SWIFT, Sarah	138	TOBY, Maria	143
SWIFT, Content	155	SWIFT, Sarah	141	TOBY, Martha	145
SWIFT, Ebenezer	149	SWIFT, Seth	149	TOBY, Mary	144
SWIFT, Ebenezer	150	SWIFT, Silas	153	TOBY, Mary	145
SWIFT, Elesabeth	133	SWIFT, Susanna	152	TOBY, Mehetabel	155
SWIFT, Elisabath	133	SWIFT, Temperance	149	TOBY, Mercy	144
SWIFT, Elisabeth	150	SWIFT, Thankfull	150	TOBY, Nathan	139
SWIFT, Elizabeth	141	SWIFT, Thomas	150	TOBY, Nathan	142
SWIFT, Elizabeth	147	SWIFT, William	128	TOBY, Nathaniel	144
SWIFT, Elizabeth	149	SWIFT, William	130	TOBY, Reliance	145
SWIFT, Elizabeth	150	SWIFT, William	131	TOBY, Remember	143
SWIFT, Epherim	128	SWIFT, William	133	TOBY, Remember	144
SWIFT, Ephraim	133	SWIFT, William	138	TOBY, Ruth	142
SWIFT, Ephraim	138	SWIFT, William	150	TOBY, Samll.	142
SWIFT, Ephraim	141	SWIFT, William	152	TOBY, Samuel	142
SWIFT, Ephraim	149	SWIFT, Zakeas	149	TOBY, Samuel	143
SWIFT, Ephram	133	SWIFT, Zebulun	155	TOBY, Sarah	142

TOBY, Silas	155	TUPPER, Martha	150	WING, Daniell	131
TOBY, Susannah	142	TUPPER, Mary	132	WING, Ebenezar	134
TOBY, Tabitha	142	TUPPER, Mayhew	150	WING, Ebenezer	139
TOBY, Temperance	155	TUPPER, Medad	131	WING, Ebenezer	140
TOBY, Thomas	142	TUPPER, Mehetabel	150	WING, Ebenezer	148
TOBY, Thomas	145	TUPPER, Meribah	139	WING, Elizabeth	148
TOBY, Wm.	142	TUPPER, Prince	150	WING, Experience	149
TOBY, Zacheus	142	TUPPER, Robert	126	WING, Hanna	131
TOBYE, Abia	142	TUPPER, Samuel	132	WING, Hannah	148
TOBYE, Deborah	143	TUPPER, Samuel	139	WING, Hannah	149
TOBYE, Elisabeth	143	TUPPER, Thankful	139	WING, Hepthzibath	131
TOBYE, Garshom	140	TUPPER, Thomas	126	WING, Jashub	136
TOBYE, Jemimah	142	TUPPER, Thomas	131	WING, Jashub	147
TOBYE, Joana	142	TUPPER, Thomas	132	WING, Jashub	149
TOBYE, Jonathan	143	TURNER, Mary	148	WING, Joana	139
TOBYE, Nathan	142			WING, Joanah	139
TOBYE, Remember	143	— V —		WING, John	131
TOBYE, Samuel	142			WING, John	134
TOBYE, Sarah	142	VINSENT, Henry	130	WING, Joseph	149
TOURNER, Anne	134			WING, Joseph	153
TOURNER, Susana	134	— W —		WING, Joshua	148
TUPER, Elizabeth	139			WING, Keziah	153
TUPPER, An	132	WANTON, Stephen	154	WING, Leidia	131
TUPPER, Ann	132	WARRAN, Elles	128	WING, Mary	136
TUPPER, Ann	140	WEEKS, Jonathan	153	WING, Mary	149
TUPPER, Benjamin	150	WHEATEN, Elizabeth	140	WING, Matthew	134
TUPPER, Bethiah	132	WHEATEN, Martha	140	WING, Mercy	131
TUPPER, Eldad	131	WHEATEN, Martha	147	WING, Nathaniel	153
TUPPER, Eldad	140	WHITE, Susanna	148	WING, Oseth	132
TUPPER, Eldad	147	WILLASSON, Rachell	133	WING, Rebecca	148
TUPPER, Eldad	150	WILLIS, Bethiah	126	WING, Saml.	149
TUPPER, Elead	140	WILLIS, Elchanan	126	WING, Samuel	136
TUPPER, Eliakim	132	WILLIS, Elchanan	127	WING, Samuel	148
TUPPER, Elisabeth	132	WILLIS, Elehanan	126	WING, Samuell	131
TUPPER, Elisabeth	139	WILLIS, Judeth	130	WING, Sarah	148
TUPPER, Elisha	131	WILLIS, Mary	131	WING, Sarah	153
TUPPER, Elisha	132	WILLIS, Nathanael	126	WING, Sarath	134
TUPPER, Elisha	150	WILLIS, Nathanael	130	WING, Stephen	134
TUPPER, Elizabeth	139	WILLIS, Nathanaell	131	WING, Stephen	148
TUPPER, Henry	126	WILLIS, Nathanail	127	WING, Steven	131
TUPPER, Ichabod	131	WING, -----	136	WING, Steven	132
TUPPER, Isaiah	150	WING, ----s	139	WING, Thomas	139
TUPPER, Israel	139	WING, Abigal	149	WING, Zachery	149
TUPPER, Israell	131	WING, Abigirl	134	WING, Zacheus	149
TUPPER, Israell	132	WING, Anne	149	WINGE, Stephen	134
TUPPER, Jane	131	WING, Barnabas	149	WINSLOW, Ruth	133
TUPPER, Jane	132	WING, Batchelder	139	WORDDEN, Mary	130
TUPPER, Jemima	150	WING, Batcheler	139	WORTHILAKE, Alce	147
TUPPER, Martha	131	WING, Bwela	131	WORTHYLAKE Mary	147
TUPPER, Martha	132	WING, Content	149	WRIGHT, Mercy	131
TUPPER, Martha	136	WING, Daniel	149	WRIGHT, Nicolas	131

INDEX - SANDWICH

WRIGHT, Peter 132

www.ingramcontent.com/pod-product-compliance
Lightning Source LLC
Chambersburg PA
CBHW082038300426
44117CB00015B/2526